4TH EDITION

Business Ethics

Dedicated to my mother
Rina Rossouw
in appreciation of her gift of life and love.

DEON ROSSOUW

To my mother
Hannetjiie van Vuuren
for showing me the magic of the written word.

LEON VAN VUUREN

Business Ethics

4TH EDITION

Deon Rossouw
Leon van Vuuren

OXFORD
UNIVERSITY PRESS
SOUTHERN AFRICA

OXFORD
UNIVERSITY PRESS
SOUTHERN AFRICA

Oxford University Press Southern Africa (Pty) Ltd

Vasco Boulevard, Goodwood, Cape Town, Republic of South Africa
P O Box 12119, N1 City, 7463, Cape Town, Republic of South Africa

Oxford University Press Southern Africa (Pty) Ltd is a subsidiary of
Oxford University Press, Great Clarendon Street, Oxford OX2 6DP.

The Press, a department of the University of Oxford, furthers the University's objective of
excellence in research, scholarship, and education by publishing worldwide in

Oxford New York

Auckland Cape Town Dar es Salaam Hong Kong Karachi
Kuala Lumpur Madrid Melbourne Mexico City Nairobi
New Delhi Shanghai Taipei Toronto

With offices in

Argentina Austria Brazil Chile Czech Republic France Greece
Guatemala Hungary Italy Japan Poland Portugal Singapore South Korea
Switzerland Turkey Ukraine Vietnam

Oxford is a registered trade mark of Oxford University Press
in the UK and in certain other countries

Published in South Africa
by Oxford University Press Southern Africa (Pty) Ltd, Cape Town

Business Ethics 4th edition
ISBN 978 0 19 598269 5

Publishing manager: Alida Terblanche
Assistant commissioning editor: Marisa Montemarano
Managing editor: Lisa Andrews
Editor: Jacqueline de Vos
Designer: Sharna Sammy
Proofreader: Allison Lamb
Indexer: Ethné Clarke

Set in Photina MT Std 10pt on 13pt by Oswald Kurten
Printed and bound by ABC Press, Cape Town
115803

Acknowledgements
The authors and publisher gratefully acknowledge permission to reproduce copyright material
in this book. Every effort has been made to trace copyright holders, but if any copyright
infringements have been made, the publisher would be grateful for information that would
enable any omissions or errors to be corrected in subsequent impressions.

CONTENTS

ACKNOWLEDGEMENTS

I t has been a long, but exciting journey since the first edition of the book was published in 1994. The evolution of the book mirrors the evolution of the field of Business Ethics. Over the last decades Business Ethics has moved from what some suspected to be merely a fleeting scholarly hobby of a few starry-eyed intellectuals to a well established field of study. The evolution of Business Ethics as an academic field has been complemented by a similar development in organisational practice. There has been a distinct move away from companies making vague and lofty commitments to high ethical standards in business to the active management, measurement and reporting of ethics in organisations.

Keeping track of these developments that occur both on a theoretical and practical level is a huge and comprehensive task that can hardly be accomplished by one person. I have been fortunate to be part of a network of people both from academia and business who are as intrigued as I am with these developments. Since the third edition of the book, published in 2004, I had the privilege of first presiding over the Business Ethics Network of Africa (BEN-Africa) and later also over the International Society of Business, Economics, and Ethics (ISBEE). During this time I also spent a year at Globethics.net in Geneva. Through these organisations I was able to build a truly global network with experts in the field of Business Ethics who shaped my perspectives and ideas in this field. Although they are too many to thank for their influence on my own thinking, I wish to acknowledge a number of colleagues who agreed to co-author specific chapters of this book.

My co-author, Prof. Leon van Vuuren, from the Department of Industrial Psychology and People Management at the University of Johannesburg, has a special interest in managing and institutionalising ethics in organisations. His keen interest in this field has resulted in us embarking on various joint projects and we have already published a number of journal articles as co-authors. He first joined me as a co-author in the preparation of the previous edition of this book. I am grateful to him for joining me again as co-author for this fourth edition of the book. His personal commitment to the success of this book, and his efforts to enhance the quality and usefulness thereof, is highly appreciated.

Dr. Neville Bews has done important research on intra-organisational trust. Since there is a clear link between trust and ethics, he has always been keen to explore that link. Our joint efforts in this regard have led to many intellectually enriching experiences over the years. I am grateful that he was once more willing to join me as co-author for the chapter on 'Ethics and trust' in Part Four of the book.

Daniel Malan shares my interest in the governance of ethics. As Head of the Unit for Corporate Governance in Africa at the University of Stellenbosch Business School, he has gained vast experience in this field. I always appreciate his effort to ground his practical work on solid theoretical foundations. We joined forces on a number of previous projects and I am delighted that he was willing to do so once more in co-authoring the chapter on 'Reporting Ethical Performance' in Part 6.

Dr. Charl du Plessis, who lectured in business and professional ethics at academic institutions in the USA and South Africa, joined us for the first time in this fourth edition of the book. He wrote the chapter on ethics on the macro-economic level (Chapter 2). We are grateful to him for his willingness and support in adding this new dimension to the book.

Prof. Derick de Jongh, Director of the Centre for Responsible Leadership at the University of Pretoria is another first-time contributor to the book. He co-authored Chapter 21 (Ethical leadership and organisational culture) with us. We are grateful that we could have benefited from his ideas and experience with regard to the promotion of responsible leadership.

Finally there are a number of persons who did not co-author, but nevertheless played an important part in preparing the fourth edition of the book. Prof. Piet Naude, Director of the Nelson Mandela Metropolitan University Business School has been both a staunch critic and supporter of this book over its four editions. We are grateful to him for reviewing a number of the new chapters that were added to this edition as well as for his many good suggestions on how these chapters could be improved.

In the staff of Oxford University Press, we encountered a team of professionals who worked with dedication to make the fourth edition of this book possible. In particular we wish to acknowledge the contributions that Marian Griffin, Alida Terblance, Marisa Montemarano, Lisa Andrews, Jacqui de Vos, and Allison Lamb made in their respective roles at Oxford University Press. Their personal commitment and ongoing support for this book are not only acknowledged, but also highly appreciated.

We also wish to thank countless colleagues and students who have commented on the book over the years. Your suggestions have been most valuable in shaping this fourth edition of the book.

Deon Rossouw
September 2009

PREFACE

Readers who are familiar with the previous (third) edition of this book will note a number of substantial differences between this fourth edition and its predecessor edition(s). Besides the revision of all the chapters that remained from the previous edition, a number of completely new chapters were added. The first major change is in Part 2 of the book where an entire section is now devoted to the ethical dimension of business on the macro-economic, organisational and intra-organisational levels. In Part 5 where the focus is on ethical decision-making in business, two new chapters were added. These chapters deal with the challenge of ensuring that business decisions regarding any aspect of business are ethically sound. Part 6 of the book was thoroughly revised to reflect changes to the ethics of governance and the governance of ethics that were introduced by the *Third King Report on Governance for South Africa*, published on 1 September 2009. A new chapter on the role of leadership and corporate culture was added to reflect the strong emphasis of the Third King Report on these two aspects. Finally, a chapter of case studies was added in Part 7 of the book. With all these changes *Business Ethics (fourth edition)* now has the following structure:

Part 1 introduces some important concepts and distinctions that have to be made in business ethics. Clarity on the meaning of these concepts will assist the reader in avoiding misunderstanding and confusion that can arise in the field of business ethics.

Part 2 deals with the ethical dimension of business. The many ways in which ethics is ingrained in business on the macro-economic level, in the relationship between business and society, as well as on the intra-organisational and individual level are explored.

Part 3 focuses on classic and contemporary ethical theories. These range from diagnostic theories on various modes of managing ethics in organisations, through classical ethical theories of a more philosophical nature, to theories on the moral status and obligations of the modern corporation.

In Part 4 the emphasis shifts to the importance of ethics in business. After the flaws in a number of popular beliefs that try to drive a wedge between ethics and business have been exposed, it is shown over the next three chapters how ethics is crucially important for the success and sustainability of business.

Part 5 deals with ethical decision-making in business. A decision-making strategy for ensuring that the ethical implications of business decisions are duly considered is first introduced and then applied to a case study on executive compensation and downsizing. Thereafter the RIMS strategy for resolving moral dilemmas is introduced and applied to ethical issues raised by employment equity.

Part 6 is concerned with governing and managing ethics in organisations. It first demonstrates the intimate relationship between ethics and corporate governance. Then the process of managing ethics in organisations is explained. Finally it is shown how the ethics management process needs to be supported by responsible leadership and an ethical corporate culture.

Part 7 offers a mix of real life and fictional case studies that cover a broad range of ethical issues likely to occur in business. It provides readers with the opportunity to apply the knowledge and skills gained from studying this book to specific business scenarios.

PART
1

Definitions and distinctions

INTRODUCTION

In any field of study there are a number of key concepts and distinctions that one needs to be familiar with. Such core concepts and distinctions provide the vocabulary for engaging in a meaningful discussion in any specialised field of study. The field of Business Ethics is no exception in this regard. It also has a set of core concepts that often feature in discussions about business ethics. Typical examples of such concepts are terms such as *ethics, morality, values, integrity,* and *virtues*. Although these concepts are related in some or other way, there are also some very important differences between them. If the connections and distinctions between these concepts are not clarified, it can lead to confusion and misunderstanding.

In this first part of the book we start by defining the concepts 'business', 'ethics' and 'business ethics'. Once the unique focus of the field of business ethics has been identified through the definition of these terms, we attend to a number of important distinctions that need to be made in the field of business ethics. We focus specifically on the distinction between what could be considered as ethically right and ethically wrong and how that distinction gets blurred in the case of ethical dilemmas. We also explore the relationship between ethics and the law as well as the distinction between ethics and values and between ethics and integrity. Finally, we analyse the distinction between personal and organisational ethics by employing the metaphor of apples and barrels.

CHAPTER
1

Key concepts and distinctions in ethics

I n order to talk meaningfully about business ethics there are a number of concepts and distinctions that one needs to understand. In this chapter we will discuss some of the key concepts and distinctions in the field of business ethics.

Business

The concept 'business' can have different meanings, as is illustrated in the expression that 'the business of business is business'. We will thus do well to clarify what we mean by business before defining what we mean by business ethics. Business, or economic activity, is any situation where individuals or parties voluntarily enter into transactions of economic exchange for goods or services. These goods or services can be provided by the state, public or private enterprises, and individuals. In narrow definitions of business ethics, the domain of business is confined to the economic activities of private enterprises and individuals. In broader understandings of business ethics, the economic activity of the state and public enterprises are also included. The broader understanding will be used in this book.

It has become commonplace in business ethics to distinguish three broad dimensions of business (Becker, 1992; Enderle, 2003; Goodpaster, 1992):

▣ The macro or systemic dimension – This is the economic system or the wider socio-political framework within which business is conducted. The framework is determined at national level by political decisions, laws and regulations as well as social norms that determine the contours of the economic playing field and the rules that govern economic play. When economic activity transcends national boundaries, international trade agreements also come into play. The macro-economic framework determines to a large extent what freedoms and responsibilities economic players will have and also which economic priorities will be pursued.

▣ The organisational dimension – This relates to the role and responsibilities of business organisations. Business organisations developed their own systems of governance according to which they direct and control their own internal activities. But businesses also inevitably find themselves in relationships of responsibility with a wide range of external parties such as the state, competitors, suppliers, customers, and organisations of civil society. The organisational dimension of business thus encompasses the collective behaviour of the business organisation towards both its internal and external stakeholders.

▣   The micro- or individual dimension – This concentrates on the economic actions and decisions of individuals interacting with the business organisation. Although the structures, policies and culture of a business organisation pose distinct constraints within which employees, suppliers, contractors and other stakeholders have to operate, they never totally constrain the freedom and responsibility of these individuals. To the contrary, they retain considerable freedom to display initiative and discretion.

Although these three dimensions are clearly distinguishable in theory, in practice they are interrelated. Often a single phenomenon has simultaneous implications for all three dimensions of business. A good illustration is economic empowerment for women. Creating conditions that will ensure that they take their rightful place in the economy might become a strategic objective in the government's macro-economic policy. On the organisational level, a company might decide to change its hiring, promotion, and procurement practices in order to support the empowerment of women. On the individual level, employees, suppliers and other stakeholders of the business will be affected by both the government policy and organisational practices related to the empowerment of women. Individuals might decide to support, openly oppose or silently sabotage the business in its endeavour to support the economic empowerment of women.

With a better understanding of what we mean by business and the three dimensions thereof, let us do a similar exploration of what we mean by ethics.

Ethics

Sometimes people try to maintain a distinction between the meaning of the concepts 'ethics' and 'morality'. In ordinary language, however the two concepts are almost indistinguishable. People tend not to make any fine distinctions between ethical and moral behaviour on the one side or between unethical and immoral behaviour on the other side. In this book both words will be used to mean the same thing.

Ethics concerns itself with what is good or right in human interaction. It revolves around three central concepts: 'self', 'good', and 'other'. Ethical behaviour results when one does not merely consider what is good for oneself, but also considers what is good for others. It is important that each of these three central concepts be included in a definition of ethics.

Should the concept 'good' be neglected, the unique nature of ethics collapses: ethics is not merely concerned with the interaction between a 'self' and an 'other', but with the quality of interaction. It wants to determine whether the interaction between the self and the other is good or bad for one or both of the parties.

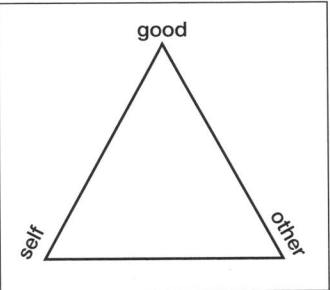

A similar distortion occurs when the 'self' is excluded from the definition of ethics. Then the concern is merely about what is good for others, without taking the interests of the 'self' into consideration. This form of altruism is probably unattainable, as it is almost impossible for someone to ignore their own interests. It is also dangerous to neglect your own interests, as a sense of your own wellbeing is a prerequisite for balanced and ongoing interaction with other people.

Alisdair MacIntyre captured this insight well when he said: 'Self-sacrifice is as much of vice [...] as selfishness' (1999:160).

Equally, the 'other' cannot be excluded from the definition of ethics, as this will result in selfishness. A concern merely for what is good for the self neglects the very nature of ethics, which is to ensure the interests of both oneself and others.

Ethical behaviour thus can be self-interested but not merely selfish. When you know your behaviour may have negative consequences for others, but care only about what is good for yourself, such action is selfish and unethical. If, on the contrary, you seek to serve your own interests, whilst simultaneously caring about the interests of others, then your behaviour is self-interested whilst also being ethical.

Business ethics

When ethics is applied to business we consider the implications of business on the interests of all who are affected by its activity. Business ethics is about identifying and implementing standards of conduct in and for business that will ensure that the interests of its stakeholders are respected.

Business ethics thus refers to the values and standards that determine the interaction between business and its stakeholders. From this definition it is clear how the three concepts of the 'self', 'good' and 'other', which are integral to the definition of ethics, also apply to business ethics. Business ethics is about a conception of what is good (values and standards) that guide the business (self) in its interaction with others (stakeholders).

Consequently, what is at stake in studying and practising business ethics is to give content to the 'good' (ethical values and standards) and to determine whether the interaction between the self (business) and others (internal and external stakeholders) lives up to these ethical values and standards.

Right, wrong and dilemmas

Ethics is often perceived as a grey area where there is little clarity about what is right or wrong. This perception of ethics is mistaken. There is a broad consensus within and amongst societies about what is considered to be either ethically right or wrong. Both within and across societies there is, for example, a consensus that the protection of innocent life and telling the truth is ethically right. There is a similar consensus that the killing of innocent people and blatant lying is wrong. The same goes for ethics in business. There are certain behaviours that are considered ethically right, such as the respect for the dignity of employees and for company property. On the other hand discrimination against employees and theft of company property is considered wrong. Whether companies and their employees live up to these standards is another question, but they would generally agree to these standards of behaviour. However, difficult situations in business arise where it is hard to tell what should be considered right or wrong in a given situation. These tough choices are called moral dilemmas.

Consequently it is important in business to distinguish between what is ethically right, what is ethically wrong and what is an ethical dilemma. Companies need to be as clear as possible on what they consider to be ethically right or acceptable behaviour. They need to be equally clear on what they consider to be ethically wrong and regard as unacceptable behaviour. They also need to acknowledge that ethical dilemmas arise and should provide guidance on how moral dilemmas need to be approached.

Moral dilemmas arise when the distinction between what is ethically right and wrong becomes blurred. From time to time incidents arise in business where people are no longer certain whether an action should be considered right or wrong. It is typical of moral dilemmas that when different people look at the same issue, some would regard it as morally right, whilst others would regard it as morally wrong. Privacy in e-mail use is a typical moral dilemma in business. Whilst some would regard the monitoring of employees' e-mail as unethical, others would justify it as a legitimate managerial prerogative.

Dilemmas can be either interpersonal or intrapersonal: they do not only occur between people, but a person may experience a dilemma within her or himself. This happens when an individual is faced with more than one option, but finds it hard to decide which option is morally the best. Both social (interpersonal) and personal (intrapersonal) dilemmas are characterised by the fact that there is no longer a choice between right and wrong, but between conflicting moral options.

The challenge that faces businesses when it comes to the above distinction between right, wrong and dilemmas, is to provide clarity on what is right and wrong and guidance on how to deal with dilemmas that arise from time to time.

right   dilemma   wrong

Ethics and the law

There are obvious similarities between ethics and the law, but there are also significant differences. Both ethics and the law strive towards determining what is right in human interaction and society. The law does so through a public and political process and employs the power of the state to ensure that all abide by the stipulations of the law. Ethics emanates from personal values; as such the sense of obligation to do what is right is internal as opposed to the external pressure of the law.

Although ethical and legal behaviour often coincide, they also sometimes differ, as illustrated in the following table.

	Legal	Illegal
Ethical		
Unethical		

Actions can be simultaneously ethical and legal. An example of this would be when a company publishes accurate statements of its income. This is both the right thing to do and in accordance with the law. Exceeding the speed limit in an effort to get a seriously injured colleague in time to hospital can be considered an example of ethical, but illegal conduct. An example of action that is legal, but unethical is where a company dumps toxic waste in a river in a developing country where there are no laws preventing companies from harming the environment. Actions can also be both unethical and illegal as in the case of bribing government officials in countries where bribery is illegal.

It is clear in the preceding examples that legality and morality do not always coincide. Because such discrepancies between ethics and the law exist, we cannot simply hide behind the law to justify our business actions. Acting morally responsibly might at times imply that companies need to go further than the prescriptions of the law or, in extreme cases, that they should challenge the existing laws when they are perceived to be unfair or corrupt.

Ethics and values

Although there is a definite link between ethics and values, the two concepts are not identical. Values can be defined as relatively stable convictions about what is important. Since it is possible to have values that have either nothing to do with ethics or that run counter to ethics, values cannot be equated with ethics.

It is not only individuals that have values. We also find values within organisations. By looking at the different kinds of values that we typically find within business organisations, the relation between values and ethics will become clear. Normally, three different kinds of values can be distinguished within business organisations. They are strategic values, work values and ethical values.

Strategic values refer to the shared conviction of the organisation about its desired objectives. As such, strategic values indicate the direction in which the organisation wishes to move. The strategic values of organisations are usually reflected in their vision and mission statements. In order to move the organisation in the direction indicated by its strategic values, all members of the organisation need to do their jobs in a specific manner. The priorities that organisational members should adhere to in their jobs are called **work values**. Typical work values include punctuality, innovation, and quality. For any organisation to function optimally, good relations and interactions between stakeholders are required. In order to ensure that such good relations and interactions are maintained, members of organisations need to commit themselves to specific **ethical values**. Typical ethical values include respect, transparency, and fairness. Adherence to ethical values ensures that stakeholders inside and outside the organisation get along well with one another. Ethical values are thus a subset of values within the broader set of values of an organisation.

Integrity

Integrity is so closely aligned to ethics that it is sometimes used as a substitute for ethics. Persons with a strong commitment to ethical standards are often referred to as persons of integrity. Similarly, the term organisational integrity is often used to refer to the organisational ethics. Despite such equations between ethics and integrity, integrity is a much more restricted concept than ethics.

Integrity refers specifically to the moral character of a person or organisation. A person is regarded as someone with integrity when s/he consistently adheres to a set of ethical standards. For this reason integrity is often associated with concepts like fairness, consistency, uprightness and wholeness. These characteristics make a person of integrity reliable and trustworthy as others know that the person of integrity will always adhere to her or his values. The same applies to organisations with moral integrity.

Apples, barrels and warehouses

A last important distinction in business ethics is the one between personal (apple) and organisational (barrel) ethics (cf. Ashkanasy, Windsor & Trevino, 2006). Unethical behaviour is often attributed to the defective moral up-bringing of an individual. Such individuals are termed 'bad apples' as it is believed that their upbringing has spoiled their moral character and they cannot be changed into morally responsible persons (good apples). This is a gross oversimplification. Individuals are affected by the organisational cult-ure in which they find themselves, in the same way that apples are affected by the environment in which they are stored. The business organisations (barrels) that individuals work in can also have either a constructive or a corruptive influence on their moral character. People with dubious or even good moral character can turn to unethical behaviour if they find themselves in organisations where unethical conduct is the norm. Thus bad barrels can corrupt dubious or even good apples. The opposite is equally true. Dubious or even bad apples can be restrained from unethical behaviour should they find themselves in organisations that do not tolerate unethical behaviour, but reward ethical behaviour. Refer to the table below for an illustration of this point.

	Good barrels	Bad barrels
Good apples		
Bad apples		

The distinction between apples and barrels reminds us that ethical behaviour should not only be addressed on the individual level, but also on the level of organisational culture and practices. Organisations are not isolated from the broader society and social norms within which they operate. It therefore makes sense to introduce the notion of the warehouse in which the barrels are kept, thus acknowledging the interplay between business and the broader socio-cultural setting. Here there is also an intricate interplay between business and society. Once more this relationship can be constructive or corruptive. It is however important to emphasise that this relationship between business and society is bidirectional. Society can corrupt or conserve the barrels, but given their immense power, business can also contribute towards corrupting or improving the moral fibre of society.

Conclusion

The concepts and distinctions introduced in this chapter will be an important part of the vocabulary that you will need to understand the rest of the book. They are also important in making you fluent in ethics discourse.

PART

2

The ethical dimension of business

INTRODUCTION

In the first chapter a distinction was made between three different levels of economic activity. The three levels that were identified are the macro-economic, the organisational and the intra-organisational levels. Each of these three levels of economic activity has its own ethical dimension. In this second part of the book we explore what ethics entails and implies on each of these three levels of economic activity.

In Chapter 2 we investigate the ethical dimension of the macro-economic level by analysing the ethical justification of economic systems and macro-economic policies. We focus specifically on the ethics of capitalism and socialism as the two major competing economic systems of our time. The ethical gains and deficits of the two economic systems are discussed.

In Chapter 3 the focus shifts to the organisational level where we attend to the ethical responsibilities of business organisations towards the broader environment within which they operate. We investigate the different types of roles and obligations that businesses are expected to fulfil in relation to their economic, social and natural environments.

In Chapter 4 we move to the intra-organisational level where we consider various manifestations of ethics within organisations. We examine the crucial role of ethics in intra-organisational relations and the role that it plays in building trust in organisations. We also explore the role that ethics plays in the performance of organisations.

CHAPTER 2

Ethics on the macro-economic level

*With Charl du Plessis**

As we study business ethics, the question will often arise: 'When is enough enough?' How do we justify that a leading import agent for sought-after brands such as Cartier, Gucci and other luxury perfumes is going through a messy divorce where his spouse spent in excess of R1 million a month on clothes, and that in a country where people are dying of hunger?

Generally, we can agree that at minimum, everyone needs food, water, shelter and air. But how much more should each individual get, and how do we determine that? And what do we make of the fact that of the four critical elements of survival mentioned, at least two, namely shelter and food (and increasingly water) are by-and-large supplied through private sector markets, and with market activity encroaching on the quality of water and air supply available to the global population? Clearly, business has an important impact on the most fundamental elements of our human existence.

During the past 25 years, the world economy has grown exponentially, and there has never been as much wealth created in such a short period of time as what we now have available to the world and its almost seven billion people. In South Africa, there are now more than 55 000 high net worth individuals (HNWIs), i.e., people whose net asset value, excluding their primary residence, exceeds $1 million (The World Wealth Report). Only Singapore had a higher percentage growth in HNWIs than South Africa's 14% growth rate in the last reported year (2007). During this same period, however, the gap between rich and poor nations, and the gap between rich and poor within each nation has increased.

More than 1,2 billion people globally get by on less than $2 a day, and thousands die of hunger despite the world producing more food than what its population can consume. US Senator, and once presidential candidate, George McGovern (2002) explained that we do not have a food problem.

---

* **Dr Charl du Plessis** has lectured in business and professional ethics at academic institutions in the USA and South Africa. He has more than 20 years of experience in the workplace: as entrepreneur, manager and management consultant in both private and public sectors in South Africa, USA, UK, Nigeria, Angola, Mozambique, Malawi, Guinea and Namibia.

Rather, we have a distribution problem, which is really a political problem. And Nobel Prize winner, Amartya Sen (2000), points out that there has never been a famine in a democratic state.

The high-level political choices made in society, including the choice of economic system, directly impact the citizens of each country, and when we study macro-ethics, we concern ourselves with the morality of these choices. Not merely as interested citizens, but also as business people who have to operate according to the rules and assumptions that underpin the choice of economic model. There are several considerations that inform the economic system choice. First and foremost, societies seek economic growth and development, because in a world of scarce resources, there is not a nation that need not concern itself with finding the optimum return on its citizens' labour with the endowment of capital (natural resources, land, talent, skill and relationships with trade partners) that they have been dealt.

But, there is also a second and equally important dimension, namely asking what the moral ramifications are that guide the choice of a macro-economic model. Is it inherently fair, just and sustainable without political contest? What systems deliver fair results? How do we morally justify part-icular elements of a specific political-economic system, should the system be regulated or completely free (laissez-faire), and who should be responsible for regulation if that is the choice? Would it be government or industry itself? And how does the choice for a particular economic system influence the operating environment of the business that is conducted in that society, and how does that affect the rights and obligations of individuals and groups?

It is quite possible to assume that if these most fundamental questions regarding the intrinsic justice and fairness of our choice of economic system go unanswered, that the resulting system and its organisations and participating individuals (which we study at meso- and micro-level) may function under moral tension.

There is hardly a rich choice between different economic models in this world. Capitalism in one form or the other is by far the most prevalent in modern society, yet it means a lot of different things to different people, and it plays out quite varied in different societies. In the next section, we will distinguish a variety of economic models and consider the defining elements and the moral justification of each. We place significantly more emphasis on the free market model, which is operant in our own society and dominates the global economic landscape. In a subsequent section, we will contrast certain critiques against each of these systems.

The free-market system

The defining elements of capitalism are that capital goods are privately owned, and that decisions about how or whether to use these capital goods rest solely with the private owners in a free market. There is no impediment to competition, and the free market generally encourages it. Capitalism endorses the private pursuit of profit, and there are unique vehicles, such as the joint-stock, limited-liability corporation, through which to pursue the maximum profit with the minimum risk.

Capital, by definition, are the assets used in the process of the further production of goods and services, rather than being exhausted through consumption. We generally think of land, raw materials, and machinery and equipment as capital goods. This might be an overtly simplistic approach, and de Soto (2000) points out that there are plenty of capital goods in the hands of the poor across the world, but that their assets are held in defective forms and therefore cannot count as capital:

> *Because the rights to these possessions are not adequately documented, these assets cannot readily be turned into capital, cannot readily be traded outside of narrow local circles where people know and trust each other, cannot be used as collateral for a loan, and cannot be used as a share against an investment.*

Property rights

The key to converting movable or immovable assets into capital appears to be the quality and protection of the property rights assigned to the rightful owners of the assets. For the private individual to be capable of deciding how and when to deploy certain assets in the productive process, it is an absolute requisite to have clear and uncontested ownership of such an asset. Or else planning the enterprise becomes too risky and cumbersome if the private owner may fear some future claim against his or her productive assets. In the West, where landholding requires title, raising a mortgage on the privately-held family home is one of the most frequent ways by which entrepreneurs fund their start-ups, and is recognised by law because of the intrinsic trust in our systems of land title and register.

The marvel of the pricing system

A centrally-planned economy, such as with Communism, tries to set pricing and production schedules for the whole market, and loses the benefit of thousands of little adjustments that private entrepreneurs can make when closer to the market. Nobel Prize economist Kenneth Arrow referred to these productive adjustments as the 'marvel of the pricing system' (1974). By rapidly and repeatedly adjusting either the price or the quantities produced, the entrepreneur forever moves closer to the optimum production capacity. When this phenomenon plays itself out many times every day, and over many years, the rate of the expansion of an economy, and the overall prosperity in a society would accelerate beyond that which a centrally-planned, and arguably a very slow and bureaucratic process of price and production planning could achieve.

Regulation

There is no completely free market anywhere in the world. Each country has some form of regulation in place to ensure that the rights of other individuals are not affected by the nominal right of each individual to enter the market in any way he or she pleases.

Regulation is often enforced to guard against so-called 'externalities,' i.e., when a company manages to shift a cost associated with its production onto other parties, and most likely the unsuspecting public. The best example is pollution, where companies may be spewing dangerous emissions into the air, without having to account for the negative side effects to the general public's health. Through emissions taxes or the sale of emissions credits, a government can force a particular polluting industry to clean up its act or to make a contribution towards the cost of health care that the public health system will incur in treating victims of the pollution.

Another form of regulation occurs at industry level, where certain industries undertake to become self-regulated. For instance, the auditing profession sets its own standards by which new members of the profession are allowed to enter practice, and guides its members by holding their conduct to a particular code. In this manner, the public who wishes to use the services of such members are ensured of a certain quality of service and integrity in conduct.

Markets also have a way of regulating themselves. If an entrepreneur had to decide to open a type of business inconsistent with the community's norms and values, private protest by members of the community, or simple lack of support for the business may eventually force the entrepreneur to shut it down. An area such as Camps Bay in Cape Town does not allow any liquor stores within its boundaries, and several communities have previously banded together to shut down strip clubs or adult shops close to their children's schools.

Despite the opposite claims by laissez-faire libertarians, people who are ardent proponents of the free market with the absolute minimum government interference, this interference by government in the commercial sphere is not inconsistent with the views of the father of the free market, Adam Smith, who dedicated several sections of *The Wealth of Nations* (1776) to the role of government in ensuring justice in the market.

At minimum, our understanding of the concept of free markets entails that each individual may choose which business to open, where to open it, and with whom he or she wants to trade. One needs to remain mindful though that these choices may affect the rights of other parties, and it is in this grey area where regulators often need to step in to ensure a just solution for all affected parties. The dramatic meltdown of the global financial system towards the latter part of 2008, with governments having to pour billions of dollars in to try and keep the system afloat, is one of the clearest signals in many years about how the lack of proper checks and balances, and oversight of the market, may lead to problems.

Competition

Capitalism promotes healthy competition. The assumption is that when several producers compete directly against one another, they become more efficient and productive at what they do, put downward pricing pressure on each other to the benefit of the consumer, and have to improve the quality of their product or service to remain competitive. All three of these elements eventually work, not only to the advantage of the consumer, but when multiplied across several industries and geographical markets, they increase the economic gain to society at large.

The opposite of free competition is to allow monopolies to dominate a particular market segment. Monopolists can extract higher prices from the market, and may even reduce their production output in order to optimise their profit. This happens at the expense of the consumer and of society at large. In South Africa, we have been particularly tolerant of monopolies in certain sectors, in part, because the survival of these firms has been perceived to be of strategic interest to our country. However, very few consumers today would support the continuation of economic dinosaurs such as Telkom without healthy competition.

Profit and personal motivation

Under a centrally-planned economy and in the absence of the profit motive, there is little inspiration for the individual to get out of bed early, and to work harder, longer and more efficiently than the next person, as the individual might not share in the gains of the extra effort. The combination of the profit motive and the free choice of economic activity jointly drive output upwards in the free-market system. When the entrepreneur knows that he or she will personally reap the benefits of the harder work, there is a true incentive to perform better. Even if the entrepreneur has no interest in the social wellbeing of society, it is through his or her reaching for their own dream that the overall welfare of the economy and of society improves. Adam Smith (1776) put it succinctly when defending the free-market system in his famous book, *The Wealth of Nations*:

> *It is not from the benevolence of the butcher, the brewer, or the baker that we expect our dinner, but from their regard of their own interest. We address ourselves not to their humanity, but to their self-love and never talk to them of our own necessities, but of their advantage.*

It is worth remembering that personal motivation could consist of more than just the wish for more profit. The privately-held business enterprise is a vehicle through which individuals in the free market can create meaningful change in their own lives and in society, and still make a profit for themselves. Smith himself saw justice, rather than self-interest as the more important objective. Donaldson et al. (2002) explain how to Adam Smith, a father of Capitalism, there could only be large-scale social gains from the private pursuit of wealth when economic actors acted with restraint, prudence, fair play, and respected the basic principles of justice and the rights of others.

'To Adam Smith, a father of Capitalism, there could only be large-scale social gains from the private pursuit of wealth when economic actors acted with restraint, prudence, fair play, and respected the basic principles of justice and the rights of others.'

The joint-stock, limited liability corporation

'A revolutionary idea' – that is how historians Micklethwait and Wooldridge (2002) describe the modern corporation, an essential element of our economy and perhaps the major contributor of economic growth in the West for the past 160 years.

The modern corporation as separate legal entity owes its origin to an Act of the English Parliament in 1862. Courts have subsequently upheld the idea that corporations are separate legal personae, and may have an infinite life beyond the inconvenient mortality of their shareholders. There is a strong school of thought that the corporation even has its own moral agency, independent of its officers, and that the corporation should be held liable for its own ethical failures. In the extreme, consumer advocates in the US, under the leadership of Ralph Nader, have argued for the death penalty in the case of recidivist corporations. That is, the termination of the licence to operate that society grants the corporation, in the event of the corporations repeatedly flouting to laws of society.

There are two real reasons why the concept of the corporation has contributed so immensely to economic expansion in the West. Firstly, because it is a 'joint-stock' entity, it allowed for the pooling of investment by multiple parties in one venture, thereby creating the ability to achieve scale and reach that would have remained beyond the capabilities of most individuals. Today, we take the concept of owning shares in a company, along with thousands of other unknown individuals, for granted, and we can trade in and out of a corporation within seconds through the click of a mouse.

The second reason for the success of the corporation and its contribution to society is its ability to limit the liability of each individual investor to the sum total of his or her investment. The only part of your fortune at risk is that which you used to purchase your shares in the company. Prior to 1862, mavericks and adventurers could wipe out their whole estate on one misguided or failed venture.

Through limiting risk and allowing the pooling of resources, along with the perpetual lifespan of this legal construct, the corporation has become the dominant institution in our societies. Robert Phillips (2003) describes how the church or the King's palace dominated urban landscapes in earlier times, and now you see corporate headquarters first before you head into a new city.

Of course, the revolution brought by the limited liability, joint-stock corporation would not have been possible without the essential underpinnings of the capitalist ideology, namely property ownership and the pursuit of profit.

Justification of the free market

In this chapter so far, there has been constant reference to the success of capitalism in expanding economic growth, improving social gains, and generally leaving nations better off than what was the case under communism. These are the *productive* successes of capitalism.

However, we are struck by the obvious inequality that is the direct result of this system. Some nations are far richer than others and the gap between rich and poor nations is forever increasing. Likewise, in almost all rich and poor nations, the gap between rich citizens and poor citizens too has been getting progressively larger. Clearly, the manner in which the gains from capitalism's productive successes have been distributed across populations is highly problematic.

There is no agreement on what is just and fair under capitalism, or even whether capitalism is morally sound. There are several theoretical approaches to argue for economic justice under capitalism, which might be useful in guiding each of us individually towards some resolution of these tougher questions.

Philosopher, John Rawls (1999), explains why we need to seek justice in our economic affairs:

> *Then, although society is a co-operative venture for mutual advantage, it is typically marked by a conflict as well as by an identity of interests. A set of principles is required for choosing among the various social arrangements which determine this division of advantages and for underwriting an agreement on the proper distributive shares.*

To seek out the set of principles on which society can agree as just, however, is a more difficult task, and as Rawls continues, 'what is just and unjust is usually in dispute'. What he claims most people could agree on as a requirement of justice, at minimum, is that a system is just when it does not draw any arbitrary distinction between individuals, and when competing claims for justice can be heard in an unbiased manner, for example, in the courts.

Before we consider two different sets of claims upon what the content of economic justice should be, we need to clarify what is understood under 'equity' and 'equality.'

Equity and equality

There are some economic principles for which there is broad support. Most of us would agree that every person should have an equal opportunity to compete fairly in the marketplace. That we would refer to as a 'level playing field'. Some would go further and insist that everybody starts with the same opportunity and resources, yet would be entitled to more gains and a better life if they used their opportunities and resources better than the next person. This state we could refer to as 'the same starting line'. Few of us would still agree, as was the case under communism, that all of us should end up with exactly the same amount of wealth and opportunity, which could be called 'full equality', as this state leaves the case of moral free-riding, i.e., riding on the back of other people's effort, unanswered.

The classic example of moral free-riding is motor insurance. Here, multiple motorists pay monthly premiums in order to pool resources so that in the event of one of them being involved in an accident, this pool of funds can pay for any damages and reduce the impact of the cost to the one motorist who was involved in the accident. But now, knowing that the cost is spread across several people, the moral free-riders will be the ones less cautious about how they drive, because other people's money can help take care of any potential adverse consequences to their blameworthy behaviour.

The difference between *equity* and *equality* is explained by Phillips (2003): Equality implies similar outcomes; that is, that regardless of the level of the playing field, or of the nature of the starting line-up and each economic agent's efforts, each individual gets exactly the same in the end. Equity, on the other hand, finds some acceptable metric or ratio on which the population can agree, whereby the distribution of goods may be determined. For example, if society decides that an acceptable wage rate is R25 per hour, it would be seen as equitable if Paul works 10 hours and therefore earns R250, while Susan works 100 hours and therefore earns ten times more than Paul did. Capitalism strives for equitable solutions, having left the full equality aspirations of communism behind in its wake.

The problem of wealth distribution, however, still remains unresolved, regardless of the attempt towards equity, because the metrics and ratios by which economic gains may be distributed do not enjoy broad consensus. Wage rates are hardly ever uncontested, for example. Furthermore, the case becomes even more convoluted, because despite our theoretical approval of the notions of 'level playing fields' and 'the same starting line', some people are simply better endowed than others. This is what John Rawls (1999) called the 'natural lottery'. Should society try and make amends for the fact that some people have better talents than others when they enter the economic race? And should parents not be allowed to do their very best to give their children a head-start in life? Why should the next generation be forced to start on the same line-up if their parents were prudent in making provision for them, or worked as slaves, like many first generation immigrants tend to do, in order for their children to have better opportunities?

Utilitarianism

The utilitarian movement was borne from the restrictive guilds and other trade practices of the late 18th and early 19-century England, and concerned itself not only with social gains, but also with the freedom of the individual to participate freely in the trade of choice. John Stuart Mill, a leading utilitarian, completed one of the finest treatises ever written on this subject: *On Liberty* (1859).

The utilitarian idea is that the greatest good for mankind is happiness, and from this they derived what is called 'The Greatest Happiness Principle'. This is a consequentialist theory, which means that it asks us to judge our actions according to their effect and consequences, and in particular, to seek for solutions where the greatest amount of pleasure and the least amount of pain would result from the action. This approach is not altogether inconsistent with the way in which most of us are brought up, namely to judge our actions by their consequences.

In the economic sphere then, the utilitarian approach would support any economic arrangement whereby the result is the greater happiness of society. The problem with utilitarianism is that the measurement of utility is almost impossible, and that it requires a very rough approximation of what society might value. One interpretation might assume that people generally prefer more goods than less, and that therefore, any economic arrangement whereby more people have more goods would meet the challenge. But, given that there is some diminishing return on utility, it becomes futile. To explain, ask yourself whether R1 in the hands of a hungry street child has exactly the same value or utility than it might have in the hands of a busy executive who earns R250 000 per month.

Even if we found a way of accurately measuring utility, and lived in a society where preferences never changed, the utilitarian approach could still not escape what has been arguably its fiercest criticism, namely that it does not take the rights of the individual seriously (Rawls, 1999). Take the case in point of affirmative action. Let's assume that the implementation of affirmative action meets the utilitarian standard, namely delivering more happiness in society than what it causes pain. Then, how do we explain to the young individuals who fall outside of the targeted affirmative action population why they cannot be considered for positions for which they are qualified?

Despite these obvious critiques, the applied form of utilitarianism, namely cost-benefit analysis, is rather ubiquitous in both the private sector and in the policy environment and is often used to justify the decisions made.

Justice as fairness

John Rawls was a fierce critic of the utilitarian position, because it affects the rights and liberties of the individual. He developed a theory of justice called 'Justice as Fairness' and derived his proposed principles of economic and social justice through an interesting construct called the 'Original Position'.

This is what he argued: assuming that citizens had to decide on the rules applicable to their societal arrangements, he suggested that they enter through a 'Veil of Ignorance' to go back to the 'Original Position'. In this hypothetical state, they have no knowledge of their future place in society, nor of their talents and endowment, and now have to agree on a set of rules that could work for each of them, independently of eventually finding yourself to be a king or a pauper.

Rawls concluded that through such an exercise, two principles would emerge: the first principle everyone would agree to would be the openness of opportunity. Everyone should have the chance to participate in the same fashion. The second principle he proposes is that everyone would agree that people should be allowed to pursue any opportunity for their own benefit, as long as the result of their actions still leaves the worst-off in society in a better position. This second principle he called the 'Difference Principle'.

The principles of justice proposed by Rawls would allow for the private pursuit of profit by all individuals in society, as is generally understood under capitalism. It is his second principle that is more problematic, because we are generally not attuned towards assessing our economic opportunities on the basis of their impact on the worst-off in society. It is also an open question whether simply being better off than before, while becoming progressively worse-off in comparison to the more affluent members of society would offer a tenable and sustainable social arrangement for people at the bottom of the economic ladder.

Command systems

The essence of the free-market system discussed above was entrepreneurial opportunity to identify a particular demand and then to make the decision to supply that demand at a particular price. Where supply and demand come into equilibrium, price and quantity is determined.

In a centrally commanded economy, such as the old-style soviet communist state, the decision about what to produce, the quality and quantity of each, the capital required for such production, and the price and distribution of such goods rested solely with the central government. Technically speaking, the government held all of society's assets in trust for its people communally, and hence the moniker 'communism' by which the system has become known.

Given that during the Cold War, the world split geo-politically between the West and the East behind the so-called 'Iron Curtain', the battle between economic ideas took on a larger meaning than a mere competition between systems. In the West, to this very day, there is still a huge resistance to some of the ideas of socialism and communism, not so much for their intrinsic nature, but more so for the threat to a certain way of life in the West that they have represented since the Russian Revolution in October 1917, through to the collapse of the Soviet Empire under Mikhail Gorbachev in 1991.

Communism

Ideologically, there is a certain appeal to communism, in that this system tries to ensure that everyone in society operates on an even playing field. Unlike with the capitalist system, the state is the sole owner of capital goods and therefore the seemingly unfair advantage that 'haves' hold over 'have-nots' in society is removed. The medical doctor performs her talents for much the same price as does the mechanic. Personal enrichment is discouraged and the motivation to work is often derived from a higher cause such as duty to the state and to one's fellow citizens. When visiting countries, such as Cuba and Mozambique, both in transition to free-market systems, one still detects traces of personal duty towards fellow citizens and the state – elements all too often lacking in the free-market democracy with its emphasis on personal gain.

When production in society takes on the austere functionality of a centrally commanded system, there is little room for competition and differentiation. No need is seen to produce the more than 1 000 kinds of motoring models that we can choose from in the South African market. The most functional and cost efficient products are produced and that is what is available in the market to powerful and meek alike. There were no advertising agencies in the old soviet states – they did not have any role to play in shaping the desires that lie at the heart of the ever-outward-shifting demand curve of free-market societies.

The socialist state

How do we measure the success of a society or nation state? Some would argue that the only measure is the production of Gross Domestic Product

(GDP), where by all accounts, the USA, with $14,58 trillion in 2008 (CIA World Factbook), is the undisputed richest country in the world.

Another approach is to estimate the per capita GDP in each nation, where some of the world's largest economies such as the USA ($45 800), the United Kingdom ($35 000), and Japan ($33 500), significantly lag behind small offshore tax havens, such as Bermuda ($91 477) or Jersey ($57 000), oil-rich states such as Qatar ($87 600) and Kuwait ($55 900), and the small European nation of Luxembourg ($97 000). Even a perceived poor country, such as Ireland, which has been the source of cheap immigrant labour to both the USA and UK for the past few centuries, excels at $46 600. It is interesting to compare these figures with South Africa ($9 700), and then some of the poorest countries in the world situated on the African continent: Malawi ($800), Sierra Leone ($600), and Liberia ($500). (CIA World Factbook, 2007)

A far more nuanced approach looks at a combination of quality of life elements. Foremost in this effort is the United Nations Development Programme (UNDP) which states on their website:

> *Human Development is a development paradigm that is about much more than the rise or fall of national incomes. It is about creating an environment in which people can develop their full potential and lead productive, creative lives in accord with their needs and interests. People are the real wealth of nations. Development is thus about expanding the choices people have to lead lives that they value. And it is thus about much more than economic growth, which is only a means – if a very important one – of enlarging people's choices.*

The Human Development Index, which the UNDP developed, considers aspects such as life expectancy, infant mortality, educational enrollment, literacy, and income to determine the relative quality of life of citizens in each country. Using these analytical tools, the mighty rich USA now only ranks 15th (UNDP UNHDI 2008 Rankings), with Iceland, Norway, Canada, Australia and Ireland at the top. Other Scandinavian states such as Sweden, Finland and Denmark, who have become the symbols of the socialist state, all outrank the USA and the UK (21st). South Africa ranks a lowly 125th on this list.

The major ideological underpinning of the modern socialist state (which we should add, has become significantly more market-friendly than with what the founding fathers of socialism would have been comfortable) is to provide a basic safety network of essential social benefits for its citizens to improve their quality of life. Sometimes, the state will even operate in the market as participant, when it owns major enterprises such as a national airline, arms manufacture, electricity, telecommunications, rail, or other industries where the prohibitive capital cost might render private ownership of such essential infrastructure prohibitive.

'The emphasis on more equality and life quality in the socialist state means that the state includes in its safety net elements such as free healthcare, education, and some retirement income.'

The emphasis on more equality and life quality in the socialist state means that the state includes in its safety net elements such as free healthcare, education, and some retirement income. Furthermore, where the socialist state relies on the free market for its productive capabilities, one may find that there is a highly graduated tax regime in place, with top earners contributing a significant share of their income to the state to pay for all of society's needs. In some Scandinavian countries, income disparity is discouraged, and guidelines exist in terms of how big a difference may exist between the lowest labour rate and the highest executive pay. In South Africa, this ratio is not regulated, and the average CEO earns approximately 157 times more than the average labourer.

Finally, as socialism in its base ideology contests the rights of the owners of capital to shape the rules of the economic game to their own benefit, labour rights are strongly protected in the market place by socialist regimes. Health and safety in the workplace, fair compensation, dismissal procedures, discrimination in the workplace, and a myriad other issues that have a direct impact on the manner in which every business organises its affairs, emanate from this movement. Compare this to the gradual, yet definitive, erosion of labour rights in the major Western economies since Ronald Reagan in the USA and Margaret Thatcher in the United Kingdom, and you find a phenomenon such as the American 'work-at-will' arrangement. Under this regime, workers can be fired with immediate effect and no reason.

The moral dimensions of different economic systems

The three different economic systems and their respective economic and moral gains have been discussed above. Each of these three macro-economic systems also has a darker moral side, which will be outlined below.

Critiques against the free market

The first major moral concern with the free market is the manner in which it trumpets individual rights over that of the common interest. When people such as Donald Trump or Jack Walsh are heralded as truly successful, the only measure that is applied is how much money they accrued as individuals, and questions are hardly raised about how many lives and livelihoods of others they might have destroyed in their race to the top.

Secondly, the major assumption on which the free-market system rests, namely that all individuals are profit-maximising economic agents, tends to simplify human behaviour to a ridiculous extreme. People have richer dreams and hopes for the world in which they live, and even the core management theory that drives the free-market model specifies that meaningful work delivers better results. There is no denying that each person aims to earn a certain necessary or desired threshold of income, but money is hardly an end in itself as this assumption would have one believe.

Thirdly, the free-market ideology assumes that everything can be regulated through market forces, and that there is no need for the state other than providing the minimum level of security to its citizens. This assumption has been proven wrong time and again, as most recently demonstrated by the dramatic failure of the global financial and banking industries, yet this assumption persists amongst free market advocates.

The most enduring criticism against the free market remains its inability to ensure an implicit fair distribution of society's gains. Owners of capital hold power and can use this power to accrue even more wealth and capital through extracting rent (an economic term that denotes the difference between the value added by a labourer and the actual wage received for adding that value) from its labour force.

Capitalism has spawned a consumerist society that is at odds with the major tenets of most mainstream religions. Competition in the marketplace demands a constant effort by manufacturers to come up with new product innovations, many of which the true benefit to society is seriously in doubt. The advertising industry manipulates the aspirations of the public in order to keep the demand curve for more products and services shifting outwards, creating more production opportunities for the owners of capital. In the process, the sustainability of our natural environment gets put under growing pressure.

Finally, capitalism promotes the ideas of externalising cost and internalising profit within the firm. Although capitalism does not stand alone in its responsibility for the ecological devastation that has been caused all over the world and that threatens the very sustainability of life on earth, capitalism does not have the preservation of biosystems, ecosystems nor species as central concern. The extinction of many a species can be directly attributed to some economic agents' pursuit of profit. It remains an open question whether an industry should be allowed to pay for the right to destroy any natural environment (therefore internalising the ecological cost of production).

Critiques against communism

There are several moral and practical reasons why a centrally commanded economic system presents a problem. The first concern is the lack of freedom for the individual. We take it as a given today that one should have the free choice of economic activity and opportunity, and in fact, that right is enshrined in the UN Universal Declaration of Human Rights and in our own Constitution. Yet, under a centrally controlled regime, such choices did not necessarily pertain and the opportunity to switch careers, or to pursue one's own economic fortunes, simply did not exist. If we had to hold individual freedom as a morally justifiable right, communism would per definition be immoral.

The second concern relates to the inefficiency of such a system. In the absence of the pricing system, there is a lag between real supply and demand and production adjustments were often made too late, if at all. The result could either be the scarcity of some basic commodities, of which the bread-lines in the soviet states became the symbol, or else, there might have been an over-supply and waste of other goods. All in all, the ability of such an economy to move close to optimal production efficiency has been proven problematic. There is an assumed moral duty on the part of the state, in a world of scarcity, to ensure a political platform that enables maximum productivity in its economy for its citizens, or then at minimum, to counter waste. Hence, we could raise a moral critique against the deliberate choice of a system that does not deliver optimally.

Finally, if the true ideological underpinning of the central command systems was justice in distribution of society's gains, the real scourge of the system developed in the abuse of power by the people entrusted centrally with allocating society's assets. Corruption and bribery by powerful officials become all too easy in such a system, in the absence of both the discipline of market forces and of democratic pressures for accountability. Several moral principles are at stake here, mostly our deep-held aversion to dishonesty, the dereliction of duty, self-enrichment at the expense of others, and the abuse of power.

Critiques against the socialist state

The first of the two biggest critiques generally raised against socialism is that it removes the motivation and incentive for individuals to perform at their absolute best. Why would someone work harder just to be over-taxed and to see his or her taxes being allocated to the benefit of others in society? The basic moral argument is that each of us should get awarded according to our merit, i.e., for the quality and quantity of our labour. This might be a fair critique, yet it is interesting to note that production has not ground to a halt in the socialist-style economies of heavily-taxed Scandinavian states, and that this critique might therefore not necessarily hold true in all cases. People might get out of bed for more than just money. Perhaps there is merit in it for some people to work harder in order to help provide for the less fortunate in society.

The second concern, and one often heard in the South African context, is the so-called 'moral free-rider' problem. Where a government provides free healthcare to all its citizens, which effectively gets paid for by the taxes raised by government, is it fair that healthy triathletes pay the same taxes as someone who eats junk food, never exercises, and smokes and drinks a lot – all to the detriment of his or her health? Surely, the latter person is taking less responsibility for the possible costs to be imposed on the national health system, yet pays a similar kind of tax rate as the super-healthy.

The current government in South Africa has embraced the requirement for a nominally free-market model in order to attract foreign investment, yet infuses this model with a strong socialist agenda, given that the ideological history of the liberation movement was steeped in socialism. One should note that the previous government also participated actively in the economy as incumbent, and was hardly a bastion of the unfettered market model. Perhaps the most significant difference between the two periods of government has been the expansion of the social safety net to all citizens through housing, public health, water and electrification supply, and the introduction of income grants for unemployed, disabled and elderly citizens. From a moral perspective, current government policy tries to strike a fine moral balance between the rights of individuals to pursue their own aspirations in a free-market system, and the state's obligations to provide for the marginalised in society who hold neither the financial nor social capital to make use of the opportunities in the free market.

Macro-ethics and moral challenges to the enterprise

This final section explains how the macro-environment may impact business, and sets certain constraints on strategic and operational options for the owners and managers of the enterprise. We will look at the macro-economic policy of Black Economic Empowerment (BEE) and Employment Equity and their impact on business enterprises in South Africa.

In South Africa, we have a variety of political influences that give our economy its particular flavour. During the height of the apartheid days, certain jobs were reserved for individuals of a particular race, and people of colour were further limited to where they could open their shops. Some industries, such as the production of sorghum beer, were closed to certain races. As political organisations in opposition to apartheid were eventually banned, the only remaining place for political organising was in industry, through a militant labour movement. National strikes and stay-aways were the political tools of the 1980s, and it hurt the owners of capital in the same manner as the international trade sanctions against the country did.

No surprise then that after our democratic transition of 1994, the African National Congress took the helm with the support of both the labour movement and the South African Communist Party, and faced an interesting challenge in balancing the realities of competing globally within the ideological framework of these three alliance partners. From this balancing act, several macro-economic policies emerged that tried to address the imbalances of the past. Amongst these policies are Black Economic Empowerment and Employment Equity, which influence the day-to-day management of South African enterprises.

Firstly, with the government laying out clear goals for Black Economic Empowerment (BEE), companies have been tasked to ensure that the owner-ship of capital no longer remains in white hands alone. Government has played an active role in redirecting their procurement to these BEE com-panies, and there are several guidelines about how the transfer of capital towards other population groups should be achieved.

Secondly, given the restrictive business and educational opportunities of the past, South Africa has chosen the employment equity (or affirmative action) route towards levelling the playing field. Under the Employment Equity Act, companies set goals to eventually employ a personnel com-plement that is truly reflective of the broader demographics of our society, and are tasked to give preference to the hiring of so-called 'Previously Disadvantaged Individuals' (PDIs) in their hiring of new staff.

Neither Black Economic Empowerment nor Employment Equity is without its detractors, yet the underlying idea is to establish a just and fair economy, based on a principle that most people on both sides of the argument can normally agree on, namely that everybody should have the same opportunity to participate freely in the economy.

These two examples are merely illustrative of how the world of com-merce cannot be divorced from ethical questions about justice, fairness and equity on the macro-economic level.

Conclusion

The choice of a country's macro-economic policies and political system directly influences the day-to-day strategic and operational choices that the modern organisation has at its disposal. Macro-ethics concerns itself with issues of justice associated with these choices, on the understanding that if the macro-system is morally flawed, it creates an untenable tension for corporations and individual agents in the economy to consistently act in a moral manner.

Capitalism has by and large proven its mettle as the most productive economic system, yet there remain significant problems with configuring the fair distribution of society's gains. The resulting inequality poses a serious challenge to business at large, as well as to the long-term health and survival of the capitalist state, because a growing number of citizens in our own society do not experience the benefits of this system in their daily lives.

The individuals who operate in the economy and the organisations that they form to this effect have a definite stake in ensuring a sustainable and just system. As Austrian economist Joseph Schumpeter warned, it may be way too early to judge the success of capitalism, and it may require hundreds of years to reach a conclusion (1942). Beyond sustainable survival, all players in the economy may also carry a moral duty towards their fellow citizens in these affairs. In the following chapters, we will explore the content of that moral duty.

CHAPTER
3

The social responsibility of business

Business companies are part of societies and therefore always find themselves in relationships with the societies in which they operate. Companies potentially can have a big impact on society. They can add value by providing employment, wealth and development opportunities for the societies in which they operate, but they can also damage societies by exploiting employees, corrupting local communities or by damaging the natural environment. The relationship between business and society therefore always has an ethical dimension. Companies inevitably find themselves in relationships of responsibility with the societies in which they operate.

The way in which this relationship between companies and societies is conceived differs not only from company to company, but also from society to society. Some companies try to keep their responsibilities to society as minimal as possible or even to evade their social responsibilities, while other companies take their responsibilities to society seriously and even venture beyond the minimal expectations of society. In similar vein, some societies have limited or informal expectations of companies, while others have extended and formal expectations – often written into laws, regulations and codes – that companies have to comply with.

In this chapter the various responsibilities that businesses might have towards society will be systematically unpacked. We will start with the most basic economic expectations that societies have of companies and then move on to the legal and other formal requirements that companies are expected to comply with. From there we will move to more informal social and ethical expectations of society and finally into the discretionary domain where companies can decide how much they want to invest in society and what role they wish to play as corporate citizens of their societies.

Economic responsibility

The first and most basic responsibility that a company has towards society is to be economically successful. Merely by remaining a viable business, a company can contribute in various ways to the wellbeing of society. By being economically viable the company creates value for a wide range of stakeholders. It provides a return on investment for shareholders as well as income for those who are employed by the company. It also provides work for its suppliers, and goods and services for its customers. The community and society benefit from levies, taxes and other contributions that companies have to pay to local or national governments, which in turn can be invested in the development of local and national infrastructure. Stakeholders stand to lose substantially should a company fail to remain economically viable.

We just have to consider the consequences and dire impact that the economic failure of companies, such as Fidentia in South Africa, Parmalat in Italy, and Enron in the USA, had on their communities – not only locally but also further abroad. In such cases of spectacular failure, shareholders, managers, employees, suppliers, customers and local communities all suffer damages. The detrimental consequences of such spectacular economic failures are well publicised in the media, but these negative consequences are no less real in the case of economic failures of small and medium enterprises that are unlikely to attract media attention.

The first responsibility of a company to society is thus to take due care of its own affairs in order to ensure that it remains a viable economic operation. Irresponsible behaviour by shareholders, managers and employees that jeopardises the economic survival of the company is not only irresponsible to the company, but also to the society.

Formal obligations

A second social obligation of companies is to comply with formal standards imposed by society. The purpose of such formal standards is to prevent companies from engaging in irresponsible behaviour that can jeopardise the functioning of the market, society or the environment. These controls can also be intended to protect vulnerable stakeholders of companies, such as minority shareholders, employees, suppliers, customers, local communities and the environment.

These formal standards that companies have to comply with can be articulated in various ways. They can take the form of laws, such as anti-competition laws or they can come in the form of regulations such as insider trading regulations issued by a financial services board. Stock exchanges also can make special rules by which listed companies have to abide, such as rules that determine what listed companies have to disclose to their shareholders and to the public at large. Other forms of formal standards that companies have to adhere to are laws, rules or codes that stipulate the rights of workers, customers or that set standards for how companies should act with regard to the environment.

The question can be raised whether obeying a law, or standard set by an external party, should be regarded as socially responsible behaviour by business, or whether it should merely be seen as a duty that companies, like all other members of society, have to fulfil. Those who deny that obeying rules counts as responsible behaviour, argue that one can only meaningfully talk about responsibility when a person (or company) has the freedom to decide what they wish to do (cf. Carrol, 1999:277). There are, however, two problems with this argument. The first problem is that we do accuse companies of irresponsible behaviour when they do not comply with specific standards of, for example, safety, health or environmental protection. Thus we do associate non-compliance to formal standards with their responsibility. The second problem with this argument is that it creates a wrong impression that companies that operate in societies with very lax legislation or standards of business behaviour have much more scope for socially responsible behaviour than companies that operate in highly regulated societies. The problem with the argument is that a company that adheres to a specific standard of, for example, employee safety in a society where such standards are enforced by the state will not be regarded as socially responsible, whereas a company who adheres to the very same standards of employee safety in a society where such standards are not regulated by the state, will be regarded as socially responsible. It is exactly this untenable distinction that led Matten and Moon (2008) to distinguish between implicit and explicit corporate social responsibility. Implicit corporate social responsibility refers to the social responsibility that companies perform when they adhere to formal external standards, while explicit corporate social responsibility refers to social responsibility that companies perform in the absence of formal external standards.

Social expectations

Besides the formal social obligations that companies have to adhere to, there also are informal social expectations that companies have to respect. There are mainly three different reasons why companies have to respond to these informal social obligations. Companies have to heed these informal social expectations, firstly, in order to gain legitimacy, secondly, to enhance their strategic interests, and thirdly, to honour their ethical obligations to society. Each of these considerations for honouring the social expectations of society will be discussed below.

Legitimacy considerations

The first reason why companies have to consider and respond to the informal social expectations of society is because their acceptance by society (or legitimacy) as a business depends on whether business is perceived by society as acting in the interest of society (cf. Garriga & Mele, 2004:57–58). It is often suggested that a business exists merely to make a profit for its owners.

Although this is certainly an important – and often the most important – consideration for starting a business, it is not sufficient to lend legitimacy to a business. For a company to be considered as a legitimate business operation, it has to do more than merely make profit. It also needs to be seen at a minimum not to harm the wellbeing of society.

An example to illustrate the point: Take the case of someone starting up a new company that abducts children from their homes and exports the abducted children as sex slaves to other countries at a huge profit. It is highly improbable that this operation will ever be recognised as a legitimate business operation. The fact that it yields excellent profits will not alter the situation in any way. Making profit is not a sufficient condition for being recognised as a business. The legitimacy of any company (or industry) that clearly violates the interests of those affected by its activities or products will be questioned by society.

A legitimate business can be defined as an enterprise that makes profit by providing goods and services in such a way that it respects the interests of society. When it becomes apparent that a business violates the interests of society its legitimacy is eroded. The predicament facing the tobacco industry at the moment is a good illustration of how society can question the legitimacy of an industry and restrict its operations when it is perceived not to be acting in the best interests of society. This approval that companies need from society in order to be accepted as legitimate business operations is sometimes referred to as a company's 'licence to operate'. In contrast to days gone by when a company's licence to operate consisted of a certificate issued by a public official, the modern company's licence to operate also consists of the approval by society that the company respects society's basic interests.

Strategic considerations

Companies always find themselves entangled in a web of social relations. In order to survive and flourish, companies need to win and retain the co-operation and support of their stakeholders. For example, companies rely on the state to provide them with a regulatory framework that protects their operations and assets. They also rely on the government to provide them with the infrastructure required to run their operations, such as transport and communication networks. Companies often require external funding by the government, banks, or investors to start or expand their operations. They depend on society to provide them with human resources to staff their operations. In addition, companies rely on suppliers to provide them with goods or services that are required in rendering the specific services or products that companies offer their customers. Companies obviously depend on their consumers to purchase their products and services. They also rely on the natural environment to provide them with resources for production and, indeed, with the basic conditions for their very existence.

Given this social network of relationships on which companies depend, it does not surprise that they require the co-operation and support of all these stakeholders in order to survive and flourish. There are thus sound strategic reasons why a company has to take the interests and social expectations of their stakeholders into consideration. Should a company be perceived as disregarding the expectations of their stakeholders, they run the danger of alienating and losing the trust and co-operation of a specific group of their stakeholders. Such alienation can translate into a variety of measures that can either impose additional costs on the business, such as additional taxation, legal restrictions, and fines, or it can lead to substantial decline in income in the case of strikes, non-delivery of services by suppliers or consumer boycotts.

It is thus in the interests of companies to strengthen their ties with their external stakeholders. This process of building strong and reliable relationships with stakeholders is sometimes referred to as 'social issues management' (cf. Clarkson, 1995:94) or 'stakeholder engagement' (cf. Greenwood, 2007:315). Whether it is called social issues management or stakeholder engagement, the basic intention remains to be in touch with social expectations of stakeholders in order to enhance the strategic interests of the company.

Ethical obligations

Both of the above considerations for respecting the social expectations that society and specific stakeholder groups have of business revolve around the self-interest of the company. It is thus in the enlightened self-interest of the company to heed these social expectations. Both these considerations treat the social expectations of society and stakeholders' groups as instrumental to the success of the company (cf. Donaldson & Preston, 1995:66–67). The implication of such an instrumental approach is that society and stakeholders need to be respected as long as they exercise a strategic influence on the company. This, however, also implies that when it can be established that a specific stakeholder group has no power to influence the strategic objectives of a company then such a stakeholder group can be ignored.

Besides the above strategic considerations that treat the interests of stakeholders in an instrumental manner, there also are ethical considerations that companies need to consider. As members of society, companies share in the basic ethical obligations that all members of society have. That is the obligation not merely to care for one's own interests, but to also consider how pursuing one's own interests affects the interests of others. All members of society need to be treated with respect and decency irrespective of their status or the social power that they can exert over companies. These basic standards of respect and decency are mostly unwritten and simply presupposed by societies. Some of them are, however, formalised in human rights charters, such as the United Nations Universal Human Rights Declaration or the Bill of Rights in the South African constitution. These moral obligations give a normative dimension to the relationship between a company and its stakeholders. The company needs to fulfil its ethical obligations to all its stakeholders, irrespective of whether it is in the short- or long-term financial interest of the company to do so.

Social investments or philanthropy

All of the previous forms of social responsibility fall into the categories of responsibilities that companies have to fulfil, or ought to fulfil. There are, however, further responsibilities that companies can fulfil should they wish to do so (cf. Leisinger, n.d.:7). These latter responsibilities are often called the discretionary responsibilities of companies (cf. Carrol, 1999:284). Such discretionary responsibilities consist of companies donating funds to causes that they wish to support.

There are various reasons why companies might want to engage in such discretionary donations to society. They may be donated merely out of sympathy for the suffering of less fortunate members of society, such as in the case of the poor or victims of natural or human-made disasters.

They may also be donated because the company stands to benefit from such donations in the long run. When a company makes donation to society in the hope that not only society will benefit from the donation, but that the company will also benefit, it is referred to as a corporate social investment. Examples of social investments are when companies sponsor schools or bursaries for students because they stand to benefit from a society that is better educated or who have more well educated people that they potentially can employ. It might also be that the company does not benefit directly from the outcome of the social investment that they are making, but that they benefit indirectly by gaining a good reputation in the communities where they invest socially. Such reputational gains cannot only cement existing stakeholder relations, but also attract both potential employees and customers to the company. They can also ease relationships between the company and local or national governments.

A form of social investment that has recently gained in prominence is 'bottom-of-the-pyramid investment' (cf. Garriga & Mele, 2004:54–55). The pyramid refers to the socio-economic strata of society. At the bottom of the socio-economic pyramid are vast numbers of low-income earners, who are often overlooked by companies since companies tend to focus on the middle- and high-income groups (or the middle and top of the pyramid). Companies have started to realise that by investing in the development of the bottom of the pyramid, they do not only support the development of society, but also open opportunities for themselves to market and sell their products and services to the largely untapped markets at the bottom of the pyramid. Examples of such bottom-of-the-pyramid social investment are banks who invest in communities in the hope that they will be able to 'bank the unbanked' – that is, to turn vast numbers of low-income earners who have never had a bank account before into future accountholders at the bank. Other examples are communication and information technology companies who develop affordable less sophisticated products that nevertheless are useful for poor communities. In this way, new opportunities are presented to the company as well as the bottom-of-the-pyramid communities.

Social development (corporate citizenship)

Corporations are playing an ever bigger role in society. Large corporations in particular have a considerable impact on the societies in which they operate. Bigger influence by business inevitably creates bigger expectations from society and bigger responsibilities for business. Although it has been indicated above that companies are expected to be decent members of the societies in which they operate, it is also clear that their responsibilities are often bigger and broader than those of individual members of society. This is especially true in an era where on the one side the sphere of influence of nation states are shrinking and where globalisation on the other hand is creating spaces of interaction that lie beyond the sphere of influence of nation states (cf. Garriga & Mele, 2004:54; Matten, Crane, & Chapple, 2003:115).

Corporations, consequently, find themselves from time to time in situations where they are being called upon, or where they are being presented with opportunities, to fulfil roles that have previously been associated with the role of the state. This is the case when companies, especially in developing countries, are expected or feel compelled to provide facilities and infrastructure, like roads, hospitals and schools. It is also the case when companies are being called upon or feel obliged to protect the basic human rights of vulnerable people, such as when they operate in political regimes where human rights are abused or when they find themselves in societies where there is armed conflict or genocide. Similarly, when companies operate in jurisdictions where there is very lax or no environmental regulation, companies are either expected to be responsible, or they feel resposible, to set their own standards of sound environmental policy.

These are examples of companies that play a role (or companies that are expected to play a role) previously associated with the state. Matten, Crane, & Chapple (2003) have proposed that we use the term corporate citizenship to refer to this political role that companies either play or are expected to play. The term citizenship has a distinct political connotation and therefore it makes sense to reserve the term corporate citizenship to refer to the political role that companies are expected to play in distinction from other roles that they are playing in societies.

The political (or corporate citizenship) role of companies is much more controversial than the other social responsibility roles of business in society. The reason for the controversial nature of this role is that companies are playing a role that was previously performed by the government, but unlike governments they are not accountable to the people whose lives they are influencing. The leaders of companies are not elected by society and are therefore not exposed to a regular process of re-election where dissatisfied voters have the opportunity to vote them out of office. Obviously there are other avenues open to people who feel that companies are abusing their political role, such as public protests and consumer boycotts, as have been witnessed recently in, for example, anti-globalisation protests around the world. Nevertheless the issue of the abuse of political power by corporations looms large. In this regard corporations find themselves in a precarious position. On the one hand they are often called upon to step into spaces where governments have failed to deliver or to protect their citizens. And on the other hand they are often accused of abusing their power to gain and exercise undue political influence over societies in which they operate. It has almost become a case of 'damned if you do and damned if you don't'. Consequently we can expect to see more guidelines emerging that will attempt to provide companies with guidance on their appropriate corporate citizenship role in society. The United Nations Global Compact is one such attempt to provide guidance to corporations on their responsibilities with regard to human rights, environmental responsibility and corruption prevention.

Conclusion

This chapter made it clear that whether businesses like it or not, they always find themselves in a relationship with society. This relationship between a business and its social environment has the potential to make or break a business. It is therefore not surprising that businesses are much more aware, careful and meticulous in how they actively manage their relationships with specific stakeholder groups and society at large.

CHAPTER
4

Ethics in organisations

While ethical policies and practices of governments and corporations across the globe provide the content for analysing business ethics at the macro- and meso- levels of ethical enquiry, it is often what happens *within* corporations that determines their ethical impact on the physical, economic and social environment. The modern business organisation is often perceived as an entity that practises amoral management. Such an entity would display little of the intrinsic ethical obligation it may have towards society (Rossouw, 2008a). Corporations are, of course, free to take up whatever social and environmental responsibilities they decide to pursue (for philanthropic or strategic considerations), but might discard them again whenever they wish to do so. This is not to deny that state and society can impose social and environmental obligations upon corporations by which they simply have to abide, but then such obligations are exactly that: imposed obligations and not intrinsic moral obligations.

The third level of ethical enquiry (the first two levels were addressed in the preceding two chapters), the micro-level of enquiry, is aimed at understanding ethics *in* organisations. In this chapter an intra-organisational perspective is presented. It will be shown that ethics cannot be divorced from business activity.

Business without ethics

Popular myths are believed by many people in society. While a myth may express a partial truth, it may also conceal some reality (De George, 1999). The prevailing myth in modern organisational thinking is that organisations are inhabited by *homo economicus* – the rational person only driven by the desire to further his or her economic self-interest. This reductionist perception of human motives results in business practices that serve economic self-interest to the detriment of other human priorities and social and environmental concerns. It further creates a sentiment among members of an organisation that ethics and business cannot mix. This sentiment could manifest as a way of thinking and doing that is devoid of ethical concerns.

Shareholder value dominance

In the business environment one group of stakeholders, namely the share-holders, has, according to Mintzberg, Simons and Basu (2002:69), 'muscled out all the others'. Despite indications that corporate governance philosophies around the world assume the consideration of the interests of *all* stakeholders, and not only that of owners or shareholders, the belief that shareholders' needs come first is still pervasive. Although (customer) service excellence appears in virtually every set of organisational values, and employees are purportedly 'our greatest asset', shareholder value often remains the bottom line. Organ-isational decisions and actions that benefit shareholders are given priority. In fact, shareholder value has become the mantra in many boardrooms (Noam Cook, 2005). With some notable exceptions the shareholders are not partial to 'how ethically' their returns are generated.

A shareholder-focused morality often results in a belief that 'the business of business is business' – and therefore not ethics. The premise of a share-holder morality is built on the notion that serving the shareholders results in what is best for all. Such a limited belief causes a neglect of the legitimate interests of non-shareholder groups. Although business decision-making and action can never be totally value-free, that is devoid of any ethical dimension, the selective morality that underpins a stakeholder-dominant sentiment, feeds the myth of amoral management in business. Businesspeople act out these beliefs by being primarily concerned with profit. This type of orientation is the so-called bottom-line mentality. Businesspeople and managers that dis-play such a singular focus are not immoral or unethical *per se*. Nor are they evil people driven by opportunism at the expense of others. Nor do they intend harm, abuse and exploitation. They merely hold the firm belief that ethical considerations are inappropriate in business (De George, 1999) and in essence view the organisation and its activities as ethically neutral.

Ethical neutrality may result in thinking and doing that is based on the notion that business is amoral. This leads to a reluctance to discuss ethical issues or to engage in moral debate. A blind eye is then cast to clear ethical concerns that may arise. There is also an aversion to heed to calls to consider ethics in business decisions and actions. Such organisational members may be 'well-intentioned, but are morally casual or careless, or may even be morally unconscious' (Carroll & Buchholtz, 2006:191). They just do not think ethically.

Motives of ethical neutrality

Organisations are currently being rewarded for short-term annual (and often even quarterly) financial performance. In an attempt to maintain the illusion of perpetual short-term growth, financial performance and records are massaged to portray upward financial performance. To ensure that corporate executives align themselves to this trend of perpetual short-term growth, their compensation is increasingly linked to, and dependent on, their ability to produce perpetual short-term gain. It is no secret that short-term gain can easily collide with longer-term growth and economic, social and environmental wealth.

It is simply easier to be concerned with facts, profits and losses, and products or services, than to spend energy on an abstract notion like business ethics and the value judgements that are perceived to be part of it. It is also easier for investors, business partners and prospective employees to evaluate the success of a business in monetary terms or by the products produced. Shareholder value can also be easily and objectively measured by returns on equity valuation (Noam Cook, 2005).

Goodpaster (2007) identifies a paradox that may threaten ethics in business when he states that it appears to be 'essential, yet somehow both dangerous and perhaps even illegitimate to guide business decision making by moral values' (11). *Essential* in the sense that business ethics is required to temper the intensely goal-directed behaviour that blinds individuals and organisations to the consequences of their focus. And *illegitimate* because of legal and rules-based expectations that limit managerial discretion. He notes that 'managers who appeal to ethical values, if they are not looked upon as questionably sincere are often looked upon as *going beyond their authority*' (2007:11) (author's emphasis). Scepticism about the place of ethics in business is still widely evident, especially if it means incurring costs or foregoing opportunities for profit (Sharp Paine, 2003).

Amoral managers

Managers who hold an amoral belief that the business of business is business, are however, often decisive business leaders that display perseverance and determination. Decisiveness is, after all, a criterion that weighs heavily in decisions to appoint or promote leaders. Although they do not have an intention to deliberately cause harm to stakeholders, they do either (a) make a conscious decision to disregard ethics in their decision making, or (b) pursue goals without balance when blinkered by their pursuit of bottom-line aspirations. Their lack of balance undermines organisational wholeness or integrity and they are often unaware of ethical implications of decisions.

Carroll and Buchholtz (2006) distinguish between intentional amoral management and unintentional amoral management. *Intentional amoral management* is practised by managers who believe that business and ethics cannot mix and that moral judgement does not apply in business. Such cynicism leads to the labelling of business ethics as an oxymoron. 'There are countless reports of successful businesspeople who claim *the only immoral act in business is to lose money*' (Kelley, 1999:18) (authors' emphasis). Although *unintentional moral managers*, similarly to intentional moral managers, do not think about business in ethical terms, they 'are simply casual about, careless about, or inattentive to the fact that their decisions and actions may have negative or deleterious effects on others' (Carroll & Buchholtz, 2006:189). They lack ethical sensitivity and do not waste time at work on thinking about the ethical dimension of business.

Amoral beliefs and business language

Some current amoral business beliefs make it very difficult to express ethical sentiments in the business context. The jargon used to describe certain business practices is analysed to illustrate this.

The notion of *strategy* in business only became part of the vocabulary of business leaders about 40 years ago. Prior to that it was only used in a military sense to mean 'that which a manager [read *general, major* or *captain*] does to offset actions or potential actions of competitors [read *enemy*]' (Steiner & Miner, 1982:18). The word strategy, from the Greek *strategos*, literally means 'the art of the general' (Steiner & Miner, 1982:18). This word, together with some favourite war-like colloquialisms used in business, for example: 'sales tactics', 'we take no prisoners', 'we launch products', 'we target consumers' (Visser & Sunter, 2002), probably emanated from the reading of the book by Sun Tsu (500 BC), *The art of war*, which is compulsory reading in many business schools.

And, of course, there is the ubiquitous 'we must be lean and mean'. Mintzberg et al. (2002:71) question the adage of lean and mean that is so prevalent in modern organisations in the following way: ''Lean and mean' is a fashionable term these days, a kind of mantra for economic man. 'Lean' certainly sounds good – better than fat. But the fact that 'mean' has been made into a virtue is a sad sign of the times.' For amoralists 'ethical language is simply not the language of business' (De George, 1999:5).

Whilst it cannot be denied that the words used in business circles provide leaders with focus and goal-oriented direction, and that no business can survive without a clear focus on the bottomline and decent returns for shareholders, the problem with excessive use of war-talk is that it leads to myopia and short-termism. This may catalyse an exclusion of other legitimate stakeholder interests.

Cases illustrative of amoral beliefs in business

Facilitation fees in developing countries

Until the late 1990s, France and Germany allowed corporations doing business in developing countries to claim tax rebates for 'facilitation fees' they paid to foreign governments to secure business deals. Company executives were acting amorally by doing business within the parameters of the law and ensuring good return for shareholders.

Marketing alcohol to teenagers

Alcohol producing companies market fruit-flavoured alcoholic drinks to a borderline teenage market segment. Although the companies' advertisements portray young (over 18) adults, the themes of such advertisements show young people having fun induced by their products. The fact that the drinks contain alcohol, of which the levels sometimes exceed those contained in standard beer, is added as an afterthought only when required by law. These companies conduct their business within legal requirements, and probably show good financial returns, but they may be acting unethically by encouraging underage drinking.

Stereotyping in advertising

Albeit very subtly, some companies' marketing campaigns continue to utilise female sexuality to draw male attention in advertisements. In the process, stereotypes are reinforced. A legal, yet unethical approach.

Selling arms to those who really should not have them

In many countries there are no laws to prevent armament manufacturers from selling their products to governments guilty of human rights abuse. The companies offer the argument that it is not their responsibility to exert control over the use of the products. They show good returns for shareholders, within legal limits, but again, amoral thinking.

Impact on stakeholders

Being good to employees, customers, suppliers and other stakeholders on the condition that it is good for the shareholders or owners, is an approach that typically results from the belief that only shareholder value matters in business. Within such a mindset, the interests of employees, for example, can easily be neglected if it does not have a direct impact on the creation of shareholder value. This phenomenon is not limited to periods of economic recession, but may occur at any given time as a quick fix to enhance shareholders' opinions of the organisation's balance sheets. Cutting salaries, benefit related and even training costs, make the books look better. Frequently, and not as a last resort – as organisations often claim during announcements of downsizing and retrenchments – employees are costs to be cut to ensure continued benefits for shareholders or owners. Organisational decision-makers often have little empathy for employees who lose their jobs and thus their life-sustaining incomes. The trauma experienced by employees and the effect on the workplace climate is also negated.

Reward for the board

A South African food supply company, with a long and reputable history of being a good employer and business partner of its suppliers, failed to realise profit for a number of years. As a remedy, the board implemented a strategy to do asset stripping (selling off unwanted or marginally useful company assets). For the first year in many, the company showed a good profit. Without further ado the board awarded its members bonuses that totalled 57% of the profit shown. Soon thereafter it announced the retrenchment of 600 employees. Both these actions benefited the shareholders and were legal. The effects on employee morale were, however, devastating.

Customers are seen as sources of income for the organisation and not as persons with legitimate and ethical expectations to reliable and safe products and services. An instrumental view is held about customers. How will being good to them help us make money? Providing excellent service is a forced strategy implemented to decrease costs that may be incurred by customer complaints or migration.

Mobile phone packages

Certain mobile network companies offer very attractive monthly call packages (which may include some free talk time). Their customers sign 24-month contracts on these deals. A problem arises when a *caveat emptor* (buyer beware) approach is adopted whereby customers are not informed or advised that they are actually losing money on their current packages and that other cheaper packages that would be much more cost-effective given the scope of the customer's monthly usage are available.

Providing credit to customers

Prior to the National Credit Act of 2006, many South African banks and retailers provided credit to customers that could not really afford it. A number of retailers went as far as actually mailing to some of their customers, that had repaid previous debt in quite a disciplined way, a type of credit card that allowed the customers to purchase goods for large amounts which they could then pay back over a number of months. Some of the customers were relatively unsophisticated and lacked personal credit management experience. The retailers also never educated their potential debtors on proper personal financial planning and management prior to offering them credit. The customers proceeded to purchase goods on credit without being able to afford it. When they failed to repay the debt the companies swiftly laid claim to some of the customers' other possessions, which were then sold to defray 'expenses'. The customers were, however, then still obliged to pay the companies further money owed. The retailers did good business, but caused a lot of grief in many poor households.

In organisational climates dominated by a lack of ethical considerations, suppliers are not viewed as business partners. They are seen as dispensable entities that should be grateful for doing business with the company. The lowest cost supplier is often selected with little regard for product quality, unless product quality and safety are determined by law. Suppliers are listed on the company's debtors' books as entities that can wait for their money while 'we draw interest on *our* money' for as long as possible, or while we use 'their money to finance new ventures'.

Controlling of suppliers

A retail group is notorious for the way in which it treats its suppliers. Since doing business with the retail group is potentially extremely lucrative, suppliers vie for the 'privilege' of doing business with the group. The suppliers are initially lured by fair prices for their goods. As time goes by the group makes deals with their suppliers to purchase more product units, but at lower prices. Eventually the group purchases, at very low profit margins for the supplier, as many of, or even all the units, the supplier can produce. Further demands by the group for lower prices, together with stalling tactics to pay suppliers' accounts, result in the suppliers having to close their businesses. The retail group views its actions as good business and shows good return on investment for its shareholders.

Should beliefs that satisfying the needs of shareholders by and large prevail in an organisation, stakeholders other than employees, customers and suppliers will also be affected. As such, little consideration will be afforded to the legitimate ethical expectations of local communities, which provide employees to the organisation, and local governments, which implement and maintain the infrastructure within which the organisation operates. The natural environment as a stakeholder may be considered only to the extent that the organisation complies with environmental regulations and laws, but does not take a longer term view on environmental issues and ultimately, sustainability.

The ethical dimension of the organisation

It appears as if opting for the belief that ethics is not required in business has shown enough success in the form of satisfaction to 'make it a real option for clever, powerful individuals ... especially in the shorter term' (Prozesky, 2007:86). The purpose of this section is to provide a counter-logic for this belief. It will be shown that ethics is an integral dimension of business organisations as well as of corporate success. Recognition of the ethical dimension of an organisation does not equate to crusades, jihads or sermons. Ethics is inherently part of business. It is not an add-on or nice-to-have when time and money permits.

The relational nature of business

There is no disputing that law and regulation are needed to prevent business from collapsing into chaos. However, a mere reliance on law and regulation can never constitute a successful business. Organisations are also social institutions that rely on people and their intrinsically *human* relations to collectively ensure success.

Business, and life in organisations, can never be solely based on cold, legalistic rule or policy requirements. An organisation consists of persons. These persons form relations amongst themselves and with others outside the organisation. Relations with those outside the organisation are determined by the quality of the relations within the organisation. The default mode from which relations are created, are positive in nature. This mode excludes greed, selfishness, a lack of empathy, evil intentions and lying as the basis of relationships. On the contrary, the basic premise is that of values, beliefs and behaviours that show concern for other persons. Without concern for the other the relational nature of organisations will collapse.

The basic *values* of human interaction – integrity, honesty, fairness, compassion and responsibility – are relatively stable convictions of what is important to maintain relations. One finds it hard to believe that the pre-vailing values, beliefs and behaviours in organisations exclude the building of relations based on trust and honesty for example. As such, a singular focus on the 'truth' that the enhancement of shareholder wealth is all that matters in business, nullifies many other truths in the relational setting of the organisation. These other 'truths' are, however, more real in societies and organisations than such a singular focus. When organisations are dominated by leaders who believe that ethics is not required in business, the relational dimension in business will suffer. This goes against needs and preferences that emanate from default human values, beliefs and behaviours.

As human beings, we interact with other people. We operate as part of human systems. In organisations, these systems take the form of dialogue, teamwork, and other forms of organisational behaviour. Human systems contain ethical standards which are required to create harmony, mitigate conflict, ensure fairness and evoke trust (Noam Cook, 2005). Ethical standards give form and direction to human activity. The actions people take and the choices they make reflect their values. The way people treat each other is evidence of their worldviews, values and accountability to other human beings. By the same token, ethics is a core dimension of decision making; not only decision making aimed at solving people related issues, but business decisions that could affect not just the bottom line, but human beings as well.

Systems cannot function *technically* only. 'Ethical values act as 'controls' or 'regulators' that we draw on to decide what is a desirable configuration of a human system and an acceptable direction to go with it' (Noam Cook, 2005:135). Surely human flourishing also depends on the ethical expectations and stability of others?

Business has an integral relational dimension. Since all relationships are built upon expectations and behaviour, and because ethics determines the value-based quality of the relationship, business is also about the ethics of relationships. These relationships are created for the sake of the business within and between individuals, groups and organisations. The extent to which business leaders and their organisations recognise and embrace the ethical imperative of relationships determines the trust of stakeholders.

Ethics is core to all relationships. When relationships are built on integrity, honesty, fairness, compassion and responsibility, levels of fear decline, confidence rises, and effort and energy are released that bring about balanced goal attainment. Prozesky (2007) suggests that a life of inclusive concern (concern for self and others) is better equipped to yield positive longer-term experiences and stability that people desire not only for themselves, but also for those around them.

The co-operative nature of work

Working within a business means working with other people. This is true for even the smallest of businesses. It is true even of the one-person business that starts up with no outside funding. That one-person business will still find itself in a relationship with at least one supplier and/or client. Actions performed within any business have an impact on all who work in and with that business. Since ethics is at the core of relations, such actions are never ethically neutral, but are always ethically laden. They can impact positively or negatively on the interests of others. This is a brutal and undeniable fact of work.

Ethics is also the foundation of teamwork. There are some things that people can do as groups that they cannot achieve at all as individuals. That is why organisations have divisions, departments, sections and teams. These are designed to function in specific ways. Since these functions can have a positive or negative effect on the wellbeing of people, they are open to moral evaluation whether managers believe it or not. The sustained wellbeing of multiple stakeholders cannot be achieved without harnessing the efforts of multiple contributors in the organisation (Prozesky, 2007), or creating the 'we'. The interdependence between individuals and groups is based on the quality of the ethical dimension of the relationships, and not only on the shared goal of financial success.

Groups cannot function without norms. The extent to which group norms are built upon ethical principles will determine the extent of conformity and cohesion in a group. Optimal cohesion facilitates the collective performance of groups, which is usually greater than the sum of the performances of individual group members. Collective performance is dependent on the levels of respect, empathy, openness, sharing of information and consequently, the levels of trust that exist among members. The trust that ensues in a group with strong ethical norms will enhance effective socialisation of new group members by the setting of boundaries of acceptable behaviour, thus eliminating uncertainty. Where group members' interdependency is based on ethical norms, the outcomes of positive group dynamics, for example, social support, workload sharing, and a sense that individual contributions are valued, are greatly enhanced.

Trust

Corporate ethical dysfunction does more than just hurt stock performance (Lennick & Kiel, 2005). It affects others in the relational domain. Building relationships that rest on strong ethical foundations create sustained trust. Even when one of the parties makes a mistake, 'the context of a trusting relationship is more likely to elicit understanding' (Kuper, 2006:71). Ethical relationships bring about positive collaboration, so much so that a 'we' is created, as opposed to an 'us versus them' mindset that so often exists in business. Kuper (2006) goes as far as suggesting that intrinsically good relationships give the 'we' a competitive advantage, as barriers to exit from the relationship are established. Ethical relationships go beyond profit and establish balance in interaction.

The time and effort it takes to establish trust-based relationships with employees and external stakeholders enhances a stakeholder mindset built on a realisation of the 'we'. Such mindsets are 'more ethically comprehensive' (Goodpaster, 2007:46), as they create room for joint decision-making on the norms that define these relationships. Goodpaster (2007) suggests that one should 'realise' the other through identifying with the other through association. This results in a somewhat adjusted take on the adage 'the greatest good for the greatest number', as balance is achieved through determining 'what is best for most'. (The crucial role that ethics plays in building trust relationships is explored in Chapter 11.)

Commitment and quality of work

For most people, work occurs within a specific organisation and the business practices of that organisation affect their lives. Ethics is crucial to the job performance of individuals. The employment contract that an employee enters into with an employer might stipulate the kind and quantity of work that is expected from an employee, but it cannot, however, determine the quality of work: the loyalty, dedication, and creativity with which employees will perform their stipulated tasks. These are determined by the ethical relations within a business.

People who feel that they are respected, who receive recognition for good work, and who sense that their creative contributions are appreciated, tend to work with more dedication than those who are not treated in the same way. They are much more likely to utilise their potential for the benefit of the business.

The opposite is equally true: people who are humiliated, who never receive recognition for their efforts, and who sense that their own ideas are not appreciated, tend to work with less dedication and less creativity. They do only what is expected of them. For them, their employment contract is the sum total of what they do.

Ethical organisations are characterised by the respect that they show to all their stakeholders. In the Peters and Waterman (1982) study, *In Search of Excellence*, the researchers isolated the mindset of *respect for the individual* (the employee) as the most pervasive theme in the excellent companies scrutinised. A mindset of respect for the individual is of course a fundamental ethical value as Immanuel Kant already emphasised centuries ago. An organisation's commitment to its people arises out of the respect for the worth and dignity of individuals who devote their energies to the business and depend on the business for their economic wellbeing. Even in crisis situations such organisations will minimise whatever hardships have to be imposed in the form of workforce reductions, relocations and the loss of income (Kreitner & Kinicki, 1992:111–112).

Conclusion

In this chapter the intra-organisational, or micro-, dimension of business ethics was explained as ethics *within* organisations. What then is the real relation between ethics and an organisation? An organisation is not an isolated, enclosed, or necessarily tangible, system. It consists of people that determine the quality of each others' lives as well as the lives of those beyond the boundaries of the organisation. Ethics is no longer viewed as 'just another aspect' of the organisation that hinders financial performance. On the contrary, it is regarded as an integral part of the organisation without which it would be unable to fulfil its purpose, mission and goals.

The narrow and shallow perception that the organisation provides a home for *homo economicus* is not only out of step with our most basic experience and intuitions about organisational members' motivations. It also deprives organisations of calling on other motives that might inspire employees as well as shareholders, clients and suppliers. Recognising within business that people care not only for financial success and gain, but also for their own psychological wellbeing and the wellness of their families, friends, societies and environment, can create new avenues for tapping into the creativity and support of all stakeholders of business.

PART

3

Theories on ethics and business

INTRODUCTION

Theories in any field of study are sense-making devices that assist us in getting a theoretical grasp of the field of study. They enable us to better understand, evaluate and sometimes even predict matters in the field of study. Without theories, any field of study is amorphous and difficult to navigate. For this reason we introduce a number of theories that are important for making sense and gaining a deeper understanding of the field of business ethics.

There are different types of theories. Two types of theories are particularly important in the field of business ethics. They are descriptive theories and normative theories. Descriptive theories in business ethics describe and explain states of ethical affairs. Such descriptive theories enable scholars and practitioners to gain deeper insight into specific states of ethical affairs in business and thus open the opportunity to plan management interventions based on these descriptive theories. In Chapter 5, a descriptive theory that classifies ethics management approaches into five categories and explains the nature, purpose and inner logic of each of these approaches is introduced.

Normative theories in the field of business ethics, in contrast to descriptive theories, go beyond mere descriptions of ethical states of affairs, and venture into the domain of how specific ethical affairs ideally should be. They thus make value judgements that set a specific standard for how things should be ethically speaking. In Chapter 6 we discuss three classical theories of ethics, namely the virtue theory of Aristotle, the deontological theory of Immanuel Kant and the utilitarian theory of J.S. Mill. These theories provide us with standards for judging whether an action or state of affairs could be considered ethical or not. These theories are theories on ethics in general and provide a basis for more applied theories in specific fields of ethics.

In Chapter 7 we provide a number of normative theories that are specifically applied to the field of business ethics. These theories identify the moral status and moral obligations of corporations. Amongst others, these theories provide insight into whether corporations should be considered as moral agents or as amoral institutions, what social responsibilities corporations should take care of, and for whose benefit corporations should be run.

CHAPTER 5

A model of managing corporate ethics

There always is an ethical dimension in business enterprises. In the previous chapter we saw how ethics permeates business organisations. Business leaders and managers have to choose how they wish to deal with the ethical dimension of their organisations. In analysing how the ethical dimension of business is dealt with, we find – on the one end of the spectrum – business leaders who endorse and nurture unethical business practices because they believe that is how you need to practise business if you wish to succeed. On the opposite side of the spectrum, we find business leaders and managers who endorse and nurture ethics in their businesses because they believe that it is the only way in which success in business can be sustained. There are thus different ways or modes of managing ethics in business.

In this chapter we present a descriptive model of the different modes of ethics management that one can expect to find in business (cf. Rossouw & Van Vuuren, 2003). A **mode** can be described as 'the preferred strategy of an organisation to manage its ethics'. It is suggested that five relatively distinct modes can be discerned with regard to preferred strategies for managing ethics. In total five different modes are identified:
- the immoral mode
- the reactive mode
- the compliance mode
- the integrity mode
- the total aligned mode.

The nature, purpose and predominant strategy of each of these modes are described. Also, the unique challenges associated with each of these modes of managing ethics are discussed, as it is exactly these challenges that often facilitate a transition to another mode of managing ethics. There is no developmental logic in the model that presupposes that a business will over time become more or less serious about managing ethics. A synopsis of the modes is provided in the table on the following page.

Table 5.1 The Modes of Managing Morality (MMM) model

	Immoral mode	Reactive mode	Compliance mode	Integrity mode	Totally Aligned Organisation (TAO) mode
Nature	• Unethical conduct is good business • The business of business is business, and not ethics	• Token gesture of ethical intent is shown (a code of ethics) • Unethical behaviour is ignored and remains unpunished	• Commitment to manage and monitor ethics performance • Rule-based approach to ethics • Disciplining unethical behaviour	• Internalisation of ethical values and standards • Value-based approach to ethics • Encouraging and rewarding ethical behaviour	• Seamless integration of ethics in corporate purpose, strategy and operations • Non-negotiable morally responsible interaction with stakeholders
Purpose	• Ethics has no place in the singular pursuit of the bottom line • Unethical behaviour is espoused as good business	• Protection against dangers of unethical behaviour • Sceptics and critics are silenced (temporarily) by the existence of ethics standards	• Prevention of unethical behaviour • Desire to have a good ethical reputation	• Raising level of corporate ethical performance • Pro-active promotion of ethical behaviour • Ethics regarded as a competitive advantage	• Ethics is embedded in corporate culture and purpose • Ethics is entrenched in discourse and decision-making
Ethics management strategy	• A Machiavellian orientation that denies the need to make decisions concerning ethics • No ethics management strategy or interventions	• Laissez-faire ethics management • Unwilling to manage ethics in a concerted manner • Corporate (ethical) values are words on paper	• Transactional approach to managing ethics • Code clear and comprehensive and corporate ethics management structures and systems are introduced • Unethical behaviour is penalised	• Transformational approach to managing ethics • Stakeholder engagement • Ethics 'talk' prevails. • High-level ethics management functions and systems	• Everyone is responsible for ethics performance • Ethics function/office serves as 'rudder' • Ethical heroes celebrated; ethics stories told
Challenges	• Financial consequences of immorality becomes unaffordable • Increased dissonance between personal and corporate values • Stakeholders are alienated	• Susceptible to ethical scandal • Stakeholders convey frustrated expectations • Corporate ethical reputation is below par	• Mentality of 'what is not forbidden is allowed' • Personal moral autonomy and responsibility is undermined • Proliferation of ethical rules and guidelines	• Discretion is abused. • Moral autonomy leads to moral dissidence • Powerful leaders undermine ethics drive • Lack of clear corporate identity undermines integrity mode	• Ethical complacency/arrogance; moral laxness • Neglect ethics induction of new employees • Lack of co-ordination in managing ethics

The immoral mode

Nature

Organisations in this mode usually espouse unethical conduct as good business and ascribe to the cynical viewpoint that business ethics is an oxymoron. They embrace the popular myths (see Chapter 8) that many corporate leaders and business ethics scholars have already dispelled during the past few decades. Examples of such myths are 'dog eats dog' (the business environment is a hostile world and you either trample on others or you yourself will be trampled on); and 'survival of the fittest' (the competitive nature of business means that you cannot afford to focus on the interests of others).

Purpose

Organisations in this mode aim at maximising profit at all cost – all that matters to them is the bottom line. This mode justifies winning at all cost. Where more ethically aware organisations realise that the above-mentioned credos are merely myths. A central feature of immoral mode organisations is that they view these myths as part and parcel of 'good business'. When this happens managerial philosophies and behaviours assume unethical proportions.

Management strategy

Immoral mode organisations are typically characterised by a Machiavellian orientation in that management does not see the need to make decisions concerning ethics. There is therefore no commitment to deal with ethics. In such organisations there is a lack of sensitivity to ethical issues and a reluctance to engage with them. Although there may be some varied dissonance about the eventual effects of unethical conduct, it is nevertheless endorsed as good business and goes unpunished.

Immoral mode organisations also have little inclination to be sensitive to stakeholders' ethics expectations. Since members of immoral mode organisations generally share beliefs regarding the prevalence of myths such as those described above, the corporate culture makes little provision for an ethical way of thinking. The ethical climate is virtually non-existent in that managers and employees can be described as morally mute (Waters & Bird, 1987). 'Ethics talk' is frowned upon and perceived as wimpish behaviour that does not belong in an organisation characterised by hardline philosophies such as a desire to be 'lean and mean' and a 'we take no prisoners' orientation. Any attempts to question the ethical dimension of decisions are thwarted by peer pressure characterised by a singular focus on the bottom line.

Consequently there is an absence of a proper ethics management strategy in such organisations. No ethics management interventions exist – not even the most rudimentary ones such as a code of ethics.

Challenges

Organisations in the immoral mode face three kinds of challenges that eventually may facilitate movement beyond this mode.

- The real financial consequences of immorality may become unafford-able. It may, however, also be that the perceived probable costs of immorality become an overwhelming threat in that organisations fear being found out or exposed. Change may also be triggered by scandal and the implosion of myths.
- An increased dissonance between personal and corporate values may surface. Employees, for example, may develop severe cognitive dissonance if they perceive the unethical inclination of the organi-sation to be contradictory to their own ethical value systems. They may then either remain in the organisation in a state of alienation and passivity, or they may move on to other companies that appear to have more sound ethics. The effects of the latter on the organisation's morale may be devastating.
- Other stakeholders, for example shareholders, customers, suppliers and the local community, may experience similar feelings of disso-nance and alienation. This may lead to severing ties with the immoral mode organisation. When this happens the organisation's social net-work may be in danger of complete collapse.

Immoral mode organisations either continue in their ways to a point-of-no-return self-destruction, or they may be compelled by the above-mentioned challenges to rethink their preferred unethical mode and to do at least something about their ethics, albeit reactive.

The reactive mode

Nature

Organisations often enter a reactive mode of morality as a knee-jerk reaction to the challenges posed by the immoral mode. In order to avoid rejection, such organisations make a confession to ethical business, but do not proceed beyond that (Rossouw, 2002:42). The reactive mode is prompted by awareness that something needs to be done to avoid the risk and dire consequences of unethical conduct. Such organisations have a naïve belief that a show of commitment (the presence of a set of ethical values) will create a sufficient context for ethical behaviour. In the process, these organisations profess to be ethical without actively managing their ethical standards. This may be ascribed to an inability to manage ethics. Although reactive mode organisations recognise the importance of ethics, unethical behaviour still prevails. A blind eye is turned to unethical behaviour and, at best, if unethical practices are detected, they remain unpunished but are not endorsed.

Purpose

Reactive mode organisations have a desire to protect themselves against the dangers of unethical behaviour in that they sense the potential risk of unethical behaviour. They also fear rejection by their stakeholders. Organisations in reactive mode become sensitive to the consequences that unethical practices may have for their reputations. By professing ethical behaviour they hope to avoid threats of litigation, boycotts, strikes and shareholder alienation. The possibility of government intervention or even enforced curatorship may be another motivational force to acquire some 'inoculation' against unethical behaviour. The enforcement of corporate governance standards by regulatory institutions also may coerce organisations into reactive morality. This mode of managing morality merely signifies a defensive corporate approach to business ethics. Although cognisant of the consequences of unethical behaviour, they may still condone a bending of the rules (for example: creative accounting).

Management strategy

Since attempts by a reactive mode organisation to manage ethics are seldom based on the conviction that ethics is good business, but rather on a desire to protect against investigation and punitive action, the organisation will formulate standards that display rejection of unethical behaviour. Although value judgements exist, they lack application. There is therefore no attempt to complement formal ethical standards with enforcement. Nor do these organisations develop any form of corporate ethics management capacity.

Senior management of organisations in the reactive mode may obviously have a desire to mend their attitudes and ways. A result of such good intentions may be a strategic planning session that results in the generation of a number of corporate ethical values. Although these values signal a commitment to integrity, respect and organisational ethics, they do not have the impact to create an ethical context in which employees can operate. Ethics management interventions by reactive mode organisations are usually limited in scope and depth. Such organisations often hasten to institute the minimum measures of ethics management interventions in an effort to avoid paying a high price for immorality. This effort can at best be described as window dressing. A feature of organisations in this mode's attempt to manage ethics is the design of a corporate code of ethics.

The focus is, however, often on the final product rather than on a proper inclusive process to produce it. As such, code design is likely to be delegated to either a single member of the organisation or to a function such as internal audit, risk management, legal services, the company secretariat or human resources. Some reactive mode organisations may engage external consultants to draft the code. It is also not uncommon for reactive mode organisations to obtain existing codes from other companies and to adapt these for their own purposes. The development of the code is an event rather than a process in the sense that it is often produced in unilateral fashion without participation of relevant internal and external stakeholders. Although the code may eventually be of high quality and may have good potential for application, the code is not worth the paper it is written on insofar as application is concerned. The code is likely to remain on a shelf without assuming living document proportions. Having most probably not been involved in the code design exercise, employees do not identify with the code, nor do they know how to apply its contents to their jobs.

Ethics management in reactive organisations therefore rarely progresses beyond code design interventions and can be described as laissez-faire ethics management, both in philosophy and in application.

Challenges

The challenges facing reactive mode organisations are as follows:

- Reactive mode organisations display a gap between talking and walking ethics. This leads to a serious credibility problem with stakeholders. Both internal and external stakeholders find their expectations frustrated and have difficulty trusting an entity whose words and actions are not aligned. They are therefore likely to formally or informally convey frustrated expectations regarding the organisation's ethics.
- In the absence of the security and predictability that an ethical context can provide for employees, the organisational morale may be very fragile.
- Like organisations in the immoral mode, an organisation in reactive mode is very susceptible to scandal. Since there is a gap between espoused ethical standards and the actual behaviour of the organisation, this might easily be exploited. Dissatisfied employees may, in the absence of internal channels for dealing with ethical failures, opt for blowing the whistle on unethical practices, which in turn can trigger scandals.
- Reactive mode organisations are also likely to discover that token gestures to ethical performance do not satisfy institutional investors, consumers and talented employees. The cost associated with their lack of confidence in the organisation might become a compelling factor in convincing the reactive mode organisation to revise its ethics strategy.

◙ Since the mere existence of a code of ethics does not guarantee ethical behaviour, nor provide the context for moral discourse, ethically aware employees might demand more pro-active engagement with ethics. They might specifically demand training in dealing with ethical dilemmas and in moral decision-making that will assist them in applying the organisation's code of ethics.

When these challenges gain sufficient momentum they have the potential of compelling the reactive mode organisation to moving beyond reactive gestures onto managing ethics in a concerted manner.

The compliance mode

Nature

The compliance mode of managing ethics represents a substantial move away from the reactive mode. Companies in compliance mode commit themselves to monitoring and managing their ethics performance and en-suring that all members of the organisation abide by the ethical standards of the company. The code of ethics is not merely for the sake of pacifying stakeholders. When deviation from the code of ethics occurs, the company takes corrective action by disciplining or penalising the transgressors. Alternatively, the company may opt for not only penalising transgressions of its ethical standards, but also for rewarding those who consistently abide by its code of conduct. The compliance mode thus represents a rule-based approach to managing ethics.

Purpose

The managerial purpose of the compliance mode is to prevent unethical behaviour by the business. The driving force behind this commitment to eradicate unethical behaviour can either be found in the desire to avoid the cost and damage associated with unethical behaviour (Moon & Bonny, 2001:26), or in the quest to benefit from having a good corporate ethical reputation. An example of the former is a company that insists on com-pliance in order to avoid costs associated with discrimination, fraud or a business scandal, while an example of the latter is a company that wishes to use its good ethical reputation to attract investors, ethically discerning consumers or talented employees.

Management strategy

Compliance mode organisations make a conscious decision to enforce ethics and display a commitment to eradicating unethical behaviour. Given the central role of the code of ethics in the compliance mode, management first needs to ensure that the code is sufficiently distinct and detailed in order to provide clear guidance on ethics to members of the organisation. If the current code is insufficient in this regard, one can expect that it will be revised to provide clarity on ethical standards and guidelines for behaviour. Unless the code is very clear and specific, it will fail in serving as a standard for evaluating ethical performance.

The code needs to be complemented by an ethics management function that will manage and drive the process of compliance to the code. This ethics management function can be the responsibility of a dedicated corporate function created specifically for this purpose (for example: an ethics office or compliance office) or it can be delegated to an existing management function in the company (for example: risk management, human resource management, or company secretariat). This ethics management function takes responsibility for all the processes and systems required for ensuring adherence to the code. This includes processes such as communication, training and the induction of new employees to the code. It requires that systems be designed for monitoring, appraising, and rewarding ethical performance. Also systems whereby employees can safely report unethical or morally suspicious behaviour by employees can be implemented. The management process in this mode may also include accounting, auditing and disclosure of ethics performance.

In sum, ethics management in the compliance mode may be described as a **transactional** approach – the emphasis is on rules to be complied with in order to avoid punishment for non-compliance, rather than on embracing and entrenching the ethical values and standards that underpin these rules.

Challenges

The compliance approach may result in a number of side effects that can potentially pose a serious challenge to the viability of this approach. These potentially harmful side effects include the following:

- It breeds a mentality of 'what is not forbidden is allowed'. Given the rule-based nature of this approach, organisational members can rely merely on the existing rules for moral guidance.
- It undermines personal moral autonomy and responsibility. As the code of ethics is enforced upon the organisation, the locus of moral control resides externally in the code and in the ethics management function. The ethical values and standards of the company are likely not to be internalised.
- Since this mode implies a comprehensive and diligent attempt to enforce ethical compliance, it may over time assume bureaucratic proportions with a proliferation of ethical rules and guidelines for conduct. Since there are so many rules, it would then be almost impossible

to recall all these directives. Consequently the rules may have very little impact on actual corporate behaviour.

◉ It tends to disempower employees (Sharp Paine, 2002:135). A compliance approach does not rely on the moral discretion of employees, but on their almost blind adherence to the rules of conduct. This undermines their ability to cope with issues and grey areas that are not addressed in the code of ethics.

If these challenges are not adequately addressed, they can erode the viability of the compliance approach to managing ethics. If they are dealt with adequately, their negative impact can be alleviated. It is, however, often these exact challenges that facilitate the transition to the integrity mode.

The integrity mode

Nature

The integrity approach comprises a value-based approach to managing ethics. Where the compliance mode is characterised by external enforcement of ethical standards upon a business organisation, the integrity approach is marked by the internalisation of ethical values and standards. Instead of imposing ethical standards upon the organisation, it seeks to obtain the commitment of individual members to a set of shared corporate values (Moon & Bonny, 2001:26). There is therefore less need for external guidance and more reliance on the discretion of individual members of the organisation to act morally responsibly. This approach to managing ethics requires a lot more knowledge and expertise on managing ethics, since it ventures into the subtle domain of value formation and commitment. Given the delicate nature of the integrity approach to managing ethics, it is usually complemented by a limited form of a compliance approach that serves as a safety net to protect the company against gross unethical conduct.

Purpose

The purpose of the integrity approach to managing ethics is to raise the level of ethical performance of the company. Instead of merely trying to minimise incidents of unethical behaviour, it pro-actively promotes ethical behaviour. By getting organisational members to commit themselves to the corporate ethical standards and values of the company, the responsibility for ethical behaviour becomes a collective effort shared by all members of the organisation. Companies typically embark on this approach when they realise that ethical performance is of strategic importance to the company or even its competitive advantage. In such cases a defensive approach that protects the company against the damage of unethical conduct is no longer deemed sufficient. To the contrary, a concerted effort in which all members of the organisation take joint responsibility for the ethics performance of the company is required.

Management strategy

The management strategy required for the integrity approach is one that facilitates the internalisation of ethical standards in all members of the organisation. Such a strategy typically commences with a comprehensive and deep diagnosis of the corporate ethical culture and current state of corporate ethics. Stakeholders are likely to be consulted as to their moral expectations of the company. The core ethical values of the company are then identified or revisited. There are two further vital components of an integrity strategy. The first is the promotion of 'ethics talk'. Employees need to get into the habit of discussing the ethical dimension of their work and decision making. Secondly, an integrity approach also relies heavily on the example set through the adherence of the leaders to the core ethical values and standards of the company.

The integrity approach further requires a managerial system and process support in much the same way that it is required in the compliance mode. It requires ongoing communication, training and induction of new employees. Training on moral decision-making becomes much more prominent as there is an increased reliance on the moral discretion of employees in the integrity approach. Systems for evaluating and rewarding the ethical performance of the company are also required. In an integrity approach the emphasis is on the reward of ethical behaviour, rather than on punishing unethical behaviour. It is therefore to be expected that ethical performance will be perceived as a key performance area to be included in performance management and appraisal. In addition, the aspects of ethical reporting, auditing and disclosure that were introduced in the compliance mode will remain. Once well established, the corporate ethics function may require fewer human and other resources, as the need for monitoring compliance diminishes.

An integrity mode of ethics management has **transformational** proportions – as such deep cultural organisational change is affected over time. Internalisation of values occurs in that employees are empowered as well as enabled to manage ethics in their own roles and jobs.

Challenges

The integrity mode also poses a number of challenges to ethics management. The most prominent challenges are as follows:

◉ The greater discretion granted to employees can be abused and unethical conduct can increase, thereby eroding the integrity approach, which risks gradually reverting to a compliance approach.

◉ The promotion of moral autonomy that results from an integrity approach can also lead to moral dissidence in a company. Given the differences in personal moral values that one is likely to encounter in bigger companies, serious moral differences are more likely to emerge.

☉ The integrity approach relies heavily on the integrity of its leadership. If they do not set both the tone and the example, the integrity approach can easily be discredited. Since those leaders who undermine the integrity approach are most probably in positions of considerable power, it may be very difficult, or even impossible, to overcome the challenge that they pose.

☉ The integrity approach also presupposes a clear sense of corporate identity and priorities (Sharp Paine, 2002:135). The individual discretion upon which the integrity approach is premised can only be properly exercised when core ethical values are aligned with corporate identity and priorities. A lack of clarity about corporate identity and priorities thus lurks as another obstacle that can jeopardise the sustainability of the integrity approach.

All these challenges can potentially be addressed within the integrity approach. Failure to do so may result in a return to a compliance approach or in disillusionment with the endeavour of managing corporate ethics. It is, however, also possible that these challenges, if overcome, may propel the company into the totally aligned organisation mode.

The Totally Aligned Organisation (TAO) mode

Nature

The TAO mode is characterised by a seamless integration of ethics into the purpose, mission and goals of the organisation. For companies in the TAO mode, ethics is integral to how they define themselves and how things are done. This presupposes that a company in the TAO mode will have a well-developed sense of identity, premised upon non-negotiable morally responsible interaction with its internal and external stakeholders as well as its environment. Ethical behaviour is regarded as strategically important and unethical behaviour is regarded risky as it can not only jeopardise the business success of the organisation, but also undermine its *raison de être*.

Purpose

The purpose of managing ethics in the TAO mode is to reinforce ethics as part of the company's culture and purpose. Through the ongoing raising of awareness all members of the organisation recognise that ethical behaviour is not an optional extra, but is at the core of the very nature and purpose of the organisation, entrenched in corporate discourse and decision making. Members of the organisation are empowered to prevent, disclose and confront deviant, unethical behaviour.

Management strategy

The management strategy in the TAO mode is geared towards reinforcing the strategic importance of ethical behaviour for the sustained success of the organisation. It therefore becomes vitally important that all managers in the organisation play their part in reinforcing ethics as part of business as usual. All the trappings of ethics management that manifested in the integrity mode will however still remain. The essential difference here is that the managerial responsibility for ethics is no longer limited to a dedicated ethics function, but is now widely dispersed throughout the organisation and on all management levels. Ethics is an ingrained part of line management's strategic and operational activities. Although a dedicated ethics management function and structure will most probably remain, its major responsibility will be to empower managers on all levels to integrate ethics in their repertoire of managerial skills and actions.

In the TAO mode, the congruence between the purpose, vision and ethical values of the organisation is all-important. Consequently, communication becomes the primary managerial intervention. Through the formal and informal communication systems, the organisation's identity and purpose and the essential role of ethics therein is continually emphasised. The vision of the company, its history as well as the stories of its former and current moral heroes, are kept in circulation. Rather than focusing on either punishing unethical behaviour or rewarding ethical conduct, the focus is on celebrating organisational heroes who embody the vision, purpose and ethical commitment of the organisation.

Sustained stakeholder engagement forms an integral part of managing ethics in the TAO mode. As the organisation regards morally responsible interaction with its internal and external stakeholders to be part of its organisational identity, it follows that regular engagement with stakeholders to determine how they are affected and how they perceive the organisation, will be a corporate priority. This will result in ongoing two-way communication in which the organisation not only listens to its stakeholders' needs and expectations, but also regularly discloses its economic, social and environmental performance to stakeholders.

Part of the ethics management strategy in the TAO mode is to identify discrepancies between behaviour and organisational values. Wherever such discrepancies are detected, those responsible for the deviation of corporate norms are persuaded that their behaviour contradicts and undermines the values and culture of the company.

Challenges

The TAO mode creates challenges of its own. Such challenges may include the following:

◙ The TAO mode can breed a mentality of ethical complacency or even ethical arrogance. Ethical behaviour is simply accepted as the norm and therefore some may regard it as superfluous to keep on emphasising its importance. This ironically can result in a situation where ethics talk begins to diminish and is left to chance, rather than being continuously promoted.

◙ Since ethics is so well ingrained in the TAO-mode organisation it becomes almost second nature to those members of the organisation who are steeped in the corporate culture. They might then start to assume that what is so evident to them is equally obvious to others. This may result in new entrants to the organisation not being properly inducted into the organisational culture and values. Over time this can create a sub-group in the organisation with a lesser commitment to the ethical culture of the organisation.

◙ The dispersion of the managerial responsibility throughout the organisation may also result in a lack of co-ordination of the ethics management effort. Because ethics management is now the responsibility of all managers, there may be no dedicated function or person to take responsibility for the ongoing co-ordination and strategic planning of corporate ethical performance. This can result in ethical discrepancies developing within the organisation. It can also undermine pro-active planning for the sustained ethical performance of the company.

◙ Reliance on the capacity of organisational members to act with integrity may also result in the organisation ridding itself of rules and procedures that were originally designed to protect the company against moral failures. The absence of such rules and procedures may over time induce moral laxness that increases the risk of moral failure.

None of these challenges produced by the TAO mode of managing ethics is insurmountable. A reluctance to address them may however result in them becoming huge obstacles that can potentially undermine the TAO mode of managing ethics and eventually compel management to revert to the integrity or even compliance mode.

Conclusion

The Modes of Managing Morality (MMM) model assists business ethics scholars and practitioners to make sense of the differences that exist in the ways in which different organisations manage their ethics. As such, it is a useful diagnostic tool to identify the main features, purposes and challenges of a company's approach to managing ethics. At the same time it also provides the opportunity to compare a company's current approach to managing ethics with alternative approaches. This comparative view presents companies with the opportunity to decide whether they deem their current approach to managing ethics sufficient or whether they wish to make strategic changes to the manner in which they manage their ethics.

CHAPTER
6

Classical ethical theories

To make judgements on what is ethical or unethical, a standard or criterion against which specific actions can be judged is required. Ethical theories provide standards for deciding whether a specific action is ethical or not. Consequently, ethical theories assist us in making a reasoned analysis of specific actions and in providing reasons for why we consider an action to be either ethical or unethical.

In this chapter, three influential ethical theories will be discussed. Through the centuries, these ethical theories have survived and still remain influential and relevant today. The three theories are:

- the virtue theory of Aristotle
- the utilitarian theory of Mill
- the deontological theory of Kant.

The three thinkers whose theories will be discussed are not the sole representatives of the respective theories. They are part of an ongoing tradition that continues to this day. What these thinkers have in common is that they are widely regarded as the classical representatives of each of these moral theories.

Virtue theory

The Greek philosopher, Aristotle, is the figure most closely associated with virtue theory. His theories are mainly to be found in a collection of his writings known as *The Nicomachean Ethics*, which was compiled in the fourth century BC by his son Nichomachus.

Aristotle's virtue theory begins with the assumption that morality is both necessary and vital for human beings. It is impossible to live with human dignity without being a well-developed moral being. Morality is not a luxury that one can choose to have or not to have. On the contrary, morality is a pre-condition for living with human dignity. People who forsake morality are, according to Aristotle, debased beings who have not fulfilled their human potential.

Telos

Aristotle believes that everything in life has a specific goal. He uses the Greek word *telos* when referring to the goal of something. The goal or *telos* of a knife, for example, is to cut, and the *telos* of a pencil is to write. In the same, way all human beings share a common *telos*. In order to live a life of human dignity, people should strive to attain the *telos* of human life.

The Greek word that he uses to describe the *telos* of all human beings is *eudaimonia*. This is commonly translated into English as happiness. This is not always the best translation of *eudaimonia*; the original word has a more profound meaning than happiness. It suggests a life well lived. It describes the state of a person who has realised his or her full human potential.

To reach the *telos* of *eudaimonia* is no simple matter. It is not something that is automatically attained. A number of things are needed to achieve it. First of all one has to live in a society characterised by justice. According to Aristotle, it is the responsibility of political scientists and politicians to work out and implement a just social order conducive to attaining *eudaimonia*. Second, you need good friends to surround and support you in order to attain *eudaimonia* in the fullest sense. These first two conditions bear testimony to Aristotle's conviction that people are social beings who need social interaction in order to flourish. Third, you need adequate material provisions. Finally, you need to develop and cultivate your human potential. Where the first three requirements are all external, in the sense that society, friends, and material possessions are outside of the self, the fourth condition is a purely internal one. And Aristotle's virtue theory focuses on this internal dimension.

The self

For Aristotle, morality starts with the self. Morality, according to Aristotle, hinges upon the character of the individual. What matters is not what is right or wrong in interpersonal interaction, but in the intra-personal development of your own character. Morality requires people of good character. Only people with good character are able to do good.

Aristotle insists that morality begins with self-love. Unless you love yourself and are willing to invest in your own self-realisation, moral development cannot occur. He does not consider self-love as being pejorative or in opposition to morality. For Aristotle, self-love is in fact a pre-condition for morality. It provides the impetus for developing character to its fullest human potential.

Virtues

The way to develop your character is through the cultivation of virtues. A virtue, according to Aristotle, is a character trait that enables you to reach your *telos*. The example of the knife can demonstrate this. If the *telos* of a knife is to cut, then the virtues of a knife are those characteristics that enable it to cut well. These might be the strength of the material that the knife has been made of, the sharpness of the blade, and the firmness of grip provided by the handle of the knife. If the *telos* of humans is *eudaimonia*, then the virtues required by humans are those traits of character that enable them to reach their *telos*.

But what are these traits of character that are required to reach one's *telos*? Aristotle defines a virtue as 'an activity of the soul, implying a rational principle'. Underlying this definition of virtue is a very specific view of human nature. Aristotle assumes that there are two distinguishable dimensions in human beings. The one is the rational dimension and the other the irrational dimension. The rational dimension should always be the dominant dimension. A person's rational ability is the real mark of a human being: that which distinguishes us from animals and other living creatures.

Not all of our bodily functions are rationally controllable, such as appetite, breathing, and sexual desire. Certain facets of human behaviour, however, are rationally controllable. These are our inclinations to action in a given situation, for example, the inclination to run away when confronted with danger. Aristotle refers to these inclinations as our natural dispositions. These dispositions should be controlled by rational thought and should not be left to our natural instincts. Once these dispositions are tutored and controlled by rational thinking, they become moral virtues. Moral virtues are nothing other than rationally controlled dispositions that become permanent traits of character. Aristotle emphasises that virtues cannot be developed instantaneously, but that they should be developed over time and maintained throughout a lifetime.

The mean

Aristotle introduces the concept of the 'mean' to indicate what is implied by rationally controlled dispositions. Our natural dispositions tend to err in one of two directions. Either we are too much inclined to do something or we are too little inclined to do it. This implies that we either have excessive dispositions or deficient dispositions. The mean is intended to correct these defective dispositions. Aristotle describes the mean as the midpoint between excessive and deficient dispositions. This mean disposition can be achieved by taking rational control of one's dispositions.

When Aristotle refers to a mean, he does not assume that there is a universal standard that applies to all people. On the contrary, he indicates that a mean is always relative to a specific person. Let us take the example of courage. Someone can tend to have either too much or too little courage. If you have too much courage, your disposition with regard to courage will be excessive. If you tend to have too little courage, your disposition is deficient. If Person A is naturally inclined to behave too courageously, then he needs to take rational control of his behaviour in order to become less courageous. Person A's mean would therefore be in the direction of exercising less courage. Should Person B be inclined to act with too little courage, his mean would be in the direction of displaying more courage.

What applies to courage in these examples also applies to our other dispositions. With regard to all of our dispositions, Aristotle envisages a spectrum that runs from an excessive pole through a mean position to a deficient pole. The table below gives an indication of his vision of the mean position with regard to a number of typical human dispositions:

Table 6.2 Aristotle's table of virtues and vices

Sphere of action or feeling	Excess	Mean	Deficiency
fear and confidence	rashness	courage	cowardice
pleasure and pain	licentiousness	temperance	insensibility
getting and spending	prodigality	liberality	illiberality
anger	irascibility	patience	lack of spirit
self-expression	boastfulness	truthfulness	understatement
shame	shyness	modesty	shamelessness

Source: Aristotle, 1976:104

Aristotle insists that the right attitude towards pleasure is a precondition for achieving our personal mean. Pleasure can be both detrimental and beneficial to establishing our personal mean. Aristotle maintains that we tend to indulge in those things that give us pleasure. This results in excessive dispositions. Similarly we tend to avoid those things that give us the opposite of pleasure, that is, those things that cause us pain. This results in deficient dispositions. Our natural experience of pleasure and pain is the main cause of our wrong dispositions. So, we should avoid being guided by our natural instincts of pleasure. We should take rational control of our natural feelings of pleasure and teach ourselves to find pleasure in achieving our personal means. Once our sense of pleasure has been cultivated so that pleasure derives from achieving our means, it becomes conducive to our moral development. We find pleasure in doing the right thing. For Aristotle, it is obvious that reaching your *telos* by always acting in a virtuous way will provide you with a sense of wellbeing and joy. The virtuous life is a life that will bring pleasure to the virtuous person. This does not mean that every single action will be rewarded with immediate pleasure. Sometimes one will have to postpone immediate pleasure in order to act with virtue. But the result of always acting in accordance with virtue is a life characterised by the pleasure of knowing that one is doing good and therefore living the good life.

If we are inclined to act in accordance with our natural instincts of pleasure and pain, how do we come to the point where we are willing to abandon these natural instincts for the sake of finding pleasure in acting with virtue? Aristotle believes that this transition should be facilitated through education. It is the responsibility of the state to educate the youth so that they will be receptive to the ideal of a virtuous life. Should the state forsake its responsibility in this regard, it becomes the responsibility of parents to prepare their offspring for the development of virtue.

The recognition of the importance of virtue and a willingness to develop virtue must be cultivated. After this, the actual development of virtue can begin. Virtue is developed by taking rational control of one's dispositions. By practising virtuous conduct over and over again, it slowly but surely becomes part of one's character. Virtuous conduct becomes a habit.

In living the virtuous life one should always be guided by the ideal of what Aristotle calls the 'virtuous man' (he used only the masculine form in all his writing). When in doubt about the right thing to do, one should always ask oneself what the virtuous man would have done in that same situation. Who is this so-called virtuous man? Aristotle maintains that it is the man who has taken rational control of his life; has cultivated his natural dispositions into moral virtues; and has always throughout his lifetime found pleasure in acting in accordance with these virtues. Although this description may sound rather abstract, it seems to be at least as useful a criterion as the so-called 'rational person' that has been used for centuries to guide the legal profession in decisions about whether an act should be considered legal or not. If the 'rational person' is accepted as a guide for legal action, why might not the 'virtuous man' be a guide for moral action?

Deontological ethics

Where virtue ethics claims that morality depends on the moral virtues of one's character, deontological ethics insists that moral action requires conformity to rationally founded moral principles. The classical representative of this theory is the German philosopher, Immanuel Kant. His influential work on ethics is entitled *Fundamental Principles of the Metaphysic of Ethics*, first published in 1785. Kant is convinced that our moral actions cannot be guided by our practical experience. He insists that the moral 'ought' cannot be deduced from the practical 'is'. In other words, it is impossible to determine what people ought to do by studying what they in fact do. People might be involved in severely corrupt practices, which cannot possibly offer moral guidance. Moral guidance should be sought outside the sphere of practical experience. It can only be found in the sphere of purely rational thinking.

The dual nature of human beings

Kant believes that humans are simultaneously natural beings and rational beings. As natural beings, they are under the control of their natural instincts and needs. In this respect they are like animals who obey the laws of nature. It is their ability to think rationally that distinguishes humans from animals. As rational beings, people can be creative and make free choices. Instead of being subject to raw instinct, they can gain insight into the laws of nature and even formulate their own guidelines for behaviour. The emphasis that Kant places on the rationality of humans is of particular importance in understanding his moral theory.

Humans are prey to their dual nature in their moral actions. Kant is convinced that our natural inclinations are too unstable and unpredictable to secure stable moral judgements. The only source of stable and objective moral guidance is to be found in the rational ability of humans. Practical experience, as we have discussed, is also not a reliable source for moral guidance. So, the only source of moral guidance is our rationality outside of, or prior to, practical experience.

The 'good will'

Kant undertook an analysis of what he called our 'pure reason' – uncontaminated by practical experience – in order to find moral guidance. Although he regards pure reason as the only sufficient source of moral guidance, he nevertheless believed that something else was needed for consistent moral behaviour. That something else is a 'good will'. The concept of the good will is central to his theory. The opening sentence of *Fundamental Principles of the Metaphysic of Ethics*, reads: 'Nothing can possibly be conceived in the world or even out of it, which can be good without qualification, except a Good Will' (Kant, 2008:8). Our will is our capacity to decide what we want to do and what we wish to become. This freedom provides us with autonomy to make independent and rational decisions. It is by exercising our freedom to act with autonomy that we gain our human dignity.

The human will is, of course, influenced by both our natural and rational dimensions. It is for this reason that Kant referred not merely to the human will, but explicitly to the 'good will'. The human will can be corrupted if it caves in to the demands of our natural inclinations. Such a corrupted will can never secure consistent moral action. It may be able to do so at times, but it can never maintain consistent moral behaviour over time. Consistent moral behaviour can only be achieved by the good will. The good will is the will that obeys the universal moral law. And our rational ability allows us to cultivate such a good will. When we gain rational insight into the universal moral law, our will respects the evident moral authority of this universal law and obeys it from a sense of duty. A good will can therefore be defined as the will that obeys the universal moral law from a sense of duty. It translates the universal moral law into practical resolutions to act in a specific way. For Kant, doing the right thing from a sense of duty towards the universal moral law is the hallmark of moral behaviour.

The categorical imperative

But what is this universal moral law? Kant's quest into the domain of pure reason leads him to the discovery of a universal and objective moral law that applies to all rational human beings. His formulation of this moral law is: 'Act only on that maxim whereby thou canst at the same time will that it should become a universal law' (Kant, 2008:40). This moral law is a purely formal law that does not apply to any specific situation. Precisely because it has such a general and formal nature, it can be used as a criterion in making the specific moral judgements that we have to make on a daily basis. Kant offers an example to demonstrate how this seemingly abstract moral law can give moral guidance in making practical decisions. He wrote:

> *Let the question be, for example: May I when in distress make a promise with the intention not to keep it? The shortest way, however, and an unerring one, to discover the answer to this question whether a lying promise is consistent with duty, is to ask myself, Should I be content that my maxim (to extricate myself from difficulty by a false promise) should hold good as a universal law, for myself as well as for others? and should I be able to say to myself, 'Every one may make a deceitful promise when he finds himself in a difficulty from which he cannot otherwise extricate himself?' Then I presently become aware that while I can will the lie, I can by no means will that lying should be a universal law. For with such a law there would be no promises at all, since it would be in vain to allege my intention in regard to my future actions to those who would not believe this allegation, or if they over-hastily did so would pay me back in my own coin. Hence my maxim, as soon as it should be made a universal law, would necessarily destroy itself. (Kant, 1929:21–23)*

From this example it is clear that in applying the categorical imperative, we should be guided by the principles of universalisability and revers-ibility (cf. Harris, Pitchard & Robbins, 2005:89). The principle of univers-alisability demands that we should be willing to make the principle of our proposed action into a universal law that will be followed by all other people. The principle of reversibility then demands that we should be willing to live in a world where everyone else behaves in accordance with this universal law. If we are not willing to live in a world where the principle of our action has become a universal moral law, then the proposed action is definitely wrong.

Kant referred to this universal moral law as the 'categorical imperative'. In doing so he distinguished it from hypothetical imperatives. An imperative is something that one has to do – a command that one has to obey. In some cases an imperative only applies to me if I am interested in achieving a specific goal. Say for example, I own a business. If I want to gain a reputation for reliability, then it is imperative that I should provide reliable products and services to my customers. The imperative in this example is a typical hypothetical imperative. It only applies to me as long as I have set myself the goal of gaining a reputation for reliability in my business. If I no longer have that goal in mind, then the imperative no longer applies to me. A hypothetical imperative therefore depends on my subjective goals. A categorical imperative, on the contrary, applies to every person regardless of personal goals. It is an imperative from which no one is excused. The moral law that Kant discovered in his analysis of pure reason is such a categorical imperative.

This categorical imperative can be translated into three practical imperatives or guidelines for moral action and decision making. These practical imperatives do not introduce anything that is not already implied in the categorical imperative. They, according to Kant, merely make the content thereof more explicit.

The first practical imperative

The first practical imperative that flows from the categorical imperative states that you should 'act as if the maxim of your action were to become by your will a universal law of nature'. By this practical imperative, Kant wishes to reinforce that our moral actions should not be guided by our own inclinations, but be guided by a sense of duty to the universal moral law (the categorical imperative). Our only concern should be whether the principle of our actions might be made into a universal law.

The second practical imperative

The second practical imperative that Kant deduced from the categorical imperative exposes a dimension that is not so immediately evident. His formulation of this second practical imperative is: 'So act as to treat humanity, whether in thine own person or in that of another, in every case as an end withal, never as a means only' (Kant, 2008:50). Kant believed that this second practical imperative is logically implied in the categorical imperative. He argued that the categorical imperative requires us to act not for the sake of our subjective goals, but for the sake of an objective goal that applies to everyone. The question is whether such an objective goal exists. According to Kant there is such an objective end, and that end is the dignity of all human beings. Every person regards him or herself as an end that should not be abused for the sake of another person's objectives. Because all people share this conviction, it is a universal conviction that each and every person's dignity should be respected. Such a universal conviction, according to Kant, can only spring from our pure reason. Kant uses an example once more to show how this second practical imperative can be utilised to provide practical moral guidance. He writes:

> *As regards necessary duties, or those of strict obligation, towards others; he who is thinking of making a lying promise to others will see at once that he would be using another man merely as a mean, without the latter containing at the same time the end in himself. For he whom I propose by such a promise to use for my own purposes cannot possibly assent to my mode of acting towards him, and therefore cannot himself contain the end of this action. This violation of the principle of humanity in other men is more obvious if we take in examples of attacks on the freedom and property of others. For then it is clear that he who transgresses the rights of men, intends to use the person of others merely as means, without considering that as rational beings they ought always to be esteemed also as ends, that is, as beings who must be capable of containing in themselves the end of the very same action. (Kant, 1929:57)*

The third practical imperative

Kant's third practical imperative states that: 'Every human will is a will which in all its maxims gives universal laws' (Kant, 1929:60). By this third practical imperative, Kant wishes to emphasise that the categorical imperative is not something alien to us, but is something with which we can identify as being of our own creation. When we cultivate our will to disobey our natural inclinations in order to act in obedience to the categorical imperative we are not passive. In our freedom as rational beings we can act with autonomy and create the moral principles that should guide our lives. We are not mere subjects of the moral law by which all should live, but should consider ourselves the authors of that universal law. In this way we demonstrate our human dignity.

Kant's moral theory claims that there is indeed an objective moral rule that can guide all our moral decisions. We need to respect this moral rule, which is to be found in our pure reason, and act on it from a sense of duty.

Utilitarian ethics

The utilitarian moral theory claims that the morality of actions should be judged by their consequences. The classical representative of this theory is John Stuart Mill, whose influential book, *Utilitarianism*, was first published in 1863.

Mill is convinced that actions are good when they contribute towards fulfilling the ultimate goal of human beings. This ultimate goal of human life he defines as happiness. Therefore an action should be considered good when it results in happiness for the majority of those affected by the specific action. This conviction he formulates succinctly in his 'Greatest Happiness Principle' which states that:

> *Actions are right in proportion as they tend to promote happiness,*
> *wrong as they tend to produce the reverse of happiness. By happiness*
> *is intended pleasure, and the absence of pain; by unhappiness, pain or*
> *the privation of pleasure. (Mill, 1965:281)*

The practical implication of this Greatest Happiness Principle is that whenever we are in moral doubt, we should merely calculate which of our alternatives for action would result in the greatest amount of happiness for the greatest number of people. The option that promises to produce the most happiness and the least pain for the greatest number of people affected by our decision should be regarded as the most morally worthy course of action.

This seemingly very simple moral theory is much more complicated than it initially appears to be. This becomes clear when we consider Mill's defence of his conviction that happiness is the ultimate desire of all human beings.

Happiness

He justifies his conviction that happiness is the ultimate end of all human beings by starting with the experience of the individual. According to Mill, each of us is motivated by one end only, and that is happiness. Whatever we do, we do merely in order to experience happiness. He suspects that when questioned about our motives for doing whatever it is we do, we ultimately would have to admit that we do it for the sake of happiness. There are plenty of routes to be taken towards happiness, such as knowledge, love, power, or money. But ultimately these are mere avenues to the final destination of happiness. This he demonstrates in the following example:

> *What for example will we say of the love for money? There is nothing*
> *originally more desirable about money than about any heap of glit-*

tering pebbles. Its worth is solely that of the things which it will buy. Yet the love of money is not only one of the strongest moving forces of human life, but money is, in many cases, desired in and for itself; the desire to possess it is often stronger than the desire to use it, and goes on increasing when all the desires which point to ends beyond it, to be compassed by it, are falling off. It may then be said truly, that money is desired not for the sake of an end, but as part of the end. From being a means to happiness, it has come to be itself a principal ingredient of the individual's conception of happiness. (Mill, 1965:310–311)

From this universal quest for happiness, Mill concludes that if each individual desires his or her own happiness, then the ultimate good must be the happiness of all people. So the ultimate goal is not the happiness of the individual, but the happiness of society.

Mill is convinced that there are firm grounds for believing that individuals have the capacity to strive not only for their own happiness, but also for the general happiness of society. He bases this conviction in the first instance on the social nature of humans. Individuals regard themselves almost invariably as belonging to a community. Further, Mill thinks that there is also external pressure on the individual to take heed of the interests of other people, as everyone needs the support of others throughout their lives. Without such support they would face the threat of rejection and expulsion from their community. Finally, Mill argues that we have a natural inclination to sympathise with others. This manifests itself in our conscience, the quality that prevents us from doing harm to our fellow-beings. The combination of these three factors, Mill believes, provides sufficient grounds for the conviction that individuals have the capacity to act for the sake not merely of their own happiness, but also for general happiness. This capacity could and should be enhanced further by public education.

Defence against critics

Mill sheds further light on the meaning and implications of his moral theory when he defends his theory against attacks from his critics. We will consider six of the most important points of criticism raised against Mill's theory and his response to each of them.

Criticism one: The theory is degrading to humans

The first objection to his theory is that it degrades human beings to the level of animals because his theory suggests that people's only goal in life is attaining pleasure. This his critics regarded as 'utterly mean and grovelling; as a doctrine worthy only of swine'.

In defence of his theory, Mill argues that this accusation is better levelled at his critics. It is they who equate the pleasures of animals with those of humans. The pleasures that excite humans differ vastly from those of animals. Mill introduces the distinction between bodily pleasures and mental pleasures to argue his point. Both humans and animals enjoy bodily pleasures such as eating, drinking, and sleeping. People also enjoy mental pleasures such as learning, planning, and caring. When mental pleasure is compared to bodily pleasure, humans assign a very definite priority to the former. This is quite evident when Mill writes: 'It is better to be a human being dissatisfied than a pig satisfied; better to be Socrates dissatisfied than a fool satisfied.' When he propagates that humans should strive to increase the general happiness through their actions, he assumes that they will give preference to their mental or higher pleasures.

Criticism two: Happiness cannot be the rational purpose of life

A second objection to his theory is that the pursuit of happiness can never be regarded as the rational purpose of human life. Mill's critics list a number of noble people throughout history who sacrificed their own happiness in order to do good. They are regarded as noble exactly because they did not pursue happiness, but because they forsook their own happiness.

Mill's response to this is that they are probably regarded as noble simply because they sacrificed their own happiness for the sake of the happiness of the greater number of people. Far from contradicting the utilitarian standard, they were actually demonstrating it. If their sacrifices were not intended to serve a purpose beyond themselves, their sacrifice of their own happiness would have served no purpose at all. Utilitarianism requires that one should act for the sake of the general good, even if it runs counter to one's own happiness.

Criticism three: Utilitarianism encourages selfishness

A third criticism levelled against Mill is that utilitarianism propagates that one should be concerned only with maximising one's own happiness. Mill's response to this charge is that his critics have their facts wrong. His theory propagates exactly the opposite of this claim. The standard of happiness that utilitarianism pursues is not the happiness of the individual, but the happiness of all. Mill writes:

> *As between his own happiness and that of others, utilitarianism re-*
> *quires him to be as strictly impartial as a disinterested and benevolent*

spectator. In the golden rule of Jesus of Nazareth, we read the complete spirit of the ethics of utility. To do as one would be done by, and to love one's neighbour as oneself, constitute the ideal perfection of utilitarian morality. (Mill, 1965:291–292)

Mill emphasises that it is part of the utilitarian ideal that the state should play its role in making social arrangements that will give equal consideration to the interests and happiness of all its citizens, so cultivating a culture where impartiality will prevail. Equally, the utilitarian ideal sees education playing a vital role in cultivating commitment in the young towards transcending their own interest in order to advance the general happiness.

Criticism four: Utilitarianism is unattainable

A fourth objection to Mill's theory is almost the opposite of the previous charge. The objection here is that the utilitarian standard is unrealistically high. Opponents claim that it is almost impossible to act always for the sake of the general happiness of society. Ordinary people will simply not be capable of constantly striving towards such a lofty ideal.

Mill's reply to this objection is that people would very rarely find themselves in situations where they have to act for the sake of the general happiness of society. Mostly we find ourselves in situations where we need to consider only the interests of the few who are affected by our proposed actions. We need to consider merely the private utility of these few and not the happiness of humanity as a whole. Only a very few have the opportunity to act for the benefit of society as a whole, and then only on very rare occasions. Only such people in such rare circumstances need to consider the happiness of the whole society.

Criticism five: Utilitarianism is self-serving

A fifth charge against utilitarian theory is that it is an immoral doctrine because it will inevitably result in expediency. Critics insist that the utilitarian principle will be applied in an opportunistic manner in order to serve the particular interests of the person making the decision.

Mill's response to this charge is that such expediency and opportunism is incompatible with the utilitarian spirit. He uses the example of telling a lie to illustrate his point. According to Mill it is unthinkable that someone would lie merely for the sake of the momentary benefit that it might hold. Each person has a conscience and a sense of veracity. Lying would violate these. This would cause so much unhappiness and pain to the liar that it would outweigh the immediate benefit that the lie might gain. What Mill does admit, however, is that his theory provides the possibility for exceptions. Say, for example, there is an accident in which a woman is seriously injured and in which her partner dies. The utilitarian theory would justify withholding the truth from her until she would be strong enough to deal with the news. Mill makes no excuse for the fact that his theory allows for such exceptions, as he believes it to be one of its strengths.

Criticism six: The theory is too time-consuming

A sixth and final objection to Mill's theory is that it would be too time consuming to apply in practice. Critics allege that it would be impossible to sit down each time a situation requires a moral decision, calculate the amount of pleasure and pain implied by each alternative course of action, and then come to a conclusion based on the utilitarian calculus. Mill's response to this is:

> *This is exactly as if any one were to say that it is impossible to guide our conduct by Christianity, because there is not time, on every occasion on which anything has to be done, to read through the Old and New Testaments. The answer to the objection is, that there has been ample time, namely, the whole past duration of the human species.* *(Mill, 1965:297)*

His point is clear. In most of the ethical issues that one is confronted with, one knows beforehand what is morally right or wrong. We know, for example, that it is wrong to lie, cheat, steal, or kill. This we have learned over years or have been taught by our elders. We need not sit down and first calculate in utilitarian fashion every time we are confronted with a decision that might have moral significance. We can simply act on the basis of the moral knowledge that we have accumulated over years. Only in the rare case where we are confronted with a new moral dilemma, do we have to go through the entire utilitarian process of deciding which course of action would produce the greatest amount of happiness for the greatest number of people.

In defending his theory it becomes evident that Mill's notion of happiness as criterion for making moral decisions is much more complex than it seems at first. His theory is built on a number of assumptions about human nature, the society in which we live, and the sentiments and values that we share.

Conclusion

The classical ethical theories that we have discussed in this chapter capture and structure a lot of our common-sense thinking about ethics. They emphasise that only persons with decent moral character can be expected to do good, that there should be certain objective standards that should guide us in making moral decisions, and that the practical consequences of actions should be taken into consideration in our ethical deliberations.

In this respect, these ethical theories are valuable and helpful. Their main shortcoming, however, is that they tend to be rather abstract and not easily applicable to the concrete situations that we face in daily life, and more specifically in business. It therefore is not surprising that a number of more applied theories have emerged in the field of business ethics that provide more direct guidance on how we should decide on morality in business. These theories that are applied specifically to business will be discussed in the next chapter.

CHAPTER
7

Theories of the modern corporation

The dramatic increase in the size and influence of modern corporations over the last century has given rise to much thought about the moral status and moral obligations of the modern corporation. Amongst the most important questions that have been raised with regard to the modern corporation are the following:

- ▣ Do corporations have moral responsibilities?
- ▣ Can corporations be regarded as moral agents?
- ▣ Whose interests should the corporation serve?

A number of theories of the modern corporation have emerged to address these types of issues. In this chapter we will discuss three of these theories, namely, corporate social responsibility, corporate moral agency, and stakeholder theory.

Corporate social responsibility

Do corporations only have moral responsibilities towards their owners (or shareholders) or do they also have responsibilities towards the societies within which they operate? This question became prominent in 1970 with the publication of an article in the *New York Times Magazine* by the Nobel Prize winning economist, Milton Friedman.

Milton Friedman

In his famous article, 'The social responsibility of business is to increase its profits', Friedman denied that business has any social responsibilities other than making a profit for its shareholders. He reacted strongly and negatively to the frequent references to social responsibility that business executives were making at the time. He regarded such talk as short-sighted and foolish. He stated that business executives who talk about corporate social responsibility are 'preaching pure and unadulterated socialism. Business-men who talk this way are unwitting puppets of the intellectual forces that have been undermining the basis of a free society.' (1993:162)

Friedman's fierce reaction was based upon his understanding of a free and democratic society. He made a clear distinction between the economic and political spheres of society. The economic sphere, he believes, is premised upon the principle of unanimity. In economic activity, parties are free to engage in whatever contracts and transactions they deem fit. There is no coercion on any party to enter into business with another. 'Society is a collection of individuals and of the various groups they voluntarily form', Friedman said (1993:166).

The principle of the political sphere, however, is conformity. In politics the general social interest dominates. Though individuals are free to express their preferences and to cast their votes, once the political decision is taken, they need to conform to it. In the political sphere, Friedman said, 'it is appropriate for some to require others to contribute to a general social purpose whether they wish to or not' (1993:167).

Friedman's main objection to the idea of corporate social responsibility was that it is an unwarranted imposition of the political principle of conformity on the economy; business should be business and politics should be politics and never the two should mix. He argues that corporate social responsibility represents exactly such an undesirable mixture between politics and economics.

He believes that the path to clearing up this unfortunate confusion lies in getting clarity on exactly what occurs when business executives engage in acts of social responsibility on behalf of corporations. Business executives are employees of the owners of corporations. In this capacity they are appointed to serve the interest of their employers, which amounts to 'make as much money as possible while conforming to the basic rules of society' (1993:162).

When business executives engage in acts of corporate social responsibility, they act outside their domain. They have no right, nor any responsibility to do so. As individuals, they have moral responsibilities, some of which might extend to society, but they have to exercise these moral or social responsibilities in their personal capacity. They can devote their own time, energy and resources to their moral obligations, but never those of the corporation. Corporations, Friedman believes, are not moral agents like individuals are, and thus do not have corporate moral obligations. Should business executive spend corporate resources on acts of social responsibility, they are actually stealing company resources to spend on illegitimate objectives.

Besides the fact of diverting money away from stockholders, employees and customers, business executives also engage in a political process of taxation that they are not equipped for. In spending corporate funds on social responsibility, business executives are effectively imposing taxes on the stockholders or any other stakeholder of the business who might have benefited from the spent money. Furthermore, in spending this money on what they regard as socially desirable causes, they also effectively decide how these taxes should be allocated. Both the acts of imposing and allocating tax, Friedman believes, are political processes.

The imposition and allocation of tax are governmental functions. In order to qualify for this function, governments need to be publicly elected. As the representatives of the majority of the population, they then have the mandate to decide on socially desirable ends and on the levels of taxation that are appropriate for society. Through its legislative, executive and judicial functions, the state is able to impose taxes, administer expenditure programmes and even mediate disputes that might arise in that respect. If voters do not approve of the way in which a government performs these functions, they have the opportunity to remove government from office at the next election.

Business executives, on the contrary, do not have this mandate, nor the expertise required. And they were not appointed for that purpose either. In spending corporate funds on social responsibility, they act as civil servants, without having been elected for this purpose by the public. Neither do they have the mandate of the shareholders or of any other corporate stakeholder from whom they are taking money away.

Friedman grants that there are certain conditions in which corporate social spending can be justified. The first condition is when an individual sole proprietor of a business should decide to spend money on social responsibility. In this case, the proprietor is merely spending his own money as he wishes. The second circumstance in which it is legitimate to spend corporate money on social responsibility is when the corporation stands to profit from such expenditure. This, for example, is the case when a company spends money on education in a local community in order to improve the level of skills of its own employees or to provide prospective employees of the company. In this case the company is merely acting in its own interest under the cloak of social responsibility. Friedman does not fault them for doing so, although he acknowledges that such tactics are deceitful.

In summary, Friedman regards talk about corporate social responsibility by business executives as short-sighted and dangerous, unless it is done in the self-interest of the corporation. By engaging in such talk, business executives play in the hand of those who allege that 'the pursuit of profit is wicked and immoral and must be curbed and controlled by external force' (1993:166). Friedman warns that if this view gains sufficient momentum it will culminate in government imposing social control on business instead of business executives who currently try to do so through their social responsibility talk and actions.

Christopher Stone

In his book, *The Social Control of Corporate Behavior* (1975), Christopher Stone took a strong stance in opposition to Friedman's view on corporate social responsibility. He argued specifically against the following three premises of Friedman's argument:

- ◙ that managers' only obligation is to maximise profits for shareholders
- ◙ that market forces are sufficient to ensure responsible behaviour by corporations
- ◙ that the law is adequate to guarantee that corporations do not harm society.

Each of these points of critique will now be discussed.

Managers do not only have an obligation towards shareholders

Stone refutes Friedman's view that managers only have an obligation to maximise profit for shareholders on various grounds. The first argument that he refutes is the one that states that the management of corporations has made an implicit promise to the shareholders to maximise their profits. He calls this the **Promissory Argument**. Stone denies that there is such a promissory relationship between managers and shareholders. Such relationships may exist, for example, between an investor and a broker. But they do not exist between managers and shareholders. Most shareholders never meet the management of the corporations in which they invest. Consequently, no promises are ever made by management to their shareholders. On the contrary, most shareholders acquire their shares in corporations by buying them from other shareholders, who in turn have bought these shares from the previous owners of the shares. Thus, Stone concludes, 'the manager of the corporation, unlike the broker, was never even offered a chance to refuse the shareholder's 'terms' (if they were that) to maximise the shareholder's profits' (1992:439).

Another version of the same argument that Stone refutes is called the **Agency Argument**. Although this argument is not premised on an implied promise between managers and shareholders, it nevertheless states that managers act as agents of shareholders. In that capacity, managers have an obligation to look after the interests of their principals, i.e. the shareholders. Stone rejects this argument because it is both *de jure* (legally) and *de facto* (factually) wrong. It is legally wrong because courts do not recognise managers as the agents of shareholders. It is also factually wrong, because if it were the case then one would have expected managers to actively seek to determine the wishes of shareholders and to act in accordance with their wishes. This, in Stone's view, is seldom, if ever, the case. Or to put it in his own words, 'it is embarrassingly at odds with the way in which supposed 'agents' actually behave' (1992:440). Through these and other arguments, Stone denies that managers only have obligations towards shareholders. Instead they have moral obligations towards all stakeholders of the corporation.

Market forces are not sufficient

Stone does not deny that markets are efficient in allocating economic resources. On the contrary, he concurs with advocates of the so-called 'invisible hand' that market forces can ensure that capital, labour and other productive resources flow to the companies and industries that will put them to the most effective use. He denies, however, that market forces are equally efficient in ensuring that the activities of corporations will serve the social needs of societies; the market mechanism is geared towards economic efficiency and not towards the satisfaction of social needs.

Furthermore, the conviction that the free operation of the market will benefit society is, according to Stone, based on the following four assumptions:

◙ that the persons who will stop supporting irresponsible corporations are aware of the fact that they are being injured by corporations

◙ that they know where to apply pressure on these offending corporations

◙ that they are in a position to apply such pressure

◙ that the pressure they apply on corporations will result in constructive changes in corporate behaviour (cf. Stone, 1992:442–443).

None of these assumptions, according to Stone, is warranted. In the complex world of consumerism with its never-ending flood of new consumer products, it is almost impossible to be aware of the health, environmental and other dangers that new consumer goods might pose. Furthermore, consumers are mostly aware of brand names, but not well informed about which corporations have stakes in the brands. Switching from one brand name to another in protest against corporate behaviour is no guarantee that the offending company will be penalised. And very often, the offended consumer is not in a position to apply pressure on the offending corporation. This can either be because no appropriate forum for applying such pressure exists, or because there are no alternative products to switch to. Finally, Stone warns that it is naïve to believe that corporations will alter their behaviour when pressure is applied. Instead of altering their offensive behaviour, they might opt to silence their critics through legal action, or they might embark on advertising campaigns to prevent damage to their reputations.

The law is inadequate

Stone also refutes Friedman's claim that obedience to the laws of the country in which a corporation operates will ensure socially responsible corporate behaviour. He denies this claim on the grounds of:

◙ time limitations

◙ the limitations of the process of law making

◙ the limitations of the process of law implementation.

The time limitation problem revolves around the fact that laws are usually made in response to existing problems. Problems first occur and only then are laws formulated to deal with these problems. Due to this reactive nature of the law a lot of damage can be done in the time period between the emergence of a new problem and the passing of a new law to deal with that problem. Stone therefore believes that there is something very wrong with a corporate mentality that believes that reliance on the law is sufficient to ensure corporate social behaviour. He says: 'There is something grotesque – and socially dangerous – in encouraging corporate managers to believe that, until the law tells them otherwise, they have no responsibilities beyond the law' (1992:444). Instead, he believes that corporations should act as moral agents who care about their impact on the social and natural environment.

The limitations of the process of law making centres around the role that corporations play in the process of making the very laws that are supposed to regulate them. The problems caused by the operations of corporations are often complex. Lawmakers tend to lack the technical expertise to formulate law with regard to these complex problems. Furthermore, the regulating body is also often cautious to formulate laws that will put them at loggerheads with industries that they have to regulate, as this can cause ongoing friction and disruptions between the regulatory authorities and the industry. Consequently, lawmakers typically involve corporations and industries in the process of formulating the laws that should govern the very same corporations and industries. It therefore is not surprising that regulations do not always reflect the best interest of society, but are often a trade-off between societal interests and corporate interest. That corporations effectively are both players and referees thus undermines the legitimacy of the lawmaking process with regard to the social responsibility of corporations. As Stone believes that this involvement of corporations in the process of lawmaking is practically unavoidable, he concludes that a mere reliance on the law is insufficient and needs to be complemented by self-initiated social responsibility of corporations.

Also, the implementation of the law is riddled with limitations. Specifically, the increasingly technical nature of society makes it difficult to implement laws effectively. Stone uses the example of the law of torts to illustrate the point. The law of torts, which regulates the process of recovering damages from someone who has injured you, works pretty well in simple cases. A simple case, for example, is where Jones ignores the pedestrian warning signal and drives into Smith who is crossing the street at the designated pedestrian crossing. Smith who is injured in the accident can now use the law of torts to reclaim damages from Jones, because he can prove:

◙ that he was injured
◙ who caused the injury
◙ the nature and extent of his injuries.

However, if this simple case is compared with a technically more complicated case, it soon becomes clear that the law of torts cannot be implemented with equal ease. The following example discussed by Stone makes it clear:

> *The food we will eat tonight (grown, handled, packaged, distributed by various corporations) may contain chemicals that are killing us, or at least reducing our life expectancy considerably. But (a) we cannot know with certainty the fact that we are being injured by any particular product; (b) it is difficult to determine who might be injuring us – that is, even if we know that our bodies are suffering from a build-up of mercury, we are faced with an awesome task of pinning responsibility on any particular source of mercury; (c) we would have a difficult time proving the extent of our injuries (the more so proving the extent attributable to any particular source). (1992:445)*

This further goes to show that Friedman's confidence in the ability of the law to ensure corporate socially responsible behaviour is misplaced. In contrast, Stone believes that only an explicit commitment by corporations to take responsibility of their social impact will suffice.

Corporate moral agency

The claim that corporations are legal persons is not disputed. As legal persons, corporations have specific rights and liabilities. It is however not clear whether corporations should also be regarded as moral persons, who have moral responsibilities besides their legal obligations.

Milton Friedman (1970) flatly denies that corporations could or should be regarded as moral agents. He argued that only individual biological persons are moral agents with moral responsibilities; corporations, on the contrary, are not biological persons, but mere artificial legal entities who cannot and should not be burdened with added moral responsibilities. He believes that only the individuals who work within corporations are moral agents and it is their unalienable right to exercise their moral agency, but then only in their personal capacity and not in the name of the corporation.

Peter French

The view taken by Friedman was challenged by Peter French (1993). French concurs with Friedman that corporations are artificial legal persons, but disagrees that this disqualifies them from being moral persons as well. His argument for the moral agent status of corporations hinges upon the distinction between legal and moral personhood.

In legal theory, a distinction is made between 'subjects of rights' and 'administrators of rights' (French, 1993:230). Subjects of rights are any entity – natural or artificial, living or dead – unto which rights are bestowed. Included in this category of subjects of rights are natural living human beings, but also unborn human beings, future generations, the deceased as well as artificial legal persons, such as corporations. The category of 'administrators of rights' is however reserved for biological living human persons. This is because administrators of rights must be agents that can take the specific actions required for exercising their rights. It has traditionally been assumed that only those beings that fall into the latter category can be regarded as moral agents. Since corporations do not fall into this category, it has been assumed that they therefore also do not fall into the category of moral agents. French, however vehemently denies this claim.

French argues that being a biological living human being is not the definitive criterion for being a moral agent. According to him, the distinguishing criterion for moral personhood resides in whether an entity can be held responsible for its actions. In this regard, French distinguishes between two notions of responsibility.

The first notion of responsibility is what he calls the 'who-dun-it' type (1993:230). This type of responsibility is at work when determining whose actions a specific event can be blamed on. The second type of responsibility is broader than the first and revolves around the concept of accountability. Accountability is established when one party finds itself in a responsibility relationship with another party and consequently has to justify its actions to that party. French believes that moral responsibility belongs to this second category of responsibility; as moral agents, we are accountable for our actions to all who are affected by our actions.

The question that French poses is whether corporations qualify for moral responsibility in this second sense. In order to be held morally responsible for an action: an agent's actions must be linked to a specific event; and the action or the event must be intended by the agent. For corporations to qualify as moral agents, corporations must be shown to have specific intentions that result in actions. It is important to understand that the term 'corporation' is not merely a convenient shorthand reference to the aggregate of individuals working within the corporation. A corporation in this context is a moral agent in its own right that constitutes more than the sum of all the individuals making up the corporation. French believes that there is a specific mechanism at work within corporations that render them moral agents in this sense. This mechanism is the **Corporate Internal Decision** (CID) structure.

The CID structure of a corporation consists of two distinct elements. First, there is the organisational flow chart (or organogram) that specifies the roles, levels and responsibilities of the various members of the corporation. Second, there are corporate decision-making rules or policies that determine what and how decisions are taken within the corporation. These decision rules are intimately linked to the purpose and business objectives of the organisation. These rules and policies ensure that decisions are taken in a manner that will assist the corporation to reach its corporate goals.

When corporations decide on a specific course of action, significant decisions are made by the board of directors of the corporation. The decisions that the board takes normally rely on input from various individuals in the organisation. The board is typically served with a variety of specialist reports from various sections in the company. Based on the information provided to them and also on their vision of the company, its objectives and priorities, they would ultimately come to a decision. This decision is not a subjective choice, but as indicated, a corporate act in which many individuals participate, and that is guided by corporate and not subjective objectives. French says in this regard: 'Simply when the corporate act is consistent with an instantiation or an implementation of established corporate policy, then it is proper to describe it as having been done for corporate reasons, as having been caused by a corporate desire coupled with a corporate belief and so, in other words, as corporate-intentional' (1993:233).

Should individuals take actions in the name of the corporation that is not licensed by either their role in the corporation, or by corporate policy, they are not acting in accordance with the CID structure. Such actions cannot be regarded as corporate acts. Consequently, individuals acting in this way are personally responsible for the actions they have taken.

The CID structure of a corporation thus turns decisions made on behalf of the corporation into corporate actions. They cannot be described as mere individual actions. They qualify as corporate actions, because they have been intended by the corporation to further or defend its interests and objectives. As these corporate acts are intended by the corporation, the corporation becomes responsible for its actions and thus accountable to those affected by its actions. Given French's earlier definition of moral agency, it is clear why he regards corporations as moral agents with moral responsibilities in their own right.

Stakeholder theory

Stakeholder theory challenges the belief that corporations should be managed for the benefit of shareholders. The name of Edward Freeman is associated with the emergence of the stakeholder theory of corporations. In a number of contributions, which he co-authored with various colleagues, he explored what the backbone of a stakeholder theory of the corporation might look like.

Edward Freeman

Stakeholder theory challenges the shareholder theory of the corporation held by, amongst others, Milton Friedman. Shareholder theory dictates that corporations should be managed for the sake of shareholders. As agents of shareholders, management should maximise the return on investment for shareholders. In an article co-authored by William Evan, Freeman challenges this assumption and critically reviews the question: 'For whose benefit and whose expenses should the corporation be managed?' (1993:76) They reject the then conventional answer to the question which stated that it should be done for the benefit and cost of the shareholders. This rejection is based on both a legal and an economic argument.

The legal argument

The legal argument for the rejection of the idea that a corporation should be managed solely for the benefit of shareholders is based upon recent legal developments. Evan and Freeman refer to a substantial number of court cases which find that corporations have duties towards stakeholders other than shareholders. In this regard they say: 'the law has evolved to effectively constrain the pursuit of stockholder interest at the expense of other claimants on the firm' (1993:76).

They refer specifically to legislation and court findings that give certain rights to employees. The management of corporations has to respect these rights of employees and thus the pursuit of shareholder interest has to be balanced with the interests of employees. This applies both to the interests of individual employees as well as to employees collectively. Employees have legally protected rights to bargain collectively, which have to be respected by management.

Similar arguments are also made with regard to suppliers, customers and local communities. Recent laws and court findings acknowledge the legitimate interests of these stakeholder groups and grant them legal protection. This further emphasises the point that recent legal developments effectively constrain management to pursue the interests of shareholders at the expense of other groups of stakeholders.

The economic argument

The classic justification of free-market capitalism is that in pursuing the interests of shareholders, the greatest good of the greatest number of people will automatically be served. This is often referred to as the 'invisible hand' doctrine. The reality of the modern corporation and its impact on society has undermined the credibility of this doctrine. Evan and Freeman point out that this doctrine has lost its credibility because 'since the industrial revolution, firms have sought to internalise the benefits and externalise the costs of their actions' (1993:77–78).

By externalities they refer to the side effects caused by corporate actions. In pursuing their goals, corporations often pollute the environment or disrupt communities. The market mechanism does not automatically correct these negative consequences of corporate activity. For this reason corporations have to be regulated to ensure that the cost of corporate activity is not only shouldered by taxpayers, or to prevent corporations from imposing extravagant costs on societies. The regulations that have consequently been imposed on corporations due to the failure of the market mechanism to deal with externalities provide further ground for the conviction that corporations are indeed constrained and cannot merely pursue shareholder interests at all costs.

Stakeholders

Based on the legal argument, Evan and Freeman conclude that different stakeholders of corporations have rights that need to be respected by the management of the modern corporation. On the basis of the economic argument, they further conclude that corporations are responsible to various stakeholders for the consequences of their corporate actions. These conclusions are then formulated into the following two principles that provide the basis for a stakeholder theory.

◙ **Principle of Corporate Rights**: The corporation and its managers may not violate the legitimate rights of others to determine their own future.
◙ **Principle of Corporate Effects**: The corporation and its managers are responsible for the effect of their actions on others (Evan & Freeman, 1993:79).

Adopting these two principles amounts to the management of corporations taking moral responsibility for the consequences of their actions on all stakeholders of the corporation.

Behind these principles lurks a new conception of the purpose of the modern corporation. Within this version of stakeholder theory the purpose of the corporation is described as:

> *... a vehicle for co-ordinating stakeholder interests. It is through the firm that each stakeholder group makes itself better off through voluntary exchanges. The corporation serves at the pleasure of its stakeholders, and none may be used as a means to the ends of another without full rights of participation in that decision. (Evan & Freeman, 1993:82).*

Stakeholders obviously become the pivotal point of the corporation in this theory. Within this version of stakeholder theory, stakeholders are defined as: 'those groups who are vital to the survival and success of the corporation'

(Evan & Freeman, 1993:79). In terms of the two principles of stakeholder theory, stakeholders can further be described as those groups who have rights or duties to the corporation and who can benefit or be harmed by the corporation. Various groups would qualify as stakeholders in terms of the above definition. Typical stakeholder groups would be shareholders, employees, suppliers, customers, local communities and managers. This network of stakeholders is demonstrated in the figure below.

Figure 7.1 Network of corporate stakeholders

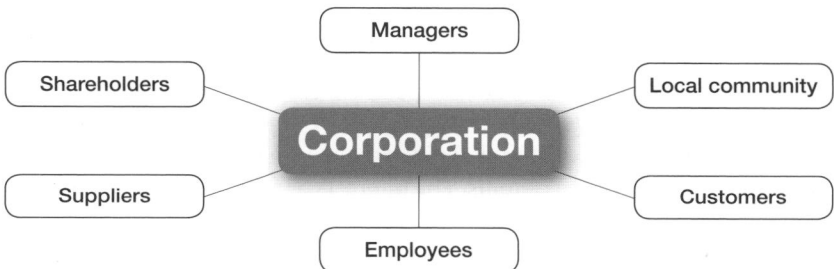

Shareholders have a stake in a corporation, because they invest their money in the corporation. Consequently they have the expectation to earn a return on their investment. If the company is poorly managed they stand to lose their investment, which in turn can have dire personal consequences for them.

Employees invest their knowledge, creativity and energy in the corporation. Without this investment, the corporation cannot survive. In return for the sacrifices that they make to the corporation, they expect management to reward them with security, wages and benefits. They also expect to be treated fairly and to be part of the decisions that affect their working conditions.

Suppliers provide the company with the raw material that will ultimately have a bearing on the quality and price of the company's products or services. They are thus vital to the survival and success of the company. In return for their contribution to the corporation, management needs to treat them with respect and pay them on time in order to ensure their loyalty and a mutually beneficial relationship.

Customers provide the lifeblood of the company as they provide the income that is needed to keep the company afloat. In return for the money that they pay, they expect quality products and decent service. Management needs to take heed of the interests of customers in order to retain their loyal support. Failure to do so might result in customers turning their backs on the corporation with detrimental consequences for other stakeholders, such as shareholders and suppliers.

Local communities provide corporations with the basic infrastructure and human and natural resources required for running a successful business operation. In return, corporations contribute to the tax base and economies of the communities in which they operate. To maintain this mutually beneficial relationship, management of corporations needs to respect local communities and act as responsible corporate citizens. Should they fail to do so, the corporation can expect to be distrusted and penalised by the local community.

Managers, of course, are also stakeholders in the organisations. They share similar expectations than other employees of the firm, in the sense that they also need to be duly compensated for their contribution to the survival and success of the company. They do, however, have the additional duty of looking after the wellbeing of the corporation as such. This implies, amongst others, the duty of balancing the claims that the different stakeholders make upon the corporation. For it is exactly in finding the appropriate balance between the claims of the different stakeholder groups that the survival and success of the corporation is achieved.

In the above version of stakeholder theory by Freeman and Evan, all stakeholders are treated as equals. The interests of no single group are given primacy over other groups. This obviously has drastic implications for how companies are to be run. It also implies that Boards of Directors need to be constituted in a way that will represent the interests of all major stakeholder groups.

It is on this point of the equality of all stakeholders that the opinions of supporters of stakeholder theory divide. A prime example of someone who subscribes to stakeholder theory, without holding that the claims of all stakeholders groups should be treated equally, is Kenneth Goodpaster.

Kenneth Goodpaster

In an article titled 'Business Ethics and Stakeholder Analysis', Kenneth Goodpaster takes issue with Freeman's version of stakeholder theory. He believes that stakeholder theory along the lines suggested by Freeman can be detrimental to both business and society.

He describes Freeman's stakeholder theory as a multi-fiduciary stakeholder conception. In this conception, managers of corporations have a fiduciary relationship towards all stakeholders of the corporation. Such a situation, Goodpaster believes, can become intolerable as the demands of various stakeholder groups can be contradictory and irreconcilable. The theory can undermine the very nature of corporations as privately owned entities with very specific economic missions. If managers were to equally cede to the claims of all stakeholders, corporations run the risk of being turned into public institutions that are no longer geared towards economic value creation for shareholders. They can effectively undermine the freedom and enterprise associated with private corporations. Thus despite its noblest intentions, Goodpaster concludes that a multi-fiduciary stakeholder approach can become a Frankenstein's monster.

On this score, Goodpaster agrees with Milton Friedman that corporations, and specifically their managers, have a special duty towards shareholders. As the agents of shareholders, managers have a fiduciary obligation towards shareholders to maximise profits.

This fiduciary obligation by managers towards shareholders does not have to result in a situation where the interests of all other stakeholders are sacrificed for the sake of shareholder interests. Goodpaster contends that besides the special fiduciary relationship of managers to shareholders, they also have moral responsibilities towards all other stakeholders of the corporation. These moral obligations can never be overridden in the name of shareholder interests. Within the framework of fiduciary obligations to shareholders, managers should find ways to respect their moral obligations to all other stakeholders of the corporation. In this way corporations can pay due consideration to their moral obligations to all stakeholders without sacrificing the private economic mission of corporations.

Conclusion

The theories of the modern corporation discussed in this chapter demonstrate how the ethical expectations that society has of modern corporations have shifted and changed in recent times. Corporations are increasingly being regarded as integral and key players in the wellbeing of society. As such, they are expected to act with moral integrity and moral responsibility. A question that inevitably arises is whether taking up these ethical responsibilities might not lead to financial failure. Is it possible to be both ethical and still profitable? We will explore this question in the next chapter.

PART 4

Business ethics matters

INTRODUCTION

The purpose of Part 4 is to demonstrate that business ethics matters in business, and that organisations and their leaders ignore the ethical dimension of business at their peril. The extent to which ethics is embraced within a business affects both the perceptions of its stakeholders and the performance of the business. The confidence of investors in organisations, the loyalty of customers to companies, and the willingness of talented individuals to offer their skills to the organisation are all factors that are influenced by the ethics of a company. Recognising and integrating ethics within a business is a crucial factor that determines its success and sustainability.

The foundation for the fact that ethics matters in business is laid in Chapter 8 by advancing logical arguments on how to dispel popular myths, in the form of slogans, which are held about ethics in business. These beliefs, if not addressed, can advocate a strict division between business and ethics.

The symbiotic nature between ethics and corporate reputation and the organisation's primary stakeholders (investors, consumers and employees), as well as its financial performance, is illustrated in Chapter 9. Ethics is proposed as the key to unlock human potential in organisations in Chapter 10. In this chapter we demonstrate how organisational ethical mindsets can facilitate human wellness, meaning and self-actualisation. A number of ethics-related factors are then suggested as prerequisites to unlocking human potential in organisations.

This part of the book ends with a discussion on the interrelationship of ethics and trust in organisations (Chapter 11). The nature of trust is first presented, whereafter the cost of distrust is counterbalanced by an illustration of the benefits of high levels of trust in organisations. The chapter ends with an explanation of how ethics can facilitate trust in organisations.

CHAPTER 8

Ethics in business: Dispelling the myths

D espite the fact that ethics has become quite prominent in business over the last few decades, there are still some who are sceptical about whether it is possible to be ethical in business. This scepticism can take one of two forms. First, there are those who believe that the very nature of capitalism excludes a concern for ethics. Second, there are people who do not regard capitalism as excluding ethics, but who are nevertheless sceptical about whether one can run a financially successful business whilst adhering to decent ethical standards. Sometimes the latter form of scepticism turns into a conviction.

Such convictions can play a powerful role in reinforcing unethical behaviour. They function as myths that legitimise and sustain unethical business practice. It is therefore imperative that when confronted with such myths, one should be able to challenge them. Failure to do so, will result in these myths perpetuating unethical business practices as 'good business' or as 'business as usual'.

The following are six myths that drive a wedge between business and ethics:
◙ dog eat dog
◙ survival of the fittest
◙ nice guys/girls come second
◙ unethical conduct is not serious
◙ when in Rome, do as the Romans do
◙ all that matters is the bottom line.

Each of these myths will be challenged to see whether they make business or rational sense. As we go through them, the case for ethics in business will simultaneously emerge.

Myth 1: Dog eat dog

This myth states that the ground rule of business is 'dog eat dog'. It portrays the business environment as a lonely and hostile environment. Either you trample on others, or you yourself will be trampled upon. To consider the interests of others would be a fatal mistake. It would leave you vulnerable and open to attack from other dogs in the pack. Thus being ethical in business is to the detriment of your own interest.

Myths normally carry an element of truth. The truth in this myth is that your own interests do play an important part in business. Many of our business decisions and actions are driven by considerations about our own self-interest. This reality was well captured by Adam Smith when he wrote in the *Wealth of Nations*: 'It is not from the benevolence of the butcher, the brewer or the baker that we expect our dinner, but from their regard for their own interest. We address ourselves, not to their humanity, but to their self-love.'

Where the myth comes apart, however, is when it claims that your own interests are all that matter in business, and that you should turn a blind eye to the interests of others. Even an elementary analysis of the nature of business activity within a market environment shows that it is almost impossible to live by this myth. Life, according to this myth, would resemble what Thomas Hobbes (the 17th-century English philosopher) termed the 'war of all against all': a situation so dangerous and hostile that it is un-bearable. When unbridled self-interest and disregard for the interest of others would prevail, life would be, in the words of Hobbes, 'solitary, poor, nasty, brutish, and short' (Hobbes, 1998:84).

Business, even in its most elementary form, always consists of a complex network of interpersonal and inter-institutional relations. Business is social in its nature. That is true of even a small business like a bakery (like the one in Adam Smith's famous quote above). The baker is dependent on a whole range of other stakeholders. The baker depends upon her suppliers, who can be, amongst others, farmers or millers. In the bakery, even if it is small, the baker depends on employees. And the baker has a relationship with her clients. The baker also has relationships with the local community, who will expect certain standards of quality and hygiene. If the baker did not have sufficient money to start the business, there might also be a relationship with shareholders or creditors. And so we could continue. It should be clear by now that it would be sheer folly to live according to the myth of 'dog eat dog' in such an intricate network of relationships. In order to survive and flourish you have no option other than to respect the interests of those who together make up the social network of a business. It is not hard to imagine what would happen if you do not respect your obligations towards suppliers, or what the consequences would be if you alienate yourself from employees, clients or creditors.

What is true for the butcher, the brewer, and the baker, also applies to the banker, the broker, and the business executive. Contrary to the myth, and because business is social in nature, finding a sound balance between concern for others' interests and concern for your own is essential if you want to run a sustainable business.

Myth 2: Survival of the fittest

According to this myth, business is essentially a competitive struggle in which only the toughest will survive. The competitive nature of business means that you cannot afford bothering about the interests of your competitors, as that will jeopardise your own chances of survival. On the contrary, one should be as tough as a nail and do whatever it takes to beat your rivals. Ethics in business is dangerous as it might undermine your competitiveness and so your chances of survival.

Competition undeniably is an important aspect of business and has a rightful and essential role to play. The major flaw of this myth therefore is not that it emphasises the importance of being competitive in business, but that it uses the fact of competition as licence for justifying anything (even unethical behaviour) in order to win.

In this respect there are three flaws in this myth:

◎   competition does not exclude ethics
◎   ethics is a precondition for ongoing competition
◎   co-operation is as important as competition.

First a discussion on the claim that competition does not exclude ethics: An analogy from the world of sport can be used to illustrate this point. It is generally accepted that sport is competitive. This fact, however, does not mean that competitors may do whatever they wish in order to win. Severe penalties and even expulsion from the sport can be expected when people break the rules. The competitive nature of sport can never be used as an excuse for unethical behaviour.

Similarly, the undeniably competitive nature of business cannot be used as an excuse to justify unethical behaviour towards competitors in business. I am not expected to further the interests of my competitors, but neither does the fact that they are my rivals give me license to treat them unethically. Beating them fairly and squarely in the competition is acceptable. But should I resort to unethical conduct in order to win, I not only transcend the rules of the game, I also jeopardise the game itself. Foul play in the name of competition is as unacceptable in business as it is in sport. That takes us straight to the second consideration, which is the claim that ethics is a precondition for ongoing competition.

For any sport to survive and flourish, the players or teams need to respect both their competitors and the game that they are playing. If they do not, they will either ruin the game, or they will be prevented from further participation in competition. Without rules, a game becomes meaningless. Imagine a soccer match where some players pick up the ball and run; others decide they don't feel like playing within the lines; and a few hold down the goalkeeper while their teammate takes a penalty kick! Spectators would lose

101

interest, other players would get fed up, and the credibility of soccer would be threatened. Rules and fair play are essential for soccer to survive. The sport depends on a minimum commitment to ethical behaviour by all who participate in it.

This point is well illustrated by the recent doping scandals in professional cycling. Because so many professional cyclists have tested positively for using banned performance-enhancing substances in major cycling events, such as the Tour de France, there is a crisis in the sport. Spectators are becoming disillusioned with the sport, because they can no longer be confident that they are watching an excellent human performance and not the effects of a performance enhancing substance on a cyclist. Television companies are showing their displeasure with this debacle by cutting down on, or even terminating, their coverage of major cycling tours. Sponsors are embarrassed to be associated with doping scandals and therefore withdraw their sponsorship. Thus, this attitude of doing whatever it takes to win is not only harming individual cyclists, but also the sport of cycling as a whole.

The same holds true for business. If ethics is abandoned in the name of competition, the future of the game of business itself is endangered. Environments in which the basic interests of economic competitors are not protected are neither conducive to competitive business, nor to the legitimacy of the market economy. This happens, for example, when companies get away with handicapping or eliminating their competitors by bribing state officials to intervene in the operations of rival companies. Business environments, where unethical conduct like corruption, fraud and human rights abuses are rampant, scare off investors who fear for their property, investment, or even their lives. Furthermore, the wider community generally shows intolerance towards unethical business practices that undermine justice, human rights and safety. Business that threatens social fairness and stability normally results in calls for stronger government intervention in business affairs. The community could even call for economic policies that would allow businesses less freedom. Thus, unethical behaviour in an attempt to win at all cost can result not only in penalties or the exclusion of certain business players, but restrictions being imposed upon businesses.

A third flaw in the myth that business is simply a matter of survival of the fittest is that it overemphasises competition and does not give due credit to the role that co-operation plays in business success. Exactly in order to be competitive, a business often has to co-operate with its rivals. Once more a sporting example is relevant. To launch and maintain a successful break away from the pack of riders in a cycling tour, the rival members of the break away group have to co-operate with one another in order to maintain and widen the gap between them and the main platoon of riders.

The same principle applies in business. Very often, and especially in the case of small- and medium-sized businesses, the key to business success lies in one's ability to co-operate with your business rivals. Successful co-operation requires a basic respect for your competitors and finding a fair balance between giving and taking in the co-operative relationship. Far from being a hindrance to competitiveness in business, ethics is rather a prerequisite both for maintaining a competitive environment and for engaging in co-operative relationships with rivals.

Myth 3: Nice guys/girls come second

This myth proclaims that it is impossible to be both ethical and successful in business. Ethics and business are seen as opposites. Either one is unethical and successful, or ethical and unsuccessful. In short, ethics is detrimental to success in business.

Once more, there is an element of truth in this myth. Ethics might come at a price. Being ethical in business might demand that you refuse business opportunities that, say, involve fraud, human rights transgressions or that jeopardise the safety of your employees. But to claim that a commitment to ethics will always undermine success in business is simply not true. On the contrary, ethics seems to be a prerequisite for sustained success, and more so for excellence in business.

Let us turn to the social nature of business again. Organisations often claim that their staff are one of their major assets. Such a claim, though often over-used and misused, is no exaggeration. The performance of any organisation is vitally dependent on employee performance. Companies who wish to be successful cannot expect to do so without the dedication and innovation of the people who work for them.

Ethics are vital for cultivating dedication and creativity in people. Dedication means that you will be willing to work hard and to make personal sacrifices for the sake of the company. Creativity means that you will go beyond what is merely expected and will use your imagination for the benefit of the company. Unethical conduct towards employees stifles both dedication and creativity. Employees who feel that their interests are ignored or disrespected tend to be resentful. Rather than being creative and dedicated, they will do the bare minimum required of them and will show low levels of commitment towards their employer.

The cultivation of dedication amongst employees requires companies to show and demonstrate respect and care for the interests of their employees. This includes respect for the dignity of each employee, recognition of people's efforts, and investment in their development through training and education. Showing respect and care to employees can enhance the performance and profitability of a company. The same argument about the role of ethics for the performance of a company can also be applied to its relationship with its suppliers and clients. The ongoing loyalty of suppliers and clients depends on the way they are treated. Unethical behaviour towards them undermines their loyalty and confidence in the company. A company that treats any of its stakeholder groups unethically runs the risk of alienating them.

One of the most obvious ways in which unethical behaviour can harm the success of a company is by damaging its reputation. A good reputation is an invaluable asset. It inspires trust from employees, business partners and customers and persuades them to enter into long-term relationships with the company. For this reason, companies are willing to invest heavily in protecting their image and reputation. Often a good reputation is what keeps them in business and gives them a competitive advantage over others. The damage that unethical business behaviour can do to a company's reputation is huge, especially if it receives media attention. Corporate scandals are by definition caused by unethical behaviour. When a company's reputation is damaged by a scandal, the trust of stakeholders in the affected company inevitably declines. Individuals and institutions tend to shun companies with bad reputations, which explains why corporate scandals are often the prelude to corporate demise.

Far from being a liability, ethics turns out to be a prerequisite not only for sustaining business performance, but also precisely for exceptional business performance.

Myth 4: Unethical conduct is not serious

This myth propagates that although unethical conduct is wrong it is not really harmful to society. Unethical conduct may not be exactly the right thing to do, but then it is not that bad either. Although unethical conduct might cause some discomfort to a few people, it will not harm society at large. In fact, there might even be some hidden benefits for society, such as the redistribution of wealth or the stimulation of economic growth. Money lost through unethical behaviour, such as fraud or bribery, will find its way back into the economy again, either through consumer spending or through investment. At least it is not as serious as other crimes like assault and murder where people are seriously injured or killed.

In the three previous myths it was not difficult to see that there was an element of truth to each of them. These myths came about as a result of distortion or isolation of an element of truth. In the case of this myth, however, it is hard to detect any truth at all. The only way in which this myth can be sustained is if one takes the view that the impact of immoral conduct in business and on its surrounding environment is superficial. For example, immoral conduct in business might lead to financial loss, but never to the loss of life. But not even this claim is true.

Unethical conduct in business is a profoundly serious matter, and can indeed result in loss of life. Two real life examples will illustrate the point. A first case is that of a fraudulent investment scheme where elderly people invested their retirement savings in a scheme that promised high returns. To their shock they discovered that the scheme was a hoax, and that they had lost most, if not all, of the money that they were to live on in their retirement. Out of desperation some of them committed suicide to escape a bleak and uncertain future.

A second case is that of corruption in a department of water affairs. The contract for water purification was granted to a private company, not on the basis of their competence, but because they bribed the official responsible for awarding the contract. The water quality in certain areas deteriorated to such an extent that a number of people died of diseases caused by drinking the unhygienic water. Unethical conduct is serious. In this case, some people paid the ultimate price for the unethical behaviour of others.

Unethical behaviour is also serious in other, less dramatic, respects. Take the example of fraud for instance. Fraud can drain a company's resources to such an extent that the company is no longer profitable, and consequently will have to retrench staff or be liquidated. This places an additional burden on society.

As a result of fraud, investors will receive a lower return on investment, because fraud has drained profits. Investors might decide to terminate their investment and move it elsewhere. Potential foreign investors are scared off from investing in countries with high levels of fraud. It is not only fraud and corruption that might affect companies and the economy detrimentally. Also the unethical treatment of employees, as we have already argued, can result in lower productivity and so lower profitability. This in turn means less money for further investment and for the creation of further job opportunities. We have also already seen the damage that unethical behaviour can do to the reputation of a business. Consequently it is clear that unethical behaviour in business is no light matter. It can lead to financial shrinkage and ruin, devastate a country's economy, and even put lives at risk.

Myth 5: When in Rome, do as the Romans do

This myth justifies unethical behaviour by arguing that it does not help to go against the tide of unethical behaviour. If unethical behaviour in business is the norm in a specific context or country, it simply has to be accepted as the way that business is being done. Anyway, what ethical difference can one person's ethical efforts make in a predominantly unethical environment. So, if you can't beat them, join them. Or, when in Rome, do as the Romans do.

This myth might initially appear to have a sense of legitimacy, because it appeals both to our duty to respect cultural diversity and to our duty to respect the will of the majority. Though it might sound legitimate at a first hearing, a deeper analysis soon reveals that it is deeply flawed.

It belongs to the very nature of democracy that we need to take heed of the wishes of the majority. However, that still does not mean that the majority always knows best. Even within a liberal, democratic society, governed by the wishes of the majority, it is accepted that the majority may not always do what is morally right. That is why specific rights and values are entrenched in a Bill of Rights or in the Constitution. In the same way that we cannot deduce from the fact that most people break the speed limit when driving, that speeding is good, we cannot infer from the prevalence of wide-spread unethical practices (like bribing or extortion) that such practices are morally acceptable.

It is a well-known fact that individuals are prone to group pressure. Therefore it is easier to engage in unacceptable practices when there are others around who do the same. The fact that group pressure is understandable does not make it excusable. It might be understandable from a psychological perspective why a young man takes part in a gang rape under the influence of peer pressure, but that does not make the deed any more morally acceptable. The fact that you indulged in immoral conduct with others provides no excuse for the immorality of your actions.

The danger of the myth, when in Rome do as the Romans do, lies in its ability to condone moral laxness and to devalue ethical leadership. When we start accepting unethical practices merely because they have become widespread, we abandon our ability to make judgements about what is acceptable and what is unacceptable. When leaders simply go with the flow of widespread unethical practices, without being willing to challenge such practices and beliefs that are clearly harmful to society, they can hardly be considered responsible leaders.

The failure of the when-in-Rome alibi is demonstrated when business leaders try to justify their companies' complicity in, for example, corruption, child labour, and toxic spills in foreign countries, on the basis that such practices are widespread in those countries. This excuse for irresponsible business conduct is simply not accepted and consequently often results in corporate scandals and consumer outrage. With affordable access to modern information and communication technology (like mobile phones and the Internet) many companies have discovered to their detriment that there is no backyard where they can engage in business practices that are not acceptable elsewhere in the world. The doing-like-the-Romans-do explanation for unethical practices in foreign countries nowadays carries very little conviction in Johannesburg, Tokyo, Sao Paolo, London, Paris or New York.

Myth 6: All that matters is the bottom line

This myth maintains that business is about one thing only and that is profit. The bottom line on your accounts, which indicates profit or loss, is the only measure of whether you are successful in business or not. Anything that impacts positively on the bottom line should be pursued and anything that distracts from it should be discarded. As ethics is not primarily concerned with the bottom line, business should not bother with ethics.

The fact that business needs to be profitable in order to continue its operations is undeniably true. There is, however, a distinct difference between admitting that profit is essential to business and the claim that profit is all that matters in business. To say that something is essential does not mean that it is all that matters. For example, to say that I need oxygen to live does not amount to saying that oxygen is all that matters to me. Without oxygen I would die, but that does not mean that the quest for oxygen automatically becomes my sole purpose in life. Similarly the need for profit to sustain business does not automatically amount to profit being the sole purpose of business. The claim that the bottom line is all that matters in business amounts to mistaking a prerequisite of existence for the goal of existence.

Claiming that profit is all that matters in business is simply not true. In our discussion in Chapter 3 of the example of a business that abducts children and exports them as sex slaves to other countries at huge profit, we already concluded that profit-making alone is not sufficient to be recognised as a legitimate business operation. To operate as a legitimate business a company must be seen to provide products or services that at a minimum are not harmful to society. This ethical relationship between business and society is often referred to as a business's 'license to operate'. The license to operate indicates an implicit agreement by society that a business is allowed to operate and make profit, but on the condition that it will not harm the society. Thus the myth that all that matters in business is the bottom line is not the whole story.

There are also other ways to prove this myth wrong. A narrow focus on financial results alone is likely to harm rather than to help a business. In our discussion of the other five myths it became clear that given the social nature of business, ethics is essential for running a successful and sustainable business. The role of ethics in maintaining the intricate set of relations between a business and its stakeholders, the role of ethics in gaining the respect, dedication and creativity of employees, as well as the vital role of ethics in protecting and enhancing the reputation of a business, makes a strong case for a link between ethics and financial success. It there-

107

fore makes no sense to eliminate ethics from business in the name of the bottom line.

Finally, there is also something condescending and degrading about this myth. It reduces and subordinates all other values to the service of business. It implies that when human beings enter the world of business they forget about all other human aspirations and become mere profit-seeking creatures. Such an assumption violates the complexity of human nature. As human beings, we are driven by a rich variety of motives that also inform how and why we work. One such motive might be to make the biggest amount of profit we can, but there might be a range of other reasons why we work, many of which will be discussed later on in this book. To imply that we trade in all our concerns and ideals to pursue profit when we enter the workplace seems a too simplistic conclusion.

Conclusion

This chapter illustrates how a number of popular myths that drives a wedge between ethics and business cannot be sustained when we start to examine them in depth. In fact, by examining these myths, something else starts to emerge: a picture of ethics as integral to business. By looking at these myths that bar ethics from business, the importance of ethics within business becomes apparent. Although there is good reason to first knock down the barriers that keep ethics out of business, it is not sufficient to stop there. One needs to go beyond the barriers and discover how ethics is ingrained in the very nature of business itself. This has already implicitly been covered in Chapters 2, 3 and 4, but in the next chapters we will deal explicitly with the reasons why ethics matters in business.

CHAPTER
9

Ethics and corporate reputation

I s there a real and growing concern in some organisations to promote ethical behaviour? Or, is the interest in business ethics being fuelled by fear that the exposure of unethical behaviour might result in organisational scandals? Early speculations on the initial cause of the interest in business ethics indicated that the interest was driven by a desire in the USA to avoid business scandals (DeGeorge, 1989). This would imply that organisations' decisions to do something about ethics may be knee-jerk reactions to avoid scandals such as those that caused the demise of Enron, Worldcom, Andersen, Tigon and Leisurenet, or seriously threatened the credibility of Nestlé, Exxon, Nike, Shell, SAA and numerous others.

If one accepts that unethical behaviour may cause high reputational risk to an organisation, it is of strategic importance that organisations avoid the cost associated with immorality. Although there are many dimensions that contribute to the perceived reputation of a business, the ethical dimension of corporate reputation has become as important, and inextricably linked to, other dimensions that constitute reputation, such as product quality and financial performance. In this sense a reputation for ethical behaviour has become a business imperative. Ethics is even perceived by some organisations as being *the* source of competitive advantage. In this chapter the nature of corporate ethical reputation is explored. Thereafter the interface between ethical reputation and the potential perceptions of a number of organisational stakeholders are analysed.

Reputation

Organisational reputation, as the attributed character of an organisation, determines the extent to which stakeholders would be comfortable to form relationships, business or otherwise, with the organisation. Reputation develops as a history of interactions. An organisation's reputation is contingent on how it interacts with others. When such interactions are consistently perceived as positive and genuine, the organisation engenders trust in its relationships. In this way reputation is inextricably linked to the trustworthiness of an entity. Kuper (2006) reminds us that reputation provides one with information about how a person or company is likely to act and react. It also affords an organisation a type of predictability when those that it interacts with know what to expect. It also mitigates risk and reduces the cost that may be incurred to acquire trust-related information.

Reputation is, however, by no means limited to organisations. Individuals, as representatives of organisations, and even countries, depend on their reputations to initiate and maintain relationships.

Reputation at country level

Attitudes to corporate governance, and to business ethics practices by implication, can vary from country to country (Dallas, 2004). These attitudes will by implication influence individual companies' attitudes toward governance and ethics. The perceptions that potential investors and businesspeople hold of a country in which it wishes to invest or conduct business operations may to a large extent be determined by the reputation that the country as a whole may have. Should the country's reputation be dubious less capital will flow into it. Such countries may even attract businesspeople of questionable integrity. Should a country consistently associate with such people, unethical business practices may contribute to a snowball effect where the country as a whole, as well as its government officials and citizens are labelled as untrustworthy.

In such countries corruption, which is the abuse of entrusted power for personal gain (Transparency International, 2009), may become endemic. The extent to which corruption becomes a norm, not only within certain countries but also in the behaviour of others that wish to do business with them, is illustrated by the following phenomenon: until as recently as the early 2000s certain European countries' governments actually allowed tax rebates for companies, registered in those countries, for money these companies had to pay to bribe foreign governments for the 'privilege' of doing business with them.

Dallas (2004) reports that multinationals, the World Bank and organisations such as Standard & Poor (by means of its Sovereign Credit Ratings), the World Economic Forum and Transparency International benchmark countries' governance. Transparency International, a global civil society organisation that aims to create a world that is free of corruption, annually publishes a Corruptions Perceptions Index (CPI). The CPI is a diagnostic tool used to rank more than 150 countries in terms of their perceived levels of transparency and corruption. Although there is severe criticism (see De Maria, 2008) about the CPI mainly because of the criteria being used to assess corruption perceptions, it is an index that is used globally to make decisions about whether to invest in a country or conduct business there. The 2008 CPI ranked Denmark, New Zealand, Sweden, Singapore, Finland, Switzerland, Iceland, The Netherlands, Australia and Canada as the top ten countries where corruption is perceived to be lowest (Transparency International, 2009).

Passow, Fehlman and Grahlow (2005:309) indicate that 'nations today are increasingly concerned with their reputation relative to other nations and turn to actively measuring and managing that reputation'. These authors developed an instrument named the Fombrun-RI Country Reputation Index. This index provides a strategic framework for effective national reputation management.

It has to be emphasised that a country's reputation, from an economic perspective, reflects the collective reputations of business and other economic players, as well as key individuals in that country. However, a positive governance and ethics environment does not guarantee that all companies within that context will govern properly and act ethically (Dallas, 2004). By the same token it is possible that companies in countries with reputations for weak governance and ethics may transcend local practice.

Reputation at corporate level

Corporate *reputation* can be defined as the collective opinion of stakeholders towards an organisation, based on its past record (Nakra 2000; TSF, 2005:1). As such, a reputation is a function of repeated interactions over time (Shapiro, 1999). It is therefore the reflection of an organisation over time as seen through the eyes of its stakeholders. A company's reputation affects its ability to sell products and services, to attract investors, to hire talented staff, and to exert influence in government circles. Good reputations are built up over years, but can be destroyed overnight (Schwartz & Gibb, 1999). However, what is the link between business ethics, corporate reputation and organisational success?

The crucial link between ethical reputation and organisational success is stated succinctly by Van Luijk (in Zadek 1998:1422): 'High ethics companies such as Texas Instruments, IBM, or Marks and Spencer ... know that behaving ethically is integral to their success. They know that their reputation – a reputation for fair dealing, which gains them the trust of their customers, suppliers, and the community at large – is crucial to their bottom line'. Mulcahy (2005:14), chairman and CEO of Xerox Corporation, is adamant about the company's ethical route: '... we all believe that we are part of an ongoing experiment to demonstrate that business success and business ethics are not mutually exclusive. In fact, we believe they are synergistic'.

The extent to which some organisations recognise the strategic importance of ethics as key to their reputations is epitomised by those organisations that actually perceive ethics to be their competitive edge. Moore, the past chairman of PriceWaterhouseCoopers, emphasises that '...ethical behavior is good business. Companies that operate ethically have a competitive edge over those that do not' (1998:7) and 'ethical behavior is at the core of our business, and it's the only way we're going to do business' (1998:9). Seidenberg (1999), the CEO and chairman of Bell Atlantic, explains that organisations can no longer rely on traditional modus operandi, and that new behaviours grounded in business ethics are urgently required to ensure continued stakeholder trust. He provides a different slant to corporate reputation, as established by the media, in explaining that organisations are increasingly being defined by the *way* in which they provide products and services. Stakeholder and marketplace confidence thus not only becomes a competitive edge, but a key factor in preserving corporate reputation. This may, in turn, ensure respect of competitors, continued investor and consumer confidence, and may place the organisation in a good position to attract talented people.

Example: The establishment of reputation

In the 1950s Motorola had an opportunity to secure a multimillion dollar deal with a certain South American government. Moorthy, De George, Donaldson, Ellos, Solomon and Textor (1998) reported that the contract would have been exceptionally profitable. When the closing of the deal was imminent, the Motorola executives realised that the deal had been structured in such a way that would suggest a kickback for that government. The executives walked away from the deal and returned to the USA. They expected to get fired for losing the potentially lucrative deal. Instead, the founder and CEO of Motorola at the time, Paul Galvin, lauded them for their actions. Galvin also declared that the company would not do business with regimes known for corruption. Had Motorola been part of such a deal it would have created the appearance of participating in corruption. The executives eventually held senior directorships in the company. By virtue of this decision and resulting action by the company, Paul Galvin had acquired a good individual reputation for ethical behaviour. With Galvin as a role model Motorola had the foundation of a company that relied on ethics to build its reputation. Clearly, potential business partners would also have felt secure in the knowledge that they would be treated ethically when conducting business with Motorola.

Johnson & Johnson is another classical textbook example of a company that enhanced its reputation through immediate ethically assertive action subsequent to the event in which contaminated Tylenol, one of their key brands, caused the death of seven people in the Chicago area in 1982. At that time, the company was listed third on the first Fortune 200 reputation list (Vergin & Quoronfleh, 1998). The company made a decision, which was ethically sound, but which could potentially have been financially disastrous – it recalled and destroyed 22 million bottles of Tylenol at a cost exceeding US$100 million. Tylenol soon reclaimed its market share however. The 1984 Fortune reputation listings placed Johnson & Johnson in fifth position with an essentially unchanged reputation score. It is interesting to note that in Fortune's Most Admired Companies survey conducted in 2009, Johnson & Johnson was still ranked in fifth position (Fortune.com, 2009). This is an example of a company that showed strong moral courage and managed to emerge with its reputation intact. Johnson & Johnson was also ranked first in the Reputation Institute's annual survey of the most reputable companies in 2008 and 2009 (Reputation Institute, 2009).

Another example of a company that enhanced its reputation through moral management is 3M. Carroll and Buchholtz (2006) report that 3M discovered during the mid-2000s that some trace elements of a chemical that the company had used in its manufacturing processes for 40 years, were present in the bloodstreams of many of its employees. The company publicly announced the crisis it faced. Many of its products, Scotchgard among others, contained the chemical, PFO (perfluorooctane sulfonate). PFO caused a serious health risk, mainly to employees. 3M decided to phase out the product at a potential cost, as a loss in annual sales, of US$500 million, before a replacement chemical was available.

At the other end of the spectrum are the effects of unethical practices or merely allegations thereof. Such practices can cause permanent damage to a firm's reputation. In some instances the damage to reputation is so severe that some existing clients will suspend further dealings with the affected company, and potential clients will withhold decisions on possible engagement. This situation is best illustrated by an analysis of the consequences of the practices of Andersen (at that stage one of the so-called 'big five' international accounting firms) at Enron. The accounting firm knowingly participated in unethical reporting practices that occurred at Enron. Immediately after Enron's demise became public, Andersen destroyed tons of documents that could implicate them in Enron's unethical practices. The firm disintegrated worldwide soon after the fall of Enron.

Ethical and socially responsible practices appear to be good business: they could result in a favourable reputation and ultimately in increased sales and decreased costs of doing business. This intimate link between ethics, reputation and organisational success explains why a 1999 UK survey of FTSE 350 companies found that the desire to improve or protect reputation was the most common factor influencing the development of business ethics activities in organisations (Moon & Bonny, 2001).

The link between ethics and reputation should, however, be clearly understood. When companies try to act ethically to achieve a good reputation, or to gain a competitive edge, ethics becomes the means to an end, but not the end in itself. Kuper (2006:3) advises that ethics cannot be adopted instrumentally, or 'purely for the sake of trust's competitive advantage'. In a sense this may not be truly ethical. As merely a means to an end, ethics is not embraced for its own sake. Powerful companies that have little competition in an industry may even use their longstanding reputation as a smokescreen when deceiving others (suppliers, customers, employees) in a quest for short-term gains or the once-off big deal (Kuper, 2006). Brennan (2003) warns that a momentary detour off the ethical path could be enough to ruin a company's reputation for many years, and perhaps even forever in some stakeholders' eyes.

Although Kuper (2006:50) warns that 'a good reputation might affect a company's wealth or talent at media management, rather than its core ethical ability', it cannot be denied that a reputation for ethics will, at the very least, pacify stakeholders. Discerning stakeholders may even make decisions in favour of dealing with the company. Seidman (2006:8) cautions organisations that act ethically to gain good reputations by suggesting that companies should build their ethical reputation *and* make money – ethics should not be applied to make money however. For a company to gain a *sustainable* advantage, ethics as an end in itself, and for its own sake, should be the way to go not only during prosperous times, but also when the company endures economic hardship.

Example: The management of reputation

During 2005 the so-called 'Boeing affair' caused potential reputational damage to the company. After receiving an anonymous tip-off on the company's whistle-blowing line, the board of Boeing forced the CEO, Harry C. Stonecipher, to resign for conducting an extramarital affair with a female colleague. Boeing Chairman, Lewis Platt (in Girion & Gaither, 2005:1) stated that certain details of the affair could hurt the company's reputation, which Stonecipher was lured from retirement 15 months prior to his resignation to repair.

The opinion of Tom Donaldson, director of the ethics and law programme at the University of Pennsylvania's Wharton School, was that 'Boeing did the right thing, because allowing a married CEO to carry on with an employee would create too much potential for Stonecipher to abuse his power, and Boeing couldn't take another scandal. We live in a period when the ethical sensors are way up. This guy didn't steal from shareholders and employees. But if it's definitely a violation of their code and culture, this is not a time period where that behavior is going to be given the benefit of the doubt' (quoted in Girion & Gaither, 2005:1)

The decision by Boeing's board clearly reflects an intention to manage the company's reputation. In this case, by dealing assertively with an ethical transgression that could taint stakeholders' trust in the corporation.

Reputation and stakeholders

Ruettgers (2003:13), Chairman of EMC, states that the bad behaviour of a relative few 'calls into question the behaviour of everyone'. It makes employees suspicious of management and suspicious of each other. As such, the reputations of a few bad apples may lead to the perception that the entire barrel is bad. Investors, consumers and employees are three key stakeholders that may explicitly or inadvertently judge a company by the ethical dimension of its reputation.

Investor confidence

The dramatic improvement of information and communication technologies in the twentieth century has shrunk the countries and continents of our planet into a global village with a truly global market. As this global market emerges and national borders become ever more perforated, investors are increasingly able to take advantage of investment opportunities wherever these arise around the globe. This has resulted in a situation where the mobility of capital has increased to unprecedented levels. Investors now have more freedom and opportunities than ever before to invest their capital wherever they believe they might receive the highest returns.

In this new situation created by a global investment market, it is not surprising that corporate governance has become prominent. Although investors are keen to take advantage of opportunities around the globe, they would not do so at any cost. On the contrary, they are continuously searching for companies that inspire confidence. Knowing that a company is being managed in a fair, accountable, responsible and transparent way generates such confidence. In short, investors desire, and often demand, proper governance.

The importance of good corporate governance for investors was clearly illustrated in the 2002 McKinsey Investor Opinion Survey. More than 200 of the largest institutional investors were asked how important they considered good corporate governance to be in their investment decision-making. These investors were managing investments in excess of US$2 trillion. The key findings of the survey were that:

▣   85% of investors consider corporate governance as important as financial performance.

◙   73% will pay more for shares of a well governed company than for a poorly governed company with comparable financial results.

◙   The premium they are willing to pay for the shares of well governed companies in Africa is 30%.

There is, however, a close link between corporate governance and ethics. The nature of corporate governance is such that the concept itself has an ethical character. It can be regarded as a moral obligation that directors have to take care of the interests of investors and other stakeholders (Collier & Robberts, 2001; Maitland, 2001). As shareholders and stakeholders have invested their capital, talents, or trust in the corporation, directors have to ensure that the corporation is governed in such a way that they receive a just reward for their investment. The moral nature of corporate governance is seen in its intention to take care of the interests of those stakeholders who have committed themselves in some way to the wellbeing and growth of the corporation (Etzioni, 1998; Rossouw, 2002).

Not only does the concept of corporate governance have an ethical nature, but the practice of corporate governance also requires sound ethical judgement by directors. They need to set morally sound corporate goals in order to protect the reputation (or symbolic capital) of the organisation. Furthermore, they need to ensure that corporate goals are being pursued in ways that would not embarrass shareholders and other stakeholders. They also need to be open and honest in disclosing information that reliably informs shareholders about the performance of their investment and foreseeable risks.

Enron and other corporate scandals in the early 2000s affected stock markets to the extent that investors acquired a sudden and substantial awareness of the companies and portfolios that they invested in. Ferrell, Fraedrich and Ferrell (2008:19) note that 'Investors today are increasingly concerned about the ethics, social responsibility, and reputation of companies in which they invest'. There are also several socially responsible mutual funds and asset management companies that assist investors to buy shares in companies that have good reputations for ethics. Brennan (2002:11), chairman and CEO of the Vanguard Group, a company that manages mutual fund assets in excess of US$700 billion, stated that 'companies that mislead or lie to their investors always pay a price eventually, *because the market ultimately does value integrity*' [authors' emphasis]. It appears that integrity has a very tangible market value. Brennan (2003) suggests that companies with sterling reputations for integrity are far more likely to attract capital and create value for their shareholders: 'Quite simply, investments in honest organisations will produce the best long-term results' (p. 14).

Ferrell et al (2008) suggest that the issue of attracting and retaining investors is a critical one for companies. They report that roughly 50% of investors sell their shares within one year. It is no surprise then that companies spend significant time and resources in communicating with their investors about their companies' reputation and financial performance. Gaining and maintaining investors trust is crucial to sustaining the financial stability of the company (Ferrell et al, 2008).

The importance of a reputation for corporate governance for investor confidence and the way in which ethics is entwined with both the concept and practice of corporate governance, illustrates once more the strategic significance of ethics for organisations.

Discerning consumers

The famous management scholar, Peter Drucker (2009) once claimed that the first priority of a business is to create a customer. This implies that financial success should be a spin-off of the processes that organisations utilise to anticipate market needs, identify potential consumers, and then provide them with high-quality products or services. A case in point is Virgin Atlantic, which estimates that it costs five times as much to recruit a new customer as it does to keep an existing one (Baker, 2000).

Davis, CEO of the utility company, Niagara Mohawk explains his organisation's ethical approach to its consumers by pointing out that 'as customers realise they have increasing options for energy service, they will become less tolerant of behaviour that might have been accepted in the past' (1999:10). He further states that ethical consumer attitudes exert significant competitive pressure on the company, which has resulted in everyone in the company being more sensitive to ethical issues and more circumspect about their behaviour. Walker, the chairman of Walker Information, is adamant that his organisation's reputation for integrity and ethics (characteristics he labels as *business practices*) is of equal importance to other factors, e.g. price, quality and service, as indicators of consumer loyalty (in Driscoll & Hoffman, 2000). According to Ferrell, et al (2008) an enduring relationship of mutual respect and co-operation with customers is an essential success factor for business. If a company treats its customers fairly and consistently, chances are that repeat purchases will occur naturally. The company's reputation for fairness and respect may also permeate the marketplace and attract new consumers.

An important dimension that has been added to the organisation-customer mix in the past few decades is that of the consumer movement, or consumerism as it is often referred to, which started in the 1960s in the USA. Consumerism is a reflection of the new counterbalancing force to capitalism (Murphy & Bendell, in Harrison, Newholm and Shaw, 2005). The one thing that concerned consumers have in common is that they are concerned with the effects that a choice to purchase has, not only on themselves, but also on the environment (Harrison, Newholm & Shaw, 2005). The fact is that consumers may at times not be adequately informed, or may be purposely misled and offered a restricted choice of alternatives or unsafe products (Du Plessis, Rousseau & Blem, 1994). Since many of these issues have their origins in unethical corporate practices, or have ethical implications, the consumer movement also provides a haven for the morally discerning, or ethically sensitive, consumer. The consumer boycott of Nike is a good example of a company whose customers deserted it upon being informed that Nike had not considered the ethical implications of their actions when it used child labour in Cambodia. De George (1999) states that consumers nowadays vote with their currency; they would therefore be discerning and only pay for products and services that provide ethical peace of mind.

A perspective on the extent to which organisations may ignore consumer opinion at their peril is provided by a survey conducted among retail consumers in the UK. A central theme derived from the responses was an increase in what could be termed 'ethical consumerism' (Zadek 1998). In this survey, 35% of the 30 000 consumers polled indicated that they had previously boycotted products as a result of ethical concerns such as animal rights, the environment and human rights. A 'yes' answer was provided by 60% of the respondents to the question on whether they would in future boycott a retail outlet or product should they suspect unethical practices.

Sensitivity to the needs of consumers who are concerned about the social and environmental responsibility and ethical practices of companies from which they buy has led to the establishment of organisations that bridge the gap between First World consumers and Third World producers. An example of such an organisation is the Fairtrade Foundation, which represents an alternative approach to conventional international trade. This foundation works from a clear set of criteria defining fair trade terms. They set up monitoring systems to ensure that these terms are met and that individual producers benefit from the trading terms applied (Fairtrade Foundation, 2009).

The Body Shop, a UK-based organisation, which sells hygiene and cosmetic products manufactured from natural or organic base materials through more than 2 400 outlets in more than 61 countries, is a typical example of an organisation that has implemented ethical consumerism as its competitive edge. Although it has subsequently emerged that the organisation has misled its consumers in its claim to use only natural products (Entine, 1995), it remains an example of an organisation that espouses ethical values and caters for the needs of ethically aware consumers. For example, the company's 1992 decision not to purchase any item made of PVC was taken as a precautionary approach to the environmental impact of PVC production and its associated health implications (Moon & Bonny, 2001). In the process of using ethics as an overt corporate strategy, The

Body Shop has the ability to broaden its customer base, attract 'green' money and recruit high-level employees with an ethical orientation.

Ethical consumerism, which is a collective noun for the potential preferences, decisions, and actions of morally discerning consumers, may therefore be a major determinant of the architecture of corporate strategy. The strategic importance of the morally discerning consumer is therefore a reality that companies cannot ignore. Companies that do not strategically account for these consumers, and neglect to build favourable ethical reputations amongst their consumers, limit their business opportunities.

Employees

Within an organisation, an individual's reputation consists of the perceptions that others accumulate of him or her over time. If employees have experienced positive interactions over time with a manager, the manager is likely to have a good reputation and consequently will be perceived as trustworthy (Lewicki & Bunker, 1996:121). Since the four dimensions of trustworthiness (openness, competence, integrity and benevolence) have very distinct ethical dimensions, and since reputation is so closely intertwined with these four factors, it is clear that ethical behaviour plays a vital role in the reputation acquired by an individual. As such, ethical behaviour becomes a pre-condition for a good reputation, which in turn is a significant factor in determining how trustworthy managers will be perceived to be.

The apples and barrels analogy provided in Chapter 1 provides a useful framework to understand the extent to which employees align their values with organisations' values. Moore (1998:8) notes that 'People who want to participate in an environment that's congruent with their own value systems will leave an unethical organisation.' He states further that 'When companies stand up for what's right, day in and day out, it has a positive impact. Positive in terms of who it attracts, *because good people want to work in ethical environments*. It simplifies decision making' [authors' emphasis] (p. 8). When companies earn the *respect* of people, it becomes a social virtue for the company (Solomon & Martin, 2004:498). Peters and Waterman (1982) found the notion of respect for people as the most pervasive theme that characterises successful companies. Respect extends beyond employees only though. Respect for employees' family is equally important (Solomon & Martin, 2004). Although many organisations include respect as a central espoused value in their value statements, not all organisations have necessarily succeeded in consistently demonstrating respect. Those that have succeeded may very well realise the importance of respect in the attraction and retention of talent.

Ethics, as it manifests in respect for people, may contribute to a company gaining a favourable reputation. This, in turn makes it attractive for prospective employees who know that the company would probably treat them with respect and preserve their dignity (Moorthy, De George, Donaldson, Ellos, Solomon & Textor, 1998). Although an 'employer of choice' or 'one of the best companies to work for' label that signifies many organisations may be earned by various means, it stands to reason that the way in which an organisation treats its people may contribute significantly to this reputation. Although such reputations may reflect companies' size, brand, strength, success, the willingness to pay competitive salaries, and the pervasiveness of its marketing campaigns, prospective employees are becoming sufficiently astute to also factorise the following into their perceptions: in-company relations between co-workers, an emphasis on wellness of employees and their families, the opportunity to engage in meaningful work, encouragement of personal growth and development, respect for diversity, corporate social responsibility actions, and possibly even the opportunity to make a difference. All these factors have a strong ethical dimension.

It may also be argued that in good economic times marked by low levels of unemployment, employees may be sufficiently discerning to rank companies in the so-called 'sin' industries low on employer-of-choice-status. The 'sin' industries are identified as alcohol-producers, arms manufacturers, gambling concerns, tobacco producers and even the extractive industries. Oil and petroleum companies, for example, may be less preferred by discerning employees due to their poor environmental track records. Clouder and Harrison (2005) report that chemical engineers are shunning BP in the UK and accepting job offers from companies in other sectors. Companies in the tobacco industry are finding it increasing difficult to attract the best minds. A case in point is tobacco company Philip Morris that has to pay a premium in employee salaries to recruit talent (Byrnes & Balfour, 2009). These examples serve to illustrate that the ethical reputation of a company may extend beyond its reputation for how it treats its employees or customers, to the inherent ethical nature of the product it manufactures or service it provides.

Reputation and financial performance

Top management often want to know whether adopting an ethical way of doing business, and managing ethics within the company accordingly, will contribute to enhanced financial performance. Larsen (2002), Chairman and CEO of Johnson & Johnson at the time, said that the company's commitment to being ethically responsible to consumers, employees and the community in this order, had the natural effect of also satisfying the expectations of its shareholders through sound and sustainable financial performance.

Erfle and Frantantuono found that firms that were ranked highest on their records of social performance also had greater financial performance

(Makower, 1994). The social performance consisted of charitable contributions, community outreach programmes, environmental performance, the advancement of women and the promotion of minorities (also see Hartman, 2002). The financial performance of the firms in the study was better in terms of operating income growth, sales-to-assets ratio, sales growth, return on equity, earnings-to-asset growth, return on investment, return on assets, and asset growth (Hartman, 2002). In a rigorous study of the empirical linkages between financial and social performance in 469 companies across several industries, and using a variety of social performance indicators, Waddock and Graves (1997) found corporate social performance to be positively associated with previous as well as future financial performance.

It is expected that companies that have codes of ethics that are actually implemented, should have climates conducive to ethical performance. An interesting finding in this regard was generated by a Webley and More (2003) study. They compared the ethical commitment and corporate social responsibility of companies with their financial performance. Their sample was taken from 86 FTSE 350 companies for which full and comparable company data was available for the years 1997–2001. The sample was divided into two groups: those who had had codes of ethics for five years or more and those who explicitly said they did not. Webley and More found that those companies with codes of ethics outperformed those without on three out of four measures of financial performance, namely economic value added, market value added and price-to-earnings (P/E) ratio. Companies with a code of ethics also experienced far less P/E volatility over the four-year period. Generally, the study indicated that that larger UK companies with codes of ethics, i.e. those that are explicit about business ethics, outperform those companies who say they do not have a code (Webley & More, 2003). A similar study in the US by Verschoor (1998) indicated that the 26,8% of the 500 largest US public corporations that commit to ethical behaviour toward their stakeholders or emphasise compliance with their code of conduct in their annual reports, significantly outperform the other corporations on eight publicly-reported measures of historical financial performance.

A USA-based study revealed that companies whose employees perceive them to have integrity had an average three-year return on investment for the shareholders of 101%, as opposed to a return of 69% realised by companies whose employees ascribe a low level of integrity to their employers (Galvin, in Ferrell, et al, 2008). It is evident that a company's reputation among its employees may also contribute to efficiency, productivity and sound financial returns.

Fortune favours the responsible. (Noreena Hertz, quoted in Dempsey, 2003:10).

Although it appears from the research reported on the previous page that fortune favours the ethically responsible, it cannot be stated unconditionally that good ethics will guarantee a good reputation, or good business. A case can be made that there is a symbiotic relation between ethics, financial performance and reputation (Carroll & Buchholtz, 2006). Although these factors are clearly interrelated, it is not always easy to determine which drives the process. In the words of Hartman: 'The jury remains out on a concrete linkage between social performance and financial performance' (2002:224). Of course, one of the problems in research that aims at exploring this linkage is that of the cause-and-effect relationship. However, what is clear from the research is that there are strong indications that those organisations that take their ethics seriously have a better chance to perform financially well on a sustainable basis than those that do not. An example of such research is the 2003 study by Gompers (in UNEP Finance Initiative, 2007) that produced findings indicating a strong positive correlation between organisations' emphasis on good corporate governance and returns on stock in the 1990s. Another study reported by UNEP Finance Initiative (2007) includes research by Goldman Sachs that established a strong link between management's ability to account for environmental, social and governance issues and 'its ability to steer the company towards sustained growth and profitability and accordingly, enhanced stock valuation' (51).

Conclusion

In this chapter the link between ethics, reputation and stakeholders' trust and willingness to engage with an organisation, was presented. If the indications that ethical performance, and a good and known reputation for it, is related to financial performance are interpreted together with the effect an ethical reputation may have on investor confidence, discerning consumers and employees, there should be irrefutable evidence that ethics is good business. Even if the reader decides that there is doubt about the correlation between ethics, reputation and financial performance, the cost of unethical behaviour and resultant tainted reputation cannot be refuted. If the role that ethics can play in the unlocking of human talent, and in the cultivation of trust as explained in the next two chapters is considered in addition to the role that ethics plays in building good corporate reputation, the business case for ethics makes resounding sense. Once organisations have bought into the business reasons for building an ethical reputation, they need to decide how to build an ethical capacity and manage their ethical performance. The way this can be achieved is discussed in the last section of the book.

CHAPTER
10

Ethics and human potential

Organisations of the 1980s and 1990s relied to a large extent on their ability to attract and spend capital wisely. The current league of successful organisations is by and large dominated by those companies with superior technology. In real terms, however, technology is becoming cheaper. What then will distinguish successful organisations from less successful ones in future? In the words of Walt Disney, 'You can create, design and build the most wonderful place in the world ... but it takes people to make the dream a reality'. Over time, it is human capital that creates financial capital, not the reverse. It is increasingly recognised that it is the people, or human resources, of the organisation that are most likely to supply the core competencies, which will be the primary source of sustained competitive advantage and successful long-term financial performance.

Although many organisations describe people as their most important asset, a large proportion of these organisations do not practise this credo. The phenomenom that people are regarded as assets but not treated as such remains a mystery. Unfortunately, many senior managers fail to appreciate the impact that the thinking, attitudes and actions of people at all levels can have on profits, growth, efficiency and relationships. It is clear that organisations that invest in their human capital, develop it and reward people for performance, make more money than those who place less emphasis on human capital.

The Peters and Waterman (1982) study, which is described in their book *In Search of Excellence*, remains a landmark in studies seeking to establish what exactly it is that makes superior organisations tick. Having analysed several high-performing companies over time, they identified the effective utilisation of people as a central criterion for excellence (financial and otherwise) in all the companies they investigated. Thus, people – if managed properly – can be an organisation's greatest competitive edge.

If, therefore, people are perceived to be assets, and are perceived to be an organisation's competitive edge, the business case for investing in, nurturing and developing human talent is clear. Companies that do not do this may survive, and may even achieve success in the short run. Their long-term sustainability may, however, be at risk. The way that companies think about their people, and what they choose to do (or not to do) in unlocking their human potential, determines their future sustainability.

In the remainder of this chapter we will analyse the role that ethics can play in unlocking human potential. The discussion commences with the notion of ethical neglect as the phenomenon whereby some organisations disregard their workforce as an asset. The use of ethics in the unlocking of human potential in organisations is then suggested as a remedy for ethical neglect. The chapter is concluded with a number of ethics-based strategies that may be useful in unlocking human potential.

Ethical neglect

When inadequate ethical mindsets exist, or are absent in organisations, a condition of ethical neglect, in a mild to severe form, may be observed. Ethical neglect occurs when organisations negate the effect that their actions may have on the legitimate rights and expectations of stakeholders to be treated ethically, i.e. with trust, fairness, honesty, empathy and consistency. Ethical neglect often manifests as job dissatisfaction. Job dissatisfaction may also vary in intensity. This may severely inhibit the organisation's employees from flourishing and reaching their full potential.

The organisational mindset that cultivates a state of ethical neglect is characterised by an unethical organisational culture, or lack of ethical conscience. The mentality that often prevails in such organisations is described by Lantos (1999) as a 'business is war' mentality. He states that:

> *This philosophy is held by basically 'good guys' who are moral in their personal lives but are convinced that business is a game, sport, or even war, governed by its own rules of fairness, and therefore must be played outside the realm of individual morality and societal mores (all's fair in love and war!). (223)*

Business leaders are often sceptical about the need for business to be concerned about the goodness for 'the other'. In the process they, sometimes irrevocably, contaminate the trust of their stakeholders. The employee as an important stakeholder requires 'goodness' (fairness, honesty, justice, empathy, recognition and respect) to experience trust and security. If organisations, through their leaders, fail to demonstrate a cognisance of the importance of ethics and fail to incorporate it into the life of the organisation and its employees, a harsh business culture may prevail. In short, organisations that have no culture of ethics may be guilty of ethical neglect.

Ethical neglect may vary markedly from workplace to workplace. Neglect could vary from mild neglect caused by ignorance about employees' rights, at the one end of the spectrum, to severe neglect caused by deliberate denial at the other. The latter results in treating employees as mere resources to be used to achieve organisational success.

The impact of ethical neglect on employees may manifest from feelings or perceptions of slight or moderate discomfort about the organisation to deviant employee behaviour. The discomfort that is experienced may manifest as *job dissatisfaction*. Job dissatisfaction can be described as an affective (emotional) attitude of dislike towards one or more job- or organisationally related dimensions (Newstrom & Davis, 1997:256). Since attitudes, and negative attitudes in this case, are reasonably good predictors of behaviour, a wide variety of consequences, from mild to destructive, may follow. The milder forms of dissatisfaction include psychological withdrawal (feelings of inadequacy, apathy, fear, depression and frustration) or physical withdrawal (tardiness and absenteeism). Another consequence of ethical neglect is the deliberate or inadvertent withholding of effort or performance. This includes wasting time, shirking, job neglect, social loafing and free riding (Bennett & Naumann, 2005), and a reluctance to be creative. Dissatisfaction clearly has an extremely adverse impact on individual, group and organisational performance.

Even worse are the detrimental and harmful consequences of serious dissatisfaction. As Ciulla (2002) states, individual workers are now able to do greater harm and greater good than ever before. Destructive and overt forms of dissatisfaction, as a result of ethical neglect, is prevalent in many organisations. This category of work behaviour has received particular attention in organisational behaviour literature of late and is labelled as deviant behaviour (Kidwell & Martin, 2005; Thorne & Jones, 2005). Deviant behaviour consists of 'voluntary acts that defy organisational norms and standards and threaten the wellbeing of the organisation and/or its members' (Robinson & Bennett, 1995, cited in Kidwell & Martin, 2005:5).

'Deviant behaviour' is used as a collective term for what is also labelled by other authors in Kidwell and Martin (2005) as organisational antisocial behaviour, counterproductive behaviour, dysfunctional behaviour and organisational misbehaviour. The central themes of deviant behaviour, under whatever label it is presented, appear to be the severity of the behaviour and the harmful nature of its consequences. Deviant behaviour thus represents the 'dark side' of employee behaviour (Kidwell & Martin, 2005). Typical forms of deviant behaviour are overt acts of aggression and retaliation, lying and dishonesty, alcohol and substance abuse, workplace violence, theft, sabotage of equipment and processes, verbal sabotage (bad-mouthing others and rumour mongering), abuse or destruction of property, harassment, and fraud and corruption.

The productivity and cost implications of an inability to deal with all these manifestations are obvious. Less obvious though is the effect of ethical neglect on human wellbeing which, in turn, inhibits the optimal utilisation of human potential. And, where neglect is continuous and pervasive, it is unlikely that the people in the organisation, and the organisation as an entity, will reach their full potential.

Ethics as the key to unlock human potential

The discussion in the previous sections, although disturbing, reflects the state of life in many organisations. Of course, since 'we are particularly fascinated by immorality' (Ciulla, 2002:345) or even obsessed with the negative, it is the stories and reports of ethical neglect and deviant behaviour that reach our ears. Thus the topic of ethics mostly surfaces in organisations in the way of ethical *problems to be solved*. This is clearly evident from the preferred approach to managing ethics by rules and compliance evident in many organisations. These are attempts to 'control' behaviour, and thus to prevent unethical behaviour. The restrictiveness of measures of this type results in frustration for the knights (often the majority) in organisations that are subjected to increasingly rigorous controls aimed at dissuading the knaves (often a minority) from acting unethically. The 'big brother' and 'we don't trust you as employee' managerial mindsets inhibit many factors that could contribute to the unlocking of human potential. In this part of the chapter we will show that ethics is not a problem to be solved, but in fact an opportunity to be embraced. We will also show why embracing ethics as an opportunity is the key to unlock human potential.

Ethical organisational mindsets

What constitutes an ethical organisational mindset? An organisation with an ethical mindset has *a strong ethical value orientation,* lives these values and practises them when engaging with all stakeholders. An organisation with an ethical mindset is characterised by a seamless integration of ethics into the purpose, mission and goals of the organisation – ethics is integral to how the organisation defines itself and how things are done. Ethics is no longer viewed as just another aspect of the organisation that needs to be managed. Such an organisation has a well-developed sense of ethical identity. An organisation's sense of identity is its self-defined distinctive character in response to the question 'What are we for whom?' The ethical identity, or the ethical fitness for purpose of an organisation, exists as the ethical dimension of the organisation's character that circumscribes the organisation's inclination to treat the 'whom' ethically. The 'whom', or 'the other', are the organisation's internal and external stakeholders.

An organisation with a well-developed and espoused *ethical identity* is in constant responsible interaction with its 'other' – in this case its employees. Consequently ethical behaviour is a manifestation of the character of the organisation and unethical behaviour is regarded as jeopardising not only the business success of the organisation, but also the very identity of the organisation.

In an organisation with an ethical identity the *ethical culture* is an integral and natural part of the organisational culture. Culture evokes notions of rules, codes, rewards, leadership rituals and stories, which Trevino, Butterfield and McCabe (2001) describe as sense-making devices that guide and shape behaviour. If organisational culture is described in the way that it often is as 'the way we do things around here', ethical culture may be described as 'the way we do things around here even when no one is watching'. This is more formally described by Trevino et al. (2001) as that which 'characterises the organisation in terms of formal and informal control systems (for example: rules, reward systems, and norms) that are aimed more specifically at influencing behaviour)' (308). Evidence of the existence of such a culture, in relation to the employees, includes high levels of trust, the presence of spontaneous discussions on ethical matters, the continuous consideration of ethical implications of decisions at all levels, the presence of several ethical role models in key positions and ethical human resource management practices. Ethics is thus recognised as part of business as usual and is entrenched in corporate discourse and decision making.

Inherent to the ethical culture integral to an ethical organisation, is *moral conscience* (or moral reflection): 'Conscience is our primary check on the unbalanced pursuit of goals and purposes' (Goodpaster, 2007:4). It is most likely the mindset of conscience that provides a platform for ethical organisations to optimally balance the three types of values (strategic, work and ethical) that constitute its core values (see Chapter 1). When such a balance is established, employees have clarity on the importance of performing their duties in an ethical way, even when there is a high work ethic in the organisation and its goals are challenging. Research by Joseph (in Carroll & Buchholtz, 2006) revealed that employees identify their organisation's concern for ethics as an important reason for them to continue working there. John Galvin of Motorola (Ferrell, Fraedrich & Ferrell, 2008) reports that organisations that are viewed as ethical by their employees are six times more likely to retain their workers.

Ethical organisations are characterised by the respect that they show to all their stakeholders. An organisation's commitment to its people arises out of the respect for the worth and dignity of individuals who devote their energies to the business and depend on the business for their economic wellbeing. Even in crisis situations, such organisations will minimise whatever hardships have to be imposed in the form of workforce reductions, relocations and the loss of income (Kreitner & Kinicki, 1992:111–112).

Organisations with respect for the individual as a core value are likely to fulfil the ethical obligations they have towards their employees as a core stakeholder group. This fulfilment of ethical obligations creates a context in which people can find a sense of coherence, predictability in decision making, and meaning in their work – this context is of course the direct opposite of a context marked by job dissatisfaction. In such environments employees have a sense of security, as they experience no ambiguity regarding expectations of their ethics. Ethical focus is consistent. Consistency, of course, invokes a sense of predictability, as employees know what their ethical boundaries are. As such, a sense of trust is established between employer and employee.

Organisations that have high levels of trust are potentially more innovative because employees are not afraid to take risks (Ciulla, 2002). Furthermore, employees are trusted in terms of their competence to do their jobs and to do them ethically. 'When leaders trust in their people's competence, they influence and empower their employees to go beyond current beliefs about their personal limitations. Their capacity for trust in themselves and others expands' (Reina & Reina, 1999:108). The knowledge that they are trusted, that their creativity is appreciated, that they will be treated fairly and the certainty that the organisation will care for their physical needs (for example: safe working conditions) and psychological needs (such as recognition) culminate in 'quality-of-worklife' (QWL). QWL, in turn, facilitates the unlocking of human potential. People with unlocked potential experience growth and development in their competencies and careers and they enjoy sufficient freedom to meaningfully pursue integrated work and personal goals. QWL also contributes to fulfilling the need for self-actualisation, which is a key indicator of 'unlocked potential'.

When human potential is unlocked, a context is created in which the business imperatives of profit, market share, growth and competitive advantage will fall into place as they did in the companies Peters and Waterman (1982) analysed. If organisations succeed in unlocking human potential, they not only build ethical organisations, but also create a competitive advantage.

People-related outcomes of organisational ethical mindsets

In the endeavour to explain human behaviour, the discipline of psychology has created a rich legacy of paradigms and theories that help us to better understand people. Many of these theories identify specific factors that contribute toward the optimal fulfilment of human potential. Three of these paradigms that serve as indicators of optimal fulfilment of human potential are presented below. The three paradigms are *human wellness*, *finding meaning* and *self-actualisation*. They represent three different, but not mutually exclusive, perspectives on human potential.

Human wellness

A recent contribution by psychology is the *positive psychology* paradigm. Positive psychologists wish to promote values that enhance personal and institutional development (Pawelski & Prilleltensky, 2005). Positive psychology represents a movement away from 'what is wrong with people' (Youssef & Luthans, 2005:1) to a school of thought that yearns for the positive, what is good, worthwhile, sustainable and authentic. The discipline of industrial-organisational psychology as the applied science of psychology in organisational contexts has adopted *positive organisational behaviour* as a paradigm to understand and change human behaviour in the workplace. Positive organisational behaviour is 'the study and application of positively-oriented human resource strengths and psychological capacities that can be measured, developed, and effectively managed for performance improvement in today's workplace' (Luthans, 2002).

We learn from positive psychology that *human wellness* can be equated with wellbeing and optimal human flourishing. It is a positive state that is broader than mere happiness or even a full life. It can be achieved through a meaningful life where the application of one's strengths and virtues are cultivated into something much larger than oneself (Pawelski & Prilleltensky, 2005). These authors suggest that the wellness of individual workers is contingent upon the fulfilment of personal needs, collaborative relationships, and supportive and effective environments.

In the post-corporate scandal era of the early 2000s, and within the realm of positive organisational behaviour, business ethicists have increasingly focused on morally sound approaches to ethical performance at the self/individual, group/team and organisational levels. This is culminating in a positive (business) ethics movement that elevates ethicists to a level beyond a fascination with immorality, a focus on the negative, why people are unethical, and organisational ethics as a problem to be solved. An outcome of a focus on these constructs is the evolving of people in organisations (human resources) as *positive ethical capital*. People who (a) are aware of their virtues and develop them, (b) have confidence and competence in their ethical capacity and courage, (c) display sound ethical judgement, (d) make good ethical decisions, and (e) act as moral agents in the organisation, can be described as positive ethical capital. They experience ethical wholeness. Such people have an internal locus of control, are resilient, display hope and optimism, and have a propensity for forgiveness.

The unlocking of human potential should be a process of natural evolvement if employees are viewed to be positive ethical capital and if they act accordingly. Optimal unlocking of human potential, or reaching true wellness, can only occur if people are treated ethically and are given the trust and support to develop their ethical capacity.

Finding meaning

Viktor Frankl contended that human beings are constantly searching for meaning in their lives. Humans, he said, possess a *will-to-meaning* (de Vos, 1995). A central aspect of finding meaning is finding meaning in one's work. The search for meaning is reflected in the following questions related to work: 'Why am I doing this work?', 'What is the meaning of the work I am doing?', 'Where does this lead me to?' and, 'Is there a reason for my existence and the organisation's?' (Krishnakumar & Neck, 2002:156). Fairholm (1996:11) suggests that work is the place where most of us find our fullest sense of meaning: 'The organisation in which we work becomes our most significant community. For some, work is replacing family, friendship circles, church and social groups'. The opposite is equally true. Naylor (Krishnakumar & Neck, 2002:156) states that a lack of meaning in work can lead to 'existential sickness' and even 'separation/alienation from oneself'.

Finding meaning in one's work

Upon visiting a construction site, a reporter asked three brick masons what they were doing. The first answered gruffly, 'I'm laying bricks.' The second replied, 'I'm earning my week's pay'. But the third mason said enthusiastically and with obvious pride, 'I'm building a cathedral'. (Neck & Milliman, 1994:9)

Solomon and Martin (2004:428) remind us that finding meaning in one's work is the key to modern character – jobs define what and who we are. Work thus plays an important role in people's search for meaning. That it is difficult to find meaning in work situations where there is ethical neglect and a lack of respect for people is obvious. The opposite is equally true. Ethical organisations can provide a fertile context for the cultivation of meaning.

People find meaning in the workplace when they are given the freedom to apply their ethical capacity in a positive ethical climate. The moment that employees realise that they are making a real difference in terms of striving towards the common, sustainable good, they start experiencing meaning. The meaning they find produces a collective optimism (hope). They then view themselves as responsible agents of change who can contribute meaningfully towards the organisation and the broader society.

Collins and Porras (1994) contend that people want something to believe in, have meaningful work, and feel that they contribute towards an organisational mission that makes a difference to others. The sense of community that comes about when organisations recognise their role as corporate citizens and live these roles, promotes the feeling of partnership

within. Should employees also understand their individual sense of responsibility and contribution to something beyond merely the creation of wealth
for shareowners, such an understanding may enhance their chances of
creating meaning in their lives through their contributions at work. Not
only will individual employees find meaning, but so will the teams in which
they function. A collective meaning may also be created by teamwork.

Employees' individual sense of responsibility will probably be more
profound if they are members of an organisation that practises corporate
citizenship. An organisation's fulfilment of its responsibility to ensure a sustainable society is known as organisational citizenship. When employees
find meaning through sensing that they are making a difference towards
the good of society, they view themselves as practising individual citizenship
within a context of organisational citizenship. By having shared core
values and looking beyond the fences of the organisation, and endowing
their employees with this same worldview, organisations will have a better
chance of optimising human potential.

Self-actualisation

Abraham Maslow is generally regarded as the father (or single parent) of
the concept *self-actualisation*. Maslow views self-actualisation as a higher-
order human need that requires fulfilment. He describes it as 'The desire to
become more and more what one is, to become everything that one is capable
of becoming' (du Toit, 1986:206). Self-actualisation is a state where people
are truly psychologically healthy, and where they have reached their own
fullest true potential (Baron, 1989). Self-actualisation implies being aligned
with who you are. It is seen as the highest state of human development.

Since work is a central part of one's existence, it can make a crucial
contribution to an individual's sense of self-actualisation. In many cases
it may even be the major factor in the achievement of self-actualisation.
When self-actualisation, and therefore the fulfilment of potential is sought
in the workplace, the work environment must provide a context where
certain psychological states are present. Hackman and Oldham (Beehr,
1996) identified three psychological states that are prerequisites for optimal
human self-actualisation: the experienced meaningfulness of the work, the
experienced responsibility for outcomes of the work, and knowledge of the
actual results of the work activities.

In a benign work environment that allows one to become everything
that one is capable of becoming, self-actualisation can emerge. Such environments are characterised by predictability, security, creativity and opportunities to make a difference, both to the organisation and its stakeholders.
Human misery and pathology, on the other hand, are fostered by environments where people's natural tendencies towards self-actualisation
are frustrated. Once more it is clear that organisations characterised by

ethical neglect will frustrate self-actualisation, while ethical organisations will foster it.

From examining the people-related outcomes of the unlocking of human potential, the focus will now shift towards ethics-based facilitators of unlocking.

Ethics-based facilitators for unlocking human potential

Organisations are powerful vehicles of wellness, meaning and self-actualisation. They therefore need to cultivate these human strengths in the quest for human flourishing (Pawelski & Prilleltensky, 2005). Some of the facilitators that organisations can utilise to unlock the true potential of their people as positive ethical capital are ethical values management, ethical leadership, optimisation of the psychological contract, empowerment and enablement, and ethical HR practices.

Ethical values management

An organisation with a vision, mission and core values that are explicitly stated and accepted by all, has clarity on how the organisation goes about its business and what it stands for. It also provides parameters for actions and behaviours required by members of the organisation. The core values reflect the essence of the organisation. It defines what the organisation is all about and what it wishes to become. Of these, the ethical dimension of organisational values create the psychological mindset of what is ethically acceptable.

Scholars and business leaders are in agreement that organisational values have to be lived and not remain words on paper. For this to happen, organisational values have to be determined through participation with employees in particular. This will ensure that they are at least compatible with the individual values of employees.

Organisations build contexts of meaning for their employees when they align organisational goals, values and behaviour with those of their employees (Youssef & Luthans, 2005). Building an organisational consensus about values is about closing the gaps that exist between personal and organisational values (Pruzan, 2001). Values management implies that everyone in the organisation understands the values, embraces them and applies them continually. The alignment of organisational and employee values seems to provide a connection with oneself, and also a connection with others, fostering a sense of order and balance in the organisation (Korac-Kakabadse et al., 2002:177).

Values have to be made *real* for every person in the organisation though. The abstract nature of values causes them to remain vague until 'translated'.

Although many people may instinctively have a notion of the meaning of a particular value, and may engage in behaviours that display that value, the abstract nature of ethical values often makes them difficult to apply naturally in the course of doing one's job. Furthermore, the same value, for example: the value 'integrity', could hold vastly different meanings for different employees due to the diversity of cultures, religious affiliations, backgrounds, educational levels and languages in the workplace. Most employees need to be guided by leaders as to the specific interpretations required of a certain value in a specific job in a specific organisation. Values need to be meaningfully and unambiguously translated into specific behaviours required to 'live' the value.

Ethical values, such as integrity, responsibility, fairness, transparency and respect, have to be prioritised by organisations that wish to bring the best out of their people. People who are secure in their knowledge that the presence of ethical values protects their human rights, ensures justice and establishes trust, achieve a sense of accomplishment. This sense of accomplishment may contribute to individuals' perceptions of the meaning of their lives and their self-actualisation.

Ethical leadership

Values-based management also implies that leaders have to be *authentic* when dealing with their followers (Covey in Korac-Kakabadse et al., 2002:168). George (2007:12) calls for authentic leadership, which implies leading without imitating someone else. He offers the following definition of successful 21st-century leaders: 'they are authentic leaders who bring people together around a shared mission and values and empower them to lead, in order to serve their customer while creating value for all their stakeholders'.

When they are authentic and values-based, leaders become guides to help employees find meaning (Konz & Ryan, 1999). Such leaders create shared meaning with others. According to Lantos (1999:223):

> *The bottom line, so to speak, is that business leaders must impart the value of values, converting the moral agnostics and unbelievers to a conviction of the worth of virtue in the marketplace. This requires more than just the head knowledge – it also necessitates the heart knowledge. Aristotle said that virtue consists not merely in knowing what is right, but in having the will to do what is right, i.e. the power to carry out the mind's judgement into action.*

Leaders are the principal architects of corporate moral consciousness (Goodpaster, 2007). Buller and McEvoy (1999) point out that the reputation for strong ethical cultures in companies like Johnson & Johnson, Motorola,

Royal Dutch/Shell and Texas Instruments can be 'traced directly to leaders who consistently, by their words and deeds, signalled the importance of and commitment to high moral standards' (403). Leaders set formal rules, but also lead by example in showing the importance of ethical behaviour. Research by Trevino, Weaver, Gibson and Toffler (1999) indicated that strong ethical cultures exist in organisations where employees perceived that leaders regularly pay attention to ethics, take ethics seriously, and care about ethics and values as much as the (financial) bottom line. The innate ethical dimension of leadership is aptly illustrated by Ciulla (2004: ix) in her (general) description of leadership:

> *Leadership is not a person or a position. It is a complex moral relationship between people, based on trust, obligations, commitment, emotion and a shared vision of the good. Ethics lies at the heart of all relationships and therefore at the heart of relationships between leaders and followers.*

Good ethical leaders refrain from micro-managing ethics in that they establish cultures of trust. It is clear that trust in ethical and authentic leaders makes it easier for employees to do the right thing and to focus on meaningful pursuits. Leaders who treat people as a cost of doing business rather than the basis for the business' success could never act as facilitators for unlocking human potential. Employees that are unencumbered by fear, suspicion or ethical ambiguity have the freedom to pursue growth and development actions that will allow them to discover their true potential.

The psychological contract

The psychological contract that exists between organisations and their employees is described as the match between the expectations organisations have of their people, the expectations people have of their organisations, and what the organisations are prepared to offer in return (Schein, 1978). Prior to the 1980s, organisations and their employees had fairly conservative psychological contracts. Being associated with a company during that time 'was an effective way to affirm one's world' (Kets de Vries, 2001:295). Employees had commitments of loyalty and affiliation with an organisation that provided them with a sense of stability and security. The 1980s, however, saw the advent of excessive preoccupation with shareholder value, business reengineering, downsizing and large-scale retrenchments. These phenomena severely dented the traditional notion of the psychological contract, which was rooted in stability.

The demise of the psychological contract caused a loss to the psychological wellbeing of employees (Kets de Vries, 2001:295). Fairholm suggests that the 'abandonment of the psychological contract connecting workers to a life-long career with the company has effectively destroyed the security and tranquillity of the workplace. People need something to repair the damage' (1996:11).

A possible solution to this problem is a redefinition of the psychological contract. This, however, calls for corporate leadership to take a long and hard look at their ability to align personal and organisational values. If organisations are serious about placing a sense of ownership on their employees they have to pay serious attention to the personal growth and development of their people. In addition to this, the establishment of nurturing work environments (rather than prescriptive bureaucracies) where employees can feel trusted, valued and secure, seems to be imperative.

This requires organisations to imbed mutual ethical expectations and needs into the new psychological contract. For this to happen there needs to be continuous dialogue about ethics between organisation and employees. Such dialogue has to commence during the pre-appointment stage of recruitment and continue throughout the employee's life in the organisation.

Retrenchment gone wrong

Some years ago a parastatal instituted a major downsizing project. On offer were voluntary retrenchment and early retirement packages for all employees. This resulted in the company losing virtually all of its engineering and IT talent (employees with marketable skills). Realising the consequences of this brain-drain too late in the process, they had to rehire many of those employees on a contract basis. For a long time this cost the company more than the salaries of the engineers and IT staff prior to their exit from the organisation.

The effects this may have had on the trust, commitment and morale of the employees that remained in the organisation is clear. The questions that then arose are:
- Can employees align their personal values with those of the organisation in such turbulent conditions?
- Can human potential be unlocked in these conditions?
- How could an ethically-based psychological contract have prevented this intervention?

Empowerment and enablement

Jack Welch (former CEO of General Electric) contends that empowering employees to reach their full potential and own sense of values is not merely benevolence; it is a competitive necessity (Neck & Milliman, 1994). Empowerment is about giving employees the keys to drive the vehicle that you have entrusted them with. If organisations believe that employees can really make a difference, be sources of creativity, behave in self-managing ways, and accept the values and culture of the organisation, they will allow the employees relative freedom of participation, contribution, innovation and opinion. This may involve a paradigmatic change within the organisational leadership to create a climate of trust that allows employees to take responsibility, make decisions and accept accountability for them.

Merely giving someone a driver's licence does not guarantee that the person can or will drive properly. This means that giving people jobs and empowering them to be accountable for the expected job outcomes is meaningless unless they are also enabled to achieve job outcomes, experience a sense of achievement, and add real value to the company. Enablement is facilitated through training and development opportunities, mentoring, coaching and guidance. Kets de Vries (2001) and Senge (1990) call for the fostering of a sense of competence in employees. Enabled people flourish in an environment of interactive trust, shared vision and common values.

Contrary to the belief that organisations often lose good employees once they are optimally trained, many employees that are properly empowered and enabled experience a sense of accomplishment that facilitates a sense of loyalty to the organisation. This, in turn, establishes organisational environments where employees refrain from engaging in behaviour that would harm others.

Ethical human resource management practices

Those responsible for the practice of human resource (HR) management, have an ethical obligation to both the organisation and its people. This implies that HR practitioners have to be, among others, in partnership with the operating managers in the organisation in order to optimise financial success on the one hand, whilst being advocates for the people cause, on the other hand.

HR management, being the corporate function that is concerned with acquiring, nurturing, protecting, retaining and developing people, has as its main responsibility the alignment of people management strategies with the organisation's vision, mission and objectives. In doing this they have to develop strategies and systems for human resource planning, recruitment and selection, performance management, human resource development and compensation. Additional tasks are to provide a context for fair treatment of employees and employee wellness and health.

It is not only important for the company to accumulate human capital in order to forge a competitive edge. The company's people are also major stakeholders – as such they have a vested interest in the company's sustainability. In short, employees deem it important that the organisation still exists ten or 15 years down the line. Hence, managing HR with a view to designing and implementing ethically sound strategies and systems that enhance the possibility of unlocking human potential will also make sense to the employees. HR's contribution in unlocking human potential is based on its understanding of human behaviour, as well as its stewardship for fulfilling the organisation's ethical obligation to its workforce. HR has to join forces with the organisation in being sensitive to practices that may endanger value alignment, inhibit opportunities for people to forge meaning through their work and promote practices that are conducive for these desirable outcomes.

Conclusion

Unlocking human talent is vital for the success and sustainability of any organisation. This can hardly be achieved without attending to the ethics of the organisation. A neglect of ethics can undermine and smother human potential. The ethical treatment of people can have the opposite effect. It can unlock human potential and create meaning and self-actualisation in the workplace, which in turn can give the organisation a competitive edge.

CHAPTER
11

Ethics and trust

With Neville Bews*

That public trust in business corporations and their leaders is low is beyond dispute. Business leaders are obviously scorched by these findings and some do not hesitate to acknowledge that rebuilding trust in corporations and their leaders is one of their major challenges. Ewald Kist, CEO of the ING Group, said: 'Restoring trust is the principal challenge that leaders of big companies have to face' (Kist, 2002:1). That these low levels of trust are a matter of great concern for corporations and their leaders is further illustrated in the fact that the theme of the 2003 World Economic Forum meeting in Davos was: Building Trust during a time of Global Uncertainty and Mistrust. Despite the effort by the World Economic Forum (WEF) to raise levels of trust in business, it was found two years later in a 20 country study commissioned by the WEF that the levels of trust in business have dropped to an all-time low since they started tracking trust levels (WEF, 2005).

A state of distrust is a disturbing condition since trust is a precondition for the functioning of any social system. Without a basic level of trust it becomes almost impossible to co-operate and negotiate with other people. JP Morgan, who founded JP Morgan bank, once said, 'The first thing is character ... before money or anything else. Money cannot buy it ... because a man I do not trust could not get money from me on all the bonds of Christendom' (Ethical Corporation, 2008). Also, in business, trust is required both within business and between a business and its external stakeholders. The current state of trust in business has generated significant interest in the nature and functioning of trust in recent years. In these studies it became clear that there is an intimate link between trust and ethics.

The purpose of this chapter is to explore the role that ethics can play in building trust in business. We will start by examining reasons why trust has become an issue of concern to business. Then we will look at the nature of

---

* **Dr Neville Bews** is a consultant in the fields of Human Resource Management and Social Impact Assessment.

trust and also make a distinction between trust and trustworthiness. Finally, we will look at the relationship between trust and ethics and the role that ethics can play in cultivating trust in business.

The loss of trust in business

There are a number of factors that have contributed to the decline of trust in business. We can pinpoint some of the most important.

Globalisation

The first factor that has led to less trust in business is globalisation. With the emergence of the global market, businesses have expanded their activities beyond national borders. People increasingly deal with colleagues, suppliers, and customers from other cultures. They have to operate in new communities that are as alien to them as they are to those communities. Although such diversity has had benefits for businesses, trust within the businesses themselves has not always benefited as much from this diversity.

Globalisation has also resulted in a rise in what has been referred to as global virtual teams (Jarvanpaa & Leidner, 1999). Many members of virtual teams never get to physically meet each other and are consequently unable to follow the traditional route of trust formation based on a long history of interactions. Without a history of shared experiences, a basis of familiarity and a common future to base trust on, the potential for trust is reduced.

Less job security

A second factor that has contributed to the loss of trust is the decline in job security over the last few decades. This has been caused by various factors:

- Globalisation has provided businesses with the opportunity to shift their operations to wherever economic conditions suit them best. This has resulted in operations being closed and the dismissal or relocation of staff.
- Corporate takeovers as a result of investor activism have fuelled the process of job shedding in order to increase value for investors.
- Corporations themselves have restructured in order to increase their efficiency and profitability. This has been achieved at the cost of employees' jobs.

Employees who have lost their jobs feel a keen sense of betrayal. They become less willing to trust new employers who might treat them in the same way. Those who have retained their jobs feel that the experience of their dismissed colleagues underlines the fragility of their own employment contracts.

Flatter company structures

Organisations have had to experiment with new ways of working in order to remain competitive in the global economy. The need to be flexible to consumer demands and fluctuations in the market means the end of hierarchical and bureaucratic organisations. Flatter organisations with fewer layers of authority and flexible job descriptions have become common. People work in teams, where they form alliances for a specific project, disband, and then regroup into a new team for a fresh project. The volatile nature of these working conditions can jeopardise the trust that was offered by long-term, stable working conditions within hierarchical organisations (cf. Sennet, 1998:31).

Corporate scandals

Much publicised corporate scandals and collapses involving companies such as Enron, Worldcom, Arthur Anderson and Parmalat on the international scene, and Tigon, Leisurenet and Fidentia on the South African scene, also dent trust in business. These scandals and failures fuel the perception that many other companies might be involved in similar activities. This was well illustrated when senior university students were asked, shortly after the infamous collapse of Enron, whether they agree with the following statement: 'The only real difference between executives at Enron and those of other big companies, is that those at Enron got caught' (Goodpaster, 2004:1). The fact that 56% of the students agreed with the statement underlines the lack of trust in and the cynicism toward business and business leaders. The public outrage at the levels of executive compensation in the banking and financial sector that came to the fore in the international credit crisis of 2008 further emphasise the public's scepticism of and distrust in corporations.

Why business needs trust

Although it is important to understand the reasons for the decline in trust in business, it is even more important to gain insight into why this decrease in trust cannot be ignored by business. There are a number of compelling reasons for addressing trust, which will be discussed next.

Distrust is expensive

The price tag of distrust is high with regard to both internal and external stakeholders. Where intra-organisational trust prevails, a business can rely on the loyalty and care of its employees. If trust has been violated and employees feel betrayed, they will look for opportunities for revenge. Employees can no longer be relied upon to act in the best interests of the business. They need constant monitoring and all kinds of control mechanisms have to be introduced to ensure that they do not abuse company assets or cause reputational damage to the company. This is time-consuming and costly.

Also, in the case of external stakeholders, distrust translates into dis-loyalty. When customers, for example, lose their trust in a company, they are likely to turn their backs on the company. When a company is perceived to lack trustworthiness, the serious damage to its reputation is costly to reverse. Protecting trust therefore makes good business sense.

Trust facilitates co-operation

New forms of work that have emerged in the global economy pose new challenges to organisations in terms of trust. With the breakdown of hier-archical structures into flatter company structures, participative manage-ment and teamwork has become the norm. Participative management pre-supposes interaction and co-operation, and cannot work unless those who participate in managing the company trust one another. Trust is also a condition for teamwork. Team members have to form alliances and expertise needs to be shared. The absence of trust slows down the formation of teams and impedes team performance. Businesses with a stake in participative management and team operations need to understand and manage trust.

Trust unlocks knowledge

Businesses have come to recognise the crucial role of knowledge in con-temporary business. Knowledge is the new capital of business. The ability of an organisation to attract and retain people with expert knowledge has become vital for its success. A business needs to tap into the knowledge of its employees and needs to ensure that the knowledge is made available to those who can benefit from it. Access to, and flow of, information depend to a large extent on the levels of trust in an organisation. As employees come to realise that knowledge is their biggest asset, they will come to protect it. An environment of trust is needed for employees to be willing to share their expertise with others, whilst situations of distrust will have the opposite effect. Trust, consequently, is crucial to unlocking and facilitating the flow of knowledge within companies.

Trust promotes loyalty

Trust promotes loyalty within an organisation and between an organisation and its external stakeholders. The nature of trust is such that it always entails a relationship between at least two parties. By trusting another party, you rely on that party for the achievement of your goals. Consequently one transcends the narrow confines of one's own interests and involves others in reaching one's objectives. In the case of what is called bidirectional or mutual trust, co-operative alliances are formed around specific goals. This adds to the social cohesion both within an organisation and between an organisation and its external stakeholders.

When someone honours your trust you feel loyalty to that person and their goals. If managers can succeed in winning the trust of their subordinates they can expect them to be more loyal to managerial goals. The same holds true for the relationship between an organisation and its shareholders, customers, suppliers and other external stakeholders. Trust can thus inspire loyalty, which results in attitudes and actions that advance the interests of the organisation. As a result, the value of trust is particularly significant during times of organisational change (Kimberley & Härtel, 2007).

What is trust?

Trust is a social phenomenon. In our dealings with people we find ourselves, from time to time, in situations where others can determine the outcome of our projects. Such situations pose a risk to us. By trusting another person to act for my benefit, I make myself vulnerable. Should the other person react positively to my trust, I will gain, but should the person react negatively, I stand to lose. The very nature of trust is such that it presupposes an optimistic disposition. It starts from the assumption that the person in whom I have laid my trust will not abuse my vulnerability. Trust can be defined as an optimistic disposition displayed by a person pursuing a goal in taking the risk of relying on another person for attaining that goal.

A number of typical features of trust have come to the fore in the preceding description of trust. These features deserve elaboration.

Trust is a social phenomenon

Trust occurs in human interaction. It presupposes more than one party and is closely tied up with the relationships that we have with those who influence us. The two parties involved in a relationship of trust are called 'the trustor' and 'the trustee'. The trustor is the person or party who extends its trust, and the trustee is the person or party who is relied upon to respond favourably to the trust invested in it.

Trust is a process

Trust is not a single event. In trusting another person, I make myself vulnerable to the goodwill of another. Before making the investment I will calculate the risk of the investment. If the relationship endures, I will continue to monitor my trust investment. Based on my experience, I will decide whether I can risk investing more trust and making myself more vulnerable, or whether I need to be more careful and invest less or even stop trusting the other person. Trust is often based on a history of interactions that determine the future of the trusting relationship.

Trust can vary in strength

Trust can either be tentative or it can be enduring. When trustees act in ways that affirm the trust we have put in them, our trust is reinforced. Should the opposite happen, our trust is likely to wane. Should trust be abused by a trustee, the trustor might replace trust with distrust. Distrust is often accompanied by the desire to avenge the abuse of trust.

Trust is always a risk

A central feature of trust is vulnerability. In trusting another person or party, I place myself at the mercy of another. For this reason, trust always represents a risk to the trustor. As with all risk-taking behaviour, it requires an act of faith on behalf of the trustor. I need to believe that the other person or party will honour the trust I invest in them, even though I have no guarantees that they will do so. The amount of risk can vary from one trust relationship to the next. My act of trust depends on my knowledge of the trustee and our history of interaction. Our risk is normally extremely high in cases where we have little knowledge of our trustee or no option other than to trust her or him.

Consider the situation at the scene of a motor accident. The trustor, as accident victim, may be in such a condition that she has little choice but to trust the paramedics who arrive at the accident scene. Alternatively, her condition may not be particularly serious, which would allow the accident victim a greater flexibility of choice. In such a case the victim may elect to consult a specific medical practitioner with whom she has a trusting relationship rather than to rely on the available paramedics.

Trust can form swiftly

The emergence of global virtual teams as a result of globalisation (Jarvanpaa & Leidner, 1999) has accentuated the need for team members to rapidly form trust-based relationships. Members of global virtual teams are forced to rely on what Meyerson, Weick & Kramer (1996) refer to as swift trust. Hung, Dennis and Robert (2004) propose that swift trust is based on expectations fixed to roles, social categories, stereotypes, third-party information, and rules. In this sense, reputation, rather than experience built on face-to-face interaction, is central in the rapid formation of trust in virtual teams.

In the formation of project teams, members of the team are often selected based on skills, occupational categories and associations. Other team members attach expectations to these roles and categories and may be prepared to engage in trusting behaviour. For instance, an accountant from a reputable auditing firm is likely to be trusted because of her profession (accountancy) and association (being employed by a reputable auditing firm). If the accountant occupied a senior position at the firm this occupational category is likely to enhance perceptions of trustworthiness in the accountant.

Trust varies from person to person

Finally, trust is a personal issue. It depends on our feelings of optimism or pessimism about others. The propensity to trust differs from person to person. Some are generally optimistic in their expectations of others, whilst others tend to be pessimistic or cynical. Our ability to trust is also influenced by our personal experience of trust relations. Differences are to be expected, but a total inability to trust others is abnormal and is a form of paranoia that undermines one's ability to form relationships.

Trust versus trustworthiness

Trust is an action. For that reason, some authors who write about trust prefer to use the word 'trusting', to emphasise that trust is not only a noun, but also a verb. Trust, or trusting, needs to be distinguished from the related concept of trustworthiness. Where trust is an action taken by a trustor, trustworthiness is a characteristic of a trustee. It is an evaluation of the quality of a person as a trustee. A trustworthy person is one who is judged to be worthy of the trust invested in her or him (Brien, 1998:399; Brenkert, 1998:300).

Studies on trustworthiness have revealed that a person's or party's trustworthiness depends upon a number of characteristics. Those who display characteristics such as openness, competency, integrity, and benevolence are judged to be more trustworthy than those who lack these qualities. This suggests that trustworthiness can be developed and enhanced. Later in the chapter we will consider ways to do this.

Personal and impersonal trust

Impersonal trust refers to trust in institutions or social practices. Such trust underlies our social practices. An example is my trust in the banking system. When I enter a bank, I assume that when I deposit my money, it will be safe in the bank. Similarly, when I order a meal in a restaurant, the staff assume that I will pay for what I have ordered. Without these basic assumptions, neither banks nor restaurants could function in a normal fashion. This trust in a system or a practice is normally taken for granted. It provides the minimum amount of security necessary to make these social practices work. Individuals and institutions can abuse this basic trust and when this happens, the legitimacy of such practices is called into question. This basic form of trust is a necessary ingredient of social intercourse.

Personal trust refers to trusting relationships between persons. Within the category of personal trust we can distinguish between unidirectional trust and bidirectional trust. In the case of unidirectional trust there is an asymmetry of power. One person is the trustor and relies upon the other person who is the trustee. The trustee has power over the trustor in the sense that the trustee is in a position to harm the interests of the trustor, whilst the interests of the trustee are not at stake. This kind of unidirectional trust sometimes occurs between managers and their subordinates. Bidirectional trust refers to trust-relations where two parties have to trust each other. This is sometimes also called mutual trust. Here, there is symmetry of power: each party relies upon the other to attain their goals. Mutual trust is found amongst equals in organisations, but is also common between managers and their subordinates, where each relies upon the other to perform well in their respective jobs.

The ethical dimension of trust

The nature of trust, as we have discussed, might suggest that trust and ethics always go hand in hand. To honour trust, the trustee needs to consider the interests of the trustor. We might assume from this that trust equals moral behaviour, because the consideration of another person's interests is a core element of ethical behaviour. This is not necessarily the case. To make sense of the morality of trust, it is useful to distinguish between the internal morality and the external morality of trust.

The internal morality of trust

The internal morality of trust lies in the moral nature of the interaction between the trustor and the trustee. Here, to honour trust, the trustee must respond positively to the interests that the trustor has entrusted in her or him. The honouring of trust means that the trustee assists the trustor in attaining her or his goals. This creates the impression that the trustee behaves morally in respecting the interests of the trustor. The problem, however, is that there are no constraints on the goals of the trustor. If the goals of the trustor are moral goals, then one can indeed agree that this is moral behaviour. If the trustor's goals are immoral, however, the honouring of trust does not amount to ethical behaviour. Someone who commits fraud, and relies upon another person to attain this goal is an example of this. To simply honour the trust of a trustor does not amount to ethical behaviour. External morality is needed before trust can be considered ethical.

The external morality of trust

The external morality of trust refers to the impact of a trusting relationship on people outside that relationship. Without considering this dimension, the moral evaluation of trust remains incomplete. Trust is not moral if it is instrumental in pursuing unethical objectives. Once more, a case of fraud can illustrate the point. Should a person involve another in plans to defraud the organisation they both work for, they stand to benefit from this trusting relationship. Their actions will, however, be detrimental to the interests of everyone else in that organisation, and so their trust relationship cannot be considered moral.

This demonstrates the moral ambiguity of trust. Trust can be both moral and immoral. When trust is used in pursuit of unethical objectives, it constitutes a moral abuse of trust. This is the case when it is used to protect the interests of an in-group. Nepotism, cronyism, favouritism, racism, and sexism are all examples of trust used to the detriment of those excluded from the trusting relationship. As well as being immoral, such abuse of trust can also undermine the competitiveness of a business because the pool of talent is restricted to the in-group. Trust is also abused when it provides a veil of secrecy for immoral practices such as corruption.

> The CEO of a company discovers that the company is in serious financial difficulty. It seems inevitable that some employees will have to be retrenched to save the company. However, the CEO is uncertain about how this situation should be handled. Should she disclose this information as soon as possible to employees, it will give them more time to find alternative employment and come to terms with their retrenchment. On the other hand, if this information is disclosed, it might impact negatively on the ability of the company to land new contracts and to protect existing jobs, as clients might be wary of dealing with a company perceived to be in trouble. Not disclosing the information to employees violates the trust of employees, while disclosing the information will damage the trust of clients in the company.
>
> ### Questions for discussion:
>
> 1 Does the CEO have a moral responsibility to disclose this information to employees?
> 2 Is there a way of managing this situation in order to minimise the violation of the trust of both employees and clients?

Trust does have great potential to enhance moral behaviour. The very nature of trust is such that it promotes the transcendence of narrow self-interest. In trusting another person or party you involve them in your personal goals and projects. Trust therefore enhances your capacity for active social behaviour, which is an integral part of moral behaviour. Trust relationships offer new opportunities for co-operation, harmony, and social cohesion. When honoured, trust can offer us the benefits of co-operation and mutual assistance. So, although trust can never be an unconditional value, its moral potential is vast.

The role of ethics in building trust

Research done in Africa and elsewhere has shown that there are a number of factors that influence the trustworthiness of a person. Neville Bews (2000) found that the following factors have a significant impact on how trustworthy managers are perceived by their subordinates:

- openness
- competence
- integrity
- benevolence
- reputation.

It is possible to extend these factors that determine the trustworthiness of managers to organisations. It is fair to assume that the characteristics that inspire trust in persons will also inspire trust in organisations.

Each of these factors that facilitate trustworthiness has an explicit or implicit moral dimension. A more detailed examination of each of them will reveal their respective moral dimensions. Since these factors are all moral in nature, it implies that specific ethical behaviours can impact positively on raising the trustworthiness of managers and organisations. This relationship between ethics and trust building will also be spelt out in the following discussion of the factors that determine trustworthiness.

Factors that enhance trustworthiness

Openness

Openness refers to how freely persons or parties make information available to those who have a direct stake in the particular information (Mishra, 1996; Robbins, 1997). A person or party that stands in a relationship with an organisation requires information to fulfil their specific stakeholder function. Employees need information to do their jobs, investors need information to assess their investment in the company, suppliers need information to be able to provide the company on time with new supplies, and so on. Withholding such information from employees, shareholders, suppliers, customers or other stakeholders will undermine their trust in the organisation.

Openness has a distinct moral dimension as it can contribute towards enhancing the interests of employees and other stakeholders who interact with an organisation. Failing to be open in the sense of not sharing functional information with stakeholders will be perceived as uncooperative and undermining. Should organisations withhold information that their stakeholders need in order to perform their respective roles towards the organisation, stakeholders will find it hard to trust the organisation. They will experience the lack of openness as unfair and immoral, thus undermining the trusting relationship.

Openness is a personal and organisational attribute that can be modified. A manager or company can introduce systems and procedures that facilitate more openness in communication between managers and their staff and between the company and its external stakeholders. If a company, for example, insists on regular meetings between managers and their internal and external stakeholders it is likely that the company will be perceived as being open. Procedural transparency and fairness in processes, such as promotions and procurement, make it easier for managers to communicate with those affected by such procedures. By taking these and other measures, openness in communicating information is enhanced, which in turn impacts positively on the trustworthiness of managers and the organisation.

Competence

Competence refers to the knowledge and skills needed by a person or party to influence the domain for which they are responsible (Mayer et al., 1995:717). With regard to competence in organisations two kinds of competence need to be discerned, namely, technical competence and people management competence.

Although technical knowledge does play a role in the trustworthiness of managers and organisations, it is the competency to manage people that has the bigger impact on trust. Managers often lack competence in the latter as they are often promoted to management positions on the basis of their technical expertise rather than their people management competence.

Competent people management is tied closely to ethical behaviour. To manage people well requires that one be approachable by and sensitive to people. Herein lies the moral dimension of people management competency. Being sensitive and caring to other people is one of the hallmarks of ethical behaviour. Poor management of people is mostly experienced as immoral behaviour by staff and other stakeholders.

People management skills are a competency that can be developed. By offering managers feedback on their current level of people management skills or by providing them with training in areas where they need it, their competency to work with people can be improved. Since people management is so intimately linked with ethical behaviour, training on the role that ethics can play in good people management (within and outside the organisation) should be included in the training of managers. An investment in the people management skills of managers will thus be an investment in the trust-worthiness of managers.

Integrity

We ascribe integrity to a person or party when they consistently act in an ethical manner (Husted, 1998; Mishra 1996). One can rely, with confidence, on the actions and decisions of a person or organisation of integrity as you know that they are unlikely to deviate from their ethical standards. The link between integrity and ethics is so intimate that the two concepts are often used as synonyms.

The two central components of integrity are a set of ethical values and consistent adherence thereto. There are various steps that organisations can take to ensure that there is clarity on the ethical values of the organisation as well as consistent adherence thereto. It already commences with recruitment and selection procedures that assist the company in hiring people of integrity. But it goes beyond that to the improvement of the integrity of managers and staff. Various steps can be taken to enhance the integrity of companies. Central to these steps that can be taken is the identification of ethical values and standards that all staff members should adhere to. Active steps should be taken to ensure that these ethical values and standards are embraced and respected by all in the company. To ensure that all consistently adhere to the ethical standards of the company various mechanisms can be used, including reward for adherence or disciplinary action against those who deviate from it. In Chapter 19, the process of institutionalising ethical values and standards in companies is discussed in detail. Besides the other benefits that a company stands to gain from actively improving the integrity of its members, it will also contribute towards improving its trustworthiness.

Benevolence

Benevolence is demonstrated in actively showing concern for others. In order to be perceived as trustworthy, a trustee should not take advantage of the vulnerability of a trustor. Although not taking advantage is a necessary condition for benevolence, it is not sufficient. The trustee should take an active interest in the wellbeing of the trustor (Mayer et al., 1995; Mishra, 1996). Benevolent managers and organisations are those who demonstrate that they are sensitive to the needs of those that they interact with, and who care about their wellbeing. Also, the ethical nature of benevolence as a factor that impacts positively on trustworthiness is obvious.

Like openness, people management competence and integrity, benevolence is also a disposition that can be cultivated and enhanced. As benevolence is closely tied to good people management skills, managers can be trained to become sensitive to the needs of their subordinates and stakeholders. Benevolent behaviour can manifest in the workplace on both a psychological and material level. On a psychological level, managers will be perceived as benevolent when they respond in a sensitive and supportive way to the emotional needs of their staff, suppliers, clients and other stakeholders. On the material level, they will be perceived to be benevolent when they offer managerial support to their staff, clients and suppliers in their respective interactions with the organisation.

When employees experience personal crises or trauma, benevolence by managers will manifest in showing compassion and demonstrating care. Emotional support might be sufficient, but in extraordinary circumstances, material or financial assistance might be required. In this respect companies with Employee Assistance Programmes (EAP), which are specifically designed to assist employees in crisis, can strengthen the hand of managers in assisting their staff. Such assistance sends out a signal to all employees that they can rely on the benevolence of managers and the company in difficult times. Benevolent behaviour, whether in the ordinary run of work or in times of crises, is one of the most significant factors that determines how trustworthy managers are being perceived.

Reputation

A person's or organisation's reputation consists of the perceptions that others accumulate over time about them. A reputation is thus developed through a history of interactions. If employees have experienced positive interactions over time with a manager, the manager is likely to have a good reputation and consequently will be perceived as trustworthy (Lewicki & Bunker, 1996:121). The same holds true for the interaction between an organisation and its suppliers, customers, shareholders and other parties that it regularly interacts with. The experiences that build the reputation of a manager or organisation consist of exactly the kind of factors that have been discussed. Reputation is determined by factors such as openness, competence, integrity, and benevolence. If managers and organisations wish to improve their reputation, they need to perform well on these factors. Should they fail on this score they will suffer reputational damage. Since all four of the factors have very distinct ethical dimensions, and since reputation is so closely intertwined with these four factors, it is clear that ethical behaviour plays a vital role in gaining a good reputation. This makes ethical behaviour a pre-condition for a good reputation, which in turn is a significant factor in determining how trustworthy managers and organisations will be perceived.

Conclusion

Ethics plays a crucial role in the formation of trust. Companies and managers who are serious about the cultivation of trust have no option other than to explore how ethical behaviour can make managers more trustworthy. Ethical behaviour can contribute to the level of trust in an organisation and can open it up to the benefits associated with such trust. It is crucial, though, that trust and ethical behaviour should not be regarded as mere managerial tools. A superficial commitment to ethics will be unmasked as opportunistic behaviour that undermines trust even further. For trust to endure, a balanced approach is needed where both the organisation and its internal and external stakeholders stand to benefit from their trust relationship.

PART
5

Ethical decision-making in business

INTRODUCTION

In the preceding parts of the book we identified the ethical dimension of business and also demonstrated that it is important to attend to this ethical dimension. An important part of attending to the ethics of an organisation is to ensure that ethically sound decisions are made by those who act on behalf of the organisation.

We distinguish between two types of ethical decisions that need to be made in business. The first type of ethical decision-making revolves around ensuring that business decisions are ethically sound. The focus is thus on the ethical implications of business decisions dealing with any aspect of business as well as on ensuring that the ethical implications of such decisions are properly understood and considered. The second type of ethical decision-making focuses specifically on ethical issues that arise in business in the form of ethical dilemmas and how such ethical dilemmas can be resolved.

In Chapter 12 we present ethical decision-making that focuses on ensuring that business decisions are ethically sound. Four criteria are developed that could be applied to business decisions to ensure that due care is taken of the ethical implications thereof. In Chapter 13 we analyse a case study where a company decides to simultaneously raise executive remuneration and downsize their workforce. This decision of the company is then subjected to ethical scrutiny by testing the decision against the four criteria for ethical business decisions that were introduced in Chapter 12.

In Chapter 14 the focus shifts to resolving ethical dilemmas in business. The RIMS (Rational Interaction for Moral Sensitivity) strategy for resolving moral dilemmas is introduced and the three basic steps that it consists of are explained. In Chapter 15 the RIMS strategy is applied to a case study that deals with an ethical dilemma that emerged in a company around the issue of employment equity. It is shown how the RIMS strategy can be used to generate creative proposals that can resolve the deadlock caused by the ethical dilemma.

CHAPTER
12

Making ethical business decisions

I n business, there do arise, from time to time, distinct ethical dilemmas that
need to be resolved through proper ethical deliberation. Such situations
are, however, not the only situations that call for ethical decision-making.
There are also normal day-to-day decisions that need to be made about
procurement, sales, marketing, remuneration, client service and hiring, etc.
that have ethical implications. These decisions also have to be made in a
manner that addresses the ethical side of such decisions.

The adage, referred to in Chapter 1, that 'the business of business is
business', cannot be used as an excuse for not attending to the ethical side
of ordinary business decisions. The discussion of the ethical dimension of
business on the macro-economic level (Chapter 2), the business and society
level (Chapter 3), and the organisational level (Chapter 4), has made it
clear that on all these levels, business always has an ethical dimension and
impact. Consequently, business decisions need to be made in a manner that
will reflect ethical awareness and responsibility. In the chapters that dealt
with the importance of ethics for business (Chapters 8 to 11) it has become
clear that businesses that do not act with ethical integrity run the risks of
ruining their corporate reputations, breaking down trust relationships, and
alienating important stakeholders who they are dependent on for their survival and prosperity.

When dealing with the ethical side of business decisions, the ethical
issue at hand might be quite apparent, for example, when customers com-
plain that a product that they have bought from a business is unsafe to
use. At other times the ethical issue(s) might not be so obvious. It might
appear as if you are merely dealing with a straightforward business issue
that does not have any apparent ethical implications, for example, decisions
about executive salaries. While it might look like a private matter between
a company and an employee at a first glance, it might turn into a full-scale
ethical issue. This can happen when the salaries of executives are regarded as
extravagant or when the ratio between salaries on the lowest tiers and those
on the top tiers of a company is unrealistically skewed or when executives
receive salary increases whilst employees are being laid off because of tough
economic conditions. How a seemingly ordinary business decision can
turn into a significant ethical issue was well demonstrated when a South

African printing company was approached to print promotional pamphlets for an organisation and signed a contract to do so. A very ordinary business transaction turned into a very inconvenient ethical issue for the printing company when it was revealed later on that the pamphlets were for Zimbabwe's ZANU PF party and were intended for use during Robert Magube's infamous presidential campaign of 2008 where he stood accused of using his presidential powers to prevent opposition candidates from engaging in a free and fair contest in the presidential election. Not only was this incident embarrassing to the printing company, but it also caused reputational damage to the wider group of companies to which the printing company belongs. In the end, the printing company donated all the profit that it made from the transaction to charities in Zimbabwe thus forfeiting the financial gain that it had gained from the deal.

The above incident reveals how companies can easily fall into the trap of disregarding the ethical significance and implications of their ordinary business decisions. Since there is a distinct danger that businesses might be prone to such ethical blind spots, it is a good practice to develop an approach to decision-making in business that will ensure that business decisions are ethically sound. One way of achieving this is to develop a decision-making procedure that attends specifically to the ethical side of business decisions. There is a host of ethical decision-making processes available in the field of business ethics (see, for example: Markkula Center for Applied Ethics, 2009; McDonald, 2001). In this chapter, we will explore one decision-making procedure that can assist us in making more ethically sound decisions in business. This procedure consists of assessing whether a business decision meets a set of normative criteria. The following questions should be asked to judge the moral soundness of a decision:

- Is it legal?
- Does it meet company standards?
- Is it fair to all stakeholders?
- Can it be disclosed?

In the remainder of this chapter, each of these criteria will be discussed in more detail. In applying these criteria, you do not first have to complete a business decision and only then start to apply the criteria for ethical business decisions. On the contrary, it is preferable that the criteria form a constant mindset that is infused in the normal business decision-making process. It should thus become almost second nature to keep these criteria in mind when making business decisions.

Is it legal?

The first criterion that a business decision has to meet in order to be considered ethically sound, is that it should be legal. In an ideal world the law lays down a standard of acceptable behaviour which all citizens need to abide by in order to ensure a safe and just society. Since businesses are corporate citizens of the societies within which they operate, they have an obligation to ensure that they abide by the laws of their societies. The fact that businesses have to make a profit or that they are engaged in fierce competition with their business rivals, does not hand them a licence to operate above the law. It is therefore imperative that as decisions are made in business, this first criterion of ethical decision-making is kept in mind.

Determining whether a planned business decision is legal can range from a fairly uncomplicated process to an extremely complicated one. In many, if not most, work environments, the legal standards that apply to a specific work environment are common knowledge. Human resource personnel, for example, are usually familiar with the standards of labour law that govern recruitment, retirement and dismissal, civil engineers are familiar with standards of safety for construction and design and those involved in marketing and advertising understand the legal parameters within which they can design and run marketing and advertising campaigns. When you operate in such an environment where legal standards are common knowledge, the application of this first criterion is straight forward. If a decision is in conflict with the law it should be abandoned, unless there are exceptional circumstances, which will be discussed later on in this section.

When the legal standards that apply to a specific work environment are not common knowledge amongst staff, it might be because they have been inadequately trained. In such situations this can be rectified by training interventions that will equip them with the required general legal knowledge that pertains to their work environment. There are, however, circumstances where legal standards are simply unclear. This happens, for example, in fast developing fields such as information technology, where the law is unable to keep up with the speed of technological innovation. Consequently, existing legal standards are vague and ambiguous and there often is no common knowledge about legal standards. In such environments, applying the first criterion of ethical decision-making becomes a complicated process. The same holds for doing business in other countries with different legal jurisdictions. In such cases where legal standards are not common knowledge, it is advisable to call on internal or external legal advice to settle the question on whether a decision that is being considered is legal or not.

The fact that legal standards are sometimes not clear, and thus not common knowledge, is one of the reasons why the legal criterion can never be the only criterion in determining the ethical soundness of a decision.

157

Another reason why the legal criterion on its own is inadequate for determining the moral soundness of business decisions is that in some cases the law might be morally flawed. It has been said above that in an ideal world the law lays down a standard of acceptable behaviour which all citizens need to respect in order to ensure a safe and fair society. However, as we are all too aware of, we do not live in an ideal world and therefore we do from time to time and in certain circumstances encounter laws that are flawed and unfair. Anyone who is familiar with the apartheid laws in South Africa or the media laws in Zimbabwe under the Mugabe regime would intuitively sense that legality does not always equal morality. It is exactly for this reason that the legal test for ethical decision-making needs to be supported by the tests implied by the remaining three criteria for ethical business decision-making.

Thus, in cases where legal standards are clear and such standards are generally perceived as fair, decisions that imply a transgression of the law should be considered ethically unacceptable. However, when there are no clear legal standards or when legal standards are perceived to be unfair, the legal test on its own is not a sufficient standard for determining the moral soundness of a business decisions. In such cases, the other three criteria for ethical decisions have to be brought into play.

Does it meet company standards?

Secondly, decisions need to be tested against the ethical standards of the company. The ethical standards of a company are usually formulated as a set of company values, in a code of ethics, or in policy statements dealing with specific issues, like procurement, expense accounts or the giving and receiving of gifts. Since these documents are intended to prevent irresponsible behaviour or to promote responsible behaviour, it is clear that they should play a central role in determining the ethical soundness of business decisions.

Applying the company standards test to business decisions can be a fairly simple and straightforward process when a company's ethical standards are formulated very clearly and precisely in either a detailed code of ethics or in policy documents that deal with specific matters in detail. The company standards test is somewhat harder to apply when company standards are formulated in the form of core values that stipulate general standards of behaviour, such as honesty, transparency and respect, without spelling out what such standards imply in business practice. Applying the company standards test is also difficult when a code of ethics or a policy is vague and general.

The above observations should, however, not lead to the hasty conclusion that detailed codes of ethics and policies are preferable to value statements when it comes to making ethically sound business decisions. Both a rule-based approach (as you would often find in detailed codes of ethics and policy documents) and a value-based approach have their respective benefits and drawbacks when it comes to ethical decision-making. Rule-based standards of ethics have the benefit of being very clear and specific and can thus provide clear guidance in making ethical business decisions. For example, when a company's code of ethics states explicitly that accepting kick-backs from suppliers is unacceptable, it makes it much easier for company staff who have to take decisions in situations where suppliers try to lure them into signing a contract by offering them a kick-back on the deal. However, when companies follow a strong rule-based approach with regard to ethical standards, it always runs the risk of undermining employees' sense of personal responsibility. As has been indicated earlier (in the discussion on the compliance mode of managing corporate ethics in Chapter 5) a strong rule-based approach to ethical decision-making can undermine personal discretion and responsibility for ethical decision-making by cultivating a mentality of 'what is not forbidden is allowed' among employees. The strength of value-based codes, on the contrary, lies exactly in their ability to invoke personal ethical discretion and responsibility in the staff members of a business. However, their drawback lies in their generality, which prevents them from providing guidance on specific issues.

When the company standards test is applied and it turns out that a decision is clashing with the company's ethical standards, it is a strong indication that the decision needs to be abandoned. When it is not clear whether a decision contravenes a company's ethical standards or not, it is advisable to discuss the decision with other colleagues in order to see how they interpret the company's ethical standards with regard to the issue at hand. If the doubt still prevails, it becomes imperative to invoke the remaining two criteria for ethical business decisions that will be discussed in the remainder of this chapter. There are also two further reasons why applying only the company standards test might not always be sufficient to ensure ethically sound business decisions. The same two deficiencies that haunt the law, will always haunt company standards as well: first, company standards might be incomplete as they can never keep up with all new developments that the company has to face; second, company standards might be ethically flawed and despite their best intentions, nevertheless give rise to unethical decisions.

Is it fair to all stakeholders?

Making ethical decisions in business amount to ensuring that the interest of all parties that are likely to be affected, are considered and respected. A decision to launch a product that can potentially bring in huge profits for a company, but that is unsafe for consumers and harmful to the natural environment, is a clear example of a decision that only considers the immediate interests of the company, but fails to consider the interests of the affected stakeholders. In order to ensure that business decisions are ethically sound, the fairness test needs to be applied. This means that you have to consider the possible impact that a decision might have on those who are likely to be affected by the decision.

Applying the fairness test, requires more creativity on the part of the decision maker than applying the legal and the company standards tests that have been discussed. It requires that you should determine how the decision will be perceived and experienced by those who will be affected by the decision. The two most important ways of discerning the possible impact of decisions on the interests of others are through moral imagination and stakeholder engagement.

Moral imagination within the context of the fairness test refers to the ability to think beyond your own perspective and to speculate about how the decision might be perceived and experienced by all other parties who stand to be affected by the decision. It first of all involves identifying all those who might be affected, and then putting yourself in their shoes in order to get an idea of how the decisions would be experienced from their perspective.

Stakeholder engagement within the context of the fairness test refers to the process of interacting with persons and parties who are likely to be affected by the decision in order to determine how they foresee that the decision is likely to impact on them. It means that stakeholders are being given the opportunity to voice their concerns and to express what the decision looks like from their vantage point.

What both moral imagination and stakeholder engagement have in common is that both methods assist you in moving beyond your own or the company's immediate self-interest and to discover how other persons and parties might be affected by corporate decisions. Should you discover via these ways of applying the fairness test that the company will benefit at the expense of other stakeholders of the company, then the red lights of an unethical business decision are clearly flashing and the decision should best be reconsidered or abandoned. Should you, however, sense that the decision would be fair to all stakeholders, and in accord with the law and company standards, you could feel confident that the decision would be ethically sound. It would however be prudent to also test the decision against the one remaining criterion, which is the disclosure test.

Can it be disclosed?

The disclosure criterion assesses whether you would be comfortable in doing a public or private account for the decision that you have taken. If you are comfortable to explain and defend your decision to significant persons in your life or on a public forum, it is a good indication that the decision is ethically sound and justifiable.

The disclosure test should preferably be applied in two ways. The first version of the disclosure test is the public one. In the public version of the disclosure test, you should ask yourself, whether you would be morally comfortable if the decision and (consequent action) is reported in the newspaper, on TV or the Internet (or for that matter in any other media that is publicly accessible). The purpose of the first form of the disclosure test is to determine whether you would be willing and able to provide in public, good and socially acceptable reasons for taking a specific decision. Should you cringe in the face of such a prospect, the ethical alarm bells should start to sound.

The second version of the disclosure test is the private disclosure test. It adds a more personal and emotional element to the disclosure test. In this version you should ask yourself whether you would feel morally comfortable to disclose your decision to the most significant persons in your life. For this purpose you should identify one or more persons in your life that matter most to you, like your best friend, your parents, a special colleague or your partner. Once you have identified the most significant person(s) in your life, ask yourself the following question: Would I feel morally comfortable if they know what I am about to do?

Should you feel confident to disclose and defend a decision both in public and in private, it is a strong indication that the decision is ethically sound. Introducing the disclosure criterion to the ethical business decision-making process adds an important dimension to what has not come to the fore in the other three criteria, namely the personal conscience dimension. It emphasises that our business decisions should not only be in accord with the law, company standards and stakeholder interests, but also in accord with our own moral consciousness. When all four of these concerns match, you can feel confident about the ethical soundness of your business decisions.

Conclusion

Ordinary business decisions often have ethical implications that were not foreseen when the decision was made. Should a business decision be perceived as unethical, it can embarrass the company, alienate stakeholders and damage the reputation of individuals and the company as a whole. It therefore makes both business and personal sense to ensure that business decisions are ethically sound. Subjecting business decisions to the four criteria that we have discussed in this chapter will assist in preventing business decisions turning into ethical embarrassment. Subjecting business decisions to the legal, company standards, fairness and disclosure test, will go a long way in ensuring that business decisions are ethically sound. When a decision passes all four of these tests, you could feel confident that the decision to be taken is morally sound.

There is always the possibility that a decision being considered passes some of the tests, but fails the others. It is, for example, possible that a decision might meet the legal and company standards criteria, but fails the fairness and disclosure criteria. In such cases, a situation develops where a decision can be justified morally on some grounds, but also rejected morally on other grounds. Whenever this happens we are faced with a moral dilemma (see Chapter 1). Resolving moral dilemmas requires a different decision-making approach from the one that has been discussed in this chapter. In Chapter 14 a procedure for resolving moral dilemmas will be introduced.

CHAPTER
13

Ethical business decisions:
Executive pay and downsizing

Kgosi Malan, general manager of Bon Voyage Wineries (BVW), in the Western Cape region of South Africa, knew that the board of directors had some tough decisions on their agenda. With the international financial meltdown, the sales of BVW took a serious turn in the wrong direction. For the five years preceding the financial meltdown, BVW benefited from a strong growth in wine exports to the UK and Europe, to the extent that by the beginning of 2008 just over 60% of the value of their sales was generated by export to these markets. However, with the global recession now in its second year, their exports to these markets were almost halved over the last 18 months. Also the local demand for wine is dwindling. The raise in sin tax on wine that the minister of finance announced in his budget speech last month did not exactly make life easier for BVW who already had to cut deep into its reserves to keep the company afloat.

Despite knowing that the board had to come up with an innovative strategy for coping with this awkward situation, the board's decision took Kgosi by surprise. The CEO of BVW, Sarie Williams, came out of the board meeting a few minutes ago and asked Kgosi, with a wry smile: 'Do you want to hear the good news or the bad news first?' Without waiting for his response she informed him that the board has decided to downsize the workforce by 40%, while at the same time giving the entire executive management team a 20% raise in salary in order to motivate them to stick with the company during this challenging period. Kgosi Malan was not sure whether he had to laugh or cry. Obviously the 20% raise in salary would bring some much needed relief as he was also feeling the pinch of the economic recession, but as general manager of BVW he would also be responsible for overseeing the downsizing of the company.

Kgosi has always taken pride in the good staff relations at BVW. In the seven years that he had been with the company, he has developed good relationships with the shop stewards of both the unions who were represented in the company. Just recently he told a friend who was complaining about a stay-away in their supermarket group that BVW did not have a single strike since he has joined the company. 'We are almost like a family.' he boasted to his friend. Sitting behind his desk, engulfed in a whirlpool of emotions, he looked up to the *BVW Business Principles* that was standing in a frame on his desk:

> BVW Business Principles
> We make wines of the highest quality that delight our customers.
> We encourage our clients to enjoy our wines in a responsible manner.
> We adhere to high standards of corporate governance.
> We are socially responsible and care for our community.
>
> We respect the dignity of each employee.
> We do not tolerate any form of unfair discrimination.
>
> We protect our natural environment and are committed to
> environmentally sound practices.

When the board made their decision to downsize the staff of BVW by 40% and to raise the salaries of the executive team by 20% they did so in an attempt to keep the company afloat in the difficult economic conditions caused by a global recession. Although a pure business decision, it was nevertheless a business decision with important ethical implications. We will assume that the ethical dimensions of their decision were overlooked by the board of BVW. In this chapter we will apply the set of criteria for ethical business decisions that were introduced in Chapter 12 to the decision taken by the board of BVW. We will investigate how their decision stands up to the following set of criteria for ethical decision-making:

- Is it legal?
- Does it meet company standards?
- Is it fair to all stakeholders?
- Can it be disclosed?

Executive remuneration

Executive remuneration has become a very contentious issue in recent years. Not only has the income of corporate executives increased steadily and substantially, but also the gap between salaries on the top level and those on the bottom levels of companies has widened. The ratio between remuneration on the non-management (worker) level of companies compared to those on the highest level (CEO) was 1:42 in 1982, by 1990 the worker-CEO ratio had grown to 1:107 and by 2004 it reached a level of 1:431 in the United States (cf. Sahadi, 2005).

The factors that contribute to the growth in executive remuneration include:

◙ Growth in the sheer size and value of corporations.
◙ Competition between companies to get and retain the best persons for the top positions in companies.
◙ Incentive schemes to motivate executives to achieve outstanding financial performance or shareholder value.
(cf. Knowledge@Wharton, 2006.)

As a result of the sharp increase in executive remuneration, more attention from both shareholders and stakeholders has been focused on executive compensation packages. Pressure on companies has been mounting to be more transparent about executive remuneration and to ensure that there is a direct correlation between company performance (or shareholder value) and executive compensation. In South Africa *The Third King Report on Corporate Governance for South Africa* emphasises the importance of establishing a direct link between the performance of executives and the remuneration packages that they receive. The report also calls for transparency in corporate remuneration policies as well as for corporate disclosure of executive pay (IoD, 2009:52).

Is it legal?

The first test that the decision by the BVW Board has to be subjected to is the legal test. The question is thus whether the decision of the board to lay off 40% of the staff of the company, as well as their decision to increase the salaries of their executive team at the same time by 20%, is within the bounds of the law.

Starting with the question about the legality of employee dismissal, the Basic Conditions of Employment Amendment Act of 2002 (Section 41.1) (cf. Department of Labour, 2009) recognises that 'operational requirements' of employers constitute valid grounds for dismissal of employees. Economic needs of an employer are mentioned specifically as an operational requirement that provides valid ground for dismissal. No guidance is given in the same or other laws on levels or ratios that pertain to executive remuneration in companies. South African law is thus silent on the issue of executive remuneration. It can thus be safely concluded that the board of BVW's decision about employee dismissal and executive pay passes the legal test.

However, as indicated in the previous chapter, passing the legal test is not sufficient for considering a business decision as ethically sound. It is only a first hurdle that needs to be cleared on the way to determining whether a business decision can be considered as ethical or not. It is therefore imperative that we submit the decision by BVW to the second test.

Downsizing

Companies often opt for downsizing (or dismissing workers) as a strategy for coping with difficult economic conditions. Downsizing is also used in an effort to rationalise or restructure an organisation in the quest for greater efficiency. Furthermore it often follows in the wake of mergers and acquisitions.

In a study of the impact of downsizing on companies and individuals the International Labour Office (ILO) identified the following consequences of downsizing:

- ◻ It can affect corporate performance adversely.
- ◻ It can trigger further downsizing in the same company.
- ◻ It can lead to a decrease in corporate morale, trust and productivity.
- ◻ It can undermine the commitment of remaining employees who have survived the downsizing.
- ◻ It can disrupt the local community.
  (cf. Rogovsky & Schuler, 2007:5 & 8)

Does it meet company standards?

The standard that BVW sets itself is articulated in the *BVW Business Principles*. These business principles are aspirational standards (see Chapter 18; cf. Sullivan, 2009:30) that BVW formulated to guide the company in its decisions and actions. It is thus appropriate to determine whether the decision of the board on executive pay and employee dismissal lives up to these standards.

Aspirational standards typically are value-based general guidelines. As such, they provide general guidance on standards that can be applied to a wide variety of situations and issues. Consequently these standards have to be applied and interpreted to determine their meaning for a specific situation or issue. This is also true for the *BVW Business Principles* and their meaning for the decisions that the BVW board has taken. When we take a closer look at the *BVW Business Principles* there are especially three standards that have a direct bearing on the decisions that the BVW board has taken. These standards are:

- ◻ We adhere to high standards of corporate governance.
- ◻ We are socially responsible and care for our community.
- ◻ We respect the dignity of each employee.

Let us test the decision taken by the board against each of these standards.

'We adhere to high standards of corporate governance': Within the South African context, the King Reports on Corporate Governance (of 1994, 2002 and 2009) have become synonymous with standards of corporate governance. One can therefore safely assume that by committing themselves to high standards of corporate governance, BVW means that they will adhere to the standards of corporate governance as articulated in the last King Report on Corporate Governance – which would be the King III report of 2009. The King III report does not provide any guidance specifically with regard to employee dismissal caused by economic distress. It does, however, state that a board of directors needs to be guided by the values of responsibility, accountability, fairness and transparency in all its decisions. Furthermore the King III report also calls on companies to be good corporate citizens that play their part in ensuring that their decisions and actions contribute towards economic, social and environmental sustainability. BVW's commitment to high standards of corporate governance thus implies that the board should not only have looked at the desperate financial situation of the company, but that they should also have considered whether their decision is fair and responsible towards other stakeholders of the company and towards society. Adhering to these standards does not imply that workers cannot be dismissed when tough economic conditions prevail. It does, however, imply that decisions on dismissal cannot be taken as a first resort and can only be taken after the impact of dismissal on both the employees and the society has been considered. The board should thus have taken these matters into consideration in order to ensure that they are able to justify their decision with regard to the standards of corporate governance to which BVW subscribes.

Concerning the matter of increase of salaries of the executive management team in order to retain their commitment the company, the King III report does recommend that executive remuneration should be linked to performance, but it also allows for incentives to retain the services of key executives 'when companies face the risk of losing key employees' (IoD, 2009:51). It thus seems that at least as far as the King III guidelines are concerned, the board's decision might be aligned with the standards of corporate governance to which the company is committed.

The statement, 'We are socially responsible and care for our community' in the *BVW Business Principles* clearly impose an obligation on the board to ensure that their decisions are not merely taken to benefit the performance of the company, but also obliges the board to balance the interests of the company with the interests of the community in which the company operates. Given the negative impact and burden that we safely can assume the economic meltdown already had on the community within which BVW is located, it would imply that BVW should also take community interests into consideration when making decisions. Once more it does not mean that considering the interests of the community precludes taking decisions about dismissal or a raise in executive pay. It only means that such decisions can only be taken after also considering the impact thereof on the community.

With the statement, 'We respect the dignity of each employee', the BVW code imposes an obligation on the board to ensure that their decisions do not violate the dignity of staff. The board's decision to raise executive salaries is less likely to offend the dignity of employees, than their decision to dismiss 40% of BVW staff members. In our society where the status of persons are to a large extent determined by the work roles and positions that they occupy, the loss of a job amounts to more than the mere loss of a steady income. It also has a negative psychological impact on the people who have lost their jobs. It detrimentally affects the affected individual's sense of self-worth and dignity (cf. Encina, 2009). This consideration of the impact of dismissal on the dignity of employees is thus a consideration that the board also should have reckoned with as part of assessing their decision against the company standards test.

The above discussion makes it clear that decisions that adhere to company standards ensure that a number of significant ethical considerations find their way into the business decision-making process. These considerations contribute towards ensuring that the ultimate business decision is not only a good business decision, but also an ethically responsible one. As important as it is to assess business decisions against company standards, it is still not a sufficient criterion to ensure ethical business decisions, since company standards may neglect important areas of ethical concern. For this reason it is important to also introduce the fairness test to the business decision-making process.

Is it fair to all stakeholders?

Applying the fairness test in business decision-making means that we should consider how the decision that one is about to take would impact on, and be perceived by, all stakeholders that are likely to be affected by the decision. As explained in the previous chapter, this can be done either be engaging directly with stakeholders to find out how they perceive the situation or issue at hand, or it could be done by applying one's moral imagination, i.e., trying to imagine how the situation might be experienced or perceived by others. Since we do not have the opportunity to engage directly with the stakeholders of BVW, we have to rely on our moral imagination.

In order to determine the impact on others, we first have to identify the stakeholders that are most likely to be affected by the decision of the BVW board. The most obvious parties to be affected by the decision are shareholders, executive managers, employees and the local community. There are also other stakeholder groups that will be affected, but for the sake of this exercise we will restrict our analysis to these four core stakeholder groups. Let us now try to imagine how each of these parties is likely to experience or perceive the decision to raise executive salaries whilst simultaneously laying off 40% of the staff of BVW.

Shareholders who are only interested in short-term financial return of their investment in BVW most probably will approve of the decision by the BVW board. The drastic step taken by the board will, at least in the short run, reduce the losses that the company has been suffering over the last 18 months. Shareholders that take a longer term view of their investment might be less positive, because they would realise that such a drastic down-sizing of staff might hamper the company's ability to bounce back and take advantage of new opportunities that might arise when the economy is moving out of recession. There might also be some shareholders who are not only interested in the financial performance of the company, but in the company's performance on the triple bottom line. These shareholders might harbour serious doubts about how the board's decision will affect, particularly, the economic and social performance of BVW.

One might expect that executive managers, as a second group of stake-holders, might also welcome the board's decision, because it is likely to turn around the bad financial performance of the company for which they are ultimately responsible. It would also be quite understandable that they would welcome the salary increase – especially in the middle of the cur-rent recession. But as the CEO, Sarie Williams, aptly remarked, the board's decision is not only good news for executive managers. There is also bad news. As CEO and executive management team, they have to carry the responsibility for downsizing the company. The whirlpool of emotions that Kgosi Malan was experiencing when he first heard about the board's decision is a stark reminder of this reality. Dismissing staff is never easy, nor pleasant. Bearing the ultimate responsibility for overseeing this task most probably will mean sleepless nights for a person like Kgosi Malan and other members of the executive team.

The employees and non-executive managers of BVW are a third stake-holder group that will be directly affected by the board's decision. The decision will have an impact both on those who will be dismissed as well as on those who will remain in the company after the downsizing has been completed. Those who will be dismissed will suffer in a number of ways. The most obvious effect of the dismissal will be the loss of a steady income. Given the tough economic conditions as a result of the global recession, and adding to that South Africa's already high unemployment rate, the danger of personal economic hardship and financial insecurity will loom large. In many a case it might translate into not having enough food on the table or not being able to provide children with decent educational opportunities. In addition to the material consequences of losing a steady income, these workers who have been laid off, are also likely to suffer psychologically. Losing one's job is humiliating and can amount to a loss of social status, especially in our society where job roles and position forms an integral part of one's identity and sense of self-worth. These employees are likely to harbour deep negative feelings towards the company – especially considering the fact that the executive management is receiving a 20% raise in salary at the time when they are losing their jobs. They inevitably will ask the question: Why could BVW not have used that money to rescue at least some of the jobs that are now being shed.

It is, however, not only the dismissed employees who will raise this question. The same question will most probably also be asked by their co-workers who will remain in the company. Lay-offs do not only affect those who lose their jobs, but also those who remain in the company after the downsizing. The survivors often also suffer from what is sometimes called 'survivors' syndrome' (Horton & Reid, 1991; Mumford, 1995), which refers to the guilt, insecurity, low morale and lack of confidence that is often found amongst staff that have survived a downsizing. Inevitably, such low morale and feelings of suspicion and negativity makes life difficult for managers on all levels, since they are the ones who bear the brunt of dealing with employees who display negative attitudes.

The impact of the dismissals will also inevitably spill over to the local community in which BVW is located. The dismissed workers are consumers of public and private goods and services, parents of children who attend local schools, members of religious or social groups. Their diminished income is thus likely to have an impact on the local municipality, shops, schools, congregations, and social and sports clubs in the community amongst others. Since all these institutions will be indirectly affected by the negative experience of the dismissed workers, these institutions will take more notice of the decision that has been taken by the BVW board. This, in turn, might have an impact on how they perceive BVW as a company. It is therefore not unthinkable that BVW might suffer reputational damage as a result.

Analysing a decision like the one taken by the BVW board for its impact on all affected stakeholders reveals whether the decision can be considered fair towards all stakeholders. The ideal is to reach decisions that are, as far as possible, fair to all stakeholders who are affected by a decision. However, in cases where it is impossible to reach a decision that is fair to all affected parties, one should opt for the decision that will be fair to most affected stakeholder groups and also be able to explain why one considers the decision as the fairest possible option.

Can it be disclosed?

The final criterion against which the board's decision should be tested is the disclosure test. The disclosure test can be applied in two ways. The one version is the public disclosure test and the second is the private disclosure version.

The public disclosure test for the ethical soundness of the board's decision consist of determining whether the board, or its representatives like the CEO, Sarie Williams, would feel comfortable disclosing the board's decision in the public media. Would she be able to provide convincing and socially acceptable reasons for the board's decision?

To get full value out of the public disclosure test, the board could imagine a situation where the chairperson of the board or the CEO of the company is facing a media conference where they have to announce the board's decision to a group of (cynical) journalists. They should consider what grounds they would provide to justify the board's decision. In particular, they should anticipate how they would react to stinging questions like: 'Could the board not have used the money that they are spending on salary hikes for executive managers to save more jobs of ordinary workers?' or 'Aren't the executive managers who failed to steer the company through the recession now being rewarded, whilst innocent workers are being punished?' Should the board feel that they can provide good reasons for backing up their decision in the face of such tough questions, they can feel confident that their decision is on solid ethical ground. Should they however cringe at the prospect of facing such hard questions, it is an indication that they find themselves on shaky moral ground.

In the private version of the disclosure test, board members should ask themselves whether they would feel comfortable in telling significant persons in their lives about the decision that the board has taken. Sarie Williams, for example, should ask herself how she would feel should she inform her spouse or children or parents or best friend that she is about to receive a 20% salary increase and that 40% of the employees of BVW are being laid off. Emotional discomfort would once more act as a moral red light, while emotional ease would be a moral green light.

The disclosure test should not be interpreted as an excuse to avoid tough and challenging situations. The question is not whether you would rather avoid such tough situations. It is to be expected of leaders that they stand up to tough and difficult challenges. The crucial question, rather, is whether they would be able to give good and convincing explanations for their decisions and actions in such situations, i.e., explanations that will make them comfortable when looking others and themselves in the eyes.

Conclusion

The benefit of using a disciplined procedure (like testing decisions against a set of criteria as we have done in this chapter) to ensure that business decisions are ethically sound, is that it systematically introduces ethical considerations into the business decision-making process that otherwise could have been easily overlooked. By considering the criteria for ethical decisions that have been discussed in this chapter, one can avoid the embarrassment, harm and reputational damage that could result from unethical or irresponsible business decisions. The ideal is that the criteria for ethical decisions should become a mindset rather than a procedure that should be imposed upon business decisions. It is typical of companies with strong ethical cultures that the kind of ethical criteria that we discussed in this chapter are a natural and logical part of making proper business decisions. In such companies, ethical criteria have become an ever-present mindset, and consequently do not have to be enforced as a procedure. Instead of seeing ethical criteria as a hindrance in business decision-making, it is regarded as essential aspect of good business decisions.

CHAPTER
14

Resolving ethical dilemmas

I n the previous two chapters we were concerned about ensuring that business decisions are ethically sound. The focus was not on dealing with ethical issues as such, but with the ethical implications of business decisions. However, in the introductory chapter (Chapter 1) we already mentioned that from time to time ethical dilemmas do arise in the workplace. When ethical dilemmas arise in business we have to deal with and resolve difficult ethical issues. It is typical of moral dilemmas that they compel us to choose between conflicting moral options. When faced with moral dilemmas, the line that we are normally able to draw between right and wrong becomes blurred. When this happens we need to make difficult ethical decisions. And for this we need a dilemma-resolving strategy to guide us through that process.

In this chapter we will introduce the Rational Interaction for Moral Sensitivity (RIMS) strategy for resolving moral dilemmas (cf. Rossouw, 1994). We will first explain why the RIMS strategy is appropriate for a situation marked by moral dissensus. Against this backdrop the strategy itself will be described along with some objections that might be raised against it.

The RIMS approach is designed as a dilemma-resolving strategy that can be used for both social and personal ethical dilemmas in the workplace. Social dilemmas arise when different people make conflicting judgments on what is considered to be morally right with regard to a specific situation. Personal dilemmas occur when a person has conflicting moral views about what the most appropriate moral decision should be in a specific situation. The purpose of the RIMS strategy is to structure a process of rational interaction between the rival points of view in a moral dispute that will result in morally sensitive decisions. Before outlining the strategy in detail, we will first explain the phenomenon of moral dissensus in order to gain a better understanding of the nature of moral dilemmas.

Moral dissensus

Alisdaire MacIntyre, author of *After virtue: a study in moral theory* (1985), elucidates the nature of 'moral dissensus'. According to MacIntyre, the current moral dissensus dates back to the 15th century, the period regarded as the beginning of the Modern Era. In the Middle Ages (the fifth to the 14th centuries) moral dissensus was not only uncommon, but even the slightest indication of moral dissensus was regarded as a dangerous defect. The Middle Ages was characterised by two distinguishing features. First was the dominant position of the church, and second was the part that reason played in providing a rational foundation for the convictions of the church. Reason was expected to reconcile different theological dogmas in order to build a theological system that would be rationally coherent. Any human idea that did not accord with the dogma of the church was discredited and the life of the thinker was in danger. Consider for example Galileo's predicament in this regard.

A good example of the role played by reason is to be found in the concept of morality that was dominant in the Middle Ages. By the 12th century, Aristotle's scheme of ethics was dominant. MacIntyre shows how Aristotle's ethics could be located within a threefold scheme consisting of:

- human nature in its natural and uncultivated state
- ethical guidelines that could transform and cultivate human nature
- human nature in its fulfilled and cultivated stage. (cf. MacIntyre, 1985:52)

The function of moral guidelines within this scheme was to transform individuals from their untutored state into a morally cultivated state. This threefold scheme was the model for Christian, Jewish, Islamic, and other moral systems during the Middle Ages.

MacIntyre maintains that this scheme was radically altered from the time of the Renaissance (the late 14th and the 15th century) as a new ideal of reason came to dominate. After the Reformation in the 16th century, Protestants in particular began to insist that reason could not conceive the true end for humankind. The power of reason had been destroyed by humankind's fall into sin. The theological doctrine of original sin maintains that each and every aspect of human nature – including reason – is corrupted by sin. Reason is therefore no longer seen as fit to design the end for which humans should live. Aristotle's scheme was rejected as deficient because it was based on his rational insights, and not on theological revelation.

The demise of Aristotle's scheme was taken one step further during the Enlightenment of the 18th century. The dominant philosophy of science ascribed a new function to reason. According to this new philosophy of science, the purpose of reason was not to determine the ends of human life, but quite a different function. MacIntyre outlines its new role:

Reason does not comprehend essences or transitions from potentiality to act; these concepts belong to the despised conceptual scheme of scholasticism. Hence anti-Aristotelian science sets strict boundaries to the powers of reason. Reason is calculative; it can assess truths of fact and mathematical relations but nothing more. In the realm of practice it can therefore speak only of means. About ends it must be silent. (1985, 54)

The result of this new view was that reason was limited to making statements about 'what is' and forced to abandon considerations of 'what ought to be'.

MacIntyre asserts that once the Aristotelian notion of ethics had collapsed, ethics was in a severe crisis. Both the church and modern science denied that reason had a place in determining human ends. And without such ends, there also could be no moral guidelines. The Aristotelian scheme of ethics was abandoned and a new way of thinking emerged, which no longer depended on ends to determine ethics.

The new way of thinking about ethics, according to MacIntyre, was based on what was considered the appropriate role for reason to play. The key features of this new standard of rationality were subjectivity and universality: knowledge should no longer be based on the authority of the church, but on the rational insights of the individual (subjectivity). The rational claims of the individual should be checked and scrutinised by other independent and rational individuals in order to determine whether it applies universally (universality). This effectively reduced the areas in which human reason could make truth claims to logical or mathematical relations and empirical statements. This new concept of rationality had severe implications for the status of moral statements.

Philosophers of the Modern Era took up the challenge of developing a new concept of ethics, within the restrictions imposed upon them by modern rationality. MacIntyre suggests that Kant's deontological ethics is a particularly fine example of such an approach. It is an attempt to meet the two criteria proposed by the modern concept of rationality. On the one hand it states that the rational individual is the source and authority of moral laws. In this it meets the demand that the source of knowledge should be the rational individual (subjectivity). Kant attempts to meet the further demand that statements should be universally acceptable by insisting that the individual who formulates the moral law should determine whether they themselves are persons willing to accept that law as one which all should obey (universality).

Although Kant's proposal did conform to the parameters of modern rationality, it did not succeed in becoming the dominant ethical approach that could fill the vacuum left by the demise of the Aristotelian scheme. Other ethicists devised alternative ethical theories that also met the standards of modern rationality. While Kant took the rational ability of the individual as his starting point, Mill opted for taking the pleasure experienced by the individual as his starting point. Mill also based his theory on what he regarded as an empirical fact: all people strive towards maximising pleasure. By insisting that each person should consider the impact of his or her actions on the happiness of all other people, he gave a universal character to his approach (see Chapter 6).

MacIntyre maintains that a serious problem arose as a result of these developments. There was no way in which the rival claims of the different ethical theories could be settled, as all of them formally met the demands of modern rationality. There was no shared objective norm against which the merits of the rival ethical theories could be judged. In this way the Modern Era produced moral dissensus (or the lack of moral consensus) without the possibility of curing it.

Coping with moral dissensus

One of the more promising attempts to deal with moral decision-making in the context of moral dissensus is offered by the German philosopher, Jürgen Habermas. According to Habermas (1993), modern rationality excludes vast areas of human life from rational discourse. Instead of the empirical verifiability that modern rationality demands, Habermas proposes consensus within an 'ideal speech situation' as the criterion for ethical knowledge. According to his alternative conception of rationality, knowledge is made in conversational agreement through the interaction of rational participants. The big difference between Habermas's approach to ethics and the prescriptive ethical theories discussed earlier (in Chapter 6) is that the previously discussed theories focus on the content of our moral considerations, and Habermas's theory focuses on the process by which ethical decisions are made.

The obvious objection to his concept of rationality is that it opens the door to relativism and so cannot be seen as a serious substitute for modern scientific rationality. It makes it seem as though any consensus established through discussion might legitimately be considered knowledge. Habermas denies this by indicating that there are certain rules that apply to this discursive process of knowledge formulation.

The 'ideal speech situation' provides the context for the process of knowledge formation. This ideal speech situation does not refer to the personality or skills of the participants, but to the structural features of the discussion. In a simplified way it could be portrayed as that situation where all participants in the discourse are treated as if they are truly equal and in which all forms of coercion or force have been removed. The only force allowed in this situation is the force of the best rational argument. Against the background of this ideal speech situation, the basic rules of the process of knowledge formation are the following:

▣ The only evidence that participants may introduce into the discourse is empirical experience, which is objectively accessible.

◙ The process of communicative interaction is driven only by the force of the strongest rational argument.

◙ Only those experiences, arguments, and norms that can attain consensual agreement are regarded as knowledge.

◙ Any knowledge formulated in this way is always open to future revision.

'The only force allowed in this situation is the force of the best rational argument.'

The obvious advantage of this broader rationality proposed by Habermas is that it readmits most of the areas excluded by modern rationality into the domain of knowledge. Because experiences about culture, values, and norms are widely shared amongst human beings they are, according to Habermas's conception of rationality, appropriate sources of experience that can be introduced into the process of knowledge formation.

Habermas's moral theory offers valuable insights that can be utilised in developing a strategy for moral decision making in business. It, of course, needs to be tailored to suit business practice. One objection to his theory might be that an ideal speech situation is an unattainable dream within corporate life. Businesses are traditionally organised into hierarchies in which people at the top have more power than people lower down. Habermas himself admits that his conditions for an ideal speech situation are not realistic. His is rather an ethical appeal to participants to act as if they are equals. So, within the business environment, participants in a moral dispute would be asked to put aside power relationships when entering into the moral decision-making process.

Assumptions behind the RIMS strategy

Habermas's moral theory forms the backbone of the RIMS strategy. It however provides only the broadest of outlines and needs to be fleshed out with a further set of assumptions.

Assumption one: Moral dissensus is a given

The RIMS strategy begins with the assumption that moral dissensus is an inescapable feature of current culture. Modernity, in its attempt to find secular and rational grounding for morality, has produced any number of varying moral theories. All of these modern moral theories are rationally justifiable and defensible. This has resulted in the current condition of dissensus, where no competing moral theory can succeed in gaining superiority over another. All need to be taken equally seriously or all need to be rejected. The first option forms the first assumption of the RIMS strategy.

Assumption two: Moral dissensus does not equal ethical relativism

The RIMS approach assumes that moral dissensus does not necessarily result in ethical relativism. Moral dissensus only equals ethical relativism if it is assumed that discourse between the rival moral viewpoints has become meaningless. This is not the case in the RIMS strategy. The RIMS approach assumes that interaction between rival moral viewpoints is not only necessary, but is also an important source of creativity that can help to find morally sensitive answers.

Assumption three: Dialogue can produce solutions

The RIMS strategy assumes that, through dialogue, conflicting moral views can be creatively harnessed to produce morally sensitive solutions to moral dilemmas. The preconditions for such a dialogue are that:

▣ the reality of moral dissensus is understood and accepted by all participants in the RIMS decision-making process

▣ participants commit themselves to finding a solution within this context of moral dissensus.

Once these preconditions have been satisfied, the rivalry between moral viewpoints no longer frustrates moral decision-making. It becomes instead a creative resource that allows us the chance to find more inclusive and morally sensitive solutions to the problem than any one moral viewpoint can achieve on its own.

Assumption four: Focusing on motives is futile

A further assumption is that focusing on the motives underlying moral viewpoints cannot solve moral dilemmas in a situation of moral dissensus. If we accept MacIntyre's argument, ethical theories are ultimately based on subjective commitments to certain basic ethical values. A focus on the subjective ethical commitments underlying the various moral standpoints cannot solve moral problems. At most, a focus on the underlying motives can illuminate the various moral viewpoints, but it cannot overcome the rivalry between conflicting viewpoints. For this reason, the RIMS strategy advises that motivations underlying moral views should not dominate the process of ethical decision-making. The focus should rather be on finding solutions that can accommodate the concerns of all parties in the dilemma.

Assumption five: Only moral arguments are allowed

Only moral arguments can be included in the dialogue. That is, only arguments that meet the minimum requirements of a moral argument will be allowed. To qualify, an argument should display a concern and respect for others and not be merely selfish. It thus excludes any socio-centric or ego-centric arguments. It is only on the basis of ethical considerations that one can expect to arrive at ethical decisions.

The RIMS strategy

The RIMS strategy begins with 'rational interaction'. This is a rational debate between two or more rival views on the moral issue under discussion. In such a debate the rival points of views should be presented, analysed and discussed in a rational and tolerant way. By 'rational' it is meant that points of view are based on reasons that will make them understandable to others. These reasons are not restricted to empirical evidence, but also include values, culture, religion, and emotions, which can provide support for a point of view. Rational arguments of this type are the only valid means of persuasion permitted.

Tolerance is required to respect all points of view and to recognise them as valid perspectives that can contribute towards the resolution of the problem. Participants have to allow one another freedom to express their points of view as well as the opportunity for countering and criticising these views. Participants in such a dialogue are not required to give an account of the specific moral tradition to which they belong or the moral theory, if any, to which they subscribe. Such a qualification would only lead to an elitist conception of moral dialogue that would exclude vast numbers of people who can make valuable contributions.

The steps in the RIMS strategy

The RIMS strategy for moral decision-making can be summed up in three basic steps:

Step one: Generate and evaluate all points of view

Any moral point of view that satisfies the following three criteria should be taken into consideration in the decision-making process:
- It should be a moral argument and not selfish.
- It should be clear and intelligible to all.
- It should be factually correct.

> ### Step two: Identify implications
>
> The focus should not be on the motives behind the various points of view. Instead the focus should be on identifying the positive and negative implications articulated in the different points of view.
>
> ### Step three: Find solutions
>
> Participants should co-operate in finding solutions that will keep negative implications to a minimum, while retaining the positive implications.

The above strategy can be used for resolving both social and personal dilemmas. In the case of social dilemmas, the different points of view are likely to be presented by different parties. It therefore makes sense in social dilemmas to use a competent facilitator to guide and structure the process according to the RIMS strategy. In the case of personal dilemmas, the different points of view will be articulated and mediated by the person confronted with the dilemma. The individuals will therefore have to structure their thinking according to the steps of the RIMS strategy as outlined above.

Objections to the RIMS strategy

It will not surprise if some object to the RIMS strategy on the grounds that:

- it is too time-consuming
- no one can be forced to use it.

None of these objections pose a serious threat to the viability of the RIMS strategy, as will be demonstrated below.

Objection one: It is too time-consuming

A first objection might be that the RIMS approach takes too much time. This is not a legitimate criticism because the fact that it requires time has less to do with the approach itself, than it has to do with the area within which it operates. Any person who understands the processes of change in ethical attitudes, values, and judgements will confirm that there are no lasting quick-fix solutions in this area. Change is more than the adjustment of a few nuts and bolts. Change always takes time to achieve, and experience has shown that the quality and durability of change is enhanced when people actively participate in such processes of change. The RIMS strategy offers such an opportunity. Consequently, it is par for the course of ethical dilemma resolution to expect processes of ethical decision-making to be time consuming.

Objection two: No one can be forced to use it.

A second concern that might be raised against the RIMS approach is that it is doomed to failure if people are not willing to participate in the process. This objection poses an interesting challenge. On the one hand it could simply be dismissed as unimportant, because it is true of most processes of change: if people do not want to play the game, the chances of success are very poor. On the other hand, this objection sets up the challenge of how to motivate people to engage in the RIMS process. There seem to be a number of strategies that could convince people:

- ▣ It might help to explain that the current situation of moral dissensus means that there is no objective ethical authority available. Solutions need to be worked out through a process of rational discussion between all points of view. This will help people to understand that moral disputes need to be approached in a different way from other decision-making processes.

- ▣ People could be told of similar situations where this approach was used and was successful. Success stories seem to give credibility to any approach.

- ▣ Possibly the most compelling way of motivating people is to explain that participation in the RIMS approach enables them to actively shape the values, norms and standards of behaviour within which they have to work. Through participation in this process, they become co-creators of their working conditions.

Conclusion

The RIMS strategy is an instrument devised especially for coping with difficult moral dilemmas that arise within business. It acknowledges that although the prevailing moral dissensus complicates moral decision-making, the opportunity of resolving dilemmas nevertheless remains if the parties to a moral dispute can harness their differences constructively within a process of dialogue. It is not to be denied that a well-established set of corporate ethical values or a well-institutionalised code of ethics can play a role in easing the process of dealing with moral dilemmas. Important as such ethical values and codes might be, they never will be sufficient to deal with all possible ethical dilemmas that might emerge in business. In the ever-changing world of business, new issues will always crop up. Whenever moral dilemmas emerge in the workplace a strategy like RIMS is needed for guiding the process of resolving moral dilemmas.

CHAPTER
15

Ethical dilemmas in business: Employment equity

Moral dilemmas arise in the workplace when two or more parties hold morally conflicting views about an issue, policy or practice. An issue that often evokes such conflicting moral views in the workplace is employment equity. The issue of employment equity (or affirmative action) tends to fuel heated debate. This is because while it creates new opportunities for some people, it often excludes others from opportunities for appointment or promotion. Affirmative action has the potential to unlock potential in an organisation. But it also carries the potential of demoralising and dividing a workforce if it is not implemented with moral sensitivity. When confronted with such an emotionally charged dilemma, a sound strategy is needed to avert potential disaster. In this chapter the RIMS strategy will be applied to moral issues raised by a policy of employment equity.

Why affirmative action?

Africa's colonial history is blemished by acts of large-scale exploitation and discrimination against black people. In South Africa, the apartheid regime heaped further prejudice and injustice upon black people. In contrast to the situation in the USA, where minorities were victims of discrimination, in Africa the majority suffered discrimination. At the same time, discrimination against black people coincided with extensive discrimination against women. This gender discrimination was, and still is being caused by cultural beliefs and gender stereotypes, amongst other factors. When the first democratically elected government came into power in 1994 they had to address the inequality caused by the discriminatory practices of the predecessor regimes. They opted for a policy of affirmative action to redress the discrimination of the past. This policy was written into law with the promulgation of the Employment Equity Act of 1998 (cf. Department of Labour, 2009). This law explicitly states that it wishes 'to achieve equity in the workplace by: (a) promoting equal opportunity and fair treatment in employment through the elimination of unfair discrimination; and (b) implementing affirmative action measures to redress the disadvantages in employment experienced by designated groups, in order to ensure their equitable representation in all occupational categories and levels in the workforce' (cf. Department of Labour, 2009).

Table 15.1 Top management positions in South Africa: Race comparison 2003 vs. 2007

Population group	2003	2007	% difference
Africans	14,9 %	18,8%	+3,9 %
Coloureds	4 %	3,9%	-0,1 %
Indians	4,9 %	6,1%	+1,2 %
Whites	76,3 %	68,2 %	-8,1 %

Source: Employment Equity Report of South Africa, 2008

In South Africa (as elsewhere where affirmative action has been written into law) the debate has moved beyond the question whether there should be affirmative action or not. The focus is rather on the form that it should take.

Distinguishing affirmative action from related concepts

Affirmative action only makes sense against a backdrop of prolonged injustice where discrimination has disadvantaged specific groups of people. A consequence of such discrimination is large-scale inequalities between those who reaped the benefits of discrimination and those who were deprived by it. Affirmative action is an intervention intended to overcome this legacy of inequality as it manifests itself in the workplace. As such, it needs to be distinguished clearly from two related practices with which it can be easily confused. They are equal opportunities and reverse discrimination.

Equal opportunities versus affirmative action

In an equal opportunities dispensation, all persons compete on an equal footing for available opportunities. Individual merit is the only criterion for determining to whom opportunities should be awarded. The person best qualified for a specific opportunity will get it. Advocates of an equal opportunity policy justify it on the grounds that it is non-discriminatory and therefore fair to all members of society.

Advocates of affirmative action would agree that an equal opportunities dispensation is the ideal approach for awarding opportunities, but only in situations where relative equality prevails. In situations scarred by deep inequalities an equal opportunities approach would be unfair. It will serve to perpetuate inequality rather than break it down. Those who benefited from the previous discrimination will invariably be the best qualified people for the better jobs. To opt for an equal opportunities approach in situations of severe inequality amounts to preserving such inequality. In order to overcome the inequality inherited from the previous discriminatory dispensation, special attention needs to be given to those who were victims of prejudice in the past.

Affirmative action is seen as a mechanism that can bridge the gap between the situation of inequality caused by discrimination and the ideal of equal opportunities. As such it is a temporary intervention, only intended to facilitate the transition from a situation of severe and unfair inequality to a situation where such inequalities have been rectified to the extent that everyone competes on an equal footing. Should affirmative action lose its character as a temporary transitional device and become a permanent policy of favouring the previously disadvantaged, it turns into something else, namely reverse discrimination.

Reverse discrimination versus affirmative action

Although the term 'reverse discrimination' was previously used as a synonym for affirmative action, the current tendency is to reserve it for situations where one form of unfair discrimination has been traded in for another form of unfair discrimination. When this occurs, the only difference between the situation before and after reverse discrimination is the target of discrimination. The groups who benefited from the initial discrimination now become victims and the previous victims become the beneficiaries. An element of retaliation is evident in a policy of reverse discrimination. This is not what affirmative action wishes to achieve, as will become clear in the definition of affirmative action that follows.

Defining affirmative action

Affirmative action can be defined as a temporary intervention of preferential treatment to rectify the consequences of discrimination in order to enable people to compete as equals for opportunities. This definition is not merely descriptive; it is normative in that it establishes certain criteria that need to be met in an affirmative action programme. Such a normative definition enables us to distinguish between poor and proper forms of affirmative action. Without such a normative definition we are compelled to accept anything that carries the name irrespective of its intentions.

So, we have defined affirmative action as a temporary intervention of preferential treatment to rectify the consequences of discrimination in order to enable people to compete as equals for opportunities. The following four components of this definition need additional clarification: 'temporary intervention'; 'preferential treatment'; 'consequences of discrimination'; and 'enable to compete as equals'.

Temporary intervention

Affirmative action is a mechanism intended to bridge the gap between an unfair past and a future dispensation of fair employment. As such it has the character of a temporary intervention. Once the major deficits have been eradicated, affirmative action should be phased out in favour of an equal opportunities dispensation. Should this not happen and affirmative action be allowed to continue indefinitely, it inevitably turns into reverse discrimination. It is therefore imperative that affirmative action programmes should be tied to defined time limits and/or numerical goals.

Preferential treatment

The purpose of affirmative action is to redress imbalances caused by prolonged discrimination. It requires that constructive action be taken to redress these imbalances. This normally consists of targeting the most disadvantaged groups for preferential treatment. Special attention is being paid to them in order to assist them in overcoming the constraints of the past. It is for this reason that affirmative action has an aggressive and temporary character – it is intended to accelerate the process of access to opportunities for members of previously disadvantaged groups. To achieve this objective it is imperative to determine the needs and deficits of such disadvantaged groups and to attend to them.

Consequences of discrimination

As affirmative action is an attempt to rectify the imbalances caused by discrimination, it is extremely important to identify who has been adversely affected by discrimination and what kinds of deficits have been imposed upon them. Statistical analyses and profile comparisons are particularly helpful in this regard:

- Statistical analysis can reveal discrepancies in employment patterns. It can, for example, indicate discrepancies between the demographic composition of a company and that of the community where it is located. Or it can reveal that the more lucrative positions in a company are concentrated in the hands of specific groups.
- Profile comparisons between, for example, different race groups of a specific age group in a company can reveal discrepancies in terms of education, experience, opportunities, financial resources, and psychological aptness. Whenever such discrepancies can be related to discrimination they become legitimate targets for eradication through affirmative action.

Once identified, these detrimental consequences of discrimination can be rectified by enabling and empowering the victims of discrimination.

Enable to compete as equals

In order to eradicate or alleviate the consequences of discrimination those who were affected detrimentally need to be given special opportunities. This will often take the form of being offered preferential education and training opportunities. But such opportunities should not be restricted to education and training alone. Special opportunities also need to be created to ensure that, once appointed, people are able to cope with the demands and pressures of new and sometimes hostile working environments. Structural changes to the power structures may also be required to ensure that the previously powerful no longer dominate an organisation and perpetuate discrimination.

Enabling persons from previously disadvantaged groups to compete as equals in the employment market is something radically different from a mere quota system where jobs are created and filled simply to reflect societal demographics. Any form of appointment that ignores individuals' abilities to fulfil the requirements of the position to which they have been appointed, serves neither the goals of affirmative action nor the interests of the appointees. Offering special opportunities to persons from disadvantaged groups that will empower them to compete with competence in the employment market is an essential component of affirmative action.

Objections to affirmative action

The clear need for affirmative action in a situation marked by a legacy of discrimination against specific groups in society does not mean that its implementation presents no practical or moral problems. If the implementation of affirmative action is not managed with care and moral sensitivity it can easily turn into a moral minefield that can destroy the well-intended objectives of affirmative action.

Given the situation in South Africa where affirmative action is already a well-established practice, it makes little sense to detail in depth all the arguments that can be raised in support of affirmative action. It makes more sense to focus on the problems associated with affirmative action. Such a focus can reveal potentially negative outcomes that one should attempt avoiding. However, before outlining these objections, it is important to remember that affirmative action is intended to:

- redress imbalances and inequalities caused by discrimination
- break down discriminatory practices and stereotypes
- enable members of previously disadvantaged groups to compete with competence in the employment market.

With these objectives in mind, we can now turn to the objections that are most commonly levelled against affirmative action.

It can generate negative feelings

Affirmative action can cause feelings of envy, hatred, and resentment among the previously advantaged group. They may feel affirmative action is an injustice, because despite their contribution to the organisation they stand little chance of being promoted or rewarded for their performance. Such negative feelings can easily translate into sabotage of the working environment. The disgruntled employees are likely to make life difficult for affirmative action appointees and can undermine their confidence and motivation. This will undermine the morale of the company. Affirmative action thus can affect both the previously advantaged group and affirmative action appointees negatively.

It can harm those it is supposed to help

Affirmative action may not only be detrimental to those whom it excludes, but it can also hurt those who are supposed to be its beneficiaries. The argument is that those who have been targeted for preferential treatment will always know in their heart of hearts that they have not been promoted on merit. They might suffer psychologically as a result and feel inferior to their peers who had been appointed on merit. Studies on affirmative action indicate that affirmative action appointees experience more problems than do their colleagues who were appointed on a non-affirmative action basis (Villere & Hartman 1989). They tend to reveal less organisational commitment and job satisfaction, as well as a greater sense of role conflict and ambiguity. Whenever this is the case, affirmative action is neither beneficial to the psychological health of affirmative action appointees, nor to the company.

Affirmative action appointees can be stigmatised

A related objection is that those promoted through affirmative action might have difficulty in gaining respect from co-workers. They will always be regarded as token appointments. Consequently they stand little chance of becoming role models for others. The experience of being stigmatised is likely to have a negative effect on their work performance. Once again, this does not benefit the employee or the company.

It can cause standards to drop

A further objection is that affirmative action might result in the lowering of standards of work. Given the educational and training deficits associated with discrimination, combined with the pressure to promote members of previously disadvantaged groups, affirmative action might result in the appointment of people who are not fit for their new jobs. This could mean lower standards of product or service quality, a decline in safety, or a decrease in productivity.

It can aggravate negative stereotypes

A final argument against affirmative action is that, whilst it may change the demographic profile of companies, it will not succeed in stamping out the underlying prejudices that live in the hearts and minds of people. Policies and rules can change practices, but they cannot change attitudes. On the contrary, affirmative action can have the opposite effect. The resentment and envy experienced by those excluded from it, coupled with the feelings of disrespect experienced by its beneficiaries, may aggravate prejudice and reinforce negative racial and gender stereotypes. Working conditions characterised by prejudice are obviously not conducive to productivity.

Table 15.2 Top management positions in South Africa: Gender comparison 2003 vs. 2007

Population and gender group	2003	2007	% difference
African men	11,2 %	12,9 %	+1,7 %
African women	3,7 %	5,9 %	+2,2 %
Coloured men	3,1 %	2,9 %	−0,2 %
Coloured women	0,9 %	1 %	+ 0,1 %
Indian men	4,2 %	5 %	+0,8 %
Indian women	0,7 %	1,1 %	+0,4 %
White men	67,5 %	58,4 %	−9,1 %
White women	8,8 %	9,8 %	+1 %
Total men	86 %	79,2 %	−6,8 %
Total women	14,1 %	17,8 %	+3,7 %

Source: Employment Equity Report of South Africa, 2008

Given these objections that can and often are raised against affirmative action, the challenge is to find ways of implementing affirmative action that will minimise the force of these objections. To demonstrate how this can be achieved, the RIMS strategy for the resolution of moral dilemmas will be applied to the affirmative action case that follows.

Affirmative action case

Sales Unlimited, a product marketing company, was started almost 30 years ago. In the early years of the company's existence almost 90% of employees were men. Over the years there was a steady increase in the number of women who joined the company. Recently the number of female employees reached an all time high of 47%. They were however mostly employed on the lower job levels in Sales Unlimited. In response to a complaint about the low level of representation of women on management levels in the company, an analysis of the gender distribution on management levels was commissioned that revealed the following gender profile.

Table 15.3 Gender profile at Sales Unlimited

Level	Males	Females
Junior management	65%	35%
Middle management	80%	20%
Senior management	91%	9%
Executive management	100%	0%

These statistics as well as the pressure by government on companies to empower women resulted in the company embarking on an aggressive affirmative action programme. The company set itself the target of bringing the representation of women on the various management levels on par with their overall number in the company. At the current stage the target is to have at least 47% of management posts on all levels occupied by women within three years.

When the affirmative action programme was announced three months ago, it was frowned upon by most men in the company. Upon learning about the negative reaction by males the CEO of the company sent a personal letter to each employee. This letter read:

Dear staff member,

It has come to my attention that some members of our staff have reacted negatively to our recently announced affirmative action programme. I deem it important that this programme is supported by all employees in our company.

Although our affirmative action programme will cause some in-convenience in the short term, we need to understand that we will all benefit from it in the long run. It will assist us in overcoming the inequalities and discrimination against women that have existed in our company over many years. By granting our female colleagues their due place we can expect that they will bring new thinking and doing to the management cadres of our company. Our company will, at the same time be complying with government requirements on the empowerment of women in business.

I call on all staff members to support this programme.

Peter Mwangi
CEO: Sales Unlimited

Initially the letter seemed to have the desired effect as less negativity was heard. However as the affirmative action programme started to kick in and women moved into positions previously occupied by men, the negativity started increasing again. Some men made no secret of the fact that they believed that certain of the newly appointed women managers did not deserve their positions and had merely been appointed because they were women. They moaned that management was allowing standards to drop. Others complained bitterly about reverse discrimination. Overall, the interaction between men and women grew tenser and the Human Resource Department registered an increase in unsavoury incidents between men and women in the company.

Even some of the women who had recently been appointed, started expressing doubts about the feasibility of the affirmative action programme. The continuous negative reactions from the men were starting to get to them. They complained that the negative reactions from their male colleagues were undermining their self-confidence, motivation and work satisfaction.

Applying RIMS to the affirmative action case

The situation that had developed in Sales Unlimited bears all the marks of a moral dilemma where parties within the company are holding conflicting moral views of the policy and practice of affirmative action that the company has embarked upon. We will now explore how the RIMS strategy can be used to ameliorate the situation that has developed in Sales Unlimited. Let us first remind us what the RIMS strategy entails.

The three basic steps in the RIMS strategy for resolving moral dilemmas are as follows.

Step one: Generate and evaluate all points of view

Any moral point of view that satisfies the following three criteria should be taken into consideration in the decision-making process:

▣   It should be a moral argument and not selfish.
▣   It should be clear and intelligible to all.
▣   It should be factually correct.

Step two: Identify implications

The focus should not be on the motives behind the various points of view. Instead the focus should be on identifying the positive and negative implications articulated in the different points of view.

Step three: Find solutions

Participants should co-operate in finding solutions that will keep negative implications to a minimum, while retaining the positive implications.

These three steps will now be applied to the affirmative action scenario in Sales Unlimited.

Generate and evaluate all points of view

The first step in this decision-making process is to identify all the moral points of view that came to the fore in the Sales Unlimited case. An analysis of the scenario reveals the following moral points of view:

In his letter to the staff, Mr Peter Mwangi mentioned the following three reasons for pursuing the affirmative action initiative:

1 Affirmative action is required to overcome inequalities and discrimination that were caused by previous discriminatory hiring and promotion practices in the company. It can thus be regarded as a form of compensation for the wrong done to women in the past.
2 Affirmative action can unlock human potential that was up until now neglected in the company. He believes that women 'can bring new thinking and doing to the management cadres of our company'. As such it will broaden and deepen the talent pool to the benefit of the company.
3 Affirmative action will also result in supporting the economic empowerment of women. This is an objective which the government has also identified as a national priority. Thus the company will not only serve its own interests, but also support a wider agenda of constructing a more just society.

The discontent with the affirmative action programme was mostly raised by some men in the company. Their discomfort with the programme was based on the following considerations:

4 Affirmative action is unfair because it does not appoint candidates for positions in the company on relevant criteria. Instead of appointing managers on merit, gender is now being used as a criterion for selection.
5 Affirmative action will lead to a lowering of standards. Since the personal merit of the candidate and the requirements of the job are no longer the only criteria for selection, they expect that the affirmative action programme will inevitably result in a lowering of standards.
6 Affirmative action is perceived to be a form of reverse discrimination. The males regard it as unfair that they have become the victims of what they regard as a new form of discrimination. They thus object to the fact that instead of stopping all forms of discrimination, a new form of discrimination is being introduced in the company.

It was not only men who objected to the affirmative action programme. Some female affirmative action appointees also aired reservations about it. Their concern was that:

7   Affirmative action is harming the people it is supposed to benefit. As women they have become the target of critique and negative reactions. This undermines their confidence and motivation and will most probably result in psychological damage in the long run.

A final moral consideration not voiced by any particular party, but nevertheless evident in the report of the Human Resource Division is that:

8   Affirmative action leads to an increase in workplace conflicts between men and women. It is clear that the affirmative action programme increased friction between the advantaged and disadvantaged groups. Thus instead of overcoming negative interactions between the groups, it seems to aggravate it.

The first step in the RIMS process requires that once identified, the various moral points of view raised in this scenario should be screened against the following three criteria:

▣   It should be a moral argument and not selfish.
▣   It should be clear and intelligible to all.
▣   It should be factually correct.

An analysis of the above moral points of view reveals that they can all be considered as moral arguments as each of them argue that affirmative action is either unfair to at least some groups in the company or detrimental to the company as a whole. Alternatively they argue that affirmative action is beneficial to not only the company, but also to society at large. They also meet the criteria of being clear and intelligible as we are able to understand the concern expressed in each of the moral points of view. Finally all the claims made in the various moral points of view are factually true – or at least potentially factually true. In the case of the point about the lowering of standards, for example, we do not have sufficient evidence to judge whether the claim is in fact true, but is not unthinkable that standards might drop in some cases as a result of affirmative action. We can therefore assume that all moral points of view have passed the required criteria for being included for consideration in the RIMS process. We can now proceed to the second step of the process.

Identify implications

The RIMS approach advocates avoiding the motives that one might suspect lurking behind a moral point of view. One should focus instead on the positive and negative implications of the issue under discussion. This implies that the outcomes that a person or party in a moral dilemma would like to attain should be identified as well as those outcomes that they would like to avoid.

By focusing on the implications identified in the various moral points of view discussed above, we can now isolate the positive and negative implications in the Sales Unlimited case.

Positive implications

The positive implications are those outcomes of a dilemma that one or more persons in a moral dilemma would like to attain. In analysing the above moral points of view we can identify the following positive implications (the number of the corresponding moral point of view is indicated in brackets):

- Eliminate inequalities caused by discrimination (1)
- Unlock human potential that was neglected (2)
- Economic empowerment of women (3).

Negative implications

The negative implications are those outcomes of a dilemma that participants in the dilemma would like to avoid. In the above moral points of view the following negative implications were identified:

- Unfair treatment of males (4 and 6)
- Lowering of standards (5)
- Undermining confidence and motivation of affirmative action appointees (7)
- Negative interaction between men and women (8).

Now that all the positive and negative consequences have been isolated, the process of finding solutions for the impasse created by the conflict between the positive and negative implications can commence.

Find solutions

The third step in the RIMS strategy requires that one should find solutions that will restrict the negative implications to a minimum, whilst retaining the positive implications. The way in which it will be done is by taking the negative implications one by one and proposing solutions that will eliminate or restrict their negative impact. These solutions, however, should be such that the positive outcomes of affirmative action identified above can still be retained. The negative implications are addressed in the same order as listed above.

Unfair treatment of males

The reason why some men experience affirmative action as unfair is because they think that women are not appointed on merit. Because they feel that the same standards are not applied to men and women, they believe that they are discriminated against. The question that needs to be answered is: 'What can be done to minimise the experience of unfairness felt by these males?' Given that members of this group may occupy influential positions in a company, it is of utmost importance to gain their co-operation. Failure to do so might result in them undermining the process of affirmative action. How might their perception of unfairness be changed?

Proposal: Communication

The company can improve its communication to staff on the need for the affirmative action programme. Special emphasis can be placed on the reasons why an affirmative action programme has become imperative and on what the company can gain from it. Good business reasons for affirmative action, external pressures on the company by the government, as well as the need for compensation to the previously disadvantaged, can be stressed. It is of utmost importance that employees do not perceive affirmative action to be a means of punishment for those who benefited from the previous discrimination. The key objective is to rectify unfair practices of the past so that the company will be able to operate more competitively by fully utilising its human resources. It should also be stressed that the affirmative action programme is a temporary intervention that will disappear as soon as its objectives have been met. This will undermine the perception of a permanent dispensation of discrimination against men.

Proposal: Involvement

An affirmative action programme developed and implemented in consultation with employees is more likely to meet with success than a programme that is unilaterally imposed by management. When employees participate in the making and implementation of a programme, they have the opportunity to voice their concerns and make constructive suggestions for the improvement thereof. All members of the organisation stand to benefit from their involvement in this process, but it might specifically assist resentful employees in coming to terms with affirmative action.

Proposal: Minimum requirement for jobs

The perception that there are different standards for men and women in the company can be countered by setting minimum requirements for jobs at all levels. This will undermine the charge that women are appointed merely on the basis of gender and not on merit. The charge that a woman is incompetent for the position she holds will then lose its force. It is important that these requirements should allow flexibility in terms of criteria for appointment or promotion. Academic qualifications and extended specialised experience should not be the only considerations in setting minimum requirements for jobs.

Proposal: Participatory management

Salary increases and promotion are not the only ways of rewarding performance in an organisation. Allowing people to contribute in decision making is also a way of showing appreciation for their contribution. People who feel they are making a meaningful contribution to the development of their organisation are less likely to experience frustration than those who do not have the opportunity thereto. Introducing a participatory management style in conjunction with affirmative action can serve two purposes:

- Those who are excluded from the benefits of affirmative action are nevertheless compensated with the opportunity to make a meaningful contribution to their work environment.
- Participatory management allows colleagues the opportunity to support each other. New appointees will benefit from the expertise and experience of their colleagues, and the company does not have to forfeit the contributions of those temporarily excluded from promotion.

Proposal: Reward

Lack of promotion opportunities often means little or no salary increases. This is demoralising for an ambitious and hardworking employee. This frustration might be alleviated if financial rewards are not solely tied to promotion. A performance appraisal system that financially rewards excellent performance or that rewards employees on the basis of comparable contribution to the company, can counter frustrations caused by lack of promotion opportunities. In this way financial recognition can still be given to those who deserve to be rewarded.

Lowering of standards

The proposals concerning minimum requirements already discussed will minimise the risk of lower standards. Additional steps to ensure that affirmative action does not lead to a drop in standards are discussed below.

Proposal: Work ethic

Work performance is not determined by the education, training, and skills of employees alone, but also by their values. The culture of a company can make a distinct difference to the way employees think about their jobs, as well as to the quality of their work. Investing in developing a work ethic built on values, such as effectiveness, quality, precision, productivity, and commitment, can boost the performance levels of employees whilst preventing standards from dropping. It goes without saying that developing such a work ethic must enjoy the support of employees and should be cultivated with their co-operation.

Proposal: Training

Successful affirmative action will offer members of previously disadvantaged groups opportunities they have been denied. Given past discrimination, new appointees can hardly be expected to have immediate and perfect knowledge of their new working conditions. Training is imperative. Opportunities to acquire the knowledge, skills, and attitudes required in the working environment will prepare new appointees to cope with the demands of their new job. Such empowered and well-trained people will act as an antidote to the lowering of standards.

There is nothing that prevents a company from preparing someone for a job well in advance of occupying that position. Succession planning coupled with a long-term training programme that gradually prepares individuals for senior jobs before they are actually required to take up these positions is a wise and far-sighted policy. A participatory management style will also serve to introduce people to the dynamics and demands of senior positions.

Undermining confidence and motivation

As illustrated in our scenario, there is a real possibility that the confidence and motivation of affirmative action appointees might be undermined by negative rumours about their ability. Such rumours suggest that these appointees are not really fit for the job, but are token appointments to satisfy public or political demand for a more representative work force. Over time they might internalise this critique and start to doubt their own ability. It is therefore imperative to ensure that these new appointees receive support to boost their confidence in their own ability.

The proposal made earlier on minimum requirements for jobs will go a long way in dispelling such feelings of incompetence. Once minimum requirements have been set and published, affirmative action appointees can reassure themselves that they have met the requirements laid down for the positions they occupy.

A number of other steps can be taken in addition to ensure that the confidence and motivation of affirmative action appointees is not unduly shaken.

Proposal: Personal development

Another way to minimise feelings of insecurity is to assist affirmative action appointees with personal development in their new job. Group stereotypes of personality and behaviour should be discarded in favour of an approach where the career and social needs of each individual are catered for. Personal growth and development of affirmative action appointees should not be considered a luxury, but should be an organisational goal that all managers take responsibility for. It is important that all employees know that affirmative action does involve risks and is a learning process in which mistakes will inevitably occur. Affirmative action appointees should be encouraged to set themselves realistic goals in accordance with their strengths and weaknesses. Failures should not be used to discredit new appointees, but should rather be used as growth and development opportunities.

Proposal: Disempowering attitudes

The group who benefited most from the old dispensation will inevitably fill the majority of management positions at the start of an affirmative action programme. They are the group most likely to be harmed and frustrated by it. It is therefore not surprising that they might take overt or covert revenge on new appointees by reacting with behaviour that is intended to disempower. In fact, they might not even be aware of what they are doing. In order to deal with this, personal development initiatives within companies should not be restricted to affirmative action appointees, but should be extended to include members of the previously advantaged group. In our scenario males should be guided to:

◙ become aware of the kind of behaviour that is experienced as humi-liating and disempowering by affirmative action appointees
◙ confront prejudices, negative feelings, and stereotypes that might lie at the root of their disempowering behaviour
◙ develop empowering attitudes and behaviour that will enable them to make a constructive contribution towards the development of the human resources of the company as a whole.

Proposal: Heroes

The idea that 'nothing succeeds like success' offers another positive avenue to support affirmative action appointees. Just as one can expect some new appointees to make mistakes, one can also expect some to perform except-ionally well in their new roles. It is important to spread these success stories through the whole organisation. These achievers should become the heroes of the new post-discrimination dispensation. They are the symbols that prove that the new order can succeed. There are a number of reasons why heroes are important:

◙ New appointees are motivated because they see others succeed in similar situations.
◙ Heroes serve as role models for young or aspiring employees.
◙ Success stories help to abolish the prejudices and stereotypes of sceptics.

Negative interaction

The challenge here is to implement affirmative action in a way that will not increase negative interaction between men and women in the company. Some of the proposals already discussed can address this problem, such as involvement of all employees in the implementation of the affirmative action programme; proper communication; and discouraging disempowering attitudes. A further proposal can be added.

Proposal: Conflict reduction

To ameliorate negative interactions that result from the introduction of affirmative action, conflict reduction sessions can be held for those who were involved in negative incidents. These sessions can consist of the following elements:

▣ An opportunity to air and express aggression created by the introduction of the affirmative action programme. Often just having the opportunity to air suppressed feelings goes a long way in easing tension that has built up over time.

▣ Challenging negative stereotypes that might prevail. The most effective way of challenging any kind of stereotype, including gender stereotypes, is to expose a person who holds these stereotypes in a constructive setting to members of the group towards whom they hold the stereotype. When people realise that others do not fit the stereotype, they are forced to alter their stereotypical views.

▣ Developing interpersonal skills. By improving the ability of people to get along and engage constructively with others, the probability of further negative incidents can be decreased.

There is of course no reason to wait with the introduction of conflict reduction sessions till negative interaction occurs. The company can be proactive and introduce it in order to pre-empt negative interactions.

Conclusion

Applying the RIMS strategy to the moral dilemma that developed in Sales Unlimited enabled us to approach the dilemma in a constructive manner and to generate ideas for resolving the dilemma. Probably more ideas have been generated than the company can afford to implement. Following selection from this variety of proposals, a strategy for improving the affirmative action programme of the company can then be decided upon. A useful combination of these proposals can be tailored into a revised affirmative action programme. The RIMS strategy has thus assisted in redesigning a morally sensitive affirmative action programme that minimises negative outcomes, whilst retaining the positive outcomes of the programme.

PART

6

Governing ethical performance

INTRODUCTION

Corporate governance refers to the control that is exercised over companies. This control can be exercised by regulators or other forces outside companies such as the state or local communities. Companies can, however, also control their own operations internally. In the latter case we refer to enterprise level corporate governance. In this part of the book we focus on the process of governing and managing the ethics of a company at the enterprise level.

In Chapter 16 a distinction between the *ethics of governance* and the *governance of ethics* is introduced. The *ethics of governance* refers to the fundamental ethical obligation of companies to be responsible, accountable, fair and transparent in all their dealings and operations. The *governance of ethics*, in contrast, refers to the process of governing and managing the ethics of an organisation. In line with the *Third King Report on Governance for South Africa* (IoD, 2009) a four-step process for governing corporate ethics is outlined. The process consists of (a) determining ethics risk, (b) designing codes of ethics, (c) institutionalising ethical standards, and (d) reporting ethics performance. In Chapter 17 a structured approach to the analysis of ethics risk and opportunities is proposed. How an organisation's stakeholder perceptions and expectations need to be gauged to enable the organisation to formulate an ethics risk profile, or the organisation's state-of-ethics, is explained.

Knowledge of the organisation's ethics risks informs the architecture of its organisational code of ethics. The nature and dimensions of codes of ethics, as the interface between organisational ethical values and ethical behaviour, is discussed in Chapter 18.

Merely having a code of ethics is not sufficient. Codified ethical standards need to be institutionalised. The institutionalisation of ethics at the strategic, systems and operational levels in organisations is discussed in Chapter 19.

The ethics management process does not end with institutionalisation however. In line with corporate governance requirements for *integrated sustainability reporting* (monitoring, auditing and disclosing of financial, social and environmental performance), the organisation also needs to report on its *ethics performance* to stakeholders. The principles and processes of ethics reporting are discussed in Chapter 20.

There remains, however, the danger that an ethics management process as described in Chapters 17–20 could become a compliance exercise or mere window dressing. It does not guarantee an ethical way of thinking and doing in the organisation. Chapter 21 introduces the less visible, but crucial roles of responsible leadership and an ethical organisational culture in the governance of ethics.

CHAPTER
16

Corporate governance and ethics

I n the introduction to the *Second King Report on Corporate Governance for South Africa* it was stated that the 19th century was 'the century of the entrepreneur. The 20th century became the century of management, [and ...] the 21st century promises to be the century of governance' (IoD, 2002:14). Although it might have been premature to characterise the 21st century in this way, it cannot be denied that corporate governance has received unprecedented attention in recent years. In this chapter we will start by exploring a number of crucial distinctions that can be made with regard to corporate governance and its ethical dimensions. We will then investigate why corporate governance has become so prominent in recent years. Finally we will analyse the ethical dimension of the *Third King Report on Corporate Governance for South Africa* (IoD, 2009). In this regard we will look at both the ethics of governance and the governance of ethics in the King III report.

Corporate governance distinctions

There are significant differences in how different countries and regions of the world perceive corporate governance. There are also significant differences in how corporate governance is approached around the world. In order to understand these different perceptions and approaches to corporate governance we first have to make a number of crucial distinctions that apply to this field.

Internal and external corporate governance

The distinction between internal and external corporate governance revolves around the question about where the locus of control over corporations is situated (cf. Rossouw 2008b, Rossouw, Van der Watt & Malan 2002). When the locus of corporate control resides inside the corporation (i.e., with the board of directors and executive management) we refer to *internal corporate governance*. When the locus of control is located outside the corporation (i.e. with the government and other regulatory institutions) we refer to *external corporate governance*.

Internal corporate governance refers to the way in which a company directs and controls its own affairs. A widely used definition of corporate governance on this level is the one that was introduced by the *Cadbury Report on Corporate Governance* in the UK which defined it as: 'the system by which a company is directed and controlled' (Smerdon 1998:1). This indicates that the responsibility for corporate governance lies with the board of directors and executive management of a corporation and consists of two main functions: the direction and control of the company. The board of directors and executive management are firstly responsible for determining the strategic direction and hence the ultimate performance of the company. Secondly, the board of directors is responsible for the control of the company. The board has to ensure that the management of the company pursues the chosen strategic direction effectively. Simultaneously they need to ensure that the company is governed in a fair and responsible manner and in accordance with legal, professional and societal standards that companies are expected to adhere to. This second responsibility of the board is referred to as their conformance responsibility.

These two responsibilities of the board of directors are demonstrated in the figure below:

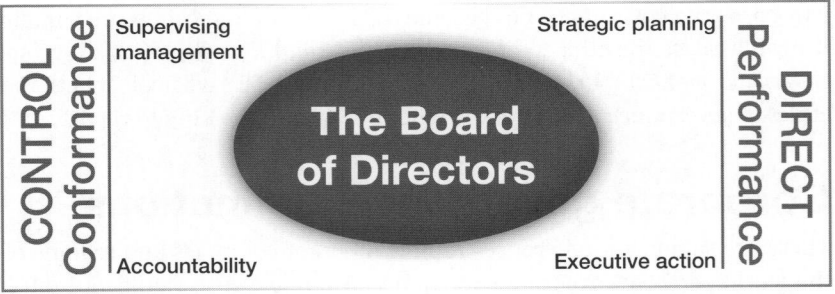

Source: Adapted from Garratt, 2003:175

The locus of control can also be located outside corporations in which case it can be called *external corporate governance*. The external control over corporations is exercised by regulatory institutions, societal norms or by the market itself. When located in regulatory institutions, corporate governance can take the form of laws, regulations, professional standards, listing requirements, etc, that are imposed upon corporations. Regulatory institutions determine the playing field on which corporations pursue their corporate objectives. External corporate governance is often mandatory and corporations who do not abide by the set standards potentially run the risk of being penalised.

External control over corporations can also be exercised in a more informal manner through societal norms that influence corporate behaviour. In contrast to external corporate governance via regulating institutions, the informal control exercised through societal norms comes in the forms of social values, practices and conventions that corporations have to heed. Although adhering to social norms is not mandatory, nor enforced through formal sanctions such as penalties, their influence is nevertheless real. Disrespecting social norms can potentially be detrimental to corporate performance and survival (cf. Rossouw, 2009:7).

A third way of external corporate control is through the market for corporate control in the form of corporate takeovers and acquisitions (cf. Gedajlovic and Shapiro, 1998:535–536). Underperforming and undervalued companies run the risk of being acquired by new owners who believe they can unlock the potential of the targeted company through better direction and control. At least in some markets the threat of takeovers and acquisitions operate as an external control mechanism that has a direct impact on how companies conduct their business.

Shareholder and stakeholder approaches to corporate governance

The distinction between shareholder and stakeholder approaches to corporate governance hinges on the question: For whose benefit should corporations be governed? When corporate governance is focused on the interests of shareholders only, internal or external corporate governance can be characterised as shareholder orientated. This exclusive focus on the interests of shareholders has resulted in this approach being referred to as the exclusive approach to corporate governance. Ever since the separation between ownership and management in corporations started to emerge, the shareholder model of corporate governance increasingly became associated with agency theory. This theory holds that managers are the agents of shareholders (or owners) and in their capacity as agents, are obligated to act in the best financial interest of the shareholders of the corporation (cf. Monks & Minow 2004:111). Shleifer and Vishny make this focus on the interest of shareholders very clear when they describe corporate governance as 'the ways in which suppliers of finance to corporations assure themselves of getting a return on their investment' (1997:737).

Approaches to corporate governance that do not merely focus on the interests of shareholders, but also on the interests of other stakeholders, can be labelled as stakeholder-orientated or inclusive (IoD, 2009:13) models of corporate governance. Such stakeholder models are premised upon stakeholder theory and conceive the corporation as a social institution (cf. Evan & Friedman 1993:82; Wieland 2006:164) where the interest of various stakeholder groups should be protected and enhanced (cf. Donaldson and Preston, 1995:67 & 71). Corporate governance is, accordingly, defined as a system that ensures that the board and management of corporations strike a balance between the interests of their various stakeholders. Collier and Roberts state that when the corporation is conceived of as a social institution, the purpose of corporate governance is 'aligning and balancing a wide variety of potentially competitive interests within the corporation' (2001:67).

Mandatory and voluntary corporate governance

Approaches to corporate governance can also be distinguished with regard to the question on whether companies are compelled to or whether they can choose to abide by corporate governance standards. When companies are compelled to abide by corporate governance standards, the corporate governance dispensation is mandatory and is often referred to as a 'comply or else' corporate governance dispensation (cf. IoD 2009:6). In the case of such mandatory dispensations, corporate governance standards are written into law and regulations that corporations have to abide by. Failure to adhere to such standards can result in sanctions like fines for corporations, imprisonment of executive managers or directors and prevention from listing or trading on stock exchanges. The Sarbanes-Oxley (or SOX) approach to corporate governance that is being practiced in the USA is often regarded as the quintessential model of mandatory corporate governance. For any mandatory corporate governance approach to be effective, corporate laws and regulations need to be clear and enforceable. It also presupposes that the state and other regulatory institutions have sufficient expertise and resources to ensure compliance by corporations to the corporate governance standards. It is exactly because these preconditions are often lacking in developing and emerging economies that a voluntary approach to corporate governance is often adopted in the latter contexts (cf. Rossouw, 2005:98).

In a voluntary dispensation, corporate governance standards take the form of recommendations on principles and practices that companies are advised to adhere to. It thus constitutes a self-regulatory approach where companies can use their own discretion on whether they wish to apply the recommended principles or practices. Although companies are free to decide whether they will apply the corporate governance standards, there is nevertheless an expectation that they should provide an explanation for their decision not to comply in their corporate reports (like annual or sustainability reports). It is exactly for this reason that the voluntary approach to corporate governance is sometimes referred to as a 'comply or explain' or an 'apply or explain' approach (cf. IoD, 2009:7). Given the emphasis on explanation in this approach, it can only be effective if companies regularly report on their corporate governance performance and disclose their adherence or non-adherence to the recommended corporate governance standards. In order to be effective this approach furthermore requires stakeholders of the corporation, like the media, shareholders and employees to critically scrutinise these corporate disclosures for accuracy and relevance.

The ethics of governance and the governance of ethics

Ethics relates in two different ways to corporate governance. The first way in which it is associated with corporate governance refers to the ethical values and principles that underpin a specific corporate governance regime. This dimension can be called the *ethics of governance*. The second way relates to the way in which corporations are expected or required to manage their ethical affairs. This is referred to as the *governance of ethics* (cf. Rossouw, 2009:6).

The *ethics of governance* of a specific corporate governance regime is not always presented in an explicit manner. Often the ethical values and principles that underpin a specific corporate governance regime have to be distilled in a second order analysis of what is presented on the surface in the form of principles or directives for corporate control and conduct. There is no doubt that all corporate governance regimes or codes have an underpinning ethic, irrespective of whether such an ethical foundation is explicitly articulated or not. The principles, regulations and directives associated with corporate governance ultimately constitute a view of the role, responsibilities and obligations of corporations towards a variety of stakeholders within a given society. Identifying the ethics of a specific corporate governance regime thus entails making explicit the moral responsibilities and obligations of corporations in society as well as the ethical values associated with these responsibilities and obligations.

The *governance of ethics* to the contrary is always presented in an explicit manner. It deals specifically with what corporations are expected or required to do in order to ensure that they act in an ethically responsible manner. Consequently the governance of ethics deals with matters such as, for example, codes of ethics, ethics training of boards of directors and staff, ethics audits, reporting on ethics performance, etc. Contrary to the ethics of governance that underpins an entire corporate governance regime in all its manifestations, the governance of ethics is just one aspect that might, or might not, be addressed within a specific corporate governance regime.

The prominence of corporate governance

The rise in prominence of corporate governance in recent years can be attributed to both the successes and the failures of modern corporations. Corporations are not simply victims of external conditions that have imposed corporate governance standards upon them. They have also created the conditions for the generation of these standards. Below we will outline a number of important factors that contribute to the current prominence of corporate governance.

Trust in corporations

There is a clear correlation between trust in business – or rather the lack thereof – and corporate governance reform. In fact, the current emphasis on corporate governance is often seen as a direct response by business to counter the devastating effects that a series of well publicised business scandals have had on the image of business in general. Corporate governance reform often follows in the wake of a major scandal that had shattered the trust of society in business. The Cadbury report of 1992 in the UK can be seen as a response to the decline in trust in business that was caused by the Maxwell scandal. Similarly, Sarbanes-Oxley in the USA can be seen as a response to the shock that was caused by the collapse of Worldcom and Enron in the USA. The declining levels of trust in business that was already referred to in Chapter 11, can thus be regarded as a important trigger for the wave of corporate governance reforms that have been witnessed in recent years. The reason for the correlation between declining trust and corporate governance reform can be found in the expectation that adherence to the principles and practices of good corporate governance might restore trust in corporations and their leaders (Payne 2004:6). As indicated above, there is always a distinct ethical undertone and foundation in corporate governance. Corporate governance reform can be regarded as an attempt to ensure that corporations conduct their business in a responsible, accountable, fair and transparent manner. And it is exactly a commitment by companies to these basic ethical values that harbours the potential of restoring trust in business. This point is well illustrated in the fact that the report on corporate governance reforms required in MCI (the former WorldCom) was titled: '*Restoring Trust*' (Breeden, 2003).

Investor demand

Dramatic improvements in communication technology have succeeded in shrinking the countries and continents of our planet into a global village with a truly global market. With the emergence of a global market national borders have become less important. Investors are able to take better advantage of international investment opportunities and the mobility of capital has increased dramatically. Investors have huge freedom to invest their money wherever they believe they might receive the highest returns. Also businesses looking for investment capital now have more scope. A business in search of investors can scout internationally.

Under these conditions, it is not surprising that corporate governance has become important. Although investors are keen to take advantage of opportunities around the globe, they will not do so at any cost. There are a number of considerations that influence their decision about whether to invest in a company or not. Investors will consider factors like:

- ▣ the vision and strategy of the business;
- ▣ the trustworthiness and capability of the management team;
- ▣ access to reliable information about current and future developments in the company;
- ▣ recourse to compensation in the case of mismanagement; and
- ▣ assurances that the business will conduct its affairs in a reputable way that will not embarrass investors.

In short, what investors look for is proper governance. Investors, and in particular institutional investors, have become increasingly demanding about improved corporate governance in order to safeguard their investments. This was clearly demonstrated by the McKinsey Investor Survey (2002). This survey among more than 200 institutional investors, who between them manage more than US$2 trillion, found that:

- ▣ 85% of investors consider corporate governance as important as financial performance.
- ▣ 73% will pay more for shares of a well governed company than for a poorly governed company with comparable financial results.
- ▣ The premium they are willing to pay for the shares of well governed companies in Africa is 30%.

Several other studies have since confirmed this link between investor confidence and good corporate governance (cf. Kim & Purnanandam, 2009; Mallin, 2007:86).

Stakeholder activism

The prominence of corporate governance is also driven by a change in attitude amongst shareholders and other stakeholders of the modern corporation. Traditionally, shareholders would have simply sold their shares when they became dissatisfied with the performance of a business. In recent years, shareholders have come to play a much more active role. Especially institutional shareholders have played a particularly significant role in this respect. Rather than exercising their right to exit when dissatisfied, they have started prompting boards and executive management of companies to improve their corporate governance standards. The Principles for Responsible Investment (PRI, 2006) is a good indication of how leading institutional investors demand good corporate governance of corporations that they invest in. Also the threat of takeovers has proved to be a stimulus for boards of directors of poorly performing companies to improve their governance standards in order to avoid becoming targets of hostile takeovers. Boards have been compelled to improve their governance in order to provide shareholders clarity about corporate objectives; access to reliable information about company performance; and confidence in the ability of the board to achieve its objectives. Proper corporate governance has become an important strategy for boards of directors to minimise the risk of hostile takeovers.

Also other stakeholders groups have become more vocal and visible in recent years. A variety of groups like consumer organisations, human rights activists, environmentalists, fair trade promoters, labour unions and anti-globalisation activists are putting pressure on corporations to act with responsibility and fairness. The disruption, boycotts and reputational damage that potentially can be brought about by such stakeholder activism have also contributed to raise awareness about the important role that good corporate governance can play in improving the relationship between a corporation and its stakeholders.

Social power

The increase in the social power of modern corporations also contributed to the current prominence of corporate governance. As corporations have increased in size and global mobility they have also increased in social influence. Businesses have a major impact on the economy, society and environment of the communities and countries in which they operate. A single large company can, for example, have a significant impact on the affluence or quality of air of the town in which it is located. The decisions that a company makes can have either beneficial or detrimental consequences for individuals and communities. Take the case of a big company which, for a variety of reasons, decided to relocate its operations. This decision might have a series of disastrous consequences for the individuals and the community where it had been previously located. Many individuals may lose their jobs; local suppliers may suffer serious financial setbacks or go bankrupt; pupil numbers at local schools will shrink; teachers will be retrenched; and the local economy is likely to start slumping.

Exactly the opposite can happen in the community where the company relocates to. New job opportunities will be created; local suppliers will benefit; new suppliers and businesses are likely to emerge; pupil numbers at local schools will increase; more teachers will be appointed; and the local economy will be stimulated.

Traditionally such public influence was associated with public institutions that were publicly controlled. National and local governments are accountable to the public for how they administer their powers. The novelty of the situation that emerged with the growth of modern corporations is that they exert enormous social influence, without being accountable to the public. This discrepancy between growing corporate social influence and a lack of public accountability has been another trigger for corporate governance reform.

The most obvious way out of this dilemma is for the state to impose stricter corporate control. The power of the state can be used to ensure that corporations do not abuse their social power. In many countries the state has indeed exercised this option in an attempt to ensure that corporations become more socially responsible (cf. Crane, Matten & Spence, 2008:11). However, this option is not the preferred one for corporations. They would rather opt for self-regulation in order to avoid government intervention in their affairs.

Another way of controlling the social influence of corporations is for special interest groups to mobilise themselves around specific issues related to the impact of corporations on society. Corporations risk disruption of their operations and harm to their reputation if they ignore such pressure.

Voluntary corporate governance reform is one way of assuring citizens and the state that corporations are willing to administer their powers in ways that are sensitive to those who are affected by them. By taking responsibility for their economic, social and environmental impact on society, corporations can wrestle the initiative for control over corporate activities away from the state and special interest groups. In this respect improved corporate governance on behalf of a company send out a signal to the government and affected stakeholders that the company takes responsibility for its social impact.

Risk management

The current prominence of corporate governance can also be attributed to the increased need for the protection of corporate assets. Boards of directors have always had a duty to protect the assets of the companies they serve and these assets have always been at risk, but in recent years both the duty of directors and the risk of companies have escalated significantly.

Modern information technology has become almost indispensable for running a competitive business, but it has also made business vulnerable to a new range of risks. Besides the risk of losing vital information, information technology has also exposed companies to confidentiality breaks, sophisticated fraud and other forms of economic crime. Boards of directors are under increased pressure and obligation to ensure that systems of governance are designed and instituted that will protect the assets of corporations.

Improved communication technology, similarly opened up many new possibilities to business, but also brought new threats to business. The risk associated with communication technologies is not principally directed to the physical or financial assets of companies, but to their symbolic assets in the form of the public reputation of the organisation. Modern communication has made it possible to expose irresponsible behaviour of a business on a global scale. Through the use of the internet, cell phones and other communication technologies, an incident of irresponsible business conduct in one country can be exposed around the world in a matter of hours. Boards of directors also have to assume responsibility for protecting their companies against this increased risk of reputational damage.

The new risks induced by information and communication technology are a further incentive for companies and industries to step up their corporate governance standards.

Sustainability

A final factor that contributed to the rise in prominence of corporate governance is the challenge of sustainability. Two versions of sustainability can be distinguished, namely, global sustainability and enterprise sustainability. Both versions of sustainability contributed towards the current prominence of corporate governance.

The notion of global sustainability grew out of the realisation that the current mode of human production and consumption is not sustainable. Through our depletion of non-renewable resources and high levels of pollution we are seriously endangering the future of life on earth. Already in 1987 the Brundtland Commission warned that development should be curbed and altered to sustainable levels. This commission coined the following definition of sustainable development: 'Forms of progress that meets the needs of the present without compromising the ability of future generations to meet their needs' (Buckley, Salazar-Xirinachs & Henriques, 2009:4).

Given the impact of modern corporations on the natural environment it is clear that business has a huge role to play in ensuring the sustainability of the earth. The dogma of an 'invisible hand' that proclaimed that society will automatically benefit from the activities of business, fell into disrepute. It was recognised that businesses produced externalities in the form of resource depletion and pollution that business should bear the responsibility for. The cost of corporate externalities cannot merely be shifted onto the state and society. Once more it is the responsibility of the board of directors to direct and control the operations of companies to ensure that corporations play their part in securing the sustainability of our planet.

The notion of enterprise sustainability grew out of the realisation that failed corporations impose a heavy cost on individuals and society alike. When a company fails and can no longer continue its operations there are detrimental consequences for employees, other contracted stakeholders, shareholders and the community in which the company operates. To counter these destructive consequences of enterprise failure, boards of directors are expected to ensure that the companies they serve are sustainable.

There is a growing awareness that business sustainability does not merely depend on the financial performance of a company. There are also so-called non-financial issues that ultimately have financial consequences for a business. Amongst these non-financial issues count the ethical, social and environmental performance of a business. If a company does not attend to and govern these aspects, it runs the risk of seriously jeopardising its sustainability. This conviction has materialised in the current emphasis on triple bottom line reporting that requires companies to report on their economic, social and environmental performance.

Both global and enterprise sustainability has made a board of directors' responsibility for directing and controlling a company a much bigger issue than it was ever before. Given all the factors discussed above that contribute to the current prominence or corporate governance, it does not surprise that some predict that whereas the 20th century was the century of management, the 21st will be the century of governance (IoD, 2002:14).

Corporate governance in South Africa

The history of corporate governance in South Africa is intimately intertwined with the King Reports on Corporate Governance for South Africa. The First King Report was published in 1994 – the same year that South Africa broke with the era of apartheid and elected its first democratic government. The Second King Report was published in 2002, and the Third King Report in 2009. The latter report was triggered in anticipation of a new Companies Act coming into effect in South Africa.

Corporate governance in the Third King Report

When the distinctions that were made at the beginning of this chapter are applied to the King III Report, the corporate governance approach advocated by the Report can be described as follows:

The Third King Report focuses on the *internal level of corporate governance*. It is thus focused on corporate governance on the enterprise level. As such the Report makes recommendations about best practice in corporate governance to 'all entities regardless of the manner and form of incorporatioon or establishment and whether in the public, private sectors or non-profit sectors' (IoD, 2009:17). Although the report recognises the importance of corporate governance on the regulatory level, it deliberately chooses not to make any recommendations with regard to the regulatory level. It rather opts for operating in the discretionary realm within companies where boards of directors can decide on how a company should be directed and controlled. The Report clearly regards the external level and the internal level of corporate governance as complementary dimensions of the corporate governance regime. In fact, in the preface to the report it is clearly stated that one of the major considerations for producing a *Third King Report on*

Corporate Governance for South Africa was to align the previous King Report with the new Companies Act of South Africa.

From the outset the Report made it clear that a *voluntary* and not a mandatory approach to corporate governance is being followed. In the preface to the Report it is stated that there is basically a choice between a statutory 'comply or else' approach to corporate governance where companies are compelled by law to adhere to corporate governance regulations, or a self-regulatory 'comply or explain' approach where companies have to provide a justification for not adhering to the principles and practices of good corporate governance. The Report prefers the terminology used in the Netherlands where the term 'apply or explain' is used (cf. IoD. 2009:7). This implies that boards of directors are to apply the principles and practices of good governance recommended by the Report to the company, but in cases where a board might judge that it is not in the best interest of a company to adhere to a recommended principle or practice, the board should provide an adequate explanation for deviating from the recommended standard. The Report motivates this choice for a voluntary approach on the ground that a too strong focus on compliance can undermine the main objective of the board, namely, improving the performance of the company.

With regard to the distinction between shareholder and stakeholder approaches to corporate governance, the Report positions itself within the tradition of its two predecessor reports, i.e., within the *inclusive (or stakeholder)* approach. The Report makes in clear that the first duty of directors is always to act in the best interest of the company. But, acting in the best interest of the company, implies that the board should take account of the legitimate expectations of stakeholders. Stakeholders are defined as 'any group that can affect the company's operations, or be affected by the company's operations' (IoD, 2009:100). It is clear that there is no dichotomy between shareholder and stakeholder interests in the Report. It is rather believed that stakeholder and shareholder interests tend to coincide in the long run.

The ethics of governance

It is stated explicitly that the Third King Report rests on a foundation of ethics:

> *Ethics (integrity and responsibility) is the foundation of and reason for corporate governance. The ethics of governance requires the board to ensure that the company is run ethically. As this is achieved, the company earns the necessary approval – its licence to operate – from those affected by and affecting its operations. (IoD, 2009:21)*

All aspects of the Report, such as the role and responsibilities of the board, audit committees, risk management and internal audit should thus be regarded as manifestations of the intention of the company to conduct its affairs in an ethical manner.

The specific ethical values that underpin all aspects of corporate governance in the report can be expressed by the acronym RAFT, which stands for Responsibility, Accountability, Fairness and Transparency (see box). This acronym indicates that these four ethical values provide the basic platform that carries all principles and practices expressed in the report.

14   The ethics of corporate governance requires all deliberations, decisions and actions of the board and executive management to be based on the following *four ethical values* underpinning good corporate governance:

14.1   *Responsibility*: The board should assume responsibility for the assets and actions of the company and be willing to take corrective actions to keep the company on a strategic path, that is ethical and sustainable.

14.2   *Accountability*: The board should be able to justify its decisions and actions to shareholders and other stakeholders.

14.3   *Fairness*: The board should ensure that it gives fair consideration to the legitimate interests and expectations of all stakeholders of the company.

14.4   *Transparency*: The board should disclose information in a manner that enables stakeholders to make an informed analysis of the company's performance, and sustainability.

Extract from *King Report on Corporate Governance for South Africa 2009* (IoD, 2009:21)

Given the inclusive (or stakeholder) orientation of the Third King Report it is clear that the four basic ethical values captured in the acronym RAFT, should guide the company in its interaction with all it stakeholders. It is repeatedly stated in the Report that the board has an ethical obligation towards the company, shareholders and all other stakeholders. A number of concepts are being used in the report to give expression to this inclusive ethical obligation of the board. These concepts are: moral duties of directors, corporate citizenship and corporate sustainability.

With the notion of 'the moral duties of directors' the Report wishes to emphasise that the first obligation of directors is towards serving the best interest of the company. The duties of Conscience, Inclusivity, Competence, Commitment, and Courage (see box) articulates the manner in which directors should fulfil their role as members of the board.

15 As a steward of the company, each director should also discharge the following *five moral duties*:

15.1 *Conscience*: A director should act with intellectual honesty and independence of mind in the best interests of the company and all its stakeholders, in accordance with the inclusive stakeholder approach to corporate governance. Conflicts of interest should be avoided.

15.2 *Inclusivity* of stakeholders is essential to achieving sustainability and the legitimate interests and expectations of stakeholders must be taken into account in decision-making and strategy.

15.3 *Competence*: A director shoud have the knowledge and skills required for governing a company effectively. This competence should be continually developed.

15.4 *Commitment*: A director should be diligent in performing his duties and devote sufficient time to company affairs. Ensuring company performance and compliance requires unwavering dedication and appropriate effort.

15.5 *Courage*: A director shoud have the courage to take the risk associated with directing and controlling a successful, sustainable enterprise, and also the courage to act with integrity in all board decisions and activities.

Extract from *King Report on Corporate Governance for South Africa 2009* (IoD, 2009:21)

In using the term 'corporate citizenship' the Report wishes to emphasise specifically the ethical relationship of responsibility between a company and the society in which it operates. As responsible members of society, corporations have to ensure that they do not undermine, but instead protect and enhance their economic, social and natural environment. This implies that companies have to play their part in promoting human rights, social and human capital, safety, health as well as in curbing climate change and the depletion of non-renewable natural resources.

The very central use of the term 'sustainability' in the Third King Report signifies the responsibility of companies to ensure that they conduct their core business in a manner that would not jeopardise the economic, social and environmental wellbeing of the community and the planet. By insisting that companies should integrate sustainability concerns in their core business strategy and business operations and by further emphasising that companies should actively manage their sustainability performance and also report on it, the Report indicates that sustainability is no longer a 'nice to have' but a core responsibility that should be shouldered by all companies.

The governance of ethics

In addition to the ethical foundation that underpins the King III report, the Report also explicitly addresses the responsibility of the board of directors to ensure that the company internally adheres to its ethical values and acts in a responsible manner towards society and the environment. The board is thus called upon to ensure that the ethics of the company is actively governed.

This process of directing and controlling the ethics of a company starts with the board of directors. The board has to set the ethical tone in the company by providing visible ethical leadership. The Report singles out the chairperson of the board and requires him/her to set 'the ethical tone for the board and the company' (IoD, 2009:32). Also with regard to the CEO the Report requires the board to appoint a person that is 'setting the tone in providing ethical leadership and creating an ethical environment (IoD, 2009:37). The board as a whole shares the responsibility to set the ethical values that should guide the company and to build and sustain 'an ethical corporate culture in the company' (IoD, 2009:24). The ethical culture of the company should permeate every dimension of the company including its vision, objectives and operations.

Although the cultivation and maintenance of an ethical culture starts with the tone and standards set by the board, it also requires a process of managing the ethics performance of the company. According to the Report such an ethics management process consists of the following four aspects (cf. IoD, 2009:25–26):

1   *Determining the ethics risk and opportunity profile of the company*
    As part of normal risk management, both the internal ethics risks
    and the ethics risks associated with the company's interaction with its
    external social and natural environment should be assessed. Through
    a process of engaging with its internal and external stakeholders, the
    company needs to identify the ethical dangers that should be avoided
    and ethical opportunities that should be embraced.

2   *Code of conduct*
    The ethical standards that are needed to guide the company in its in-
    ternal operations as well as in its interaction with its contractual and
    non-contractual external stakeholders need to be formalised in a code
    of ethics.

3   *Integrating ethics*
    The code of ethics has to be institutionalised in the company. It should
    be translated into structures, processes, practices and actions. And all
    of these should be effectively monitored and managed to ensure that
    the board and the company adheres to its ethical values and standards

– both in its internal operations and in its interaction with society and the environment. In this regard the internal audit function has a special responsibility to provide assurance to the board that the ethics management of the company is intact.

4   *Ethics performance reporting and disclosure*
    The final aspect of the ethics management process is that the company needs to report on its ethics performance as part of its sustainability reporting. All the criteria that apply to sustainability reporting thus also apply to ethics reporting. In this regard King III advocates the formalisation of sustainability reporting in accordance with international best practice standards and also recommends that sustainability reports should be subjected to independent external verification and assurance.

Conclusion

In the next five chapters the cultivation of an ethical culture as well as each of the above four aspects of an ethics management process will be discussed in more depth and detail.

CHAPTER
17

Determining ethics risk

This chapter and the four chapters that follow demonstrate that business ethics encompasses more than ethical dilemmas and business ethics case studies, and the decision-making philosophies and heuristics to solve the dilemmas and analyse the cases.

These chapters will show that ethics *can* in fact be managed in organisations. They further illustrate that it cannot merely be assumed that employees enter an organisation with their own unique sets of ethics without an organisation being able to do much about changing or influencing the ethical beliefs and behaviours of employees. The management of ethics is about addressing the ethics of the barrel, as well as the ethics of its apples.

Organisations that decide to govern their ethics have to do so in a planned and structured way. The focus of this chapter is directed at determining ethics risk, or ethics risk assessment – the first step in the process of ethics management as outlined in the previous chapter. The nature of ethics risk and the processes that organisations could employ to anticipate and mitigate such risk are discussed.

Risk management

Risk in general can be defined as conditions or behaviours that can affect a company either beneficially or detrimentally. According to Garratt the concept risk found its way into the English language via the Italian word *riscare*, which means 'to dare' (2003:194). He claims that risk 'concerns the real, or possible, events that reduce the likelihood of reaching business goals, and increases the probability of losses' (Garratt 2003:194).

That boards of directors have an obligation to direct and control the risk of companies is beyond dispute. In fact, most larger organisations have separate functions that deal exclusively with risk management. In the UK, the *Turnbull Report* recommends that directors not only consider what the significant risks are that face their companies, but also ensure that there are effective mechanisms for identifying and managing risks (Garratt 2003:195). Similarly in South Africa the *King III Report on Corporate Governance* requires directors to take responsibility for the governance of risk (IoD, 2009).

Organisational risks are often categorised by their nature or source, the most common being business and financial risk (Van der Watt, 2003). Business risks are those that pertain to competition, efficiency of production factors, demand/supply issues and economic factors. Financial risks include risks related to credit, foreign exchange, interest rate, cash flow, gearing and liquidity. An increasing number of organisations use operational risk to define their business risk (Van der Watt, 2003). Typical operational risks are reputational, compliance, sustainability, corporate social investment, employment equity, human capital and ethics risk.

Ethics risk

Boards' responsibilities with regard to risk have expanded significantly with the shift from the singular (financial) bottom-line reporting to triple bottom-line reporting. Triple bottom-line reporting requires boards to report on organisations' economic, social and environmental vision and performance. Part of this process of reporting is that boards should report not only to their shareholders, but also to other stakeholders on what they perceive to be the most significant risks in each of these three areas. They also have to report on the strategies they have adopted for dealing with these respective risks.

Where boards traditionally only dealt with financial and business risks, they are now expected to deal with a much broader set of risks, which are sometimes referred to as sustainability risks. Although there is growing clarity internationally that boards should take responsibility for a wider set of risks than they used to do, this awareness is not complemented with similar clarity on how boards should go about executing this broader responsibility. This also applies to ethics risk. Ethics risk is an integral part of the second bottom line of reporting, viz. social reporting.

Three dimensions of social reporting can be distinguished, namely internal social reporting, external social reporting and ethics reporting. Internal social reporting refers to how companies deal with social issues such as safety, health and human capital, external social reporting refers to how the company deals with external social issues such as corporate social responsibility (CSR), corporate social investment (CSI) and social transformation, whilst ethics reporting focuses on the ethics performance of a business, which is sometimes also referred to as organisational integrity. Reporting on ethics (integrity) as a component of triple bottom-line reporting is illustrated in Figure 17.1.

Figure 17.1: Ethics as a component of triple bottom-line reporting

For an organisation to comprehensively report on its ethics performance, it needs to demonstrate through internal and external reporting actions that it has adequately assessed its ethics risk. It then needs to indicate how the ethics risk as identified will be accounted for. At a minimum level, business ethics requires that one should avoid harming the interests of others within the context of a competitive market economy. Accounting for ethics risk then requires that an organisation should estimate the ethical implications of its actions for all its stakeholders (the 'other'). At an optimum level business ethics requires that one's actions should not only benefit oneself, but also those who are affected by one's actions. Accounting for ethics risk then becomes a reflection on how an organisation has not only prevented harm to others, but also how it balances its own interests with the interests of those who are affected by its actions. Reporting on ethics performance signals to stakeholders that the organisation respects the legitimate ethical expectations of stakeholders and intends to do something about it.

If one revisits Garratt's (2003:194) definition of risk, namely that risk 'concerns the real, or possible, events that reduce the likelihood of reaching business goals, and increases the probability of losses', it is clear that this view of risk is unduly negative in that risk needs not be associated with losses only. On the contrary, risk is often associated with gain. The belief that risk-taking is rewarded with financial gain is at the very heart of entrepreneurship and capitalism. Managing corporate risk consequently entails mitigating or avoiding those conditions or behaviours that can affect companies detrimentally whilst embracing those that can benefit the company. King III recommends that an organisation's board should continually monitor risk (IoD, 2009). It further suggests that risk be comprehensively assessed on an annual basis, and that accountable methodologies be used for this purpose.

What applies to risk in general also applies to ethics risk. *Ethics risk can be defined as potentially detrimental or beneficial outcomes caused by unethical or ethical conditions or behaviours respectively.* A board's willingness to concern itself with ethics risk depends largely on its understanding of the benefits and dangers of (un)ethical practices and behaviours (Schwartz & Gibb, 1999:178).

The natural undertone associated with the notion of ethics risk is negative in nature. This means that a natural default approach to ethics risk requires organisations to ask the following question: 'What can go wrong ethically?' Phrased differently, the question could be posed as 'What could affect our stakeholders' trust, or even worse, alienate our stakeholders?' Ethics risks that would emanate from such an approach are negative in nature, and could include bribery, corruption, fraud, discrimination, nepotism, harassment, disrespectful treatment, conflict of interest, and the like. Such an ethics-as-threat approach could result in a knee-jerk reaction to stomp out unethical behaviour and adopt approaches based on fear of scandal and characterised by an abundance of rules to prevent unethical behaviour. Should ethics risk be viewed in such a light only, an organisation may act ethically and enforce ethical behaviour, not because it wants to or because it is the right thing to do, but because it is forced to do so due to externally motivated forces.

There is clearly more to ethics risk than the negative connotation ascribed above. Ethics risks may also present organisations with opportunities to embrace the benefits that may be gleaned from doing business ethically. The question 'What can go wrong ethically?' can then be rephrased to 'If we are ethical, what could we gain from it?' Or, 'What could we do to ensure continued stakeholder trust?' Such an approach may be labelled as positive ethics risk, or ethics-as-opportunity. Typical ethics-as-opportunity, or positive ethics risks, would be centred around sustained stakeholder trust and loyalty. Should ethics risk also be viewed from this vantage point, and not only from an ethics-as-threat perspective, it affords organisations the opportunity to adopt ethical practices, because it wants to, and because it is the right thing to do (cf. IoD, 2009:26). Thus, an internally driven motivation to be ethical.

The value of managing ethics risk

The governance of ethics risk starts with an adequate understanding of the dangers and benefits of ethics performance or the lack thereof for companies (Moon & Bonny, 2001:33). The ways in which unethical behaviour or ethical behaviour can harm or enhance a company's reputation, and the contribution a thorough understanding of ethics risk could make to the proper governance of ethics, are discussed next.

Ethics risk and reputation

The effective management of ethics risk enhances an organisation's potential to be regarded as a responsible corporate citizen. King III defines good corporate citizenship as the 'establishment of an ethical relationship of responsibility between the company and the society in which it operates' (IoD, 2009:52). Fombrun (in Carroll & Buchholtz, 2006) suggests that corporate citizenship consists of shared ethical principles between an organisation and its stakeholders, and as a type of enlightened self-interest that balances organisational and stakeholders' needs. Although businesses are economic institutions, they remain corporate citizens that have to balance economic, social and environmental value (IoD, 2009:23). Properly assessing ethics risk, in the context of holistic risk management imperatives, may facilitate an organisation's status as a responsible corporate citizen.

As a good corporate citizen an organisation may gain a reputation that attracts ethically-minded stakeholders to interact with the organisation and that repels dubious stakeholders. Corporate reputations determine whether investors, consumers, potential employees, suppliers and governments will trust companies sufficiently to pledge their sustained allegiances to these organisations. It is, for instance, doubtful whether investors, be they large institutional or individual ones, will invest their clients' or own funds in entities with questionable reputations. By the same token, if organisations have reputations for large internal losses due to fraud, investors may frown upon these organisations' ability to pre-empt and curb this kind of unethical behaviour. Examples of the extent to which ethics risk in the form of threats (negative risk) and opportunity (positive risk) may enhance or detrimentally affect an organisation's reputation in relation to a number of key stakeholders are presented in Table 17.1 below.

Table 17.1 Ethics risk and reputation

Dimension	Poor reputation (a lack of ethics)	Good reputation (a reputation for ethics)
Investor confidence	Deters potential institutional and individual investors.	Attracts investors concerned with good governance and ethics (reflects sustainability).
Supplier loyalty	Scares off suppliers with integrity. May attract suppliers that have questionable ethics themselves.	Ensures alignment with suppliers that are equally ethically aware.
Consumers	Scares off discerning consumers. Enhances potentially fickle consumer choices.	Inspires consumer confidence. May ensure loyalty even in the face of the occasional mistake.
Employees	Deters potentially talented employees from applying. Gives current employees the impression that they can get away with unethical conduct. May result in high employee turnover.	Attracts the best talent. Gets the organisations onto employers-of-choice lists. Enhances loyalty of employees.
Governmental concerns	May result in a lack of government support, subsidies. May lead to over-regulation of industries.	Receives governmental support through easy and difficult times.
Community	A lack of trust in the business. Views organisational actions in the community with suspicion. Lack of support for initiatives.	Creates trust in the organisation. Mobilises forces at its disposal to support organisational programmes in the community.

Other benefits of ethics risk assessment

Once an organisation is cognisant of the types and magnitude of ethics threats and opportunities it faces, it could utilise this information to formulate ethics management strategies, create ethics management structures, develop ethics standards, and design ethics management systems.

An ethics risk assessment provides an organisation with a broad frame of reference within which a proper ethics management strategy can be formulated. The ethics risk assessment produces an ethics risk profile for an organisation, or its state-of-ethics (cf. IoD, 2009:26). The organisation can then position itself in relation to its current mode of managing ethics (see Chapter 5). The ethics risks, and the way in which these are currently being dealt with may give an organisation an indication as to whether the organisation is in one or more of the immoral, reactive, compliance, integrity or totally aligned modes. Different divisions or functional areas of an organisation may find themselves within different modes depending on the extent of the ethics risk the divisions or functions are exposed to and how well the risks are currently addressed. Once an organisation possesses this knowledge it is empowered to consolidate its ethics management efforts across the organisation, and choose the most appropriate mode of managing ethics henceforth.

A comprehensive ethics risk profile enables an organisation to evaluate the success of current ethics management systems to deal with unethical behaviour or promote ethical behaviour. In larger organisations this could trigger the appointment of ethics managers (officers), the establishment of an ethics committee and the restructuring and expansion of sections concerned with risk management, compliance, internal audit and human resource management. It could furthermore confirm line managers' responsibility for integrating ethics into the activities of their domains of supervision.

The most immediate and profound impact that results of an ethics risk assessment has on the management of ethics in an organisation comes in the form of ethical behaviour standards. Specific ethics risks can be accounted for by ensuring that they are adequately covered by the organisation's existing code of ethics and ethics policies that complement the code. Should the organisation not have a code of ethics or related policies, the ethics risks could be utilised to develop such documents.

Once an organisation has a proper code of ethics and policies, these need to be implemented for maximum effect as part of a comprehensive ethics management process. The existence of ethics risks and their particular character and magnitude may inform the design of specific ethics management systems that may prevent negative risks from surfacing. In addition to this, a focus on ethics opportunities could be appropriately channelled. Ethics communication strategies could be designed, and ethics could be integrated into organisational development actions, staffing practices and training and development interventions.

In summary then, organisations do not only have to anticipate and mitigate the negative consequences of ethics risks they may incur (managing threats); they also need to position themselves to utilise their reputation for ethics as a vehicle for capitalising on the positive effects of ethics risk management (managing opportunities). The first step on the road to governing ethics is to find adequate means for identifying such risk.

Identification of ethics risk

The first part of this chapter essentially focused on the Why? context of ethics risk assessment. In this section the main issues in identifying ethics risk revolve around answering the Who? What? and How? questions. These questions are discussed in turn.

Role players responsible for the identification of ethics risk

Who should be responsible for determining the ethics risks of a company? It has already been indicated that the responsibility for ensuring the governing of ethics risk resides in the board of directors of an organisation. The board should thus ensure that ethics risk is assessed, managed and reported on.

The process of ethics risk identification is typically delegated to a board sub-committee (for example an ethics or sustainability committee). This committee consists of a cross-functional group of experts that are well-versed in the intricacies of governance and ethics in the organisation. Such a committee would typically consist of functionaries from the following departments in the organisation: legal and compliance division; risk management; internal audit; corporate social responsibility; corporate communications; the company secretariat; and human resource management and employment relations. In addition to these representatives, the organisational ethics manager (officer), if such a position exists in the organisation, is usually a key member of such a committee, as well as being the coordinator of the ethics risk identification process. (The roles of the various role players and their responsibilities are discussed in detail in Chapter 19).

Types of ethics risk to be identified

What are the possible ethics risks a company could face? Risk resides in conditions or behaviours. Both the conditions and the behaviours can be internal or external to the company (as indicated in Table 17.2).

Table 17.2 Sources of ethics risk

	Internal	External
Conditions		
Behaviours		

Conditions give rise to risk when they either enhance or hinder ethical behaviour. External conditions that can have the same dual effect includes the laws and regulations within which a company have to operate, the levels of corruption in the society, industry and perhaps even the organisation, crime and poverty in society and, cultural preferences and sensitivities, etc. There are various internal conditions that may promote or prevent ethical behaviour. Amongst these count existing culture, policies, systems and procedures or the lack thereof. An organisation with a bottom-line driven culture and where there is no code of ethics will be, for instance, more prone to the risk of unethical behaviour. Other internal conditions that may give rise to risk are an overemphasis on strategic or work values, low levels of ethics awareness in the organisation and low levels of trust.

Behaviour both internal and external to the organisation can pose ethics risk. Examples of behaviours external to the organisation that can cause embarrassment to the company are suppliers that engage in unethical behaviour, such as child labour, or the use of agents that may bribe government officials in foreign countries to secure trading licences. Alternatively, suppliers may conduct themselves in such exemplary ways that the company would prefer to associate with them rather than other potential suppliers. The same applies to internal behaviours that may cause ethics risk. Typical risk laden behaviours are bottom-line driven leader behaviour that negates an ethics dimension in the organisation, amoral decision-making, inconsistent application of policies and rules, rewarding unethical behaviour, ridiculing ethics talk, underplaying legitimate stakeholder expectations, hypocrisy, retaining or protecting bad apples, inadequate application of disciplinary procedures, and leader role-modelling marked by arrogance, lack of empathy and disrespect.

Approaches to identifying ethics risk

In answering the 'how' question, there are essentially two broad approaches to the identification of ethics risk, namely a unilateral approach or a multilateral approach. When ethics risk is identified unilaterally, a person or delegated function identifies ethics risk without engaging with other internal or external stakeholders. The obvious disadvantage of a unilateral approach is that risk identification is restricted to the perspectives of the person or delegated function within the company responsible for identifying such risk. The perceptions that other internal stakeholders and external stakeholders have of the ethics of the company are thus excluded by a unilateral approach to risk identification.

It is exactly for this reason that a multilateral approach is regarded as best practice when it comes to ethics risk identification (Driscoll & Hoffman 2000:46). It is through a process of stakeholder engagement that the perceptions that stakeholders have of the ethics of the company are gauged.

Stakeholder engagement

A multilateral approach to stakeholder engagement requires that the organisation's stakeholders give their opinion of (a) the organisation's past ethics performance (ethics history or track record), and (b) expectations they have regarding the organisation's future ethical orientation and performance. It is considered good practice that an organisation involves its stakeholders in a consultative and participative manner as part of its ethics management process. Doing it in this way ensures that the organisation does not impose its own ethics or set of ethical values, rules and guidelines on others. Once an organisation has obtained meaningful and useful information regarding these ethics expectations, it has to develop strategies and systems to avoid ethics risks and capitalise on ethics opportunities to enhance the organisation's reputation over time (see Chapter 19). Thereafter it has to monitor, audit and regularly report to the stakeholders on the progress that has been made on ethics performance (see Chapter 20).

Stakeholder engagement is a process and not merely an event. It is a proactive approach of entering into meaningful and constructive dialogue on ethical issues that are important to both the organisation and those that it affects or those that affect the organisation. Stakeholder engagement should therefore be part of the environmental scanning process that is a crucial component of the organisation's overall strategic planning effort. A comprehensive stakeholder engagement strategy consists of three relatively distinct phases: stakeholder identification, planning for stakeholder interaction and implementation. Each of these phases can be subdivided into a number of sub-processes. A stakeholder engagement strategy as formulated by Mwangi (2004) is depicted in Figure 17.2.

Stakeholder identification

The first phase shown in Figure 17.2 entails stakeholder definition and identification. Stakeholder *definition* requires of organisations to be very specific on what they mean by 'stakeholder'. Freeman (1984) originally defined stakeholders as those groups or individuals who can affect the company or who are affected by the company.

The second component of the first phase of stakeholder engagement involves *stakeholder identification*. Each organisation has its own relatively unique set of stakeholders whose ethical expectations have to be gauged and satisfied. Organisations have to identify their specific stakeholders that could be internal (employees) and external stakeholders (e.g. shareholders, labour

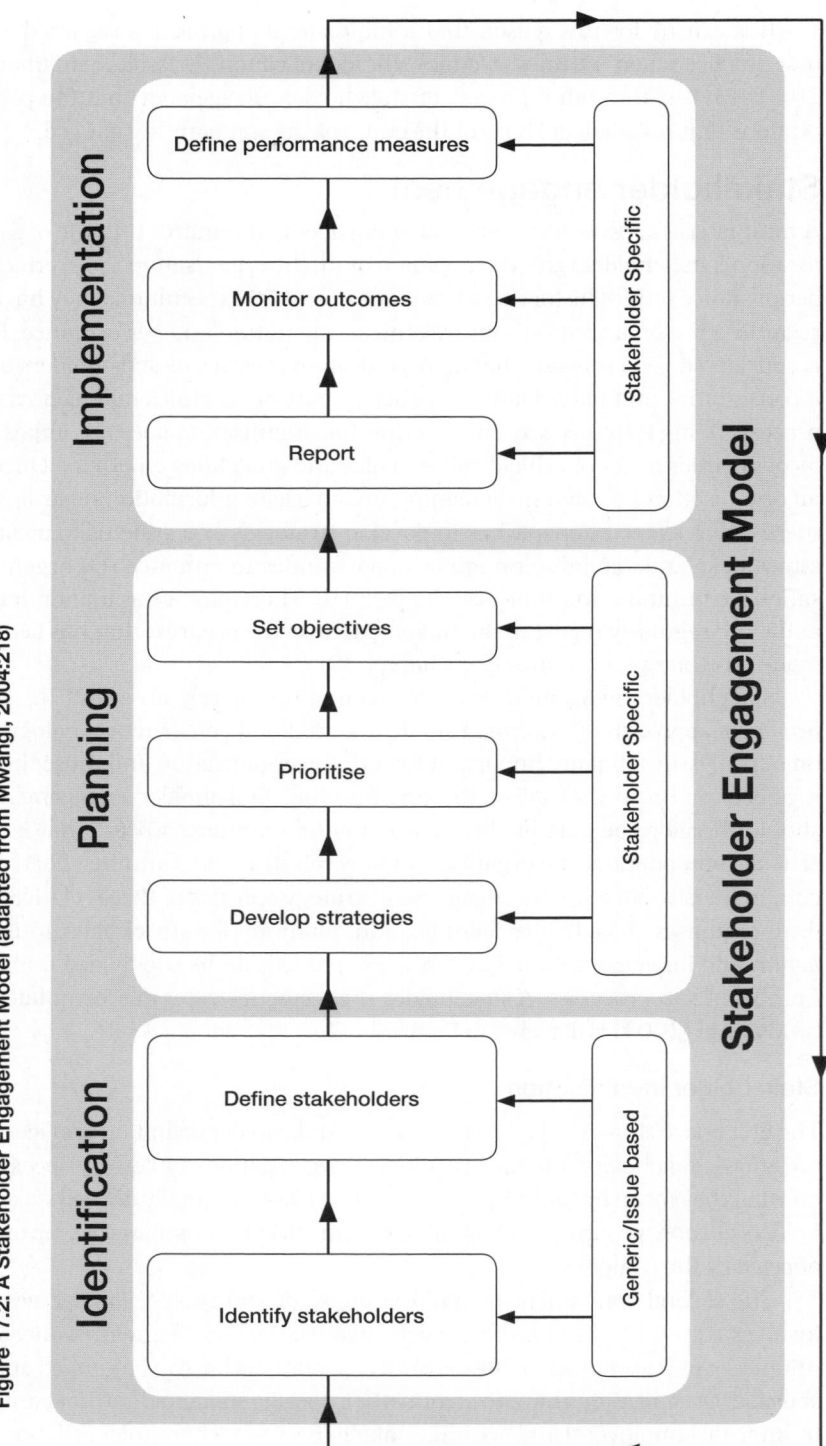

Figure 17.2: A Stakeholder Engagement Model (adapted from Mwangi, 2004:218)

unions, employer federations, consumers, the community, suppliers, NGOs, local and national government organisations, special interest and activist groups, professional organisations, and competitors). A useful approach for stakeholder identification is to design a stakeholder map to identify which stakeholders could have a stake in the ethical practices of the organisation.

Stakeholder *prioritisation* is the next logical process as part of stakeholder identification. Stakeholders can be prioritised in terms of the power (ethical, legal, voting, technological, ecological, political, etc.) that they have (see Weiss, 2003). The organisation has to determine the extent to which its ethics (ethical and potentially unethical behaviour) can influence particular stakeholders, as well as the extent to which stakeholders have legitimate ethical expectations regarding the organisation's activities; i.e. stakeholders are prioritised in terms of the ethical impact they may have on the company as well as the ethical impact that the company may have on them.

Planning stakeholder interaction

The second phase of stakeholder engagement is the *planning for stakeholder interaction* phase. The first task of this phase is the formulation of objectives. This consists of determining what the organisation actually wants to achieve with its process of stakeholder engagement. An objective such as 'To actively engage with stakeholder X on a quarterly basis to determine their perception of the organisation's ethical transformation programme' would, for example, be more conducive to a structured and planned engagement effort. The second task is to prioritise the objectives in order to ensure that energy is focused on determining material ethics risks, i.e. those that can singly or collectively endanger or enhance the organisation's reputation for ethics.

The third task of the planning for stakeholder interaction phase is the formulation of a stakeholder engagement *strategy (or strategies)*. Here one can distinguish between general strategies directed at all stakeholders and specific strategies directed at specific stakeholders.

Who will do the work and what will it cost? An important implication of strategy development, as a key step of the *planning for stakeholder interaction* phase (prior to implementation), is the allocation of human and financial resources required to implement the stakeholder engagement and communication strategies within pre-determined time frames.

Implementation

The third phase of the stakeholder engagement process is that of *implementation*. During this phase the stakeholder engagement strategies formulated in the previous phase are implemented within the constraints of the pre-determined costs and within set time frames. As a first task, performance measures need to be designed in order to answer the following questions:

How will we know that we are receiving the right amount and type of information? How do we know that we have optimally identified potential ethics risk? Implementation would consist of utilising communication channels to convey information to all or selected stakeholders and to elicit information from these stakeholders. Information received in this way needs to be analysed and prioritised in order to determine ethics risks and their magnitude.

Monitoring of the outcomes, as a second task of the implementation phase refers to the process of assessing whether objectives set for each stakeholder have been met (Mwangi, 2004). Typical measures to monitor outcomes are surveys to determine stakeholder satisfaction regarding the analysis of information and expectations they supplied to the organisation, feedback received on the analysis and whether appropriate action was taken. Reporting, as a final task of the third phase, represents a culmination of the stakeholder engagement process in that progress on managing ethics risk is reported and disclosed to stakeholders identified.

Methods to obtain information on ethics risk

How can a company identify the conditions and behaviours that constitute its ethics risk? The process of risk identification is essentially a research process. As such it should comply with the accepted norms of research in terms of reliability and objectivity. A range of quantitative and qualitative instruments can be used to determine the perspectives of internal and external stakeholders.

The organisation has to decide which method or combination of methods will be used to identify ethics risk. The choice of methods will largely be determined by the following factors:

- How serious the organisation is about doing something about ethics
- The commitment, time and resources available to identify risk
- The size of the organisation
- The diverse nature of the organisation's people, products, processes and markets
- The number of priority stakeholders that have to be polled
- The complexity of the stakeholders' expectations
- The potential sensitivity of information that may be obtained.

The methods selected for the purpose of this discussion are personal interviews, focus groups, questionnaires, document analyses, benchmarking and appreciative inquiry. These five methods are discussed in turn.

Personal interviews

By utilising one-on-one interviews with key internal members of the organisation, as well as key external stakeholders, organisations can obtain expert opinions on the organisation's state-of-ethics. Typical candidates internal to the organisation to be approached for the purpose of personal interviews are major shareholders, members of the Board, the CEO, the Chief Financial Officer, the Company Secretary, the Head of Internal Audit, the Head of the Legal and Compliance Department, the Head of HR and certain key line managers. Externally one would focus on representatives of (1) the main trade unions that represent the organisation's employees, (2) key suppliers, (3) activist groups (e.g. consumer organisations), (4) local government, (5) current and potential investors, etc.

The type of interview that works best for this type of risk identification is a semi-structured interview. This entails four or five key questions. Besides adherence to the generic protocols for preparing for the interview and conducting it, the following sample questions are useful to elicit information on ethics risk:

- What is the organisation's ethical reputation?
- What are examples of unethical behaviour that members of this organisation are prone to?
- What are examples of unethical behaviour that people employed in this industry are prone to?
- What behaviour have you witnessed that you would describe as unethical?
- How is unethical behaviour dealt with?
- Who are the ethical role models in the organisation? Why?
- How can ethics be used to get the best out of people?
- How can ethics be used to enhance the organisation's reputation?
- What ethical values are required to accomplish this?
- What ethical guidelines are required by the company to protect internal and external stakeholders?
- What does the organisation need to do to build an ethical reputation?
- How should ethics be managed in the organisation?

Questionnaires

Advantages of using this type of survey to gather information on ethics risk are that (1) the respondents may remain anonymous, and may therefore be inclined to release sensitive information, (2) results may be statistically compared to indicate significant differences between stakeholder groups, and (3) data can usually be illustrated graphically with relative ease. Major disadvantages of using this technique are that (a) the results can be easily manipulated by respondents, (b) people are often subjected to complete questionnaires for all different kinds of surveys – they may therefore be reluctant to complete 'just another survey', or they may not take it seriously, and (c) response rates for the return of voluntary questionnaires are notoriously low – response rates for compulsory questionnaires are obviously higher, but there is doubt as to whether stakeholders (e.g. employees) that are forced to complete questionnaires will do so objectively.

The questions that served as examples for use in the personal interview can be effectively utilised in the qualitative component of a questionnaire. Examples of questionnaire items that can be subjected to quantitative analyses are provided in Table 17.3.

Table 17.3 Examples of questionnaire items

	On a scale of 1 to 6 where 1 indicates total agreement and 6 total disagreement, please indicate the extent to which ...						
1.	You consciously think about ethics and ethical consequences when performing your job.	1	2	3	4	5	6
2.	You feel equipped to deal with ethical issues.	1	2	3	4	5	6
3.	There is a general awareness of ethics in the organisation?	1	2	3	4	5	6
4.	The CEO is committed to ethics.	1	2	3	4	5	6
5.	The Board is committed to ethics.	1	2	3	4	5	6
6.	Managers are committed to ethics.	1	2	3	4	5	6
7.	Ethical role-models (people you can look up to), are present in the organisation.	1	2	3	4	5	6
8.	People actually TALK about ethics in the organisation.	1	2	3	4	5	6
9.	Ethical behaviour is encouraged.	1	2	3	4	5	6
10.	The climate (atmosphere) in the organisation makes it easy to make ethical decisions.	1	2	3	4	5	6
11.	Opportunities for unethical behaviour exist.	1	2	3	4	5	6

Should organisations wish to obtain information of specific types of unethical behaviour, it could use a format that requires respondents to indicate the extent to which specific unethical behaviours actually occur in the organisation. Thereafter responses on the extent to which each of these behaviours is dealt with, and the existence of policies that may assist in preventing such behaviours or in dealing with them when they do occur, may be elicited.

Focus groups

This method of information gathering is useful when many stakeholders are to be surveyed, when questionnaires alone do not produce sufficient information, when the response rate for questionnaires is inadequate for meaningful analysis, or when qualitative data is of the essence. Focus groups usually consist of fairly homogenous representatives of a stakeholder group, e.g. a group of line managers that are at more or less similar levels in the organisation or a group of consumers that have the same product safety concerns. A focus group session is normally conducted by a trained and experienced facilitator. Some organisations even opt to make use of external facilitators to enhance objectivity. The duration of such a session usually does not exceed one hour. The questions that the facilitator may use to give some structure to proceedings are similar to those that can be used for personal interviews.

Document analyses

There are usually several documents used in organisations that have a bearing on the organisation's ethics and the organisation's engagement with stakeholders. Examples of such documents are existing codes of ethics, industry standards, legislation that addresses specific ethical concerns (e.g. human rights), annual reports, policies (e.g. employment equity, sexual harassment, psychometric testing, whistle-blowing), and minutes of meetings. Organisations can also analyse information captured through existing management systems. These include the content of and decisions made during disciplinary hearings, the number and nature of customer complaints, the number and types of queries received by the ethics helpdesk, and the number and types of reports generated by the safe reporting (whistle-blowing) facility.

Benchmarking

Through domestic and global benchmarking a company can also determine how competitors perceive their ethics risks. Although some of this information may be difficult to obtain, organisational websites and annual reports usually contain useful information that already exists in the public domain. This information can then be used to compare ethics risks and ethics management practices. Most listed companies' codes of ethics are also available on their websites.

Appreciative inquiry

A particularly useful intervention that could be utilised to identify organisations' ethics opportunities is that of appreciative inquiry (AI). Originating from an organisational development approach, it could be used as an alternative approach for developing a shared meaning of ethics, or a vision for ethics, within an organisation (Van Vuuren & Crous, 2005). An AI intervention entails a facilitated group discussion with a selected group of organisational members that have a desire to embrace ethics as an opportunity for the organisation. The group would usually consist of the executive directors, senior management and the organisation's ethics committee. The premise of AI is that it moves beyond viewing organisational ethics as a problem to be solved, to embracing ethics as an opportunity (Van Vuuren & Crous, 2005). The structured group discussion results in an ethics vision, ethical values and a strategy to fuse ethics with all organisational activities. It is a particularly useful risk assessment heuristic for organisations and professions that have made a decision to proactively build an ethical culture, rather than reacting to external pressure to be ethically compliant.

Ethics risk profile

After the methods have been applied, the information has to be collated, coded, integrated, analysed and, where appropriate, also subjected to statistical analyses. Reports on findings then have to be generated and presented, together with recommendations, to the board and other relevant parties. Findings also have to be presented to other stakeholders for comment and to elicit recommendations for adjustments. These comments have to be integrated with the final report. In this way, a comprehensive organisational ethics risk profile is produced.

Many organisations opt to use external consultants that specialise in managing ethics to coordinate and execute the methods chosen for the identification of ethics risk. By following this route the objectivity of the findings may be enhanced and the credibility of follow-up ethics management projects boosted.

Once the ethics risks have been identified and prioritised, the process does not stop. A process of risk identification is likely to produce more ethics risks than a company can afford to manage. It is exactly at this point where the board needs to determine what the most significant risks are. Indeed, some serious decisions have to be taken on the implementation of measures to avoid ethics risks that are threatening, and to embrace ethics risks that are regarded as opportunities. The natural next step in the process of managing ethics would be to capture the ethics risks in a meaningful code of ethics. This process is discussed in the next chapter.

Case study: CITICOM

CITICOM[1] is a company that specialises in providing a full range of IT services for small and medium businesses. Since it was founded in 1989 it has experienced tremendous growth. It currently employs approximately 400 full-time employees, as well as 110 sales personnel that are employed on a contract basis. The full-time employees consist of network engineers and software engineers and technicians, system building technicians, maintenance operators, call centre personnel, as well as sales coordinators and administrative personnel. On par with rest of the IT industry, CITICOM has an annual staff turnover of 22% on average. CITICOM has offices in seven locations across the country. It has a client basis of 4 500 businesses. This figure is increasing by 10% per year.

1 Fictional company - no reference to any existing company.

Rolf Brundin is the founder and CEO of CITICOM. Although some-what autocratic, he is an extremely innovative and astute business-man. He has a better reputation outside the company than he has within CITICOM's ranks. Since the company is by and large bottom-line driven, the staff work very long hours. The company does not cater for overtime pay, but pays market related salaries with good annual bonuses. Some describe working for the company as an all-consuming experience. The design and manufacturing staff are conti-nuously in conflict with those responsible for sales. The reason for this is that the sales personnel regularly sell more systems and procure more maintenance deals than the other departments can provide. Complaints by customers to the call centre have included allegations of bribery and non-delivery on promises. The sales department is considered to be the CEO's favourite department.

Since corporate governance requirements in the country expect compa-nies to have a written code of ethics the company drafted a code of ethics that was distributed to all employees at the time. Since then the code has merely been in existence, but rarely used. The company is considering listing on the Securities Exchange within the next 18 months. The newly appointed internal auditor has realised that the company needs to report on ethics in its annual report. He sent out a questionnaire to all employees to determine the nature of ethical issues they have to face in their day-to-day activities. Only 45 questionnaires were returned to his office. He is extremely frustrated because Rolf Brundin has asked him to draw up a new code of ethics for the Board's approval. The next Board meeting takes place in three weeks time.

1   Why do you think the internal auditor is frustrated?
2   Do you think the company faces ethics risks? If so, what are they?
3   What has the company done correctly insofar as managing ethics is concerned?
4   Describe the stakeholder engagement process followed by the company?
5   What additional steps would you recommend?

Conclusion

An ethics risk assessment is an important first step in managing ethics in an organisation. The aim of the risk assessment is to gauge an organisation's mode of managing ethics and to produce an ethics risk profile. The fact that multiple stakeholders' opinions are sought when ethics risk is assessed by means of multiple methods makes it an objective starting point for organisational ethics management. Since it is not only ethics threats that are assessed in a risk analysis, but also ethics opportunities, the process not only facilitates the building of an ethical reputation, but also informs further ethics management phases. It should also be noted that an ethics risk assessment is already an ethics management intervention in the sense that it creates an immediate awareness of ethics, opens avenues for debate on ethics issues and dilemmas, facilitates ethics talk, and creates stakeholder expectations regarding future organisational ethical behaviour.

The ethics risk profile informs the next phase of the ethics management process, which is the codification of ethical standards. Risk related information, which includes ethical threats as well as opportunities, provides the platform for developing a useful organisational code of ethics. It not only informs the code insofar as content is concerned, but also in terms of rationale, format, process and tone. Once a code has been developed, the organisation can actively institutionalise and manage its ethics. This all happens with a view to eventually report, and disclose ethics performance not only to shareholders, but to all relevant stakeholders.

CHAPTER
18

Codes of ethics

C odes of ethics have a long tradition. The Hippocratic Oath, which is still today widely associated with the medical profession, was drawn up more than two thousand years ago. Codes of ethics have traditionally been a distinguishing feature of the professions. Over the last thirty years codes of ethics have become part of business practice too. They have gained such prominence that they are now often mistakenly regarded as the sole mechanism for managing ethics in business.

Although there has been a sharp increase in the number of corporate codes of ethics around the world over the last three decades, the record of these codes for changing the behaviour of individuals and corporations remains ambiguous. Some studies did find empirical evidence that codes of ethics do influence corporate behaviour, but other studies failed to uncover such a link (cf. Moore, 2006:412; O'Dwyer & Madden, 2006:219). While one code of ethics might be a powerful instrument for guiding the behaviour of an organisation, another might be totally ineffectual and not worth the (glossy) paper it is printed on (cf. Sims & Brinkmann, 2003). To develop an effective code of ethics requires a special effort, which starts with the design of the code.

The purpose of this chapter is to discuss some of the most important considerations that need to be taken into consideration in designing or reviewing a code of ethics. The factors that will be discussed are the purpose of the code, the process of code development, the format of a code, the content of a code, and the tone of a code of ethics (cf. Rossouw, 1997b). Finally we will look at code implementation and limitations of codes of ethics. However, before we do this, we will first look into the reasons for the recent increase in the number of corporate codes of ethics and also determine what we mean by a 'code of ethics'.

The prominence of codes of ethics

The sharp incline in the number of corporate codes that has been witnessed in recent years can be attributed to a number of reasons. Three of the most prominent reasons for this increase are corporate governance reform, change in organisational structure, and the global impact of information and communication technology.

Corporate governance reform

The global wave of corporate governance reform over the last two decades (that was discussed in Chapter 16) contributed to the growth in the number of corporate codes of ethics. Since one of the reasons for this wave of corporate governance reform is the attempt to restore trust in business, the ethics of corporations became an important focal point in corporate governance reform. Special attention was devoted to the governance of corporate ethics, and codes of ethics are perceived to play a pivotal role in establishing and maintaining high standards of corporate ethics.

With the passing of the Sarbanes-Oxley Act in the USA in 2002, it became mandatory for listed companies to have a code of ethics that applies to their senior financial officers. Also in South Africa, the *First King Report on Corporate Governance of 1994* recommended that companies should have their own code of ethics. This recommendation was retained in, and elaborated upon in both the Second and Third King Reports. The Third King Report recommends that companies should have a code of ethics as an integral part of their ethics management programme. In this respect the Report recommends: 'The board should ensure that a company code of ethics is developed, stipulating the ethical values or standards as well as more specific guidelines guiding the company in its interaction with its internal and external stakeholders' (IoD, 2009:57).

It seems as if the recommendations of the King Reports with regard to codes of ethics have been taken seriously by listed companies in South Africa. A KPMG study (2006) on the sustainability reporting of companies listed on the JSE Securities Exchange in South Africa found that 70% of the 141 companies included in the survey, reported on their codes of ethics in 2006. This represents a substantial increase, since a previous survey done in 2004 found that more than 50% of company reports made no mention of a code of ethics (cf. KPMG, 2006:4). In a study done in 2008 by the Centre for Business and Professional Ethics at the University of Pretoria, it was found that 96% of companies on the Socially Responsible Investment (SRI) index of the JSE Securities Exchange had codes of ethics, while the figure for non-SRI companies listed on the JSE was 80% (cf. CBPE, 2008:15).

Organisational structure

In recent years there was a marked shift from hierarchical organisational structures to flatter organisational structures with project teams, adaptable networks, and flexible production and service schedules. Bureaucratic organisations with standard processes and procedures found it increasingly hard to cope with the needs and expectations of ever-changing markets.

Stability and rigidity has been replaced by an emphasis on flexibility and individual initiative (cf. Sennet, 1998:47).

This shift from hierarchical to flat networking organisations came at the price of losing central organisational control. Instead of demanding compliance with centrally issued directives, companies now have to rely to a much greater extent than before on the co-operation and responsibility of employees in multiple teams and networks. The solution to this problem, according to contemporary management theory, lies in shared values (cf. Weaver, 2006:341). When all members of an organisation can agree to a set of shared values, some form of control and focus can be restored. Control is no longer externally enforced, but is now driven by the voluntary commitment of individual members of the organisation. Commitment to a set of shared values and standards is expected to enhance the self-discipline and personal responsibility of organisational members. The prominence of corporate codes of ethics can partly be explained by the expectation that a code of ethics can be a mechanism for ensuring that all members of the workforce commit to adhering to the standards of behaviour articulated in a code of ethics.

Information and communication technology

The spectacular growth in information and communication technology (ICT) has speeded up, and eased up the flow of information dramatically. Easy and affordable access to ICT means that the impact of corporate activity on individuals, communities and the natural environment can be communicated around the globe with greater ease and lower cost than before. This new situation brought about by modern ICT, in combination with higher social and environmental expectations from corporate stake-holders, implies that corporations are now more in the public eye than ever before. Since corporate irresponsibility or negligence can be reported with ease by affected parties, corporate reputations are at greater risk than before. Consequently we have witnessed corporations becoming more sensitive to reputational risk.

In their effort to mitigate reputational risk, corporate codes of ethics have become a popular tool. Corporate codes of ethics have been adopted by companies in an effort to ensure that their operations comply with accepted standards of ethical behaviour. At the same time codes of ethics have also been adopted by companies to signal their ethical intent to stakeholders.

What is a code of ethics?

A code of ethics is a document or agreement that sets the standard for ethically acceptable behaviour in and by an organisation. It defines the ethical standards and/or guidelines that need to be respected by all members of an organisation in their decisions and actions (cf. Moore, 2006:411; Schwartz, 2001, 248; Weaver, 1993:45). A corporate code of ethics is thus a self-imposed standard for ethical behaviour that a corporation adopts. The reasons for adopting a code of ethics can vary considerably across companies. Weaver's reminder that we 'should not naively assume that firms invoke codes for morally proper reasons' (1993:53) remains relevant in this regard.

It is not only the reasons for adopting codes of ethics that vary significantly across organisations, but also the names that are used to refer to codes of ethics. There is no consistency to be found in how these terms, which are used to refer to codes of ethics, are applied in practice. Consequently we find an array of terms that are used to refer to codes of ethics, without being able to deduce any significant meaning from the term that is used to refer to a code of ethics. Some of the terms that are used to refer to codes of ethics are:

- corporate credo
- declaration of business principles
- value statement
- code of business practice
- standard of conduct
- guidelines for behaviour
- code of conduct

Extract from the Johnson & Johnson Credo

We are responsible to our employees,
the men and women who work with us throughout the world.
Everyone must be considered as an individual.
We must respect their dignity and recognize their merit.
They must have a sense of security in their jobs.
Compensation must be fair and adequate,
and working conditions clean, orderly and safe.
We must be mindful of ways to help our employees fulfil
their family responsibilities.
Employees must feel free to make suggestion and complaints.
There must be equal opportunities for employment, development
and advancement for those qualified.
We must provide competent management,
and their actions must be just and ethical.

Source: www.jnj.com/wps/wcm/connect/30e290804ae70eb4bc4afc0f0a50cff8/our-credo.pdf?MOD=AJPERES

In the section on the format of codes of ethics (that follows later in the chapter) a distinction will be drawn between aspirational and directional codes that can be used to make a distinction between different forms of codes. For now, we will turn to the five considerations that need to be taken into account when a code of ethics is being designed or reviewed.

The purpose of a code

The first decision that needs to be made in designing or revising a code of ethics, is to determine what purpose the code is to serve. Codes of ethics can serve a variety of purposes in an organisation. The variety of purposes that a code can serve can be divided into internal and external purposes. Internal purposes refer to objectives internal to the organisation, while external purposes relate to objectives that the organisation wishes to achieve with regard to its external stakeholders or social environment. We now discuss some of the most important internal and external purposes that a code can serve.

A code of ethics for internal purposes

A code of ethics can be designed to serve one or more of the following intra-organisational goals:

- To prevent unethical practices in the organisation by stipulating conduct or practices that are unacceptable in the organisation.
- To promote ethical responsibility by articulating ethical values and standards that all members of the organisation are expected to live up to.
- To provide guidance on dealing with and deciding on ethical issues that members of the organisation are likely to encounter.
- To foster a process of cultural change in an organisation by mobilising staff around core ethical values.
- To signal a change in leadership orientation.
- To boost the morale of an organisation and to communicate to staff that management rely on them and trust them.

A code of ethics for external purposes

A code of ethics can also be developed in an attempt to guide, satisfy or pacify external stakeholders of the organisation. In some instances codes of ethics are not intended for the staff of an organisation at all, but solely directed towards external stakeholders. In the case of a code of ethics for external purposes, the purpose of a code of ethics might be:

- to send a message to external stakeholders that the organisation can be trusted;
- to promote the reputation of the organisations amongst its external stakeholders;

◉ to pacify external stakeholders like special interest groups who might be concerned about specific organisational practices;

◉ to pre-empt regulation by external authorities by voluntary adopting standards that would satisfy their expectations;

◉ to set standards of behaviour that the company expects from its up-stream and down-stream value chain and industry peers;

◉ to comply with legal standards or to safeguard the company from potential litigation.

The list of internal and external purposes cited above is by no means exhaustive (cf. Moore, 2006:411; O'Dwyer & Madden, 2006:219; Weaver, 1993:46–47). The purpose of a code of ethics does not have to be restricted to any one purpose, but can consist of any combination of internal and/or external purposes. From the above list of possible purposes it should be clear that although one would expect a code of ethics to serve an ethical purpose, it is not always or necessarily the case.

The process of code development

A variety of processes can be used to develop or review a code of ethics. A key variable in distinguishing different processes that can be followed in code design is the extent of participation of internal and external stakeholders in the process of code development. A code that is developed with minimum participation by the stakeholders whom are most likely to be affected by the code, can be expected to be met with cynicism and scepticism, while a code that is the outcome of consultation with affected stakeholders is more likely to be accepted and appropriated. The appropriate level of participation in the process of code development will be determined by the purpose that the code of ethics is supposed to serve.

If the purpose of a code of ethics is, for example, to put an end to specific unethical behaviours and practices in a company, it would be sufficient to determine the executive management's expectations and formulate them into a set of directives. The process of code development will thus be geared towards articulating the behaviour and practices that management deem inappropriate for the organisation.

Should the purpose of a code of ethics be to instil trust among external stakeholders in the organisation, the process would have to be structured differently. It would have to involve some engagement with these stakeholders to gauge their expectations of the company. Should a code be intended to pre-empt regulation by external authorities, the process of code development will have to be structured in a way that will inform the company of the concerns of the relevant authority.

If the purpose of a code is to cultivate commitment to a set of shared values among members of an organisation, a consensus-seeking process of code development is required. This will call for extensive consultation with and participation by members of the organisation. Commitment to a common set of ethical values cannot be prescribed to an organisation. Members of the organisation need to be convinced of the ethical values before they will subscribe to them. The process of establishing a common set of values should therefore allow for personal identification with, and commitment to such values. If this is not allowed to happen, the chances are slim that the values articulated in a code of ethics will be appropriated by members of the organisation. The participative process of code development is thus vital to the ultimate success of the code. In the process of developing the code one is also already building support for the ethical values, standards or guidelines that will ultimately be written into it.

The format of the code

Codes of ethics come in a wide variety of formats. They range from short, concise, single page documents to lengthy elaborate documents. Drawing a distinction between aspirational and directional codes can help to make sense of the wide variety of shapes and sizes of codes of ethics. According to this distinction, codes of ethics can in terms of their format be placed somewhere on a spectrum that stretches from purely aspirational codes on the one extreme to purely directional codes on the opposite extreme. Although there are codes that can be classified as almost exclusively aspirational or exclusively directional, many companies opt for codes that display both aspirational and directional dimensions. The explanation for such a hybrid format can often be found in the fact that aspirational and directional codes each has their own benefits and limitations. We will now look at the nature, benefits and limitations of aspirational and directive codes respectively.

Aspirational codes

An aspirational code is usually a short document that spells out the ethical values, principles or standards that should guide an organisation in its interaction with its internal and external stakeholders. It is called aspirational, because it sets a standard of ethics that all members of an organisation are expected to live up to. In that sense it does not necessarily describe the ethical status quo of the organisation, but rather the ethical ideal towards which the organisation aspires.

There are several benefits associated with an aspirational code of ethics. They include the following:
- *Recallability*. It is a concise document and therefore easy to recall. Because it is easy to recall, it has the potential to become a living document that lives in the minds and hearts of people.

◉ *Discretion*. It does not spell out every ethical action or step that organisational members are expected to comply with, but instead provides a
general standard of ethical behaviour. Consequently the code communicates respect for the moral maturity of people and allows them the
discretion to apply the articulated ethical standards in their specific
work environment.

◉ *Inclusive*. As a general standard of ethics, it can be applied to all situations. Although it does not cover every single action or aspect of the
organisation it does provide ethical values, standards or principles that
can be applied to all manifestations of organisational life.

The limitations of an aspirational code are closely tied with its strengths.
The major drawbacks of aspirational codes are the following:

◉ *Vague*. The fact that it provides a general standard of ethics implies
that it does not provide specific guidance on what is expected from
organisational members in specific situations. It can therefore be experienced as too vague and general.

◉ *Enforcement*. Because the code does not go into the detail of specifying
every behaviour or practice that is ethically unacceptable, it is often
difficult to determine whether specific behaviours or organisational
practices amount to a breach of the code. This makes it difficult to
enforce the code, which in turn might undermine the credibility and
usefulness of the code.

Directional codes

Directional codes are sometimes called codes of conduct (or behaviour). A
directional code is a more extended document that provides specific guidelines about what is expected from members of an organisation in specific
circumstances. It has a definite directional purpose, as it spells out clearly
what persons should or should not do in specific situations.

A directional code has obvious strengths:

◉ *Specific*. It gives clear guidance or instruction as to how organisational
members should behave and leaves little room for misinterpretation.

◉ *Enforceable*. Since the code is very specific, it is easy to identify misbehaviour and thus to enforce the code.

◉ *Sanctions*. It can identify specific consequences or sanctions that will
follow on specific transgressions of the code.

The weaknesses of this format are:

◉ *Recallability*. Directional codes run the risk of becoming rather lengthy
in an attempt to cover all possible manifestations of unethical conduct.
When a code is too long, it becomes hard to remember all the directives
contained in the code.

◙ *Discretion.* Since the code is so specific, it carries the danger of undermining personal discretion and responsibility. This can easily cultivate a mentality of 'if is not forbidden, it is allowed'.

Given the above benefits and limitations of aspirational and directional codes, it often makes sense to design a code with both aspirational and directional elements. In such cases the code would contain both some general ethical values, principles or standards, but then also provide illustrative directives of what these ethical standards might mean in a number of circumstances, but without attempting to cover all possible scenarios that might occur in the organisation. The ultimate decision on whether a code should be aspirational, directional or a mix of these two formats will once more be determined by the purpose that the code should serve.

The content of the code

The decision on the format of the code will have a direct bearing on what content will be included in a code. Generally speaking the following categories of content can potentially be found in codes of ethics:

◙ rationale for the code
◙ ethical values, principles or standards
◙ guidelines for conduct
◙ guidelines for ethical decision-making
◙ sanctions
◙ references to resources

Rationale for the code

This is the justification for the existence of the code. It explains why the code has been developed and what purpose it is to serve in the organisation. The rationale of a code intends to persuade its readers of the importance of the code by explaining what the organisation and its members stands to benefit from adhering to the code.

Ethical values, principles or standards

These provide the norms which will guide and tailor organisational behaviour. The ethical values, principles or standards provide the ethical backbone of any code of ethics. When a code takes a purely aspirational format, it is not likely to go much beyond stating the core ethical values, principles or standards of the organisation. In a directional code the implications of these values and standards for organisational behaviour are likely to be spelt out in more specific guidelines for conduct.

Guidelines for conduct

These are more likely to be found in directional codes. They prescribe or prohibit specific actions or practices. The purpose of such guidelines is to specify what is ethically unacceptable in the organisation or to provide explicit directions about what is expected from organisational members in specific situations.

Guidelines for ethical decision-making

A code might also contain guidance on how to apply the values, principles or standards of ethics contained in the code in practice. It might, for example, propose a decision-making procedure that can be followed in cases where the code does not provide sufficient guidance on what needs to be done in a specific situation.

Sanctions

A code might also stipulate the consequences of transgressing the code. In the case of an aspirational code, sanctions are likely to be specified in a general way, while in directional codes specific sanctions for specific transgressions can be specified. A code might also specify what disciplinary procedures will be followed in cases of code contravention.

References to resources

Codes sometimes also refer their readers to specific supporting resources that can be called upon in implementing the code. These resources might be people who can provide advice on the meaning or implementation of the code such as an ethics helpline, or it might be a safe reporting mechanism (ethics hotline or so-called whistle-blowing line). Reference can also be made to other policies or documents that need to be consulted in addition to the code.

The decision on which combination of the above categories of content will be included in the code will depend on the earlier decisions that have been made on the purpose and format of the code. Directional codes are more likely to contain most, if not all, of the above categories of content, while aspirational codes are more likely to consist only of a rationale and ethical values, principles or standards.

The tone of the code

The underlying tone (spirit or mood) of a code is a very important aspect of code design that is often neglected. The tone of a code of ethics can have a marked influence on its effectiveness. In general, a code of ethics that is intended to stamp out ethical malpractice by imposing sanctions will have a negative and prohibiting tone. A code intended to inspire members of an organisation to live up to ethical values is more likely to have a positive and supportive tone.

A useful instrument for analysing the tone of codes of ethics is the Competing Values Framework that has been developed by Quinn, et al. (1991) and Stevens (1996). This framework distinguishes between the following four rhetorical dimensions of organisational communication: relational, transformational, informational and instructional communication. These four dimensions are portrayed in the table below:

Relational (trust)	Transformational (change)
Informational (facts)	Instructional (action)

Source: Competing Values Framework. Quinn et al. 1991

When applied to codes of ethics this model can assist in identifying what the dominant tone of a code is. It is, however, very important to note that the four modes of communication can stand in a competing relationship to one another. According to this model each of the quadrants has an opposite. The opposite of the relational quadrant is the instructional one, and the opposite of the transformational quadrant is the informational one, and vice versa. That implies that if the tone of a code is predominantly classified in one quadrant, then one can expect the code to be weak in the opposite quadrant. A code that, for example, has a strong informational tone can be expected to have a weak transformational tone. In designing a code one should therefore avoid conflicting tones in the code and also ensure that that the tone of the code is aligned with the purpose of the code.

Implementation of the code

Proper consideration needs to be given to the implementation of the code of ethics. Without this, the code will remain words on paper. It is vital that planning for code implementation should not start only after the code has been completed. Communication of the code, for example, does not need to wait until the code has been finalised, but should start long before that. The process of code development could already form an important part of the communication process. This can happen when a code is created through consultation, negotiation, and participation. If a code is created in a transparent and participative manner the credibility of the code is greatly enhanced.

Once finalised, the code of ethics needs to be communicated regularly and in different ways so that it is reinforced over and over again. Communication of the code does not always have to be direct. It can also be done via the discussion of moral dilemmas or case studies. In such discussions the code can be introduced as an aid in resolving the moral dilemmas or the cases at hand. The idea of a launch, where all members of an organisation are expected to make a public commitment to the code might work in some instances, but it is not enough. It needs to be followed up with ongoing communication on different aspects of the code. A special effort should also be made to ensure that new appointees are acquainted with the code and the application thereof in their jobs.

> The security manager in the IT department of a company regularly monitors employees' e-mail communications for viruses and irregularities. In doing so, she has discovered a number of incidents that she considers as inappropriate use of the company's e-mail facilities. These include excessive amounts of private messages, messages with either a sexist or racist slant, and the use of e-mail to conduct private business. In each of these cases, she has reported the incidents to the manager of the employees involved. Some employees were outraged when they discovered that the security manager was monitoring the content of their e-mail. They insisted that the security manager had no right to infringe upon their e-mail communications. E-mail messages should be considered private in the same way as telephone conversations are, they claimed.
>
> ### Question for discussion:
>
> What role can a code of ethics play in preventing abuse of electronic communication in this company?

Measures to enforce the code should also be taken well in advance. There should be clarity about what would happen if a member of the organisation were to contravene the code. If special structures need to be created to deal with such transgressions, they should be in place by the time the code is officially announced to the organisation. A code can be enforced either negatively or positively. Positive enforcement rewards those who demonstrate exemplary adherence to the code. In the case of negative enforcement, code transgression results in some form of sanction.

There are also other factors that have a marked influence on the effectiveness of a code of ethics. The code should be visibly and audibly endorsed by the leadership of the organisation and they should demonstrate their personal commitment to the code. Should a prominent person be seen to disrespect the code and then get away with it, the code's credibility will be severely damaged. The opposite is equally true. By demonstrating a commitment to the code in word and deed, the leadership of the organisation can enhance the code's credibility.

In the next section on the institutionalisation of ethics in organisations, the implementation of a code of ethics will be discussed in more detail.

Limitations of codes of ethics

A well-developed and properly implemented code of ethics can be a valuable asset to a company. It can be a powerful instrument for preventing ethical malpractice as well as for promoting moral responsibility in an organisation. Useful and important though it is, it would be a mistake to overestimate the value of a code of ethics. A code of ethics can play a vital role, but it should not be regarded as the sole instrument for managing the ethical performance of an organisation. Some of the limitations of codes of ethics are identified below.

Codes of ethics might not promote moral autonomy

Moral autonomy refers to the ability to think independently and imaginatively about moral matters. Members of an organisation are expected to live by a code of ethics. Such compliance with a code of ethics can be a very good thing, especially if the code offers sound ethical guidelines. It may, however, blunt people towards issues not covered by the code. A blind reliance on a code of ethics can mean that people do not develop or rely on their own moral judgement. Various initiatives should be taken to keep moral debate and the moral imagination of employees alive in an organisation, such as regular discussions of case studies or debate about new moral issues as they arise.

One needs skills to apply a code of ethics

A further limitation of a code of ethics is that although it can provide valuable guidance, it cannot ensure that people will be able to apply the code in situations that require ethical decision-making (cf. Rossouw, 1997a). Especially in the case of aspirational codes, but even in the case of directional codes, organisational members need some guidance on how to interpret the standards or guidelines of the code in some very specific or tricky situations. To make proper moral decisions, one needs to develop the relevant skills and knowledge required for making moral decisions or resolving moral dilemmas. Once more the code of ethics on its own is not sufficient, but needs to be complemented with training in ethical analysis and decision making.

Codes of ethics may silence other views

Codes of ethics tend to silence dissident voices in an organisation. As the purpose of a code is to promote uniformity in organisational moral behaviour, it follows that by its very nature a code of ethics will tend to silence alternative moral views. It might well be that there are other valid moral viewpoints within an organisation that are not accommodated in the existing code. In such cases, the existing code could be viewed as oppressive and intolerant by some. The debate on ethical matters must remain open and it is important to make provision for the regular revision of the code of ethics. Ironically, those codes that are most regularly opened for revision are the ones that most often survive a revision exercise unscathed.

Codes of ethics can be counterproductive

Introducing a code of ethics can also be counterproductive. This is especially likely to be the case when there is a discrepancy between the professed and actual behaviour in an organisation, or when there are very low levels of intra-organisational trust. If the code of ethics is perceived by external stakeholders as nothing but a smokescreen to conceal unethical practices, or if they regard it as an attempt to pacify legitimate moral concerns about the organisation, they are likely to react with cynicism towards the code. The same can happen within an organisation, when employees perceive the code of ethics to be an insincere effort at manipulation by management.

Conclusion

Codes of ethics can be effective instruments for promoting ethical behaviour or in constraining ethical malpractices in organisations. But a code's relevance and effectiveness is never guaranteed. Whether the code will have a significant impact on organisations depends upon careful planning and good judgement on a number of vital decisions that need to be taken during the process of code development and implementation. Even in cases where codes of ethics are effective, they will have limitations and will need to be complemented by other measures. A range of management interventions that can be introduced to institutionalise codes of ethics in organisations will be discussed in the next chapter.

CHAPTER
19

Institutionalising ethics

I n previous chapters we established that ethics is an essential part of business and highlighted the impact that ethical issues have on business. We also showed how unethical behaviour can have devastating consequences for an organisation. Conversely, ethical behaviour can contribute meaningfully to an organisation's reputation. Following the identification of ethics risk we indicated how the codification of ethics standards is an essential and useful precursor to making ethical values real in organisations. The commitment to organisational integrity that is demonstrated through the adoption of a code of ethics has to be translated into organisational practice. Managers need to set specific ethics objectives for their organisation, design and implement a *strategy* to achieve these objectives, design *systems* to institutionalise ethics, and infuse (*operationalise*) ethics in the daily activities of the organisation. In this chapter the '*how*' of institutionalising business ethics at the strategic, systems and operational levels is explained. In addition to this, the role players responsible for managing ethics in organisations are identified and their roles explained.

Even if an organisation is characterised by the presence of (a) leaders with integrity, (b) widespread internal support for an ethical way of conducting business, and (c) a sound code of ethics, this may not be sufficient to produce *sustained* ethical behaviour. An institutionalisation effort built on an ethics strategy and comprehensive ethics management programmes is required. To achieve this, an organisation has to be clear on the end-state of ethical performance it aspires to. Once it knows what it wants to achieve over time, it can institutionalise ethics on the strategic, systems and operational levels.

Institutionalisation on a strategic level

Ethical organisations manage ethics in a concerted way. They do this by formulating a vision for ethics. An ethics vision constitutes the end-state of the ethical identity the organisation intends to achieve over time. That is, to be defined not only in terms of their products, services and brands, but also in terms of the ethical way in which these are produced and managed.

Strategising for ethics implies that once an organisation has embraced business ethics as strategically important and decided to make ethics part of how it defines itself, it needs to decide on an appropriate ethics management strategy. In order to produce sustained ethical behaviour, an ethical way of thinking (ethical organisational culture) and doing (ethical behaviour) needs to be cultivated.

For ethics to be institutionalised, ethical values have to be made part of the operating consciousness of the organisation (Goodpaster, 1989). A corporate conscience needs to be institutionalised therefore (Goodpaster, 2007). Ideally, this would result in an ethical organisational culture. Since organisational change can be positioned on a continuum of superficial (first-order) change, to deep (second-order) change (Porras & Silvers, 1991), an effort to institutionalise ethics may therefore be successful only if it has second-order change qualities. This will require change that is somewhat revolutionary and characterised by multi-dimensional, multi-level interventions. It may, however, not be easy to transform the culture in organisations that have strong and established cultures – an ethical culture change therefore has to be of a deep, but gradual nature. Change of this type can be conceptualised and driven only at a *strategic level* in the organisation.

The commitment to ethics should be reflected in the vision, mission and identity of the organisation. It should be clear on this level that ethics is ingrained in the way in which the company does its business. This commitment to ethics should be communicated to all relevant stakeholders. It is also the board's responsibility to decide on an appropriate strategy for managing the ethics performance of the company. The strategy that is selected for managing ethics risk will largely be determined by whether there is merely a need to protect the company from ethical failures or whether the company wishes to benefit from good ethical performance. Four broad strategies for managing ethical performance can be distinguished, namely the reactive, compliance, integrity and total aligned strategies (cf. Rossouw & Van Vuuren, 2003). These strategies are discussed in turn. (See Chapter 5 for a more detailed discussion of these strategies)

The reactive strategy

The reactive strategy is a defensive approach to managing ethical risk. It is a type of knee-jerk reaction to do something about ethics out of fear of scandals. Consequently it does not amount to an ethics management strategy in the true sense of the word. In the past such a reactive approach has often been the starting point to managing ethics for many organisations.

When companies sense that they might alienate stakeholders through unethical behaviour, they often tend to adopt a reactive strategy. This strategy consists of publicly committing the company to ethical behaviour in the hope that such a commitment will be sufficient to avoid threats of litigation, boycotts, strikes and other forms of stakeholder alienation. Since a reactive strategy is seldom based on a conviction that ethical business is good business, but rather on a desire to protect against investigation and punitive action, the organisation will formulate standards that display rejection of unethical behaviour. Although ethical standards are articulated, they lack application. There is consequently no attempt to complement formal ethical standards with compliance procedures.

A reactive strategy has certain dangers that need to be considered in advance. Since the commitment to ethical standards of behaviour is not complemented with management interventions to ensure compliance to the formulated standards, a credibility problem is likely to develop. The chances are good that there will be a gap between talking and walking ethics. Both internal and external stakeholders might find their expectations frustrated and experience difficulty trusting a company whose words and actions are not aligned.

Furthermore, the reactive strategy is very susceptible to scandal. Since there is a gap between espoused ethical standards and the actual behaviour of the organisation, this might easily be exploited. Dissatisfied employees may, in the absence of internal channels for dealing with ethical failures, opt for blowing the whistle in public on unethical practices, which in turn can trigger scandals. Finally, a reactive strategy mostly does not satisfy institutional investors, consumers and talented employees. They are not interested in mere confessions of adherence to ethical standards. They want to see real commitment to ethical standards that is properly managed by the company.

The compliance strategy

Companies that adopt a compliance strategy normally adopt a directional code of ethics. The code prescribes ethical standards of behaviour and there is usually an emphasis on behaviour that is prohibited. Consequently the code tends to be a document of substantial proportions that is comprehensive in providing for a wide range of behaviours that are ethically unacceptable.

The compliance strategy for managing ethics represents a substantial move away from the reactive strategy. The objective of a compliance strategy is to prevent unethical behaviour in the organisation. Companies with a compliance strategy commit themselves to monitoring and managing their ethics performance. Instead of merely having a code of ethics for the sake of pacifying stakeholders, the code becomes the standard against which the company measures its ethical performance. Companies with this strategy of managing their ethics typically express their intention to ensure that all employees abide by the ethical standards of the company. In order to ensure compliance to the code, they monitor the ethical performance of employees. When deviation from the code of ethics occurs, the company takes corrective action by disciplining or penalising the transgressors.

Alternatively the company may opt for not only penalising transgressions of its ethical standards, but also for rewarding those who consistently abide by its code of conduct. The compliance strategy is a rule-based approach to managing ethics.

Since compliance is externally controlled and not self-imposed (Rasche & Esser, 2007), a compliance strategy may have a number of side effects that need to be kept in mind when considering this strategy. Firstly, it may breed a mentality of 'what is not forbidden is allowed'. Given the rule-based nature of this approach, employees can rely merely on the existing rules for moral guidance. Secondly, it tends to disempower employees to use their own discretion in making ethical decisions as it requires almost blind adherence to rules of conduct (Sharpe-Paine 2002:135). This undermines their ability to cope with issues and grey areas that are not addressed in the code of ethics. Finally, the compliance strategy can lead to a proliferation of ethical rules and guidelines for conduct. In an attempt to provide unambiguous guidance on ethical conduct, more and more ethical guidelines are issued. These rules can grow so numerous that it becomes difficult to keep track of them. Should this happen, it is almost impossible to remember all the directives, and for that reason they may have very little impact on actual corporate behaviour.

None of these side effects are insurmountable. They can all be countered with appropriate management interventions. These side effects, however, may prompt companies to adopt an integrity strategy instead.

The integrity strategy

An integrity strategy is a values-based approach that typically consists of a limited number of broad and aspirational guidelines that set the parameters of corporate ethical conduct. Driscoll and Hoffman (2000:14) describe the utility of this approach: 'Companies are embracing ethics and values initiatives because they believe that they will have a competitive advantage if they do so.' The ethical principles are cascaded down throughout the organisation and, for example, divisions or sections set their own guidelines that are based on the broad corporate ethical guidelines. In an ideal situation, employees at every level know exactly how to apply the guidelines in their particular jobs and therefore what constitutes ethical behaviour and what not.

The purpose of the integrity strategy is to raise the level of ethical performance of the company. Instead of merely trying to minimise incidents of unethical behaviour, it pro-actively endeavours to promote ethical behaviour. Companies typically follow this strategy when they realise that ethical performance is of strategic importance to the company or even its competitive edge. In such cases a defensive approach that protects the company against the damage of unethical conduct is no longer deemed sufficient. On the contrary, a concerted effort in which all members of the organisation take joint responsibility for the ethics performance of the company is required.

Where the compliance strategy is characterised by external enforcement of ethical standards, the integrity approach is marked by the internalisation of ethical values and standards by employees. Instead of imposing ethical standards upon the organisation, it seeks to obtain the commitment of individual members of the organisation to a set of shared corporate values (Moon & Bonny 2001:26). By ensuring that the locus of control resides within members of the organisation, less external control is required. There is thus less need for external control and more reliance on the discretion of employees to act morally responsible in accordance with the company's ethical values. An integrity strategy is usually complemented by a limited form of compliance, where a limited number of rules serve as a safety net to protect the company from gross unethical conduct.

The integrity strategy also has a number of side effects that need to be considered. Firstly, the greater discretion granted to employees in an integrity strategy can be abused. This can either lead to an increase in unethical conduct or it can fuel moral disputes in a company. Secondly, the integrity strategy depends heavily on the leadership of the company setting both the tone and the example of ethical behaviour. If the entire leadership does not endorse the core ethical values in their practical behaviour (i.e. walk the ethics talk), it can pose a serious challenge to the viability of an integrity strategy. Finally, the integrity strategy presupposes a clear sense of corporate identity and priorities. The individual discretion upon which the integrity approach is premised can only be properly exercised when core ethical values are aligned with corporate identity and priorities. Should there be a lack of clarity about corporate identity and priorities, the sustainability of the integrity approach might be jeopardised.

The totally aligned strategy

Organisations that opt for a TAO (Totally Aligned Organisation) type of strategy wish to seamlessly integrate ethics into the purpose, mission and goals of the organisation. Ethics is no longer viewed as just another aspect of the organisation that needs to be managed. This presupposes that a company using this strategy will have a well-developed sense of identity and purpose, which are based on non-negotiable ethical standards in its interaction with internal and external stakeholders. Consequently ethical behaviour is regarded as strategically important and unethical behaviour is regarded as jeopardising not only the business success of the organisation, but also as undermining the reason for its existence.

A TAO strategy is about congruence between the purpose, vision and ethical values of the organisation. Consequently communication gains in importance and becomes the primary managerial intervention. Through both formal and informal communication the essential role of ethics in the organisation is continually emphasised. The vision of the company, its history as well as the stories of its former and current ethical heroes, are kept in circulation. Rather than focusing on either punishing unethical behaviour or rewarding ethical conduct, the focus is on celebrating organisational heroes who embody the vision, purpose and ethical commitment of the organisation.

At this point the importance of conducting a proper ethics risk analysis becomes clear. For an organisation to decide on a strategy, it has to be clear on what its current mode of managing ethics is. There is no one ideal strategy for managing ethics that can be prescribed unconditionally for all organisations. Insofar as managing ethics is concerned, there is no one-size-fits-all. One may intuitively sense that the integrity and TAO modes may be superior to the others. However, numerous factors, e.g. the size of the organisation, the stage of the organisation's life cycle and the type of industry it inhabits, may call for a specific type of strategy. An organisation may even opt for a combination of strategies, e.g. compliance and integrity, or adopt a compliance strategy in some divisions and an integrity strategy in others.

Institutionalisation on a systems level

Once an organisation has decided on its ethics management strategy, it still has a long way to go to entrench a culture of ethics. The challenge then, for the key role players involved in ethics management, is to translate the ethics strategy into meaningful *ethics management systems*. Designing and implementing such systems are crucial to ensure that the vision and strategy for ethics are made real throughout the organisation. The systems required to do this should make provision for the introduction of an ethics dimension in the following aspects of the organisation: communication, recruitment, selection, orientation, performance management, training, and disciplinary procedures. Finally, systems for monitoring and evaluating ethics performance need to be created. Each of these systems will now be expanded on.

Communication

To really gain momentum in its quest to achieve ethical organisation status over time, an organisation has to clearly communicate its ethics expectations to all stakeholders. Also, the standards for ethical conduct that have been captured by its code of ethics have to be understood and applied by every employee. In addition, the organisation needs to know what types of ethical issues their employees are confronted with, what types of un-ethical behaviour occurs, and what the 'good news' ethics stories are. Communication about ethics forms the backbone of implementing an ethics strategy. A good two-way communication strategy that enables the organisation to convey ethics expectations and that affords its stakeholders, in particular the employees, opportunities to tell the organisation about their ethics experiences, has to be designed and implemented. Specific interventions that can be used to ensure effective communication on ethics include ethics awareness programmes, ethics talk, an ethics helpline, a reporting channel for unethical behaviour, and ethics newsletters.

Awareness programmes

Unethical behaviour is often related to ignorance about desired ethical behaviour. Employees, in particular, need to know what the organisation expects in terms of ethical awareness and ethical conduct. The code of ethics has to move beyond the point of being words on paper – it has to become a living document. An ethics awareness campaign can raise the level of ethics awareness in an organisation.

An example of an ethics awareness intervention is orientation sessions about the importance of ethics, what the code of ethics entails, how it should be applied, what the resources for advice on ethics are, and procedures in case of non-compliance. The orientation sessions could be conducted by the key ethics management role players. Such orientation sessions are of course ideal forums for top management to visibly demonstrate their commitment to ethics. Depending on the size of the organisation, such sessions could be conducted in a typical 'road-show' format. Organisations also use these sessions to give their employees an opportunity to participate in the annual code revision process. Some organisations use a comprehensive awareness campaign to launch their newly developed or revised codes of ethics.

Complementary awareness raising actions include poster campaigns, corporate clothing and stationery that promote ethical values, as well as computer screensavers and software aimed at engendering awareness.

Ethics talk

Ethics talk is the spoken or written articulation that reflects the consideration of the ethical interests of (a) the self (e.g. the company and the wellbeing of its members), and also of (b) the other (e.g. other internal and external stakeholders, other organisations, society) (Schwartzel, 2008). As the antithesis of what Bird and Waters (1989) originally coined as moral muteness, ethics talk is an extremely powerful tool to entrench ethics in an organisation. According to McCoy (2002) it is the 'stories people tell, rather than printed materials' that transmit the 'conceptions of what is proper behaviour' (p. 186).

Traditionally in the dog-eat-dog and lean-and-mean world of business, references to ethics may have been perceived to be unacceptable behaviour in organisations obsessed with financial success. The fact is that although many people think about ethics, not many verbalise their thoughts in meetings and discussions. Nor do people actually debate ethical issues often.

Although not an 'ethics management system' in the strict sense of the word, efforts at getting employees to talk about ethics and to bring it to prominence in their daily vocabulary have to be facilitated. Ways of doing this are to put ethics on the agenda when decisions have to be made, creating forums where ethics can be discussed openly and freely, making ethics part of managerial development and training, and identifying a number of credible ethical role models in the organisation that can be utilised to facilitate ethics talk.

An ethics helpdesk

Having a code of ethics is one thing. Applying it is another. Aspirational or value-based codes of ethics do not provide specific guidelines to deal with ethics issues that confront employees on a daily basis. Even those codes that are rule-based cannot cover all eventualities. For example: if an aspirational code that relies on employees to use their own discretion, forbids bribery, can an employee accept a gift from a supplier? And, what is the difference between a gift of a company T-shirt and an all-expenses paid weekend away? The reality is, employees need guidelines to deal with lesser decisions as well as issues that have more serious ethical consequences. How do they know what to do?

Many organisations across the world have instituted so-called 'ethics helpdesks' to assist employees in code interpretation or when they are confronted with difficult ethical issues. A typical helpdesk is a facility that consists of an 'office', website or telephone line that can be used by employees seeking answers to their ethics queries while remaining anonymous. Calhoun and Wolitzer (2001:72) describe an ethics hotline, or helpdesk, as a '24-hour service that employees can use anonymously or confidentially to ask questions about the company's ethics policies and practices or alert the ethics officer to an existing or potential problem'. A helpline serves as a central contact point where critical ethics related comments, dilemmas and advice are received and dealt with by the person most appropriate for handling a specific case (Ferrell, Fraedrich & Ferrell, 2008). The helpline is preferably a source of ethics guidance or specific advice. Trained ethics advisors deal with queries quickly while maintaining confidentiality and protecting the identity of the caller or person that raised the issue. Having a helpline naturally also raises the ethics awareness in an organisation – if the helpline receives many calls it does not necessarily mean that unethical behaviour is rife – it does, however, indicate that people think about ethics and are not afraid to ask questions about it.

Confidential reporting system

Not all ethical issues can be adequately addressed by the ethics helpline. There are often complicated or serious issues that require something in addition to the helpline. It may stand organisations in good stead to have a separate, anonymous facility or reporting line where unethical behaviour can be specifically reported. Such a reporting line satisfies the need for confidential reporting. Certain ethical issues pose dire consequences for organisations should these issues be made public. Rather than reading about unethical conduct in a newspaper, organisations would want to know about it before it is made public by the media. Such reporting lines, or whistle-blowing facilities, may prevent 'scandals' being exposed in the public domain and give an organisation an opportunity to deal with the issue decisively within the organisation's boundaries.

Organisations can avoid potentially harmful reputational damage in this way. Although many organisations have an internal reporting line to cater for whistleblowers, others opt for outsourcing it to external companies that specialise in providing such services. The latter approach increases the chances that the person who reports unethical behaviour remains anonymous and thus does not fall victim to potential victimisation.

It needs to be emphasised though that safe reporting, or whistle-blowing, is not in itself a cure for unethical behaviour. In a sense it represents the dark side of ethics management, whereby employees are encouraged to 'tell on their colleagues', a practice that is severely frowned upon in many cultures. Safe reporting should ideally be a last resort for employees that experience or perceive ethics problems, and should be available as an avenue to be explored when all others, e.g. advice from line managers or the ethics helpdesk, have been exhausted.

Ethics newsletters

Newsletters are useful vehicles to maintain organisational ethical awareness. Organisations could include sections on ethics in their regular newsletters as an internal communication mechanism for ethics. This could include good news ethics stories, case studies of ethical dilemmas, records of cases that indicated how unethical behaviour was dealt with or statistics relating to helpline queries or confidential reporting incidents. This type of information is an important aid in the ethics management endeavour. Although most organisations choose not to hang out their dirty linen, others publish theirs in newsletters in the hope that the employees will realise that the organisation takes ethics seriously. Case studies published in this way also provide contextualised content for ethics training interventions. A particularly creative application is the example of organisations that have created cartoon strips with ethics as the central theme, as a regular feature in their newsletters.

Recruitment

If an organisation wishes to build a new ethics culture or maintain an existing one, it has to ensure that it attracts potential employees of integrity. When devising recruitment strategies the organisation has to put out the word in no uncertain terms that it wishes to attract people that can align their ethical orientations with those espoused by the organisation. An organisation that is known for and that expresses the fact that it has unyielding ethical values underpinned by codified standards of behaviour, may actually deter candidates of dubious integrity from applying for vacancies. This approach to recruitment also builds the organisation's reputation and enables it to attract talent. It also contributes to the creation of employees' ethics awareness from the outset.

Selection

Once an organisation has embarked on an ethics journey, it has no choice but to be an ethically discerning employer. This holds particularly true for organisations that have had histories of unethical behaviour, or whose business is by nature characterised by opportunities for employees to commit fraud, bribery and corruption. Along with the growth of the high-technology age came the proliferation of opportunities to abuse technology for unethical ends. No wonder then that many organisations opt for including integrity as a criterion for the selection of new employees or when promoting existing employees to positions that require ethical accountability. Given the assumption that integrity may indeed be measurable in a quantitative or qualitative manner, it may be included as a dimension to be assessed in a number of selection methods. In the following paragraphs the inclusion of integrity as a dimension in interviews, reference checking, psychometric testing and assessment centre technology is discussed.

Selection interviews

If utilised correctly, these interviews are a useful way of establishing whether an applicant's integrity will be aligned to that of its employer. Although interviews are by no means known for possessing good predictive validity, they are still the most popular component of any set of selection tools employed by organisations. There have also been great strides in improving the extent to which interviews can meaningfully discriminate between candidates that seemingly have equally impressive resumés. Two types of questioning techniques that have contributed to the increased sophistication of interviews as selection tool are the *critical incident* and *simulation techniques*.

When using *critical incidents* to assess competence, interviewers usually ask interviewees to describe particular job-related incidents from their past.

Answers given are then analysed for the extent to which the interviewee has displayed the propensity to be competent and efficient in dealing with the particular incident (issue) in question. The *simulation technique* allows the interviewer to control the contents of the discussion by describing a potential situation to interviewees that they may encounter in the job they are applying for. The interviewee's response is then interpreted to evaluate the extent to which competence in dealing with the issue was demonstrated. Although there is a tendency for candidates being interviewed to provide socially acceptable answers, interviewers that assess for ethics usually analyse candidates' ethical reasoning rather than necessarily the correctness of the answer when using either the critical incident or simulation techniques.

Reference checking

The types of jobs that are particularly suited to reference checking for integrity are those that require of incumbents to have a level of integrity that is above reproach. Examples are jobs in the financial services sector that are susceptible to fraudulent or corrupt behaviour, jobs that require of incumbents to handle cash, jobs that require high levels of confidentiality due to the secret or sensitive nature of the information incumbents may have access to (e.g. in the arms manufacturing sector), jobs where decisions may effect peoples' lives and livelihoods, and, for that matter any job where the incumbent is faced with ethical decisions in the face of temptation on a regular basis.

Reference checking methods include written and verbal accounts of applicants' values and integrity. However, both of these methods elicit notoriously vague responses from referees and rarely require factual answers to questions relating to specific incidents of unethical behaviour. Organisations therefore need to decide whether reference checking is worth the effort. A solution to overcome the inherent problems relating to reference checking is to be very selective when deciding which jobs' integrity requirements are so crucial to the company that it has no other option than to do reference checking. Many organisations outsource reference checking to specialised external agencies. In all cases of reference checking organisations should heed the legal requirements that have been instituted to protect potential employees' rights, privacy and dignity.

The psychometric assessment of integrity

Organisations are keen to identify employees that may be prone to unethical behaviour in a timely manner, and preferably before they enter the workplace. Of all the methods that have been used to this effect the issue of psychometric testing to assess potential employees' levels of integrity has been the most controversial (Coyne & Bertram, 2002). Such questionnaire-type integrity testing (sometimes called honesty testing) has received widespread attention from researchers and business organisations alike during the recent past. One reason for this is the huge monetary losses that organisations incur because of employee dishonesty.

Meta-analytic research by Ones, Viswesvaran and Schmidt (1993) indicated the validity of all integrity tests to be .47 using criteria of counter-productive behaviour. Their findings were confirmed in later studies by Schmidt and Hunter (1998), Engleman and Kleiner (1998), Miner and Capps (1996), and Marcus, Lee and Ashton (2007). A validity coefficient of .47 is totally acceptable within the realm of utilising psychometric testing.

Integrity in assessment centre technology

Although assessment centre technology is rather expensive to develop and apply its predictive validity is very good. An assessment centre is a process of simulating a particular job by means of subjecting candidates to certain simulation exercises, or work samples, which are scored and evaluated by trained observers and assessors. Examples of simulations are in-tray exercises, group discussions, role plays and analytical exercises. Although simulations can be used for any job category, these simulations are by nature particularly suitable for the assessment of managerial potential at all organisational levels. Measuring for ethical orientation by means of assessment centre technology entails the inclusion of ethics as a dimension to be assessed. The way in which ethics may be included could vary from explicit measures where ethics case studies are included in the simulations, to more subtle measures where ethics (e.g. ethical sensitivity, insight and problem solving acumen) is assessed as a by-product when other (leadership) dimensions (e.g. decision making, judge-ment, delegation, interpersonal sensitivity, etc.) are evaluated.

Orientation of new employees

Inadequate orientation or induction correlates highly with the number of employees resigning from organisations soon after joining. Even if there had been little emphasis on ethics during recruitment and selection, the orientation or induction of new employees can be a particularly powerful intervention to create a timely ethical awareness amongst newcomers. Employees entering an organisation are susceptible to adopting the new organisation's culture. If this culture is characterised by a strong ethics dimension, new employees become aware of the organisation's expectations regarding ethical behaviour from the outset. This is also the time to explain the code of ethics and how to apply its behavioural guidelines. The new employees' supervisors and managers also play an important role at this point, as they can make or break the new employees' attitude towards organisational ethics. Coaching newcomers on using the code of ethics in their daily tasks is the responsibility of the supervisor or manager. Informal or formal mentorship is an additional useful vehicle for conveying the organisation's ethical values and standards to new employees.

Performance management and reward

If ethics is an integral component of organisational life it is also an integral responsibility of all employees when they perform their jobs. Furthermore, most jobs in organisations involve decision making. Although decisions may vary in terms of their impact on the organisation, most decisions have ethical consequences. For purposes of managing the performance of employees, most organisations have performance appraisal systems that form part of a larger performance management system. An employee's performance appraisal is usually based on a number of key performance areas that constitute a job. Employees are appraised on the extent to which they accomplish the demands defined by these key performance areas. Further decisions regarding, for example, training, rewards and promotions, are usually made based on performance appraisal results.

Ethics is not only the collective responsibility of all employees, but also the responsibility of each employee in his/her individual capacity. Ethics should therefore be 'made real' for every employee. One way in which this can be accomplished is to make ethics an integral part of every job. This can be done by making it a stand-alone key performance area for some jobs that require continuous ethical decision-making, or at the very least, to integrate ethics into one or more key performance areas. In this way employees know what ethical performance is required and the extent to which it will be measured as part of a broader appraisal process.

Rewarding performance is usually an integral component of an organisation's comprehensive performance management system. When employees are rewarded (intrinsically and extrinsically) for their performance across several key performance areas, which include ethical performance as an independent key performance area, they are then, by implication, also rewarded for their ethical performance. Organisational incentive schemes can also be designed in such a way that employees are given the opportunity to integrate ethical considerations into their decision making (May, 2009).

The converse, however, may also hold true: by design certain organisational reward systems are aimed at rewarding behaviour that violates principles of ethics (Lennick & Kiel, 2005). This is particularly prevalent in organisations where the ethics-performance tension (May, 2009) is inadequately managed.

Training

An important component of organisational ethics institutionalisation is ethics training. An advantage of a formal ethics training intervention is that trainees are exposed to a more structured learning environment than normal work situations allow for. It facilitates spontaneous discussions on ethics, and empowers learners to be confident and decisive when required to make ethical decisions.

A key focus area of organisational ethics training interventions is the training of employees to understand, interpret and apply the code of ethics. Such training is usually conducted by means of generic and company specific case studies. Employees should also be trained on their responsibilities in creating and reinforcing an ethical culture. Training on the purpose and use of helpdesks, as well as confidential reporting lines, are further components of ethics training.

Organisational management cadres are probably the most important facilitators of organisational ethics. It can be argued that managers, in particular, in addition to the usual managerial competencies required of them, also require an *ethics competence*. Although universities and business schools play an important role in teaching business ethics to managers and potential managers, few courses are, however, aimed at providing managers with an ethics competence.

Managers have three *roles* insofar as organisational ethics is concerned, namely (a) being *change agents* for organisational ethics, (b) being *ethics managers* (managing the ethics performance of employees in their departments' or sections), and (c) *being ethical* in their own jobs (job-specific ethics role). To adequately fulfil these roles, managers need to acquire three types of ethics competence. These are 1. *cognitive competence* (having analytical and decision-making skills), 2. *behavioural competence* (commitment and courage to implement ethical decisions), and 3. *managerial competence* (the knowledge and skills to direct, control and reward the ethical behaviour of others) (cf. Rossouw, 2004).

Disciplinary procedures

The downside of building an ethical organisational culture is that it is sometimes unavoidable that unethical or non-compliant behaviour be discouraged through punishment. Organisations have to resort to deterrents to unethical behaviour by dealing with transgressions, especially serious ones, in a swift, but fair and decisive way. Organisational disciplinary structures and procedures are usually sufficiently informed and well-positioned to also deal with ethical transgressions. Disciplinary procedures should be based on principles of substantive and procedural fairness to ensure fair investigations, hearings, verdicts and penalties.

Monitoring and evaluation

In order to actively manage the ethical performance of a company, it is vital that it should be constantly monitored. There are a number of measures that can be used in a monitoring and evaluation system.

Ongoing engagement with stakeholders can provide valuable feedback on whether the ethical expectations that they have of the company are met or frustrated. Changes in stakeholder expectations can be gauged qualitatively (through personal or group interviews) and quantitatively (through surveys). Incidence reports are another source that provides feedback on the organisation's ethics performance. The number of incidents of complaints, fraud, corruption, sexual harassment, allegations of racism, calls to the ethics helpdesk, and reports via the confidential reporting system all provide information on the organisation's ethics performance. This information needs to be systematically documented and analysed. So too should information provided in external indices that rate companies with regard to reputation, sustainability, or attractiveness to aspirant employees, be captured in the monitoring and evaluation system. If ethical performance is included in the performance appraisal system of the company, it also provides feedback to the company on whether levels of ethical performance are improving or declining. Another measure of ethical performance is to be found in the prevalence of ethics talk. Document analysis of the minutes of meetings and other forms of documented company communication can reveal to what extent 'ethics talk' has become ingrained in organisational life.

Feedback on ethical performance that is gained in the ways described above serves two purposes. On the one hand it provides the information required for further ethics management interventions. On the other hand it provides the data required for reporting on the ethics performance of organisations.

Institutionalisation on an operational level

Having formulated a comprehensive ethics management programme at a strategic level, and having designed appropriate systems for strategy implementation, it is important to ensure that ethical behaviour manifests itself in all jobs and interpersonal interactions.

Bennis (1999) asserts that it is the job of every manager in the organisation to set the climate for ethical behaviour based on mutual respect. Employees need to be empowered and enabled to talk about ethics. This can be achieved through the incorporation of ethical requirements in job tasks where relevant, and by using line managers and ethical role models to mentor, coach and train employees to be ethically aware, identify ethical issues, solve basic ethical problems, and display courage when making ethically sound decisions. One way of accomplishing this is to encourage an organisational climate where 'It's OK to talk about ethics around here'.

The most profound challenge for those concerned with the operationalisation of ethics in organisations is that of values translation. The ethical culture of an organisation is established over time by organisational values, norms, beliefs and practices. Of these, the ethical dimension of organisational values creates the psychological mindset of what is ethically acceptable. Examples of typical ethical values that organisations either formally conceptualise or informally endorse are integrity, honesty, respect, transparency, empathy, care, compassion, fairness and responsibility.

Whether organisations formally engage with employees (and sometimes other stakeholders) to formulate the ethical values applicable to the specific organisation, or whether top management formulate the values and cascade them down to the rest of the organisation, the values will remain vague until 'translated'. Although many employees may instinctively have a notion of the meaning of a particular value, and may engage in behaviours that display that value, the abstract nature of ethical values often make them difficult to apply in the course of doing one's job. Furthermore, the same value, e.g. the value 'integrity', could hold vastly different meanings for different employees due to the diversity of cultures, religious affiliations, backgrounds, educational levels and languages represented in the workplace.

Most employees need to be guided by leaders as to the specific interpretations required of a certain value in a specific job in a specific organisation. Values need to be meaningfully and unambiguously translated into specific behaviours required to 'live' the value.

By way of an example, if call centre consultants are asked what their interpretation of 'respect' is, they will most likely answer 'to be nice to customers'. Upon further probing though, the perception of what respect entails may become increasingly vague. Specific behaviours associated with living the value of respect should be communicated to the consultants. Examples of such behaviours could be:

Answering a call within the first three rings
Clearly stating the name of the company or division
Clearly stating one's name
Addressing customers by their preferred title
Listening carefully to the customer's rendition of the query/ complaint
Expressing empathy with customer's frustrations
Paraphrasing the customer's complaint to ensure there is mutual understanding
Never raising one's voice
Not getting into an argument with a customer
Never using expletives
Never being sarcastic or condescending
Concentrating on the customer's situation

Not putting the customer 'on hold' for too long periods without
informing them what you are doing to solve the issue
Not talking to colleagues while dealing with the customer
Keeping promises to return calls

Once employees understand the behaviours associated with respect it will be relatively easy to apply these in practice. The same process has to be repeated for other values, some of which may prove more demanding to translate, e.g. integrity. Only then could meaningful and practical behavioural expression be given to ethical values. This opens opportunities for ethics dialogue which, in turn, facilitates the establishment of a shared meaning of what 'good' or ethics implies for the specific organisation.

A further operational application of the institutionalisation of ethics relates to the way organisations use their past and present 'ethical heroes' as role models for ethical thought and actions. Ethical heroes are those individuals that have high credibility as ethical leaders and role models and that often make ethical decisions that are based on expressing strong ethical values and moral courage. In the same way that people base their personal ethics on asking questions such as 'What would Jesus do?' or 'What would the Prophet do?' in these circumstances, people in organisations may ask similar questions regarding their ethical heroes. This is illustrated by the example of the question, or so legend has it, that employees of Disney Corporation ask when in doubt, namely 'What would Walt [Disney] do?'

Ethics management role players

Ethics has to be managed (the 'why' question) and there are ways to do it (the 'how' question). An important remaining issue in managing ethics, relates to the 'by whom' question. This implies that it is necessary to understand who the role players in managing ethics could be. Although some role players may have specific functions and duties allocated to them, others may have symbolic significance and roles that are less formally defined. The remainder of this chapter provides a framework for the identification of the key role players that should be directly involved in managing ethics. Organisations that may particularly benefit from an understanding of who the key role players ought to be and what their roles and responsibilities should be, are those organisations that not only wish to entrench ethics, but have the resources required to do so.

Once the key role players have been identified, their symbolic and/or specific functions will be discussed and the necessary links between their respective roles explored. The key role players are: the board, the CEO, the ethics sponsor, the ethics champion, the ethics committee, the ethics manager and the line manager (cf. IoD, 2009:27). Since the role of the board in facilitating governance and ethics was addressed in Chapter 16, it will not be elaborated upon further in the current chapter. The role players' respective roles and responsibilities are discussed in turn, where after the links between the role players are explained.

The CEO and ethics

The role of the CEO is that of the moral leader of the organisation, not only as a symbol of ethics to external stakeholders, but also to internal stakeholders. The CEO directly portrays the ethical character, reputation and credibility of the organisation to most of its stakeholders, but especially to current and potential shareholders, investors and employees. As influencers of behaviour, opinion formers, policy makers, decision makers and role models, leaders act as representatives of the organisation's ethical credibility.

The role of the CEO implies several responsibilities including being an influencer of ethical behaviour (cf. IoD. 2009:27). This is achieved through the process of role modelling. The power of individuals in senior management positions determines the extent to which ethical behaviour will be modelled. The CEO is therefore in the best position to influence corporate ethical behaviour. 'Not only do leaders set formal rules, but by example show the importance of right behaviour or undermine it' (Steiner & Steiner, 2003, p. 216). Research by Treviño, Weaver, Gibson and Toffler (1999) indicated that strong ethical cultures exist in organisations where employees perceived that executives regularly pay attention to ethics, take ethics seriously, and care about ethics and values as much as about the (financial) bottom line. Explicit (and even implicit) ethical behaviour of the CEO is probably as important an ethical guideline as a code of ethics or policy document. Buller and McEvoy (1999) point out that the reputation for strong ethical cultures in companies like Johnson & Johnson, Motorola, Royal Dutch/Shell and Texas Instruments can be 'traced directly to leaders who consistently, by their words and deeds, signalled the importance of and commitment to high moral standards' (p. 403).

The CEO may be an active member of the ethics committee that oversees the implementation of the ethics strategy. In conjunction with the board, the CEO recommends and approves the resources, financial or otherwise, that are required to institutionalise and manage ethics. The role player entrusted with the allocation and distribution of these resources is the *ethics sponsor.*

The ethics sponsor

The presence of a powerful sponsor that can initiate, allocate, and legitimise resources for any large-scale change intervention – which is exactly what the implementation of an ethics strategy entails – is crucial for an ethics inter- vention's sustainability (Cummings & Worley, 2001). Sponsors should function at levels that are sufficiently high in the organisation to ensure access to and control of appropriate resources. They must also have the visibility and power to nurture the intervention and see that it remains viable.

The ethics sponsor is a role that comes into being when the organisation deems ethics to be important enough to allocate funds and resources to manage it in a concerted and structured way. As is the case with any organisation-wide initiative the management of ethics requires more than just a shared enthusiasm – corporate funding and other resources are preconditions for success. The corporate ethics sponsor is that person in the organisation that provides and guarantees the resources, financial and other, that are required to design and implement ethics management initiatives.

The sponsor is typically a senior member of the organisation that has a deep-set belief in the case for organisational ethics. Sponsors are usually board members, or in positions where they function close to the board. The ethics sponsor role is, however, an over-and-above role in that the sponsor remains a key executive in another functional area, e.g. finance, marketing or operations. The sponsor should not, however, be responsible for the actual implementation of the ethics management strategy. The implementation role is facilitated by the *ethics champion*.

The ethics champion

True project champions are individuals who believe so strongly in an idea that they pursue it against all opposition, and sometimes against all logic (Katzenbach & The RCL Team, 1995). Champions passionately believe their organisations must begin to adapt and they are willing to act ahead of top management's support. Champions act within the scope that they can reach and often beyond the normal bounds of their authority.

The most important role of the ethics champion is to provide the initial impetus for an ethics management drive, and to ensure that the ethics initiative retains momentum for however long is required. The champion is usually a well-respected member of the board or a person that functions close to the board. The CEO can be the ethics champion, but if not, the champion should be a person with direct access to and support of the CEO. The champion has an instrumental role in being the catalyst for the ethics management initiative. This person visibly embodies the organisation's ethics drive. The board or a board sub-committee with the approval of the board, bestows ownership of the ethics initiative upon this person. As was the case with the ethics sponsor, the ethics champion has to have a deep-set belief in business ethics as non-negotiable imperative.

The board's choice usually falls on someone with an intimate knowledge of the organisation's business, culture and activities. It requires someone of high legitimacy and credibility, usually someone that has successfully facilitated similar, perhaps culture-change type, initiatives in the past. In addition to this, and since the ethics champion role will be marked by a very high visibility, the champion has to be regarded as an ethical role model. Champions' personal commitment and even risk taking encourages others to do more and join the process (Katzenbach, et al., 1995). This image is earned over time and is the result of moral sensitivity, moral astuteness and moral courage.

The ethics champion's foremost responsibility is to provide the vision and energy that is required to launch the ethics initiative. The ethics champion also has a significant marketing-of-ethics responsibility and must ensure that the ethics initiative gains and retains prominence. A further important responsibility of the champion is to align the ethics management functions of different corporate entities, affiliates, business units or regions when the organisation's functions are decentralised and each entity has its own ethics management structure.

In many organisations the champion role is an over-and-above role, i.e. the incumbent performs the role in addition to other functional responsibilities (e.g. CEO, company secretary, risk manager, head of internal audit, etc.). The champion is, however, not responsible for the actual design, implementation and management of the ethics management systems that support the ethics strategy. That role is fulfilled by an ethics manager. Together with, among others, the CEO, ethics sponsor and ethics manager, the champion serves as a key member of the ethics committee.

The ethics committee

The *ethics committee* is also sometimes known as the ethics task group, the ethics forum, the advisory committee for ethics, ethics advisory board, or as the ombuds-committee. Irrespective of the name selected by the organisation, the core purpose of this committee is the promotion of corporate ethical behaviour (cf. IoD, 2009:27). Direct oversight of the committee's activities usually emanates from the board of directors. As was the case with the ethics champion, the committee collectively has to have a high level of perceived integrity and credibility. An organisation that has an ethics committee clearly demonstrates to all stakeholders that institutionalising ethics is a corporate priority. Besides its obvious executive role, it also has a powerful symbolic value in that it conveys the message that the organisation is genuinely committed to ethics.

An ethics committee, in the form of a cross-functional team, usually consists of a range of organisational managers at executive management level. The CEO, ethics sponsor or ethics champion acts as coordinator of this committee. In order to have sufficient power to formulate and implement an ethics strategy, it is preferable that there should be at least one board member on this committee. Should this not be possible, the committee should function in close proximity to the board and report to it. The functional areas that could be represented on this committee are the company secretariat, compliance, finance, risk management, internal audit, corporate communication, human resources (HR), human resource development (HRD), organisational development (OD), employment/industrial relations (ER/IR) and, most importantly, the ethics manager (ethics officer).

The primary roles of the ethics committee is that of (a) *providing strategic direction* to the organisation's long-term ethics initiative, and (b) *oversight* of strategy implementation. The committee will thus direct and oversee all aspects of a typical ethics management programme: determining ethical risks, developing a code of ethics, institutionalising ethics, managing and monitoring ethics performance and accounting and reporting on ethics performance. It also has an educational role in that it enhances critical thinking about ethics in the organisation (McDaniel, 2004).

Since the role players discussed thus far usually fulfil their involvement in the ethics drive on an over-and-above basis to their own functions, they should not be involved in the management of ethics at the systems level. Neither the ethics sponsor (as provider of resources), nor the ethics champion (as catalyst for the continued implementation of the ethics strategy), nor the ethics committee (in its role as provider of strategic direction and overseer of the ethics management initiative), have the specialised competence that is required to design and implement ethics management systems. That role belongs to a specialised organisational ethics management function co-ordinated by the *ethics manager*.

The ethics manager

The roles of the CEO, sponsor, and to an extent, even that of the ethics champion, are defined by a strong overt display and resource allocation for creating an ethical organisation over time. The ethics committee, although having a substantial coordination role, still consists of individuals whose involvement with ethics in the organisation is limited to their capacity to perform their functions as ethics committee members over and above their corporate roles as risk managers, HR managers, OD specialists, etc. A structured and formalised approach to manage ethics in a concerted way is, however, also required. This implies the establishment of a corporate ethics function (cf. IoD, 2009:27) managed by an expert.

An ethics officer is an individual that manages the institutionalisation of ethics in an organisation. Texas Instruments was the first company to officially create and describe, back in 1959, the job of 'ethics officer'. The notion of establishing an organisational ethics office staffed by 'ethics officers', or ethics 'managers', is nowadays commonplace in organisations across the world. Furthermore, the occupation of ethics officer is gaining recognition as an occupation with aspirations to professionalise. In the United States the Ethics and Compliance Officer Association (ECOA) act as professional association for thousands of persons that hold organisational positions where they are responsible for their organisations' ethics management activities. Whereas some larger corporations have ethics offices that consist of several functionaries performing an array of duties, other organisations' ethics offices have structures in which the overall responsibility for ethics is placed with a single corporate executive or in a legal department.

The responsibilities of the ethics manager are determined by the ethics committee. The primary role of the ethics manager, as executive member of the ethics committee, is to be the executive head and manager of the organisation's ethics function (or office). This entails the planning, coordination, implementation and control of the strategies, structures and systems required to institutionalise, monitor and report ethics performance.

In order to illustrate the comprehensive range of responsibilities the ethics manager may have, it is for the purpose of this chapter assumed that an organisation has no formal ethics function. The first responsibility of the ethics manager is therefore to establish the corporate ethics function or office.

Thereafter the ethics function coordinates the design and implementation of ethics management systems as described earlier in the chapter. This includes designing and implementing a communication strategy for ethics, introducing integrity criteria in the recruitment and selection process, ethics training for new and existing employees; integrating ethical behaviour and decision making in organisational performance and reward management systems; and enforcing the code by means of a disciplinary system when required. The ethics manager also has the responsibility to market the ethics function and its projects to the rest of the organisation.

The last, but probably most crucial responsibility of the ethics function, is to monitor, and report on the ethics performance of the company to the ethics committee. Doing this infuses discipline into the ethics management of a company, as it indicates whether and to what extent a company has attained the ethics objectives it has set for itself.

These responsibilities cannot be adequately fulfilled without the active support of other specialist staff or line functions in the organisation that can contribute special skills to the management of ethics effort and act as a support base for the ethics manager. These may include functionaries from the areas of human resource management, training, employment/industrial relations employee counselling, employee assistance programmes, risk management, internal audit, corporate communication, fraud prevention, investigation, legal counsel and compliance.

Having an ethics manager and an ethics office is but one way of formally managing ethics and promoting ethical behaviour. Members of the organisation that are ultimately responsible for ethical leadership, as well as the implementation of ethics systems, are *line managers*.

The line manager

Ethical leadership by line management 'ensures consistency between orga-nizational values and actions' (Rasche & Esser, 2007:112). The role of the line manager is thus to make ethical values and behaviour, as defined by the code of ethics, *real* for all employees. This requires an ongoing commitment to ethical behaviour by line managers. 'Buy-in' from line management regarding ethical behaviour is brought about by a process of participation whereby they are involved in codifying standards and in using the standards to promote ethical behaviour. Buy-in by line managers is crucial in the organisational quest to establish a sustainable ethical culture over time in the sense that managers need to see the value of ethics and their role in promoting it, rather having the role of facilitator of ethics being forced upon them. It is the role of line managers to mould a viable morality for their organisations.

Line managers' ethics responsibilities commence with persuading their subordinates to behave ethically by explaining the value of ethical beha-viour (the business case for ethics) and the risk and costs associated with unethical behaviour. This can be accomplished 'without the sermon' by utilising arguments premised upon good business principles. Managers have an obligation to interpret ethical standards for their subordinates (and to thus translate the meaning of codes for concrete situations (cf. Kaptein & Wempe, 2002) and advise them on preferred ethical behaviour. They also have to incorporate ethical behaviour in key performance areas for purposes of performance appraisal, management and improvement. Managers further have the crucial responsibility to *talk* about ethics and stimulate ethics talk. In essence, managers are responsible to live ethical values, and to translate the expectations around these values for their subordinates.

The link between role players

The role players as identified above, all have important responsibilities insofar as managing corporate ethics is concerned. As such, they are individually and collectively responsible for the formal and informal management of corporate ethics. As was pointed out earlier, depending on the size and other characteristics of the organisation and its particular ethics strategy, two or even more of these roles (e.g. ethics champion and sponsor), may be performed by a single person. Furthermore, the CEO, sponsor, champion, ethics manager and a number of top executives and senior line managers can all serve on the ethics committee. As explained earlier in the chapter, institutionalisation occurs at three levels in the organisation – this requires that specific role players should also operate at the three levels (strategic, systems and operational levels) of managing ethics.

The CEO, board of directors, ethics committee, ethics champion and ethics sponsor are responsible for ethics management at the *strategic* level (cf. IoD, 2009:27). At this level ethics is systematically embedded in the corporate purpose and values as well as in strategic planning efforts. It is at this level that the organisation's ethical identity is established.

Although ethics managers are key members of the ethics committee that operates at the strategic level, they have, as coordinators of the organisational ethics function, a particular responsibility at the *systems* level. At this level specific systems, as conceptualised by the ethics committee at the strategic level, are designed, formalised, implemented and aligned to the organisation's code of ethics to ensure ethical behaviour.

It follows that line managers have key responsibilities pertaining to the *operational* level of ethics management. It is at this level that ethical performance is managed and organisational ethical values given practical meaning. As such, line managers assume responsibility for operationalising the ethical values and standards contained in the code of ethics.

The nature of the relationship between the role players, and the levels of ethics management intervention (strategic, systems and operational) at which they operate, are depicted in Figure 19.1

Figure 19.1 Managing ethics in organisations – The role players

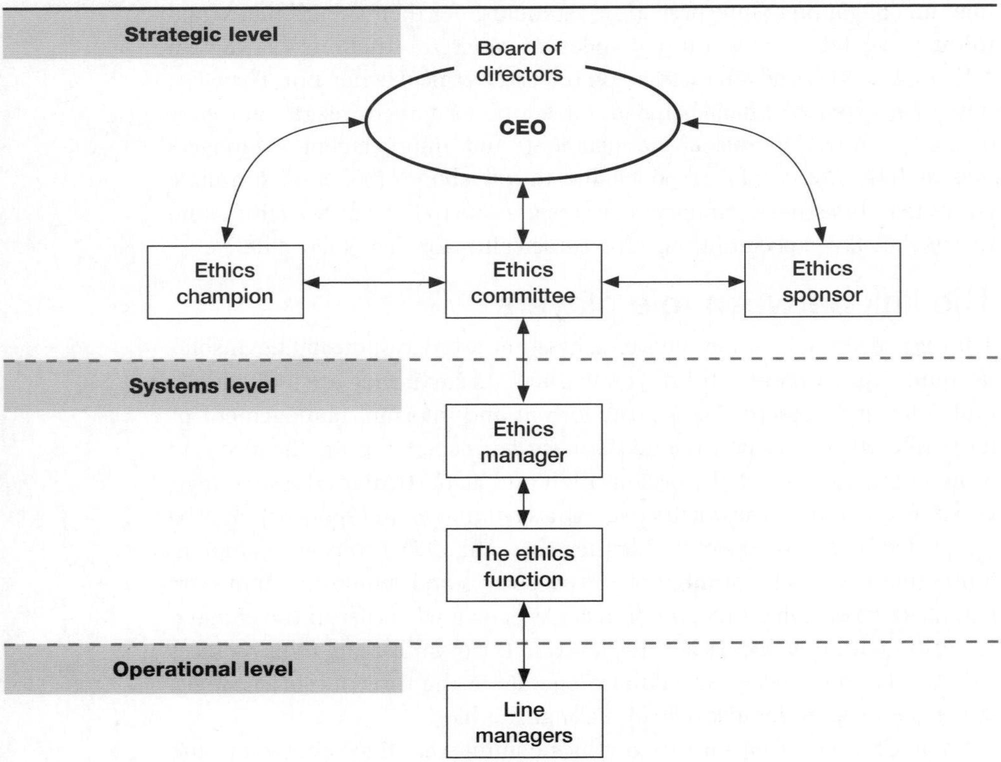

Although a rather rigid delineation of ethics management roles are presupposed by the three levels of involvement as shown in Figure 19.1, the reality is that each organisation, depending on its unique properties, resources, life cycle and existing ethical orientation, will decide on its own repertoire of role players to execute its ethics management strategy. For example, in some organisations the ethics champion, sponsor and manager roles may all be fulfilled by one person. In some organisations, the sponsor and champion roles are shared by one person. The CEO, by the same token, particularly in smaller organisations, may fulfil the sponsor and/or champion roles. The role players may also be linked somewhat differently to what is proposed in Figure 19.1 Some role players may have specific functions and duties allocated to them. Others may have symbolic significance and roles that are less formally ascribed. A word of caution may be in order here: when the ethics management role is less formally described and perhaps even rather vague, or when it becomes an over-and-above responsibility of another organisational function (e.g. risk management or compliance) an inherent danger is that the urgency of doing something about ethics may wane and even disappear over time.

Conclusion

No single strategy or process for the institutionalisation of business ethics will provide a guaranteed or quick fix remedy for ridding organisations of unethical behaviour. The quest for entrenching ethics in an organisation is a gradual process that will require not only commitment to ethical behaviour, but also sustained institutionalisation. The strategies and systems described in this chapter can put organisations on that path. It may also prepare them to report on their ethical performance. The latter will be the focus of the next chapter.

CHAPTER 20

Reporting ethical performance

*With Daniel Malan**

The final stage in the process of managing ethics is to measure and report accurately on ethical performance. Measuring and reporting on the ethical performance of a company closes the loop in terms of a corporate governance framework for managing ethics. It is part of the framework, but at the same time involves reflection on the other dimensions that have already been discussed: determining ethical risk, codifying and institutionalising ethical standards. Measuring and reporting on ethical performance is complex for many reasons. For example, often it is easier to measure *unethical* behaviour (e.g. non-compliance with a code of ethics), while ethical behaviour goes largely unnoticed. Therefore, ethical behaviour is sometimes understood to be the *absence* of unethical behaviour, which is clearly not the case. Also, ethical behaviour is closely linked to the company's values, which implies that the *attitude* of employees and their *perceptions* of their own behaviour and the behaviour of others become increasingly important. Again, these 'softer' issues are difficult to measure. The current trend is to integrate reporting on ethical performance with reporting on the social, economic and environmental performance of the company, also referred to as sustainability reporting or triple bottom-line reporting. A more generic term that is used with increasing frequency is corporate responsibility reporting.

This chapter addresses the emergence of corporate responsibility reporting, the rationale for reporting and the target audiences that reporting organisations try to reach. Finally, the different steps in the process of reporting are discussed.

* **Daniel Malan** is a Senior Lecturer at the University of Stellenbosch Business School in South Africa. He is the head of the Unit for Corporate Governance in Africa and the KPMG Special Advisor on Ethics and Governance (South Africa).

Emergence of corporate responsibility reporting

Corporate responsibility reporting has been around for longer than most people might think. Although the focus has shifted from social to environmental components and ultimately to an integrated triple bottom-line approach, the roots can be traced back more than 60 years (SustainAbility 1999:8). In the 1940s, the term 'social audit' was used for the first time by Theodore Kreps in relation to companies reporting on their social responsibilities. During the 1980s ethical investment funds in the UK and USA started screening companies based on their social and ethical performance. The 1990s saw increased reporting, e.g. the Body Shop International published its first *Values Report* (1995), including environmental, animal protection and social statements. The 1990s were described as the Transparency Decade by SustainAbility (2002:6), when a series of major incidents forced early pioneers to 'come clean' and issue reports.

SustainAbility suggested that the first decade of the 21st century could become the 'Trust Decade', based on ever-increasing transparency, accountability and reporting. The most important changes identified over the last decade are the growth in the number of reporting companies (from a few dozen to a few thousand), the shift from environmental to triple bottom-line disclosure and the rapid increase in the volume of information disclosed by companies (both printed and online). However, with more than 50 000 multinational corporations, even a few thousand reporting companies still constitute a small percentage. The challenges identified by SustainAbility relate to the following issues: the need to link sustainability issues with brand and corporate identity, the continuing disinterest in sustainability reporting by most financial institutions and the so-called 'carpet-bombing' syndrome of bombarding readers with more information, rather than more insight (Sustainability, 2002:6). If one looks at the spectacular corporate collapses that ranged from Enron in 2001 to Lehman Brothers and many other financial institutions in 2008, the reference to 'Trust Decade' certainly seems a bit optimistic. Many companies still seem to be paying lip service to transparency, accountability and reporting without aligning these concepts to their core strategic and risk management processes.

Prevalence

A KPMG survey on corporate responsibility reporting (2008) of approximately 2000 companies (including the top 250 companies of the Global Fortune 500 (GFT250) companies has revealed that 79% of the GFT250 companies currently issue stand alone corporate responsibility reports. This percentage increased from 52% in 2005.

Who is reporting?

The *KPMG International Survey of Corporate Responsibility Reporting 2008* revealed the following:

◉ Almost 80% of the largest 250 companies worldwide issued corporate responsibility reports;

◉ 75% of the largest 250 companies worldwide have a corporate responsibility strategy with defined objectives;

◉ Nearly 67% of these companies engage with their stakeholders in a structured way (a dramatic increase from 33% in 2005);

◉ More than 75% of the largest 250 companies worldwide use the Global Reporting Initiative (GRI) guidelines for reporting;

◉ 92% of the largest 250 companies worldwide disclose a code of conduct or a code of ethics, but only 59 % report on non-compliance incidents; and

◉ 40% of the reports from the largest 250 companies worldwide received formal third party assurance, while 27% of reports included other types of third party commentary (e.g. stakeholder panels or subject matter expert statements).

The top reporting companies, according to a 2006 survey performed by SustainAbility, UNEP and Standard and Poor's (2006:3) are:

1   BT
2   Co-operative Financial Services
3   BP
4   Anglo Platinum and Rabobank
6   Unilever
7   MTR and Vodafone
9   Shell Group
10 Nike and Novo Nordisk

Standards

There are emerging international standards that aim to introduce some consistency into the process of sustainability reporting. Standards in this area are mostly voluntary, but some countries (e.g. France) also have mandatory reporting requirements.

The AccountAbility 1000 Process Model (AA1000) was launched in 1999 by the Institute of Social and Ethical Accountability, a global non-profit organisation, and has subsequently been developed further into a range of formal standards, including an assurance standard and a stakeholder engagement standard. In 2008 AccountAbility published its AA1000 Accountability Principles, which are:

- the Foundation Principle of Inclusivity;
- the Principle of Materiality; and
- the Principle of Responsiveness.

The AA1000 model guides the process of engaging with stakeholders in the following areas:
- identification of issues and priorities;
- definition of performance metrics and targets; and the
- process of accounting, auditing and reporting.

The framework consists of principles of quality and process standards covering planning, accounting, auditing, reporting, and embedding. It also provides guidelines for quality assurance and offers a professional qualification. The AA1000 standard was intended to serve two related purposes: as a common currency or reference point to underpin the quality of specialised account-ability guidelines and standards, and as a stand alone system for managing and communicating social and ethical accountability and performance.

The AA1000 model is displayed below:

Figure 20.1 The Accountability 1000 Process Model (AA1000)

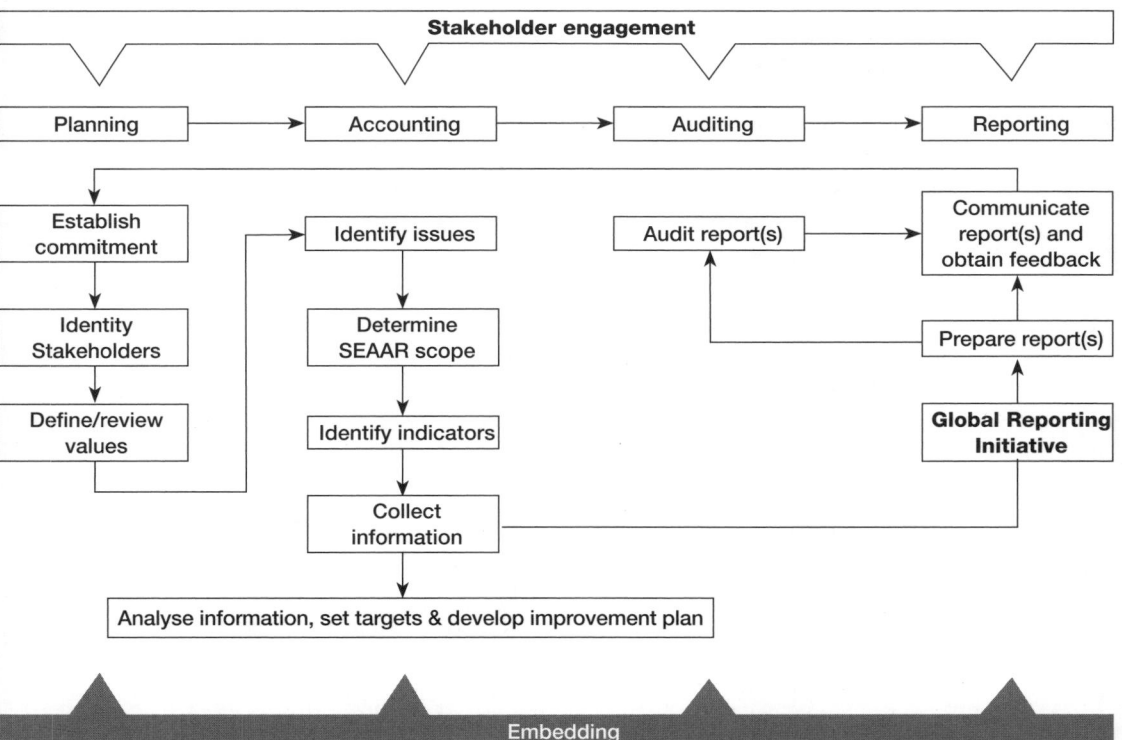

Reproduced by kind permission of the Institute of Social and Ethical Accountability

The Global Reporting Initiative (GRI) is the leader in terms of reporting guidelines for sustainability reporting. The mission of the GRI is to develop and disseminate globally applicable sustainability reporting guidelines for voluntary use by organisations reporting on the economic, environmental, and social dimensions of their activities, products and services (GRI website: http://www.globalreporting.org). The GRI embraces the principles of transparency, inclusiveness, auditability, completeness, relevance, sustainability context, accuracy, neutrality, comparability, clarity and timeliness. In 2006 the GRI published its G3 Reporting Guidelines, comprising reporting principles, reporting guidance and a set of standard disclosures on strategy, company profile and management approach, as well as specific economic, social and environmental performance indicators. These elements are all considered to be equally important.

The two key international assurance standards are the AA1000 Assurance Standard and the International Federation of the Accountants' International Standard for Assurance Engagements Other Than Audits or Reviews of Historical Financial Information (ISAE3000).

The International Standards Organisation (ISO) is also in the process of developing a guidance standard on social responsibility (ISO 26000), which should be finalised towards the end of 2009.

Rationale for reporting

The purpose of measuring ethical performance is to determine whether an existing ethics programme is successful or not, and to identify and understand the strengths and weaknesses of the programme. The purpose of ethics reporting is to ensure communication with stakeholders, both internal and external to the reporting organisation. Thus measuring and reporting ethical performance instils discipline into the management of ethics.

There are some interesting similarities and differences between financial and ethics reporting. Companies measure and report on their financial performance, not only because they are legally compelled to do so, but also because accurate measurement of performance assists the company in identifying risk areas, determining effective strategies and ultimately in improving financial performance. The same applies to reporting on ethical performance. There are some countries where reporting on non-financial performance is compulsory. For example, with effect from 2002, listed French companies have to report on their environmental and social performance. Also in South Africa the *Second King Report on Corporate Governance* recommends that companies should 'report at least annually on the nature and extent of its social, transformation, ethical, safety, health and environmental management policies and practices' (IoD, 2002). This requirement was also included in the King *Code of Governance for South*

Africa 2009 (King III), which was published in September 2009. According to this document, 'the company's ethics performance should be assessed, monitored, reported and disclosed' (IoD, 2009:21).

> In the introduction to BP's 2008 report Tony Hayward, BP's group chief executive states: 'I don't see a distinction between sustainability and performance. My aim for BP is that its performance should be sustainable – in other words everything we do each day should contribute in some way to the long-term health of BP and that of the environment and society. We measure performance accordingly, not only with financial metrics but also with the data on safety, the environment and employees ... This reflects my top three priorities as chief executive: safety, people and performance' (BP, 2008:2).

There is a growing body of empirical evidence that indicates a positive link between social and financial performance, for example the studies by Verschoor (1998) and Webley & More (2002). This is a complex relationship and should not be understood as a direct, causal link that will apply in all contexts. In 2006 Goldman Sachs released their Environmental, Social and Governance Investment Framework. The company uses the framework to integrate these issues with their existing industry analysis, primarily because they believe that such an approach will assist them to identify investment opportunities. Ittner and Larcker (2003) describe how increasing numbers of companies measure aspects like customer loyalty and employee satisfaction simply because they affect profitability even if they are not recognised by accounting rules.

Ethics reporting also leads to enhanced stakeholder relationships, improved risk management because of an increased understanding of non-financial risks, as well as improved investor relations. Institutional investors are increasingly focusing on non-financial performance when they make investment decisions. There is also a global increase in ethical investment funds and initiatives. In 2005 the United Nations Global Compact and UNEP Finance Initiative launched their Principles for Responsible Investment (http://www.unpri.org). Signatories commit themselves to incorporate environmental, social and governance (ESG) issues into their investment decisions and to report on their actions to stakeholders.

Target audience

An ethics report is prepared for the benefit of all the stakeholders of a company. Stakeholders are defined as any individual or group that has an interest in, or an influence over, the company. The identification of stakeholders is a complex process and will not be discussed in detail. A very basic model to identify and prioritise stakeholders is presented below. Based on this model, the critical stakeholders are those that are plotted in the upper right hand quadrant, i.e. high interest *and* high influence:

Figure 20.2 Prioritisation of stakeholders in terms of interest and influence

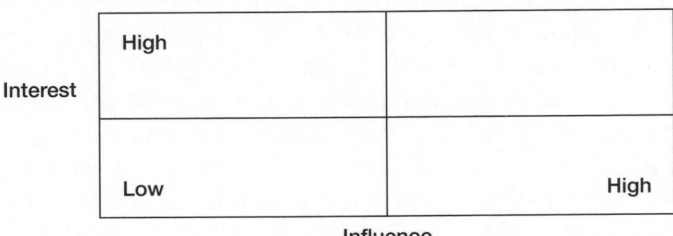

Source: KPMG 2002

Stakeholders are not passive participants in the process of ethics re-porting, i.e. they are not only readers of the ethics report. They should be consulted and engaged and – in a way – could be seen as co-authors of the ethics report. Companies who produce good ethics reports therefore usually also have successful stakeholder engagement processes in place.

It is vital to emphasise the importance of internal stakeholders – i.e. employees and, in particular, management and the board of directors. Com-panies do not necessarily produce one ethics report that is distributed to all stakeholders. For example, BP uses a tool where stakeholders can access the website and compile their own reports based on their specific interests[1]. Many large corporations nowadays use sophisticated software solutions to enable them to collate relevant information from different locations around the world.

Just as there are separate public financial reports and financial manage-ment reports, senior management should have access to ethics management reports. These reports will often have more detail than would be of interest to the external stakeholders, and could sometimes also include sensitive information. However, there is ever increasing pressure on companies to become more transparent in their reporting processes and – ironically – the more balanced, and the more comprehensive the disclosure, the more positive the impact will be on the reputation of the company. SustainAbility identifies five reporting personalities, ranging from the 'Truants' (those companies that do not report beyond legal requirements) to the 'Supersonics' (those companies that have reached the pinnacle of corporate reporting). Corporate Supersonics are described as 'having the ability to break through

---

1 http://www.bp.com/sectionbodycopy.do?categoryId=6931&contentId=7051661, accessed 1 May 2009.

transparency's glass ceiling, they operate from state of the art accountability platforms, but can still maintain the big secrets from their competitors' (SustainAbility, 2003:9).

The process of ethics reporting

The quality of the measurement process will ultimately determine the quality of the ethics report. The old axiom of 'garbage in – garbage out' also holds true for ethics reporting. Therefore, companies need a robust structure in place that will guide them through the entire process.

In the remainder of this section the main activities of ethics reporting are discussed in terms of the AA1000 process model:

Planning

The first activity required is to plan the entire process and to ensure that the basic requirements for a successful reporting process are in place. Since ethics reporting forms part of the corporate governance framework, it is not surprising that one of the critical requirements for a successful process is to get the initial support and commitment from the board of directors and senior management. Also, because the AA1000 model is inclusive, one of the early steps is to identify the stakeholders of the reporting organisation. Both senior management and stakeholders should be involved in the planning process.

Finally, to ensure consistency with its current values, the reporting organisation is required to review whether its values are aligned with its ethical objectives. In the case where a company has not yet formalised its values, it is expected to do so as a matter of priority.

It is suggested that there should be a formal structure (e.g. an ethics committee) that should oversee the planning process. This structure should have sufficient resources at its disposal and should also have credibility within the organisation. In terms of accountability, it is recommended that this structure should report, at least quarterly, to a board committee that assumes overall responsibility for the reporting process (e.g. a corporate governance or risk management committee).

Accounting

The ethics accounting process itself follows a logical sequence of events: identifying the issues that will be reported on, determining the scope of the report (e.g. for a multinational organisation the first report might not necessarily cover all its global operations, but could be restricted to a few key locations), identifying indicators that will be used, collecting the information, and finally analysing the information, setting targets and developing an improvement plan. The improvement plan is important, because the report is not only prepared for the benefit of external stakeholders, but the information will also be used as a management tool and should influence the overall business strategy of the reporting organisation.

Reporting

Once all the information is available, the report should be drafted. It has already been mentioned that an increasing number of companies are making use of the guidelines provided by the GRI when deciding on what they should report about. The specific aspects related to performance indicators are presented in the table below.

Table 20.1 GRI G3 Performance Indicators – main categories and relevant aspects

Main category	Aspects
Economic	economic performance, market presence, indirect economic impact
Environmental	materials, energy, water, biodiversity, emissions, effluents and waste, products and services, compliance, transport
Social	Labour: employment, labour / management relations, occupational health and safety, training and education, diversity and equal opportunity
	Human Rights: investment and procurement practices, non-discrimination, child labour, forced and compulsory labour, security practices, indigenous rights
	Society: community, corruption, public policy, anti-competitive behaviour, compliance
	Product Responsibility: customer health and safety, product and service labelling, marketing communication, consumer privacy, compliance

Source: GRI Sustainability Reporting Guidelines Version 3.0 © 2000-2006 GRI, pp. 25-36

Because of its broad focus on all aspects of corporate reporting, the GRI remains limited in terms of specific guidance on ethics reporting. It does not directly address aspects of organisational integrity such as the existence of a code of ethics, training programmes, ethics helplines, confidential reporting systems, etc. Consequently, the GRI guidelines need to be extended to include specific indicators on organisational integrity. The Federal Sentencing Guidelines, originally developed in the USA in the early 1990s, can for example be drawn upon to provide indicators of an organisation's commitment to organisational integrity. These indicators will be useful to any organisation, regardless of its location. In a sense, they summarise the requirements of a corporate governance framework for managing ethics. The Federal Sentencing Guidelines (2007) indicates that companies should 'promote an organizational culture that encourages ethical conduct and a commitment to compliance with the law'. This implies that companies should develop a code of ethics and then demonstrate its commitment to the code by:

◙ creating systems and procedures to introduce, monitor and enforce the code;

◙ assigning high level individuals to oversee compliance to the code;

◙ assessing the integrity of new appointees in the selection and promotion procedures;

◙ exercising due care in delegating discretionary authority;

- communicating with, and training, all employees regarding enterprise values, standards and compliance procedures;
- providing, monitoring and auditing safe systems for reporting of unethical or risky behaviour;
- enforcing appropriate discipline with consistency; and
- responding to offences and preventing re-occurrence.

Reporting on all these aspects in combination with those suggested in the GRI's guidelines will give a reasonable indication of the ethical performance of the company. If such reporting takes place in the format of detailed management reports as well as public stakeholder reports, it will successfully fulfil the dual role of a strategic and communication tool.

Auditing

Independent verification or auditing (assurance) is the process of evaluating both the contents of a report and the processes and systems that supported the preparation of the report.

Assurance can be provided either internally (e.g. by the Internal Audit department) or externally, i.e. by one or more external organisations that issue an assurance statement. Research shows that the major accounting firms have the major market share in this field, but there are many other service providers, including specialist consultancies and non-governmental organisations that are active in this field.

The environmental consulting group ERM (quoted in SustainAbility, 2002:49) has identified three different objectives for the assurance process. According to ERM, a large percentage of companies expect straightforward validation, i.e. a stamp of approval that the information contained in the report is reliable (Confirmation Seekers). A second group of companies (Active Learners) expects the assurance process to provide in-depth advice on management issues and systems, while the third group (Crowd Pleasers) considers its main audience to be the general public and retail customers. Confirmation Seekers tend to use the large accountancy firms, Active Learners prefer the specialist consultancies, while Crowd Pleasers often use non-governmental organisations or celebrity endorsements.

The following extract is a typical example of an assurance statement. It was provided by Ernst & Young for the BP Sustainability Review 2008 and this particular section focuses on the issue of materiality.

- With the exception of the subject areas listed below, we are not aware of any material aspects concerning BP's sustainability performance that have been excluded from the Report. We consider that BP could have covered the following *subject* areas in more depth in the Report:

- Disclosure of future performance targets in relation to GHG emissions reduction.
- Explanation of how stakeholder views have been taken into consideration when determining BP's response to challenging issues.
- Nothing has come to our attention that causes us to believe that BP management has not applied its processes for determining material issues to be included in the Report.

Embedding

The introduction of an ethics reporting process and framework is not easy. Quite often there is some resistance from within the reporting organisation. This resistance could be based on misunderstandings or lack of commitment and will be exacerbated if there is a perception that reporting increases the workload of those that will be actively involved in the reporting process. Therefore, the measurement processes have to be embedded within the organisation and linked to existing management information systems. This will not only increase buy-in from sceptics, but will increase the value and relevance of the information that is generated. The existence of sophisticated reporting software that ensures consistency in terms of units of measurement and automatically collates information from existing systems has proved to be extremely valuable in this regard.

Stakeholder engagement

Stakeholder engagement has to permeate the entire process. Ethics reporting addresses the relationship between an organisation and its stakeholders. If the organisation does not involve its stakeholders, or involves them only at the end of the process, the danger is always that the stakeholders will not support the process, for example by arguing that the organisation is using irrelevant indicators. By engaging stakeholders throughout the process, the organisation ensures buy-in from the early stages and strengthens the credibility of both the reporting process and the eventual report.

Conclusion

Ethics reporting is the final stage in the process of governing and managing an organisation's ethical performance. Not only does it provide essential feedback on the organisation's ethical performance. It also provides the basis upon which planning for improved ethical performance can be done. Although ethics reporting is in its infancy and the standards of reporting still emerging, its benefits are already well-established.

CHAPTER
21

Ethical leadership and organisational culture

With Derick de Jongh*

T he ethics management process described in the previous chapters (Chapters 17–20) can ensure that a company is aware of its ethics risks and opportunities, that it develops appropriate ethical standards and that it institutionalises and manages these standards in the company. There is, however, the danger that an ethics management process could become a compliance exercise or mere window dressing. If an ethics management process is, for example, instituted merely to show that a company adheres to the requirements of corporate law or to the recommendations of a corporate governance code, the ethics management process can become superficial with little or no impact on the actual ethical behaviour of the organisation and its members. This danger that haunts ethics management processes and programmes was well illustrated in the now infamous Enron case. In an article, aptly titled, *Enron ethics* (or: *Culture matters more than codes*), Sims and Brinkmann show how despite all the trappings of an ethics management process, a deep 'ethical erosion' (2003:245) pervaded the company prior to its demise.

This inherent weakness of ethics programmes is recognised in recent corporate governance developments that emphasise the importance of cultivating an ethical corporate culture that pervades all aspects of corporate life. In the USA the 2004 revised Federal Sentencing Guidelines indicated the need to 'promote an organizational culture that encourages ethical conduct and a commitment to compliance with the law' (Desio, 2006). *The Third King Report on Corporate Governance for South Africa* (generally referred to as King III) also emphasises the need for deeper and more profound change with regard to ethics: 'Good corporate governance requires that the board takes responsibility for building and sustaining an ethical corporate culture in the company' (IoD, 2009:24). This new emphasis on organisational

---

* **Prof. Derick de Jongh** is Director of the Centre of Responsible Leadership at the University of Pretoria.

ethical culture prompts organisations to move beyond ethics management programmes and to attend specifically to the organisational culture that underpins and lies beyond ethics management programmes. Leaders on all levels of the company have a vital role to play in developing and sustaining a pervasive ethical culture in a company. In this chapter, we will first explore the relationship between leadership and ethical organisational culture. Then we will examine the roles and responsibilities of leaders in the creation and sustenance of ethical culture. Finally we will analyse the functioning of ethical corporate culture and how it can be cultivated in organisations.

Governance, leadership and culture

Leadership can be exercised at various levels in organisations and also by various role players in organisations. Leadership roles also do not necessarily coincide with hierarchical position in organisations. It is exactly for this reason that a distinction is often drawn between leadership and management in organisations. Being in a management position does not necessarily mean that a person performs a leadership role. Leadership roles can be performed by those in formal managerial positions, but also by those who do not occupy such positions in organisations. Irrespective of where leadership roles are performed, they are always intimately related with the ability to envision a desired future state of affairs and the capacity to gain the commitment and cooperation of others to work towards the realisation of the envisioned state of affairs (cf. Maak & Pless, 2009:544; Palmer, 2009:527).

In the field of leadership studies various approaches to leadership are identified. One way of categorising different approaches to leadership is to distinguish between a traits approach, a behaviour approach, a situational approach and a relational approach to leadership (cf. Booysen, 2009:290–301; Painter-Morland, 2008:511–512). The traits approach focuses on the character traits that leaders need in order to be effective. In the behavioural approach the focus is on the social abilities and skills and powers of persuasion that leaders should possess. The situational approach to leadership revolves around the fit between a person (with her/his specific traits and skills) and the challenges posed by a specific circumstance. Finally, the relational approach takes a more systemic perspective where leadership is framed within processes of social interaction, and collaboration.

Within the context of corporate governance, which revolves around the responsibility of the board of directors and executive management to direct and control the company, it is to be expected that the leadership responsibility of key corporate governance role players, such as the chairperson of the board and the CEO of the company, will be emphasised. This also applies to their leadership responsibility for the ethics of the company. In King III, the ethical leadership responsibility of the chairman of the board is described as 'setting the ethical tone for the board and the company' (IoD, 2009:34), while with reference to the CEO the Report emphasises that s/he should 'foster a corporate culture that promotes sustainable ethical practices, encourage individual integrity and fulfils social responsibility objectives and imperatives' (IoD, 2009:37).

Important as the role of the board and specifically the roles of the chairperson and CEO might be, they can never be the sole owners or sole directors of ethical corporate culture. On the contrary, creating an ethical corporate culture requires a network of ethical relations in the company in which organisational members collaborate in shaping and sustaining an ethical corporate culture.

The popular characterisation of corporate culture as 'the way we do things around here' (Deal & Kennedy, 1982:4) contains an important element of the nature of culture. It accentuates that culture is unique to an organisation and also that it manifests in 'acceptable modes of behaviour' (Martin & Martin, 2009:423). Conceptualising culture in this manner is aligned to the understanding of scholars of the theory of corporate culture such as Edgar Schein, who emphasises that corporate culture is accumulated group learning that patterns the behaviour of groups. He defines corporate culture as 'a pattern of shared assumptions that the group learned as it solved its problems of external adaptation and internal integration, that has worked well enough to be considered valid and, therefore to be taught to new members as the correct way to perceive, think and feel in relation to those problems.' (1992:12; also see Lim, 1995:16). Corporate culture thus has the effect of disposing members of the culture to think and act in a specific manner (cf. Caldwell & Moberg 2007:195; Kaptein & Wempe, 2002:149).

The ethical aspect of corporate culture deals specifically with what is recognised as matters of ethical significance in an organisation and what passes for acceptable standards of behaviour. The ethical culture of an organisation is not static, but evolves over time. There is a dynamic interaction between leaders and the ethical culture of an organisation. Leaders can shape the ethical culture of an organisation, but they can also be shaped or sanctioned by the existing ethical culture. In the next section we will investigate the roles and responsibilities of leaders in shaping the corporate culture of companies.

Ethical leadership

Companies shape and influence societies in direct and indirect ways. They are thus co-responsible for creating the societies in which they operate. The ethical underpinning of this 'creational outcome' of companies' actions determines whether they contribute towards sustainable development or towards societal degeneration. Organisational leaders bear a special and unavoidable responsibility in this regard and need to understand that through their personal and institutional actions, they contribute towards the development or degeneration of society.

Developing healthy and sustainable societies requires business leaders who are capable of building balanced relationships across societal boundaries. These boundaries do not only refer to those between the private, public and civil society sectors, but also to the natural environment. In a complex world where society is characterised by a conglomeration of realities, it becomes vital for leaders to understand the inherent potential of allowing the various role players in society to be more integrated and for the boundaries between them to become more dynamic. The only way, however, for society to become more dynamic and penetrable is to create alignment between them through ethical leadership. Leaders need to understand and embrace the uniqueness of the interfaces between these societal players, as for example, between the private sector and the natural environment. Most importantly, leaders need to understand that managing this alignment within society requires ethical awareness and ethical commitment. When these interfaces are explored across societal boundaries, it will unlock great value through social collaboration that will promote both sustainable enterprises and a sustainable planet. This relational approach, as mentioned earlier in this chapter does, however, require a certain leadership mindset and characteristics. In their work based on different types of intelligence, Pless and Maak (2005) referred to this as relational intelligence. It is the ability to connect, engage and meaningfully build relationships between societal actors (internal and external stakeholders as well as the natural environment).

In order to understand the ethical parameters of their actions, leaders need to be able to deconstruct the complex world by creating connecting patterns between the various role players in society and also be capable of harnessing the powers of interdependency (Quinn & D'Amato, 2008:9). Leaders do not only have to understand these connecting patterns but also need to create them in an ethical manner. Interdependence and interconnection emerge as the binding factors in building sustainable enterprises, a just society and a sustainable planet.

In order to further build on the notion of interconnectedness as the ethical binding factor, leaders need to integrate both context and complexity (EFMD, 2005). *Contextual* relevance implies that leaders succeed in evaluating their decisions in relation to the specific aspects of their environment (e.g. cultural, economic, physical, technological, ecological). The *complexity* dimension on the other hand implies the ability of leaders to reflect on these decisions within the bigger whole (markets, societies, regions and the planet). What is thus vital is to understand the impact that an organisation has on various aspects of its economic, social and natural environment, while also taking into account the induced effects (risks, opportunities, uncertainty, etc.) it might have on the bigger whole. In order to operate in an ethical way, business leaders have to learn to shift their decision-making styles to match complex environments (cf. Snowden & Boone, 2007:74). By fully understanding the consequences of their decisions and basing them on sound ethical principles, leaders will be aware of danger signals, avoid inappropriate reactions and lead effectively in any context. Organisational leaders who therefore succeed in operating from an ethical predisposition are able to demonstrate responsibility. The relational approach covered in this section emphasises how crucially important it is for leaders to be capable of reflecting critically on the possible outcomes (positive or negative) of their decisions before making them. In the next section we will define responsible leadership and describe the roles and responsibilities of responsible leaders.

Defining responsible leadership

Responsible leaders believe in constant personal and institutional reflection of the short and long term impact of their personal and institutional decisions on society and the environment as a whole. Such leaders succeed in shaping new principles for the role of business in society, place a high emphasis on ethical fitness, believe in corporate 'statesmanship' and critically reflect on the purpose of business. Responsible leaders emphasise the importance of building sustainable organisations that do not compromise the natural, social and economic environment or the livelihood of future generations. In King III (IoD, 2009:20) strong emphasis is placed on the uncompromising role of leaders in balancing the social, environmental and economic impact of organisations' operations on society. It also underlines the importance of doing business ethically and of not aiming for the lowest common denominator, which is mindless compliance to governance regulations. On the contrary, leaders who understand the expectations of society succeed in being mindful of the impact of their actions on society. The prerequisite for responsible leadership is an ethical mindset. Sorlie (2007:22) argues that developing such an ethical mindset is the ultimate challenge to ensure that the company operates in harmony with society and the environment as a whole.

Pless and Maak (2007:438) argue for an approach to leadership 'in the larger context of leading business in society'. This approach clearly calls for a different role that responsible leaders should play in society. This role is underpinned by a deep sense of moral conviction, conscious awareness of one's own as well as societal expectations, the importance of interconnectedness, and embracing diversity. Responsible leaders therefore have to build and sustain organisations that are to the benefit of multiple stakeholders and the natural environment. They should not be, in Maak's words (2007:329), mere 'risk seeking individuals'. The challenge, however, in a stakeholder society, is not only balancing the legitimate expectations of the various stakeholders, but also understanding how these stakeholders relate to the natural environment. Maak (2007:330) points out that in an interconnected and multicultural global stakeholder society moral dilemmas are inevitable. If one adds the global environmental crisis to the mix the complexity increases further. This puts an additional demand on the ethical consciousness and responsibility of organisational leaders. What emerges is a delicate interplay between the demands of a multi-stakeholder environment in combination with those of a natural environment characterised by ever depleting resources. The decisions of leaders therefore need to reflect both human and ecosystem implications that, in turn, creates the bedrock for ethical conduct. It once again emphasises the importance of being able to reflect on decisions within the complex whole of the human and natural environment.

Characteristics of ethical leaders

Ethical leaders need to become active promoters and champions of societal and environmental sustainability. These leaders possess qualities that will enable them to be the custodians of a society where there is balance between economic and societal progress and ecological sustainability. Szekely and Knirsch (2005:631) recommends that leaders should have the qualities of vision, flexibility to change, and openness for engagement as the three key success factors to achieve a sustainable world. Table 21.1 depicts a summary of the characteristics and guiding principles of responsible leaders.

Table 21.1 Characteristics and guiding principles for responsible leaders

Characteristics of responsible leaders	Guiding principles for responsible leaders
Globally responsible conscience	Honesty
Commitment to dialogue	Freedom
Commitment to generate debate on issues	Fairness
Commitment to codes of ethics	Humanity
	Tolerance
	Transparency
	Understanding of the interconnectedness of individuals, communities, regions and ecosystems

Source: EFMD, 2005:22–25

If one considers the characteristics mentioned above it becomes clear that the emphasis is increasingly placed on accountable leadership. Leaders with an ethical mindset understand that being accountable implies responsibility beyond their own organisations. Within the context of a complex multi-stakeholder landscape combined with a depleting and stressed ecosystem, being accountable now means much more. Milton Friedman's statement in the 1970s that the social responsibility of business is to maximise profit is arguably completely outdated. The approach of being only accountable to one's shareholders has lost legitimacy. The importance for organisational leaders to fully understand to whom they are accountable, cannot be overemphasised. Being ethical and account-able implies that leaders occupy specific leadership roles, and demonstrate clear responsibilities. In the following section the roles and responsibilities of responsible leaders will be analysed.

Roles of responsible leaders

Responsible leaders have specific roles to perform. These roles relate to the complex multi-stakeholder environment within a resource constraint eco-system. These roles therefore focus mainly on weaving and creating networks of value and strengthening the relational interdependency between indivi-duals, cultures, society and the natural environment. A prerequisite for creating any external network is, however, the creation of an ethical culture inside an organisation. Leaders first need to understand the value of building and maintaining strong internal relationships before attention can be given to the external environment. Without strong, visible elements of internal ethics and values, attempting any external drive would be very difficult. An integral part of sustaining an ethical organisational culture is to highlight the interdependence between various internal role players such as business leaders, management, staff, line functions, support staff etc. Whether leaders focus internally or externally, there are a number of generic roles that responsible leaders have to fulfil. Prominent among these roles are networking and bridge building roles. Both these roles relate to the relational dimension discussed earlier, which points to the importance of leaders' abilities to build and maintain sound internal and external relationships.

The specific roles and responsibilities that have to be fulfilled by leaders in a complex multi-stakeholder, resource constraint environment are:

- *Defining the role of business in society.* Leaders have responsibilities towards society, organisational stakeholders, and the natural environ-ment. When leaders have clarity about the role of business in society, they will be able to identify whom they are accountable to and how to respond to the demands from society. Leaders should therefore be able to communicate this role of business to both internal and external stakeholders in a clear and convincing way and create systems and procedures to manage expectations and report on performance.
- *Creating new forms of value.* Leaders should not only cultivate internal

organisational values through value-based leadership, but should also create economic and social value for internal and external stake-holders, as well as environmental value to the benefit of the planet. Synergies need to be created between these different forms of value to ensure that the company, its stakeholders and the planet benefit from it. Leaders have an important role to play in raising awareness about the importance of these new forms of value both among their management and staff, as well as among the investment public, customers, suppliers and government.

◙ *Weaving value networks.* Leaders also need to facilitate interaction between and among internal and external stakeholders. They should be able to build bridges through clear and convincing communication that allows for mutual respect and collaboration. Leaders have to build trust between these various stakeholders as well as tolerance for the uniqueness and challenges that each of these stakeholders are confronted with. They have to ensure that their personal and institutional decisions support and strengthen these networks.

◙ *Shaping the future of business.* Responsible leaders have to challenge conventional business models and be critical of one-dimensional views that reduce capitalism to the creation of shareholder value. Instead they have to generate and promote new business models where short term financial success is balanced with long term sustainable development. They will be responsible for developing rules, regulations, codes of conduct and policies to deal with these new business models.

◙ *Acting with corporate statesmanship.* Leaders need to project and practise the moral character and stature associated with statesmanship. They have to reflect on the implications and consequences of their decisions for nature and society and must be willing to engage with the humanitarian challenges of our time. This requires that responsible leaders must be willing to align their personal and organisational values with the wellbeing of society and the natural environment. At the same time they should create an enabling environment for all stakeholders to act with social and environmental responsibility.

Leaders who succeed in fulfilling the roles mentioned above and accepting the responsibilities associated with these roles can be regarded as *'leaders for good'*. The double meaning of the term suggests long term sustainable outcomes that serve the best interest of society as a whole.

Ethical organisational culture

Responsible leadership is difficult to sustain if it is not anchored within an ethical organisational culture. Business ethics scholars often point to the fact that the absence of a strong ethical culture in an organisation can corrupt members on all levels of organisations, including organisational leaders. A case in point is the demise of Enron. In line with the characteristics of a typically reactive mode organisation (cf. Chapter 5), Enron had in place all the corporate social responsibility (CSR) and business ethics tools and symbols that may have created the impression that it was ethically in control. Had it been subjected to an ethics audit to assess the presence of ethical values, codes of ethics, policies and ethics officers, it could probably have convinced assessors that it complied with expectations to manage ethics. Yet the company epitomised ethical failure. Although charismatic and apparently visionary, the company's leaders were irresponsible and unethical. Enron employees were encouraged to stretch ethical limits, break the rules, be arrogant towards stakeholders and make money for the company at any cost. Unethical behaviour was not only tolerated, but often rewarded. Sims and Brinkmann (2003) suggest that Enron had a culture marked by greed, selfishness and jealousy. The company is a classical example of large-scale groupthink and widespread conformist behaviour. In this case, not conforming to the rules that had been in place, but conforming to rule-breaking practices.

As with many organisations in the reactive mode of managing ethics, ethics and CSR in Enron were no more than window dressing. Having ethics management artefacts in place, or even a rule-based compliance approach, often only addresses ethics in a superficial manner. Such ethics management 'tools' are what Sims and Brinkmann (2003) refer to as secondary catalysts. In essence, sustainable business ethics presupposes an ethical organisational culture that evolves over time under the influence of ethical leadership as primary trigger.

Characteristics of ethical organisational cultures

Organisations with strong ethical cultures have an organisational mindset based on *a strong ethical value orientation.* In such cultures there is a collective moral conscience (Sims & Brinkmann, 2003), or a 'collective mindfulness' (May, 2009:105). An ethical organisational culture represents 'a collective or institutional ethic beyond the ethics of the individual' (Goodpaster, 2007:161). The organisation has a strong ethical identity, and ethics is integral to how the organisation defines itself and to how things are done. Ethical values are neither merely seen as elements that need to be managed, nor interpreted as rules that need to be adhered to, but are made part of the *operating consciousness* (Goodpaster, 1989) of the organisation and are seamlessly integrated into organisational philosophies, practices and behaviour. In such organisations ethics is an integral and natural part of the organisational culture. If organisational culture is described in the way that it often is as 'the way we do things around here', ethical culture may be described as 'the way we do things around here even when no one is watching'.

What do ethical cultures consist of? The ethical culture of an organisation is an interdependent, interrelated dimension of the broader organisational culture. Ethical culture can be compared to an iceberg. The part of an iceberg that protrudes above the ocean is the dimension of ethical culture that is formal, often structured, and visible. The submerged, and much larger, component of the iceberg represents a more informal, tacit and not readily observable dimension.

There is also not necessarily a clear distinction between the obvious and tacit dimensions. Each of these dimensions consists of several sense-making tools or devices that guide and shape behaviour. Tools such as articulated values, clear rules, codes of ethics, policies, disciplinary procedures and ethics management structures are clearly visible and measurable elements of an ethical culture. The less obvious or submerged elements, but probably much more significant in the shaping of an ethical culture, are the organisational stories, traditions, and informal practices. These elements constitute what could be called 'deep culture' – they are not easily demarcated, articulated, measured or understood. The deep culture evolves slowly and is entrenched over time by deep-set values and beliefs, leadership behaviour, interactions with stakeholders and feedback on interactions. They do, however, play a significant role in shaping behaviour, or in influencing 'the way things are done around here'.

Deep ethical culture

The best manifestations of a pervasive ethical culture are found in a totally aligned (TAO)-mode organisations (cf. Chapter 5). A significant part of such an organisation's iceberg protrudes above the water. Clearly defined ethics management tools exist and ethics form a natural part of organisational talk, behaviour and practices. Ethical values are not only espoused, but talked about and *lived* by all members of the organisation. The ethical pillars of responsibility, accountability, fairness and transparency are seamlessly integrated within organisational practices and behaviour. Stakeholders are treated with respect and they show high levels of trust in the organisation. They are comfortable that ethical concerns may be raised without fear of retribution (May, 2009:97).

Ethical norms and standards, and subsequently resultant behaviour, are shaped by the deep culture elements of tales, totems, traditions and taboos that constitute the submerged part of the organisation as iceberg. *Tales*, or organisational stories, relate to accounts of previous ethically examplary behaviour. The historical accounts of actions by organisational ethical role models are told and retold in ethical cultures. An example of such culture forming behaviour is that of Motorola employees relaying the story of Paul

Galvin's stance on ethics in the 1950s. Moorthy et al (1998) explain that Galvin, the company's CEO at the time, had fully supported (rather than fired) Motorola employees that had walked away from a suspicious business deal that would have been the largest in the history of the company at the time (cf. Chapter 9). *Totems* are human beings or inanimate objects that elicit 'almost superstitious respect' from stakeholders and therefore serve as 'the foundation of a social system of obligation and restriction' (Kirkpatrick, 1983; 1365). As such, they contribute to the formation of ethical culture by their mere presence, or by the legend built around them. It could be said that Alan Knott-Craig, the founding CEO of Vodacom (a South African cellular phone network provider) is regarded as a totem in the company even beyond his retirement in 2008. His motto of 'we deal straight' is legendary in the industry. The Johnson & Johnson Credo (code of ethics), even though it is an inanimate object, has been afforded ever-increasing totem status, even beyond the company's boundaries, since its inception in 1943. *Traditions*, as doctrines, customs, beliefs, rituals and practices, are equally powerful foundations of ethical cultures in that they are handed over from generation to generation in organisations. Such traditions provide opportunities for 'caring and sharing, for developing a spirit of 'oneness' (Weiss, 2003:131). The tradition of certain banks to reward employees that expose fraudulent practices contributes to the norm that fraud is unacceptable and promotes employee honesty. *Taboos* act as organisational prohibitions to exclude undesirable behaviour. A typical taboo is the practice of extramarital affairs among employees that is seriously frowned upon, or even punished, in many organisations. The Boeing example related in Chapter 9 serves to illustrate this taboo.

The tales, totems, traditions and taboos are usually relatively stable phenomena that emerge gradually over a number of years. Over time they become part of the organisational establishment and contribute significantly to what is regarded to be ethically desirable philosophies and behaviour. It has to be conceded though that the tales, totems, traditions and taboos as explained could also be negative or undesirable in nature. When this is the case, the formation of ethical culture is retarded or even continuously heavily undermined. It is extremely difficult, or even impossible in some cases where unethical norms prevail, to create a culture of ethics. A popular intervention, by many organisations in the post-Enron era, is to deal with cultures where unethical norms are endemic by introducing a heavy-handed compliance (rule-based) strategy for dealing with ethics. Although such an approach may have short-term benefits in certain organisations, it does not guarantee the establishment of an ethical *culture* over time. Attempts to influence culture under circumstances where ethical behaviour is externally enforced may even be met with disdain and cynicism, particularly in fear-based, autocratic organisational environments.

295

Establishing deep ethical culture

Changing or influencing deep culture requires long term paradigmatic change intervention. Should one wish to change the ethical culture of the organisation, changing merely the visible, 'above the water' elements of the iceberg would be a necessary but not sufficient condition for ensuring substantial and sustainable change in the ethical culture. Since the visible part of the ethical culture iceberg may be adequately addressed by the ethics management process as described in Chapters 17–20, changing the submerged part of the iceberg is clearly a challenge that needs to be addressed. The challenge is characterised by the tacit and often unarticulated and inexpressible nature of the submerged iceberg. A further complication is that ethical culture is not fixed. According to Painter-Morland it evolves and accommodates, and is open to challenge and continuous reform. She emphasises that 'the tacit sense of moral propriety that informs the behaviour of an organization's individual employees does not develop overnight. It develops gradually over time and is never entirely reified' (2008:520). The way in which an organisation might acquire an ethical culture over time is by (a) confirming its moral conscience, (b) recognising and enacting an ethical culture as a social construction, (c) embracing the benefits of relational leadership, and (d) ensuring osmosis between the visible and the tacit. These four aspects are discussed below.

Organisational moral conscience

Once an organisation has embraced the necessity of building a moral conscience in order to be accountable to all stakeholders and to influence and build a sustainable society, it has to aim at a *balanced* pursuit of goals and purposes. It is most likely the mindset of conscience that provides a platform for ethical organisations to optimally balance the three types of values (strategic, work and ethical) that constitute its core values (see Chapter 1). The core values and ethical identity of an organisation give continuity and direction to 'the way we do things around here even when no one is watching'. It is this tacit sense of purpose that empowers the organisation and its members to think and act ethically. Sets of values cannot be imposed. Effecting a change in ethical culture requires that ethical values be based on a sense of common cause (identity) and normative propriety. Painter-Morland explains that 'this congruity of purpose and priority among the members of an organization has a powerful effect on their sense of common cause and normative propriety' (2008:521). The congruity of purpose and priority need to move from the tacit to the tangible however – the ethical values need to be *lived* for an ethical culture to form.

Ethical culture as a social construction

Social constructionism holds that human communication is the key process that creates and maintains realities. Organisations and their realities, in this case ethical cultures, are products of their members' worldviews as these emerge in interactions. As such, organisations' moral mindsets are continually shaped by all their members through interaction. Although there is a substantial component of ethical culture that evolves naturally over time, leaders and members that share a sense of common ethical purpose and accountability are primary catalysts in constructing the organisation's emerging social order. Role modelling appropriate behaviour and reinforcing the submerged elements of tales, totems, traditions and taboos that contribute positively to strong ethical cultures are the responsibilities of all members of the organisation, whether they are performing their job-related duties in isolation, in teams, or in interaction with others.

Relational leadership

Change in ethical culture requires a shared ethical organisational mindset. This mindset is influenced by, and is the responsibility of, every member of the organisation. There is thus a clear sense of interdependence required for the evolvement of ethical cultures. In such cultures the leaders, through modes of *relational* leadership, create communication systems that foster interdependence in the organisation. Relational leaders practice what May (2009:97) refers to as 'dialogic communication', which is open, honest and reciprocal. Such communication is non-transactional and unconditional. Employee participation in decision making is valued and stimulated.

Leaders, through their actions, directions and influence, remain primary catalysts in shaping employees' sensibilities. In terms of social learning theory, individuals pay attention to and emulate credible and attractive role models (Painter-Morland, 2008). Relational leaders, as role models, play a variety of roles in establishing stakeholder trust. As stewards, coaches, architects and story tellers they are in a position to change the tacit and often mythical status of tales, totems, traditions and taboos into organisational reality. Leaders, by influencing social processes in the organisation, create contexts and communication systems in which all members of the organisation can participate to create moral congruence.

The challenge of making ethics *real* remains, however. In this regard it is leaders, through their experience, power and competence who need to ensure that each employee understands the organisation's ethical values in job-specific context and content terms. What integrity, respect, fairness and transparency mean to each individual in terms of his/her job, and how the enactment of these values affect the organisation's ethical culture and resultant stakeholder relations, need to be understood in concrete, observable terms. Should values remain vague, unstated and unmonitored, behaviour that could be in conflict with the values might be rewarded (Ferrell, Fraedrich & Ferrell, 2008). Having a clear sense of the value of ethics and the way in which shared ethical mindsets form when the abstract nature is removed from ethical values, relational leaders help employees to 'translate' values into real, observable and measurable behaviours,

The power of effective ethical engagement, or organisational *ethics talk*, is recognised by relational leaders. As relational agents, leaders can stimulate and facilitate open discourse on ethics and the consequences of decisions. By doing this, they create a context whereby employees are empowered, or given a mandate, to raise ethical concerns. Furthermore, through interdependent communication, they shape future discourse by giving employees an ethics vocabulary.

Osmosis

In the iceberg metaphor there is not necessarily a clear distinction between the obvious and tacit dimensions of ethical culture. What is required is osmosis to shift the membrane between the obvious and the tacit to the extent that more of the submerged part of the iceberg becomes visible. Through relational leadership, osmosis is created between the observable (codes, rules and ethics management structures) and the less obvious (the tacit elements of the deep culture). Merging the observable with the tacit gives substance to tales, totems, traditions and taboos – these become vehicles through which codes are lived and ethics management systems embraced. If there is sufficient ethically positive content to tales, totems, traditions and taboos they should be brought to the fore, celebrated and thus further institutionalised. In this way business ethics programmes and tacit values, beliefs and practices are fused over time to establish organisational cultures of ethical propriety and substance.

Conclusion

The introduction of an ethics management programme as discussed in the previous four chapters (17–20) is important for governing and managing the ethics performance of an organisation. There is, however, the danger that such an ethics programme can become an exercise that results in mindless compliance, without really affecting the ethical behaviour of an organisation and its members. To ensure the effectiveness of an ethics programme, it needs the visible support of responsible leaders who care about the ethics of their organisations and who can build trusting relations within their organisations, as well as with their organisations' external stakeholders. In addition, the ethics programme needs to be embedded in an ethical organisation culture where ethical consciousness permeates the thinking and doing of all organisational members.

PART

7

Case studies

INTRODUCTION

In the final part of the book a number of case studies are presented. Some of the cases are high profile cases that received substantial media coverage, while others are less known real-life cases or fictional ones depicting typical ethical issues that arise in the workplace. The issues that emerge in these case studies include conflicts of interest, executive remuneration, anti-competitive behaviour, retrenchment, favouritism, bribery, fraud, and many more typical business ethical issues and dilemmas.

The purpose of this last part of the book is to give readers the opportunity to apply the knowledge and skills gained in previous chapters to specific situations that are likely to occur (or that have already occurred) in the workplace. There are questions at the end of each case study that will assist in the analysis and assessment of these case studies. Teachers can also use the case studies in conjunction with specific chapters in the book. For this purpose references to specific chapters have been made in the questions that follow the case studies.

CHAPTER
22

Business ethics cases

In this final chapter the reader will be introduced to a number of case studies in business ethics. The ABSA-PSL, Clover SA and South African Airways (SAA) cases are real ones that were quite extensively reported on in the media. Investigative journalists' reports that appeared in newsprint were integrated to compile the cases describing the ethics in these companies. The other cases are shorter, some being real-life incidents, and the others purely fictional. They do, however, reflect typical dilemmas and issues in business ethics as experienced by organisations, irrespective of size and power. The case descriptions are followed by a number of questions that may serve as guidelines in the interpretation of the cases. It is suggested that readers track the references to specific chapters of the book in order to interpret the cases in terms of the theory presented in the relevant chapters.

Case one: The ABSA-PSL liaison

On 30 September 2007 the *City Press* newspaper published an open letter by Trevor Manuel, the South African Minister of Finance. The letter was addressed to Steve Booysen, the CEO of Absa at the time. This bank is a listed company and is one of the so-called 'big four' South African banks. In the letter he questions, in no uncertain terms, certain dimensions of a sponsorship deal that Absa had made to sponsor the National Professional Soccer League (NSL) that conducts its affairs under the name and brand of the Professional Soccer League (PSL). The PSL is the South African premier football (soccer) league.

The Minister was prompted to write this letter when it became public knowledge that the PSL's chairperson, three other executive committee members and a consultant to the committee were due to receive R50–70 million (approximately US$5–7 million) as commission for their efforts in securing a R500 million (approximately US$50 million) sponsorship from the bank. In the process Absa had successfully outbid Standard Bank as the other major bidder.

Mr Manuel accused Absa of intending to pay commissions to the officials and consultant mentioned above. Referring to the executive committee of the PSL he stated that his 'understanding is that individuals concerned are elected into office to serve the interests of the sports code ... there cannot ever have been an expectation that they would have so acquired ownership of soccer that they have an entitlement to personal enrichment for administering the sport' (Manuel, 2007:2). In addressing Absa, through its CEO, Manuel stated: 'Making such an irregular payment is wrong, morally reprehensible and corrupt. It worries me that Absa would make such an announcement without batting an eyelid' (Manuel, 2007:2). The Minister further warned Absa: 'I surely need not remind you that corruption is a criminal offence for both the giver and the receiver. I cannot understand, though, why the same issues do not arise in your mind when dealing with sports administrators' (Manuel, 2007:2).

Tromp (2007) of the Johannesburg *Star* newspaper reported two days later that Patrick Craven of COSATU, in his capacity as spokesperson for the country's largest trade union federation, said the following about the PSL executive sponsorship committee: 'While their responsibilities legitimately include seeking business sponsorship, it is immoral, if not illegal, for them to receive huge bonuses and commissions from sponsors for performing their normal duties'.

The reactions of other members of the PSL executive committee who were not members of the sponsorship sub-committee were aligned to that of the Minister. One committee member, for example, warned that it would lead to infighting among executives to secure positions on the seemingly lucrative sponsorship sub-committee (Tromp, 2007). Another committee member accused the sponsorship sub-committee of having had no authority to do the deal without first informing the full PSL executive committee, and that 'there is absolutely nothing in the PSL constitution to suggest a 10% bonus in any deal' (Mark, 2007).

Absa subsequently vehemently denied that it would pay money into the personal bank accounts of the PSL officials. It stated further that the commission payments were an internal matter for the PSL, and that the bank could not dictate terms of corporate governance for recipients of its sponsorships. The bank therefore absolved itself of any accountability of how the money given as sponsorship would be utilised. The reason given for this was that this situation was different from other corporate social investment projects that the bank sponsored and over which control could be exerted.

Following the bank's denials, the spokesperson for the Ministry of Finance, Thoraya Pandy, reiterated that the Minister had accused Absa of allegedly turning a blind eye to the PSL's internal bonus (commission) arrangements on the sponsorship deal (Ensor, 2007). She added that it was the Minister's opinion that the bonus money would be better spent on community sporting projects. The commissions created further controversy after a survey conducted a few months prior to the announcement of the sponsorship deal and the commission to be paid to the members of the PSL executive, revealed that some players in the PSL earn as little as R1 000 (approximately US$100) per month (Tromp, 2007). Pandy reiterated that 'The minister says the ethical issues remain. These officials have been selected to serve the interests of their organisations and not for personal enrichment' (Misbach, 2007). She further questioned the magnitude of the commissions, given the dire need to fund the development of football in the country.

One of the potential recipients of the commissions and PSL sponsorship committee member, Mato Madlala, was outraged at the accusations. He was adamant that there was nothing sinister about the 10% commission for people who secured sponsorship: 'It's crazy, I don't even know what to say. In the past, we had companies that sourced sponsorship for the league and we paid them the commission. It is not true that we are doing it for ourselves' (Moholoa, 2007).

The PSL later changed the term 'commission' to 'token of gratitude' prior to rewarding the executive committee members for securing the sponsorship.

The official PSL website (www.psl.co.za) contains what is called the 'objects' (sic) of the PSL:

The objects of the league are:

6.1 to promote, organise, control and administer professional football;

6.2 to co-ordinate and facilitate the development of professional football;

6.3 to foster friendly relations amongst officials, clubs, teams and players of the League;

6.4 to uphold constitution, rules and the code of ethics;

6.5 to promote the interests of clubs

6.6 to concern itself with matters affecting professional football;

6.7 to utilise its funds in the pursuit of its objectives but not for personal gain except:

6.7.1 for the payment of staff as per their employment contracts,

6.7.2 for the awarding of honoraria to the Executive Committee as approved by clubs at the Annual or Biennial General Meeting,

6.7.3 for the payment of people employed or contracted to carry out specific tasks or work.

6.8 to do all such things as may be incidental or conducive to the attainment of its objectives.'

Source: NSL Constitution, 2007. [Online]. Available: http://images.supersport.co.za/NSL Constitution as amended 29 December 2007.pdf [Accessed on 14 April 2009]

The PSL Code of Ethics appears on the official PSL website (http://thepsl. co.za/content.asp?id=5485 [Accessed on 4 May 2009]). The date of publication on the website is not provided.

Questions for discussion

1 Are there key ethical issues that can be identified in this case, and if so, what are they?

2 Describe how ethics could potentially have been divorced from both Absa's and the PSL's objectives in the liaison described in the case study. (Chapter 4: Ethics in organisations)

3 How could the respective organisations' relations with stakeholders potentially be affected by the liaison? (Chapter 9: Ethics and corporate reputation)

4 How could the situation have been dealt with differently? (Chapter 12: Making ethical business decisions) If it had already occurred, how could it have been managed to prevent further damage?

Case two: CLOVER SA

Clover SA is South Africa's largest milk and dairy product company and processes 30% of South Africa's milk in 17 factories. It has a staff complement of 6 200 and its annual turnover is R4,3 billion (Clover, 2009). The company started in 1898 as a small creamery in the Natal province. It was eventually operated for many decades as a co-operative called NCD (National Co-operative Dairies). As a co-operative it essentially belonged to milk-producing farmers until it became a public company in 1994.

The company's core values include idealism, dedication and respect. The current vision statement reads: 'To be a leading and competitive company in South Africa and selected African countries, reaching every consumer on a daily basis with its most admired branded and trusted products, delivering improved and sustainable shareholder value by being a responsible corporate citizen and preferred employer' (Clover, 2009).

During 2004–2005 the company went through a series of unfortunate events. In 2003 Clover showed a loss of R50 million. The next year (2004) it made a profit of about R180 million on a turnover of R3,8 billion. The profit was largely due to severe asset-stripping in the company (Solidarity, 2005). According to the 2004 annual report, a number of executive directors and senior managers earned R56 million by selling shares back to the company (de Lange, 2005). This amount represented 11,56% of the company's share capital issued. They had previously purchased these shares at a price of

60c per share. The shares were then sold to the company at R6 per share (Solidarity, 2005). Soon thereafter they bought back 10,7% of the company at a price of R15,8 million (de Lange, 2005). Top management also earned R6,55 million in income from dividends during 2004.

After initially increasing the price of milk purchased from producers by 10c per litre in early February 2005, Clover then unilaterally decreased the producer price of milk on two separate occasions by a total of 20c per litre (in late February and mid-March 2005). The company justified its decision based on a statement that there was an oversupply of milk of 60 million litres on an annual basis in the country (van Rooyen, 2005). The milk producers, however, denied that there was an oversupply (van Rooyen, 2005). It also came as a huge shock to them, as feeding costs were much higher in the southern hemisphere winter months. An estimated 700 producers owned shares in the company at the time.

Also in the first quarter of 2005, Clover announced a joint venture with Fonterra (a New Zealand dairy co-operative and the world's largest exporter of milk products) (Visser, 2005). Clover's reason for the intended joint venture was that it experienced a shortage of 300 tons of milk products (Visser, 2005). In a case brought against Clover by a number of producers in the South African Competition Tribunal, judgement was eventually passed in favour of the Clover-Fonterra deal (Enslin, 2005). In April 2005 the Competition Commission also investigated Clover and other companies in the industry for collusion to control milk prices (van Vuuren, 2005).

In April 2005, less than nine months after executives had benefited from their share options deals, the company announced the retrenchment of 500 employees (de Lange, 2005). This would result in a cost-saving of about R100 million in employee costs. The CEO of Clover at the time, Robert Wesseloo, said about the cost-cutting intervention: 'The only solution is to pay less for raw materials and to take out people. This is normal business practice' (de Lange, 2005).

Questions for discussion

1 Are there key ethical issues that can be identified in this case, and if so, what are they?
2 What are possible causes of the actions taken by the management of Clover?
3 Describe the impact of the chain of events on trust relations between Clover and its stakeholders. (Chapter 3: The social responsibility of business; Chapter 11: Ethics and trust)
4 How could these situations have been handled differently? (Chapters 16–21: Governing ethical performance)

Case three: South African Airways

South African Airways (SAA) is one of the world's oldest airlines (established in 1934). It is the largest commercial airline organisation in Africa. Its vision is 'To deliver sustainable profits and to grow our market share through world-class service to our customers internally and externally' (SAA, 2009). The organisation is state-owned and employs approximately 8 000 people. Its values are: Customer Focused, Accountability, Integrity, Safety, Excellence in Performance, and Valuing our People. The value of integrity is described as 'Practising the highest standards of ethical behaviour in all our lines of work and maintaining credibility by making certain that our actions always match our words consistently' (SAA, 2009). During the 2007/2008 financial year the airline's turnover exceeded R17 billion (Approximately US$1,7 billion).

The CEOs

The last three permanently appointed CEOs of SAA have been Coleman Andrews (1998–2000), André Viljoen (2001–2004) and Khaya Ngqula (2004–February 2009). The current acting CEO is Chris Smyth.

Andrews was brought in from the United States of America by Transnet, the state-owned parent company, to turn the organisation around from its precarious financial position at the time. After his contract expired it came to light that his total compensation for his time at the helm had been R244 million. This equated to approximately R580 000 per day (de Lange, 2009a). Andrews left the organisation amidst allegations of bullying tactics during takeovers and bad judgement calls regarding exchange rate hedging manoeuvres (*Noseweek*, 2001).

Andrews was succeeded by André Viljoen, who was paid R2,4 million during his term as CEO. Viljoen took up his position at a time when the airline industry worldwide suffered huge post-9/11 losses. It appeared initially that the airline was recovering financially under Viljoen's leadership, yet after his departure it came to light that the airline was R6 billion in the red due to the accumulated effect of fuel price hedging by these two CEOs (Williams, 2007). Two years after Viljoen's contract had been terminated, a commission headed by Judge Mervyn King found that a company incentive share scheme had unfairly advantaged Viljoen and 12 other directors (Phasiwe, 2006). 'It is open to argument that management, who were also directors, acted wittingly by directing the valuations [of share prices] and effectively being both seller and purchaser' (Phasiwe, 2006). The report recommended that Viljoen and the other directors pay back the money.

In August 2004 Viljoen was succeeded by Khaya Ngqula. Ngqula had been successful at turning the Industrial Development Corporation (IDC) around, but he had no previous experience in the aviation sector. Barron

(2009) reports that although Ngqula had turned the IDC into a vehicle of black economic empowerment, his term at the IDC 'was marred by stories that some of those empowered with IDC funds may have been too close to him for comfort'. During his time as CEO at the IDC questions were asked about him facilitating a deal where ISCOR (at the time the major steel producer in South Africa) was acquired by Mittal Steel for an amount of R5 billion (de Lange, 2009b). The market capitalisation of the new group, ArcelorMittal (SA), was estimated to be R37 billion shortly after the takeover (de Lange, 2009b). During 2003 it was revealed that one of the IDC's clients had furnished Ngqula's coastal home in East London as a 'favour' to the CEO (de Lange, 2009b). During his term as CEO of SAA Ngqula served on the boards of 38 organisations (Leuvennink, 2007).

Ngqula's mandate at SAA was clear from the outset: he had to prepare the carrier for a partial listing on the JSE's Securities exchange, and to do this through cost-cutting and customer service of high quality (Barron, 2009). In 2005, when the rising oil prices had pushed SAA to the brink of adopting a survival strategy, Ngqula said he would be happy if half of the 602 senior managers on SAA's payroll at the time were to leave (Derby, 2005).

Three months after taking over the reins from Viljoen, he took a holiday as guest of billionaire Naresh Goyal, chairman of Indian airline Jet Airways (Barron, 2009). Barron (2007) reports that this was on the eve of negotiations over the lease of three Airbus A340–300s by SAA to Jet Airways. SAA leased the aircraft to Jet for R450 million. It later emerged that it could have earned an additional R110 million if it had done business with another Indian airline, whose offer Ngqula had rejected (Barron, 2009).

The June 2005 employee strike that lasted for six days and caused 60% of all SAA flights to be cancelled at a cost of R50 million per day, was a major crisis for the airline that Ngqula, as CEO, would have been expected to deal with. He was, however, holidaying with his wife at a luxury hotel near the Kruger Park for the duration of the strike (Barron, 2009).

During 2005 Ngqula explained to a transport sub-committee of parliament that he was justified in spending R500 000 on 15 helicopter trips between Johannesburg and Pretoria to attend meetings.

Between 2004 and 2008 Ngqula received R20 million in salary. Over and above this amount he also received a 'retention fee' to the value of R68 750 per month. When Ngqula was relieved of his duties in early March 2009, he repaid the retention fees. Several other SAA directors also received retention fees, most notably the directors of the support functions of human resources and legal counsel. The retention bonuses were paid at a time that followed an agreement between SAA and its major trade union, Satawu, to collectively cut costs by means of a wage freeze (Barron, 2009). De Lange (2009a) reports that SAA had budgeted R72,2 million during 2008 to reward managers for effectively applying procedures that lead to

600 retrenchments. Approximately 3 000 SAA employees were retrenched during Ngqula's time at the helm.

In November 2008 the *Sunday Times* reported that Ngqula had reinstated 691 000 expired frequent flyer miles of a consultant hired by the airline to probe fraud and luggage theft (Hawkey, 2008). The decision to reinstate the airmiles was in breach of the SAA's Voyager (frequent flyer scheme) policy. The consultant was effectively rewarded with frequent flyer miles, thus tax-free 'income', in lieu of payment for services rendered. The total frequent flyer miles available to the consultant could, for example, be used for 56 one-way business class flights to London, or 265 economy class flights from Johannesburg to Cape Town (Hawkey, 2008).

At the end of January 2009 a dossier containing serious allegations against Ngqula was handed to the Minister of Public Enterprises. This was as a result of a catering deal worth R3,5 billion between SAA and a French company, Servair. Servair's empowerment partner is Vusi Sithole, a business partner of Ngqula's wife, Piliso (2009).

Ngqula took special leave during 2009, pending an investigation (Gerwel, 2009). His contract was terminated while he was on special leave. The chairman of the SAA Board, Professor Jakes Gerwel, stated in the *Business Times* of 22 March 2009 that the board 'took the decision to terminate Khaya Ngqula's contract for very logical reasons. If the board had not decided to separate with Mr Ngqula, he would still be earning his salary and retention premiums while on special leave' (Gerwel, 2009).

The leadership team

Soon after Ngqula's appointment, Oyama Mabandla, who had been rated by independent evaluators to have been first in line to succeed Viljoen, resigned from the organisation. Within six months of Ngqula's appointment a further 11 directors and senior managers had been dismissed or resigned. Among these was the highly rated, internationally experienced Chief Operating Officer, Kyrl Acton who had been 'unable to cope with his [the CEO's] apparently autocratic, bullying style' (Barron, 2009).

According to the records of Cipro (Companies and Intellectual Property Registration Office of South Africa) the 11 SAA board members collectively held 220 directorships during 2007 (Leuvennink, 2007). This equated to an average of 20 directorships per director. One board member held 51 directorships.

Financial status

SAA posted a pre-tax loss of R8,7 billion in the 2003/2004 financial year (Derby, 2005). In mid-2007 the CEO announced a cost-cutting initiative that would save the airline R2,7 billion in 18 months.

The airline suffered a loss of R833 million in the 2007/2008 financial year (Ensor, 2009). In the 2008/2009 financial year its loss amounted to R1 billion (Ngobeni, 2009). SAA requested a R5,2 billion rescue package from the government in 2008, but was granted R1,6 billion for its 2009/2010 budget. In February 2009 SAA chief financial officer Kaushik Patel 'warned that the airline's precarious financial situation was likely to deteriorate even further as it was severely undercapitalised and burdened by debt, which exceeded its equity by 10%' (Ensor, 2009). Since SAA's level of indebtedness is higher than those of Delta Airlines and American Airlines which have been placed under bankruptcy protection (Ensor, 2009), it is clear that the carrier's sustainability is in jeopardy.

Price-fixing

In 2005 the airline faced the threat of a fine to the value of R1,6 billion for offering higher than industry standard commissions to travel agents to book passengers on SAA flights (Phasiwe, 2005). It was eventually fined R100 million. The fine was paid during 2005 and 2006.

In March 2009 SAA was facing new charges of price-fixing (Ngobeni, 2009). It is one of several airlines under investigation for partnering in a price-fixing cartel (Ngobeni, 2009). A number of airlines implicated in the cartel had already paid US$1,2 billion in fines in the US and Australia for inflating cargo shipping prices (Ngobeni, 2009). SAA had budgeted US$10 million (R100 million) in its 2007/2008 budget to make provision for possible fines by international aviation authorities (Ngobeni, 2009). The possibilities of having to settle civil claims remain. SAA executives could also face prosecution in the US.

Questions for discussion

1. Are there key ethical issues that can be identified in this case, and if so, what are they?
2. In what mode of managing ethics does SAA find itself? Provide reasons for your assessment? (Chapter 5: A model of managing corporate ethics)
3. How would you describe the ethical culture and levels of trust in SAA? (Chapter 11: Ethics and trust; Chapter 21: Ethical leadership and organisational culture)
4. What role could the governance of ethics have played if it had been in existence in the organisation? (Chapter 16: Corporate governance and ethics; Chapters 17–21: The ethics management process)
5. Assess the leadership in SAA from an ethical perspective.

Case four: Company turnaround? Or not?

Optimix, a chemicals distribution organisation (with 1 200 employees), is in the process of a successful turnaround, after having appointed Mr Alan Chiever ten months ago. Mr Chiever is a strategist with a very successful reputation for reviving struggling corporations. The company is just starting to break even and is showing excellent growth prospects. Top management is extremely optimistic and relieved that the threatened mass retrenchments appear to have been averted. The climate in the company has changed completely. Morale is high and employees are motivated and working productively.

Today, however, the ethics committee is meeting to discuss a very disturbing piece of information that has come in from the ethics hotline. It appears that Mr Chiever has been utilising a strategy that was devised by another company, Systemfix, to which Mr Chiever had access, but was bound from using by a non-disclosure clause. This fact was heretofore not known to anybody at Optimix.

Optimix is fighting for survival and has just started a recovery. In fact, it may not succeed without Mr Chiever at the helm. However, the company's reputation is at stake. Either way, the future again appears bleak.

Questions for discussion

1   Are there key ethical issues that can be identified in this case, and if so, what are they?
2   Would you classify the ethical issue in this case as a business decision with ethical implications or as an ethical dilemma? (Chapter 12: Making ethical business decisions; Chapter 14: Resolving ethical dilemmas)
3   How could the organisation go about solving this problem? (Chapter 12: Making ethical business decisions; Chapter 14: Resolving ethical dilemmas)

Case five: The death of a town

Loriston is a small town (with approximately 7 000 inhabitants) on the Sishen–Saldanha railway line in the Northern Cape. It is located in a sheep- and game-farming area. There is a local school (pre-primary to Grade 12) with 710 learners. The town is due for a R50 million development grant from the provincial government. The town square is built around the historic railway station and contains several stores, a co-op, a hotel and churches representing several denominations.

NCIS is a highly profitable iron and steelworks company (with 1 000 employees) that has been based in the town since 1963. It is in the process of considering a relocation of the plant to Kimberley, 300 km from Loriston. Should the relocation become reality, the company will merge its operations with the company's other, much bigger, plant and head office in Kimberley. Initial projections indicate a turnover growth of 20% and an effective dividend growth (payable to shareholders) of 40% over the next three years. NCIS also intends listing on the AltEx of the JSE 18 months from now. The company is willing to pay employees a once-off relocation allowance of R75 000. Rumours of the possible move have recently reached the townfolk. In turn, the CEO, Kabamba Plaatjies, has heard that a delegation consisting of representatives from different interest groups has requested an urgent meeting with the Board of NCIS to discuss the relocation, which they perceive to be imminent.

Questions for discussion

1 Are there key ethical issues that can be identified in this case, and if so, what are they?
2 Who are the stakeholders that will be affected by major decisions regarding relocation, and what are the organisation's obligations to these stakeholders? (Chapter 3: The social responsibility of business)
3 What should the organisation do to ensure an optimal ethical decision? (Chapter 12: Making ethical business decisions; Chapter 14: Resolving ethical dilemmas)

Case six: CORCON

CORCON is a large construction company that employs 3 600 people on a permanent basis. Although the company's growth has been very good, there is pressure on all employees to perform and reach difficult targets. Younger employees feel frustrated, rather disloyal and utter phrases like 'we feel leaderless' and 'there is no management in this company'. There seems to be a poor climate in the organisation. The company has also lost its reputation for being an employer of choice. Furthermore, there have been allegations and talk in the corridors about the company being targeted by a large-scale investigation about corruption in the construction industry. It appears that the company's management are divided into two camps regarding the importance of ethics: one group is of the opinion that ethics 'does not belong in business' and that the company's only obligation is towards their shareholders; the other is of the opinion that the shareholders are but one stakeholder of the company.

A new employee, Sean, has recently graduated from university with a degree in human resource management. He was fortunate enough to get a job as management trainee in the Human Resources (HR) Department (the recruitment/selection section) of the company.

During his first two days with his new employer he attended a voluntary, but quite comprehensive, induction programme. The topics that were covered included HR policies, health and safety regulations, training programmes available in the organisation, how the organisational benefits work, the organisation's disciplinary and grievance procedures, as well as information on the organisation's recreational programmes.

During the induction programme CORCON's CEO gave a short speech. The speech contained a few words of welcome, after which the CEO provided some statistics on the organisation's successes during the previous financial year. He also stated in no uncertain terms that the new employees had to realise that 'he didn't care what they had to do in the process, as long as the work got done'. He also emphasised that 'the work has to be done with a cost-cutting mindset'. He then wished them well and hurriedly left to attend a board meeting.

After the induction programme Sean was introduced to Jay, his supervisor. Jay was the manager of the recruitment/selection section in the HR Department. He gave him a hearty welcome and assured him that the HR Department was the 'best department' in CORCON, even to the extent that other departments were envious of it.

During his first week on the job he was asked to work through a batch of CVs of candidates applying for jobs in CORCON's call centre. He was told by Jay to eliminate all those candidates that were older than 30 years. When he asked why the cut-off was 30 years, Jay told him that that they already had enough dead wood in the organisation. While discussing this with Jay, the phone rang. Jay spoke to the caller for a few minutes and then put the phone down with a triumphant glint in his eyes. 'I just organised a weekend in a resort for my wife and I!' he said. 'And it's for free!', he continued. Sean later heard through the grapevine that Jay's resort trip was sponsored by Finders, a recruitment agency that often did business with the CORCON. Jay had made about 60% of all new appointments during the past year through Finders.

Later in that week Sean got a call from a person called Marvin. Marvin introduced himself as an assistant manager with Finders and told Sean that Jay suggested he call Sean and 'get to meet him'. Marvin suggested they have lunch together the same day. During the lunch, which Marvin paid for, he told Sean that he had good relations with the rugby fraternity and that he could arrange free tickets to all major rugby matches. Marvin also suggested that he seriously consider some 'excellent' candidates for the call centre position whose CVs had been sent through by Finders.

Things started bothering Sean. He felt uncomfortable deep down. He was uncertain as to how to deal with the issue regarding Marvin. The next day he approached Jay who told him that Finders 'always provided the best candidates'. Jay also told Sean that Marvin had many 'connections' and that he was 'a good person to know'. Sean, sensing that something was not above board, then attempted to find out what the company policy regarding accepting gifts from suppliers and vendors was. He was told that there were no specific guidelines in this regard. A supervisor in another department told him not to be a stirrer, and another HR manager told him to use his gut feel to deal with his uncertainties. He even phoned the Communications Department, but no-one there could answer his query about accepting gifts. When he got to his office the next day, there were two tickets to the next major rugby match in a blank envelope on his desk.

Questions for discussion

1   Are there key ethical issues that can be identified in this case, and if so, what are they?
2   Describe the state of ethics in this organisation in terms of the model of managing corporate ethics. (Chapter 5: A model of managing corporate ethics)
3   What is the effect of the behaviour of the HR Department on morale in the organisation? (Chapter 10: Ethics and human potential)
4   How could the organisation go about building an ethical corporate culture? (Chapter 21: Ethical leadership and organisational culture)
5   What ethics management systems could be institutionalised in the organisation? (Chapter 18: Codes of ethics; Chapter 19: Institutionalising ethics)
6   What arguments would you use to convince the managers that are of the opinion that ethics 'does not belong in business' and that the company's only obligation is towards the shareholders, that ethics does in fact matter in business? (Chapter 4: Ethics in organisations; Chapters 8–11: Business ethics matters)
7   What advice would you give to Sean? (Chapter 8: Ethics in business: Dispelling the myths; Chapter 12: Making ethical business decisions; Chapter 14: Resolving ethical dilemmas)

Case seven: Pay on entry

Lovemore Sibanda, the director of technology procurement of a large electricity supply organisation based in Johannesburg, South Africa, has just arrived at the international airport in Kinshasa (DRC). He has travelled via Nairobi from Singapore where he attended an electrical engineering conference. The temperature inside the airport's arrivals hall is 40°C, and the humidity is in the 90s.

Sibanda is a key decision maker in a multibillion dollar capital equipment deal. He is due to meet with potential business partners from China and France that will be in Kinshasa for one day only. Some of these businesspeople had travelled on the same flight as he did. Others had arrived earlier that morning from other destinations.

When going through customs at Kinshasa International airport he is informed that his yellow fever card expired a week ago. Yellow fever inoculation has a ten-year lifespan. Many African countries require proof of yellow fever inoculation by tourists and businesspeople wishing to enter the countries by air or ground transportation. Proof of inoculation is provided in the form of a yellow fever card, which is also yellow in colour. Immigration officials inspect travellers' yellow fever cards when they present their passports upon entering a country.

The French-speaking immigration official communicates with Sibanda in broken English. He is given the following choices: (a) to pay a bribe of US$500 to enter the DRC, (b) to return to Johannesburg on the next flight which leaves in 45 minutes, or (c) to receive a yellow fever inoculation injection. Leaning over a table behind the uniformed immigration official is another official wearing a rather soiled white coat and a stethoscope around his neck. On the table are several syringes filled with an amber-coloured fluid and some cotton balls. He notices a speck of blood on one of the cotton balls. Some of the needles are not protected by the usual plastic cover. In despair he takes his mobile phone from his pocket. He sees that there is no signal. There are several heavily-armed Congolese policemen hovering in the arrivals hall. Since this situation is holding up the queue, some of his fellow passengers are peering over his shoulder to ascertain the source of the delay.

Questions for discussion

1   Are there key ethical issues that can be identified in this case, and if so, what are they?
2   What are the implications of each of the three options offered to Lovemore?
3   What advice would you give to Lovemore? (Chapter 8: Ethics in business: Dispelling the myths; Chapter 14: Resolving ethical dilemmas)
4   How could organisations prepare their employees to deal with situations such as this one? (Chapter 18: Codes of ethics; Chapter 19: Institutionalising ethics)

REFERENCES

Ali, F. & Knox, A. 2008. Pakistan's commitment to equal opportunity for women: A toothless tiger? *International Journal of Employment Studies*, 16:39–58.

Aristotle. 1976. *Ethics*, translated by J.A.K. Thomson. London: Penguin.

Arrow, K.J. 1974. Limited knowledge and economic analysis. *American Economic Review*, 64(1):1–10.

Ashkanasy, N.M., Windsor, C.A. & Trevino, L.K. 2006. Bad apples in bad barrels revisited: Cognitive moral development, just world beliefs, rewards, and ethical decision-making. *Business Ethics Quarterly*, 16(4):449–473.

Baker, D. 2000. Another satisfied customer: Management customer relations – behind every complaint is a unique opportunity to enhance the corporate reputation. *The Financial Times*, August 2:15.

Barron, C. 2009. Hamba Khaya! (Go home). Beleaguered SAA boss trails clouds of controversy. *Business Times*. 15 February 2009.

Benatar, D. 2008. Justice, diversity and racial preference: A critique of affirmative action. *The South African Law Journal*, 125(2):274–306.

Bennett, N. & Naumann, S.E. 2005. Withholding effort at work: Understanding and preventing shirking, job neglect, social loafing, and free riding. In R.E. Kidwell & C.L. Martin (Eds.) *Managing organisational deviance.* London: Sage.

Bennis, W. 1999. *Managing people is like herding cats.* Provo, UT: Executive Excellence.

Bews, N.F. 2000. An investigation into the facilitators of the trustworthiness of managers. Unpublished doctoral thesis. Johannesburg: Rand Afrikaans University.

Bird, F.B. & Waters, J.A. 1989. The moral muteness of managers. *California Management Review*, 32(1), 73–88.

Booysen, L. 2009. Basic approaches to leadership. In S.P. Robbins, T.A. Judge, A. Odendaal & G. Roodt (Eds.) *Organisational behaviour: Global and South African perspectives.* Cape Town: Pearson Education.

BP. 2008. Sustainability Review 2008: 100 years of operating at the frontiers. [Online] Available: http://www.bp.com/liveassets/bp_internet/globalbp/ STAGING/global_assets/e_s_assets/e_s_assets_2008/downloads/bp_ sustainability_review_2008.pdf [Accessed on 8 June 2009].

Breeden. R.C. 2003. *Restoring trust.* New York: Report to the United States District Court for the Southern District of New York.

Brenkert, G.G. 1998. Trust, morality and international business. *Business Ethics Quarterly*, 8(2):293–317.

Brennan, J.J. 2002. *The market value of integrity.* The Sears Lectureship in Business Ethics. Waltham, (MA): Bentley College.

Brien, A. 1998. Professional ethics and the culture of trust. *Journal of Business Ethics*, 17:391–409.

Buckley, G., Salazar-Xirinachs, J.M. & Henriques, M. 2009. *The promotion of sustainable enterprises*. Geneva: International Labour Office.

Buller, P.F. & McEvoy, G.M. 1999. Creating and sustaining ethical capability in the multinational corporation. In R.S. Schuler & S.E. Jackson (Eds.) *Strategic human resource management*. Malden, MA: Blackwell.

Byrnes, N & Balfour, F. 2009. Philip Morris' global race. *Businessweek*. 23 April 2009. [Online]. Available: http://www.businessweek.com/magazine/content/09_18/b4129038611856_page_2.htm [Accessed on 29 May 2009].

Caldwell D.F. & Moberg D. 2007. An exploratory investigation of the effect of ethical culture in activating moral imagination. *Journal of Business Ethics*, 73:193–204.

Calhoun, C.H. & Wolitzer, P. 2001. Ethics as a value-added service. *CPA Journal*, January 2001, 71(1):71–73.

Carroll, A.B. 1999. Corporate social responsibility: Evolution of a definitional construct. *Business and Society*, 38(3):268–295.

Carroll, A.B. & Buchholtz, A.K. 2006. *Business and society: Ethics and stakeholder management* (6th ed.). Mason, OH: Thomson Southwestern.

CBPE. 2008. *Ethics reporting practices of JSE listed companies 2008: A comparison between JSE SRI listed and non-JSE SRI listed companies*. [Online]. Available: < http://web.up.ac.za/sitefiles/file/46/5232/JSE_SRI 2009_Report_PDF.pdf> [Accessed on: 16 May 2009].

CIA World Factbook. [Online]. Available: https://www.cia.gov/library/publications/the-world-factbook/ [Accessed in February 2009].

Ciulla, J.B. 2002. Trust and the future of leadership. In N. Bowie (Ed.) *The Blackwell guide to business ethics*. Malden, MA: Blackwell.

Ciulla, J.B. 2004. *Ethics, the heart of leadership* (2nd ed.). Westport, CT: Praeger.

Clarkson, M.B.E. 1995. A stakeholder framework for analyzing and evaluating corporate social performance. *The Academy of Management Review*, 20(1): 92–117.

Clouder, S. & Harrison, R. 2005. The effectiveness of ethical consumer behaviour. In R. Harrison, T. Newholm & D. Shaw (Eds.) *The ethical consumer*. London: Sage.

Clover SA. 2009. [Online]. Available: www.clover.co.za [Accessed on 18 April 2009].

Coleman, G. 2000. *The six levels of a totally aligned ethics culture*. Paper presented at the Managing Ethics in Organisations course. Waltham, MA: Centre for Business Ethics, Bentley College.

Collier, J. & Robberts, J. 2001. An ethic for corporate governance? *Business Ethics Quarterly*, 11(1):67–71.

Coyne, I. & Bartram, D. 2002. Assessing the effectiveness of integrity tests: A review. *International Journal of Testing*, 2(1):15–34.

Crane, A., Matten, D. & Spence, L. 2008. Corporate social responsibility: Readings and cases in a global context. London: Routledge.

CSR Network and D.R.Cameron-Cole. 2003. *Material world: The 2003 benchmark survey of global reporting*. Executive summary downloaded from csrnetwork.com

Cummings T.G. & Worley, C.G. 2001. *Organization development and change* (7th ed.). Cincinnati, OH: South-Western.

Dallas, G.S. 2004. Country influences on individual company governance. In G.S. Dallas (Ed.) *Governance and risk: An analytical handbook for investors, managers, directors, and stakeholders.* New York: McGraw-Hill.

Davis, W.E. 1999. *Managing ethics in today's changing utility industry.* The Sears Lectureship in Business Ethics. Waltham, MA: Bentley College.

Deal, T.E. & Kennedy, A.A. 1982. *Corporate cultures: The rites and rituals of corporate life.* Reading, MA: Addison-Wesley.

Department of Labour. 2009. *Employment Equity Act of 1998.* [Online]. Available: http://www.labour.gov.za/legislation/acts/employment-equity/employment-equity-act [Accessed on 18 April 2009].

Department of Labour. 2009. *The Basic Conditions of Employment Amendment Act of 2002.* [Online]. Available: http://www.labour.gov.za/legislation/acts/basic-conditions-of-employment/read-online/amended-basic-conditions-of-employment-act [Accessed on 21 March 2009].

de George, R.T. 1987. The status of business ethics: Past and future. *Journal of Business Ethics,* 6:201–211.

de George, R.T. 1999. *Business ethics* (5th ed.). Upper Saddle River, NJ: Prentice-Hall.

de Lange, J. 2005. Clover dank af na ruim bonusse vir base (Clover retrenches widely after generous bonuses for bosses). *Beeld,* 6 April.

de Lange, J. 2009a. SAL se enjins rook gevaarlik na vertrek van nog 'n baas (SAA engines smoke dangerously after departure of another boss). *Sake24,* 16 March.

de Lange, J. 2009b. Vakbonde stop SAL-vergrype (Trade unions halt SAA excesses). *Sake24,* 16 January.

de Maria, W. 2008. *Why is the president of Malawi angry? Business hegemony and the politics of corruption.* Paper presented at the fourth ISBEE World Congress. 15–18 July 2008. Cape Town: South Africa.

Derby, R. 2005. High oil price pushes SAA to the brink of survival. *Citizen,* 22 March.

Desio, P. 2006. *An overview of the organizational guidelines.* [Online]. Available: http://www.ussc.gov/corp/ORGOVERVIEW.pdf [Accessed on 30 November 2006].

de Soto, H. 2000. *The mystery of capital.* New York: Basic Books.

de Vos, H.M. 1995. Phenomenology and existentialism in psychology. In A.T. Möller (Ed.) *Perspectives on personality.* Durban: Butterworths.

Donaldson, T. & Preston, L.E. 1995. The stakeholder theory of the corporation: concepts, evidence and implications. *The Academy of Management Review,* 20(1):65–91.

Donaldson, T., Werhane, P.H., & Cording, M. 2002. *Ethical issues in business: A philosophical approach.* (7th ed.). New Jersey: Prentice Hall.

Driscoll, D. & Hoffman, W.M. 1997. Spot the red flags in your organization. *Workforce,* 76(6):135–136.

Driscoll, D. & Hoffman, W.M. 2000. *Ethics matters. How to implement values-driven management.* Waltham, MA: Bentley College.

Drucker, P. 2009. [Online]. Available: http://www.brainyquote.com/quotes/authors/p/peter_drucker_2.html [Accessed on 9 June 2009].

du Plessis, P.J., Rousseau, G.G. & Blem, N.H. 1994. *Buyer behaviour: Strategic marketing applications.* Halfway House: Southern Books.

du Toit, S.I. 1986. Die behoefte aan selfaktualisering (Abraham Maslow). In S.I. du Toit, M. Aronstam, J.A.K. Erasmus, E. Grobler & R. van Vuuren (Eds.) *Perspektiewe op menswees.* Pretoria: Academica.

EFMD. 2005. *Globally responsible leadership: A call for engagement:* Brussels: The European Foundation for Management Development.

Employment Equity Report of South Africa. 2008. [Online]. Available: http://www.labour.gov.za/documents/annual-reports/Commission for Employment Equity Report/2007–2008/ [Accessed on 18 April 2009].

Encina, G.B. 2009. *Firing with dignity.* [Online]. Available: http://www.cnr.berkeley.edu/ucce50/ag-labor/7article/article19.htm [Accessed on 21 March 2009].

Enderle, G. 2003. Business ethics (pp. 531–551). In N. Bunnin & E.P. Tsui-James (Eds.) *The Blackwell companion to business ethics* (2nd ed.). Oxford: Blackwell.

Engelman, D. & Kleiner,B.H. (1998). Effective employment screening practices. *Career Development International,* 3(4).

Enslin, S. 2005. Clover joint venture bodes well for African markets. *Star Business Report.* 23 May.

Ensor, L. 2007. Manuel soft-pedals on Absa PSL bribes. *Business Day.* 1 October.

Ensor, L. 2009. SAA needs big bail-out, finance chief tells MPs. *Business Day.* 19 February.

Entine, J. 1995. The Body Shop: Truth and consequences. *DCI,* 156(2):54–59.

Ethical corporation. 2008. *North America: finance – consumer trust overdrawn.* [Online]. Available: http://www.ethicalcorp.com/content.asp?ContentID=6234&newsletter=24 [Accessed on 9 December 2008].

Etzioni, A. 1998. A communitarian note on stakeholder theory. *Business Ethics Quarterly,* 8:679–691.

Evan, W. & Freeman, R. 1993. A stakeholder theory of the modern corporation: Kantian capitalism. In T. Beauchamp & N. Bowie (Eds.) *Ethical theory and business.* (4th ed.). New Jersey: Prentice Hall.

Fairholm, G.W. 1996. Spiritual leadership: Fulfilling whole-self needs at work. *Leadership and Organisation Development Journal,* 17(5):11–17.

Fairtrade Foundation. 2009. [Online]. Available: http://www.fairtrade.org.uk/what_is_fairtrade/fairtrade_foundation.aspx [Accessed on 29 May 2009].

Federal Sentencing Guidelines. 2007. [Online] Available: http://www.ussc.gov/2007guid/8b2_1.html [Accessed on 8 June 2009].

Ferrell, O.C., Fraedrich, J. & Ferrell, L. 2008. *Business ethics: Ethical decision making and cases* (7th ed.). Boston, MA: Houghton Mifflin.

Forbes.com 2009. *America's most reputable companies: The Rankings.* [Online]. Available: http://www.forbes.com/2009/04/28/america-reputable-companies-leadership-reputation_table.html [Accessed on 30 May 2009].

Fortune.com. 2009. *World's most admired companies: The Rankings.* [Online]. Available: http://money.cnn.com/magazines/fortune/mostadmired/2009/full_list/ [Accessed on 25 May 2009].

Freeman, R.E. 1984. *Strategic management: A stakeholder approach.* Boston, MA: Pitman.

French, P. 1993. The corporation as moral person. In T.I. White (Ed.) *Business ethics: A philosophical reader.* New York: MacMillan.

Friedman, M. 1992. The social responsibility of business is to increase its profits. In J. Olen & V. Barry (Eds.) *Applying ethics.* Belmont, California: Wadsworth.

Garratt, B. 2003. *Thin on top: Why corporate governance matters and how to measure, manage, and improve board performance.* London: Nicholas Brealey.

Garriga, E. & Mele, D. 2004. Corporate social responsibility theories: Mapping the territory. *Journal of Business Ethics,* 53:51–71.

Gedajlovic, E.R. & Shapiro, D.M. 1998. Management and ownership effects: Evidence from five countries. *Strategic Management Journal,* 19:533–553.

Gellermann, S. 1987. How 'good' managers make bad ethical choices. In *Harvard Business Review,* 64(4): 85–90.

George, W.W. 2007. *True north: Discover your authentic leadership.* Raytheon Lectureship in Business Ethics. Waltham, MA: Bentley College.

Gerwel, J. 2009. SAA remains a jewel in the crown. *Business Times.* 22 March 2009.

Giacalone, R.A., Jurkiewicz, C.L. & Dunn, C. (Eds.) 2005. *Positive psychology in business ethics and corporate responsibility.* Greenwich, CN: IAP.

Girion, L. & Gaither, C. 2005. Dismissal may spur new exec romance rules. *Los Angeles Times.* [Online]. Available: http://articles.latimes.com/2005/mar/08/business/fi-affair8. [Accessed on 27 May 2009].

Global Reporting Initiative. 2002. *Sustainability Reporting Guidelines.* Boston: GRI.

Goodpaster, K.E. 1989. Ethical imperatives and corporate leadership. In K.R. Andrews (Ed.) *Ethics in practice: Managing the moral corporation.* Boston: Harvard Business School.

Goodpaster, K. 1993. Business ethics and stakeholder analysis. In T.I. White (Ed.) *Business ethics: A philosophical reader.* New York: MacMillan.

Goodpaster, K.E. 1992. Business ethics. In L.C. Becker & C.B. Becker (Eds.) *Encyclopedia of ethics.* New York: Garland.

Goodpaster, K.E. 2007. *Conscience and corporate culture.* Malden, MA: Blackwell.

Greenwood, M. 2007. Stakeholder engagement: Beyond the myth of corporate responsibility. *Journal of Business Ethics,* 74(4):315–327.

Habermas, J. 1993. *Justification and application: Remarks on discourse ethics.* Translated by Ciaran Cronin. Cambridge, UK: Polity Press.

Handy, C. 2002. What's a business for? *Harvard Business Review*, December.

Harris, C.E., Pritchard, M.S. & Rabins, M.J. 2005. *Engineering ethics: Concepts and cases* (3rd ed.). Belmont, CA: Thomson Wadsworth.

Harrison, R., Newholm, T. & Shaw, D. 2005. Introduction: Defining the ethical consumer. In R. Harrison, T. Newholm & D. Shaw (Eds.) *The ethical consumer.* London: Sage.

Hartman, L.P. 2002. *Perspectives in business ethics* (2nd ed). New York: McGraw-Hill Irwin.

Hawkey, K. 2008. SAA boss in air-miles scandal. *Sunday Times.* 16 November .

Hobbes, T. 1998. *Leviathan* (edited and introduced by J.C.A. Gaskin). Oxford: Oxford University Press.

Horton, R.T. & Reid, P.C. 1991. Beyond the trust gap: Forging a new partnership between managers and their employers. Homewood, IL: Business One Irwin.

Hung, Y.C., Dennis, A.R. & Robert, L. 2004. Trust in virtual teams: Towards an integrated model of trust formation. *System Sciences, 2004. Proceedings of the 37th Annual Hawaii International Conference on System Sciences,* 5–8 Jan:11–21.

Husted, B.W. 1998. The ethical limits of trust in business relations. *Business Ethics Quarterly*, 8(2):233–248.

IoD. 2002. *King Report on Corporate Governance for South Africa 2002.* Johannesburg: Institute of Directors (IoD).

IoD. 2009. *King Report on Governance for South Africa 2009.* Johannesburg: Institute of Directors (IoD).

IoD, 2009. *Code of governance principles for South Africa, 2009.* Johannesburg: Institute of Directors (IoD).

Ittner, C. & Larcker, D. 2003. *Coming up short on non-financial performance measurement.* Harvard Business Review, Reprint R0311F.

Jarvanpaa, S.L. & Leidner, D.E. 1999. Communication and trust in global virtual teams. *Organisational Science*, 10:791–815.

Jeanne Sahadi, J. 2005. *CEO pay: Sky high gets even higher.* [Online]. Available: http://money.cnn.com/2005/08/26/news/economy/ceo_pay/ [Accessed on 25 March 2009].

Kant, I. 1929. *Fundamental principles of the metaphysics of ethics,* translated by T.K. Abbott. London: Longman.

Kant, I. 2008 (1785). *Fundamental principles of the metaphysic of morals,* translated by T.K. Abbott. Forgotten Books: www.forgottenbooks.org.

Kaptein, M. & Wempe, J. 2002. *The balanced company: A theory of corporate integrity.* Oxford: Oxford University Press.

Katzenbach, J.R. & The RCL Team 1995. *Real change leaders: How you can create growth and high performance at your company.* London: Nicholas Brealey.

Kelley, B. 1999. *Ethics at work.* Aldershot, Hampshire, UK: Gower.

Kets de Vries, M. 2001. *The leadership mystique: A user's manual for the human enterprise.* London: Prentice Hall.

Kidwell, R.E. & Martin, C.L. 2005. The prevalence (and ambiguity) of deviant behavior at work. In R.E. Kidwell & C.L. Martin (Eds.) *Managing organisational deviance.* London: Sage.

Kim, E.H. & Purnanandam, A.K. 2009. *Corporate governance and investor confidence in seasoned equity offerings.* [Online]. Available: <http://ssrn.com/abstract=1339642> [Accessed on 12 May, 2009].

Kimberley, N. & Härtel, C.E.J. 2007. Building a climate of trust during organizational change: The mediating role of justice perceptions and emotion (pp. 237–264). In C.E.J. Härtel, N.M. Ashkanasy & W.J. Zerbe (Eds.) *Research on emotion in organizations: functionality, intentionality and morality,* Vol. 3. Oxford, UK: Elsevier/JAI Press.

Kirkpatrick, E.M. 1983. *Chambers 20th century dictionary.* Edinburgh: Chambers.

Knowledge@Wharton. 2006. *CEO pay: A window into corporate governance.* [Online]. Available: http://knowledge.wharton.upenn.edu/article.cfm?articleid=1481 [Accessed on 25 March 2009].

Kohlberg, L. 1981. *The philosophy of moral development.* San Francisco: Harper and Row.

Konz, G.N. & Ryan, F.X. 1999. Maintaining an organizational spirituality: No easy task. *Journal of Organizational Change Management,* 12(3):200–210.

Korac-Kakabadse, N., Kouzmin, A. & Kakabadse, A. 2002. Spirituality and leadership praxis. *Journal of Managerial Psychology,* 17(3):165–182.

KPMG. 2006. *2006 survey of integrated sustainability reporting in South Africa.* [Online]. Available: <http://www.kpmg.co.za/images/naledi/pdf documents/mc1672 sustainability survey 36pg.pdf > [Accessed on 16 May 2009].

KPMG. 2008. *KPMG international survey of corporate responsibility reporting 2008.* Amsterdam: KPMG.

Kreitner, R. & Kinicki, A. 1992. *Organizational behavior* (2nd ed.). Homewood, IL: Irwin.

Krishnakumar, S. & Neck, C.P. 2002. The 'what', 'why' and 'how' of spirituality in the workplace. *Journal of Managerial Psychology,* 17(3):153–164.

Kuper, L. 2006. *Ethics: The leadership edge.* Cape Town: Zebra.

Lantos, G. 1999. Motivating corporate moral behaviour. *Journal of Consumer Marketing,* 16(3):222–233.

Larsen, R.S. 2002. *Leadership in a values-based organization.* The Sears Lectureship in Business Ethics. Waltham, MA: Bentley College.

Leisinger, K.M. n.d. *Corporate philanthropy: The 'top of the pyramid'.* Novartis Foundation for Sustainable Development.

Lennick, D. & Kiel, F. 2005. *Moral intelligence: Enhancing business performance and leadership success.* Upper Saddle River, NJ: Wharton School Publishing.

Leuvennink, J. 2007. SAL se baas dien in 38 direksies (SAA chief serves on 38 boards). *Sake24*, 16 March.

Lewicki, R.J. & Bunker, B.B. 1996. Developing and maintaining trust in work relationships. In R.M. Kramer & T.R. Tyler (Eds.) *Trust in organizations: Frontiers of theory and research.* Thousand Oaks, CA: Sage.

Lim, B. 1995. Examining the organizational culture and organizational performance link. *Leadership & Organization Development Journal*, 16(5):16–21.

Luthans, F. 2002. The need for and meaning of positive organizational behavior. *Journal of Organizational Behavior*, 23:695–706.

Maak, T. 2007. Responsible leadership, stakeholder engagement, and the emergence of social capital. *Journal of Business Ethics*, 74:329–343.

Maak, T. & Pless, N.M. 2009. Business leaders as citizens of the world: Advancing humanism on a global scale. *Journal of Business Ethics*, 88:537–550.

MacIntyre, A. 1985. *After virtue: A study in moral theory.* London: Duckworth.

MacIntyre, A. 1999. *Dependent rational animals: Why human beings need the virtues.* London: Duckworth.

Maitland, I. 2001. Distributive justice in firms: Do the rules of corporate governance matter? *Business Ethics Quarterly*, (11)1:129–143.

Makower, J. 1994. *Beyond the bottom line.* New York: Simon & Schuster.

Mallin, C.A. 2007. *Corporate governance* (2nd ed.). Oxford: Oxford University Press.

Manuel, T. 2007. Absa 'bribe' corrupt. *City Press.* 30 September.

Marcus, B., Lee, K. & Ashton, M.C. (2007). Personality dimensions explaining relationships between integrity tests and counterproductive behaviour: Big five or one in addition? *Personnel Psychology*, 60(1):1–34.

Mark, J. 2007. PSL draws blank cheque. [Online]. Available: http://www.iol.co.za/index.php. [Accessed on 20 April 2009].

Markkula Center for Applied Ethics. 2009. *Making an ethical decision.* [Online]. Available: http://www.scu.edu/ethics/practicing/decision/ htm [Accessed on 3 March 2009].

Martins, N. & Martins, E. 2009. Organisational culture. In S.P. Robbins, T.A. Judge, A. Odendaal & G. Roodt (Eds.) *Organisational behaviour: Global and South African perspectives.* Cape Town: Pearson Education.

Matten, D., Crane, A. & Chapple, W. 2003. Behind the mask: Revealing the true face of corporate citizenship. *Journal of Business Ethics*, 45:109–120.

Matten, D. & Moon, J. 2008. 'Implicit' and 'explicit' CSR: A conceptual framework for a comparative understanding of corporate social responsibility. *The Academy of Management Review*, 33(2).

May, S. 2009. Transforming the ethical culture of organizations. In J. Friedland (Ed.). *Doing well and doing good: The human face of the new capitalism.* Charlotte, NC: Information Age Publishing.

Mayer, R.C., Davis, J.H. & Schoorman, F.D. 1995. An integrative model of organizational trust. *The Academy of Management Review*, 20(3):709–734.

McCoy, B.H. 2002. The parable of the Sadhu. In L.P. Hartman (Ed.) *Perspectives in business ethics* (2nd ed.). New York: McGraw-Hill Irwin.

McDaniel, C. 2004. *Organizational ethics: Research and ethical environments.* Burlington, VT: Ashgate.

McDonald, M. 2001. *A framework for ethical decision-making.* [Online]. Available: http://www.compliance.co.za/documents/a_framework_for_ethical_decision. htm [Accessed on 3 March 2009].

McGovern, G. 2002. *The third freedom: Ending hunger in our time.* Lanham, MD: Rowman & Littlefield.

McKinsey Investor Opinion Survey. 2002. [Online]. Available: http://www. mckinsey.com/clientservice/organizationleadership/service/corpgovernance/ pdf/globalinvestoropinionsurvey2002.pdf [Accessed on 30 May 2009].

Meyerson, D., Weick, K.E. & Kramer, R.M. 1996. Swift trust and temporary groups. In R.M. Kramer & T.R. Tyler (Eds.) *Trust in organizations: Frontiers of theory and research.* Thousand Oaks, CA: Sage.

Micklethwait, J. & Wooldridge, A. 2002. *The company: A short history of a revolutionary idea.* New York: The Modern Library.

Mill, J.S. 1859. *Utilitarianism.* Reprint by Filiquarian Press, United Kingdom, 2007.

Mill, J.S. 1965. *Mill's ethical writings.* New York: Collier.

Miner, J.B. & Capps, M.H. 1996. *How honesty testing works.* London: Quorum.

Mintzberg, H., Simons, R. & Basu, K. 2002. Beyond selfishness. *MIT Sloan Management Review*, Fall.

Misbach, W. 2007. Manuel sticks to moral manual. *Sowetan.* 1 October.

Mishra, A.K. 1996. Organizational responses to crisis: The centrality of trust. In R.M. Kramer & T.R. Tyler (Eds.) *Trust in organizations: Frontiers of theory and research.* Thousand Oaks, CA: Sage.

Moalusi, K.P. 2001. Repositioning industrial psychology for the creation of new futures in turbulent times. *Journal of Industrial Psychology*, 27(4):17–21.

Moholoa, R. 2007. Self-enrichment? Who, us? *Sowetan.* 1 October.

Monks, R. A. G. & Minow, N. 2004. *Corporate governance* (3rd ed.). Malden, MA: Blackwell.

Moon, C. & Bonny, C. 2001. *Business ethics.* London: The Economist Books.

Moon, C. & Bonny, C. 2001. Attitudes and approaches. In C. Moon & C. Bonny (Eds.) *Business ethics.* London: The Economist.

Moore, G. 2006. Managing ethics in higher education: Implementing a code or embedding virtue? *Business Ethics: A European Review*, 15(4):407–418.

Moore, N. 1998. *Ethics: The way to do business.* The Sears Lectureship in Business Ethics. Waltham, MA: Bentley College.

Moorthy, R.S., De George, R.T., Donaldson, T., Ellos, S.J., Solomon, R.C. & Textor, R.B. 1998. *Uncompromising integrity: Motorola's global challenge.* Schaumburg, IL: Motorola University Press.

Mulcahy, A.M. 2005. *Social responsibility: Building a culture of strong ethics, good deeds and smart business.* Raytheon Lectureship in Business Ethics. Waltham, MA: Bentley College.

Mumford, E. 1995. Contracts, complexity, and contradictions: The changing employment relationship. *Personnel Review,* 24(8):54–70.

Mwangi, J.C. 2004. A strategy for stakeholder engagement in South African businesses. Unpublished doctoral thesis. Johannesburg: Rand Afrikaans University.

Nakra, P. 2000. Corporate reputation management: 'CRM' with a strategic twist. *Public Relations Quarterly,* (5)2:35–42.

Neck, C.P. & Milliman, J.F. 1994. Finding spiritual fulfilment on organizational life. *Journal of Managerial Psychology,* 9(6):9–16.

Newstrom, J.W. & Davis, K. 1997. *Organizational behavior: Human behavior at work* (10th ed.). New York: McGraw-Hill.

Ngobeni, W. 2009. SAA faces fresh charges of price-fixing. *Business Times.* 22 March.

Noam Cook, S.D. 2005. That which governs best: Leadership, ethics and human systems. In J.B. Ciulla, T.L Price & S.E. Murphy (Eds.) *The quest for moral leaders: Essays on leadership ethics.* Cheltenham, UK: Edward Elgar.

Noseweek, 2001. How SAA plotted to kill off Sunair. *Noseweek,* (36) October.

NSL Constitution. 2007. [Online]. Available: http://images.supersport.co.za/NSL Constitution as amended 29 December 2007.pdf. [Accessed on 14 April 2009].

O'Dwyer, B. & Madden, G. 2006. Ethical codes of conduct in Irish companies: A survey of code content and enforcement procedures. *Journal of Business Ethics,* 63(3):217–236.

Ones, D.S., Viswesvaran, C. & Schmidt, F.L. 1993. Comprehensive meta-analysis of integrity test validities: Findings and implications for personnel selection and theories of job performance. *Journal of Applied Psychology,* 78(4), 679–703.

Painter-Morland, M. 2008. Systemic leadership and the emergence of ethical responsiveness. *Journal of Business Ethics,* 82:509–524.

Palmer, D.E. 2009. Business leadership: Three levels of ethical analysis. *Journal of Business Ethics,* 88:525–536.

Passow, T., Fehlman, R. & Grahlow, H. 2005. Country reputation – From measurement to management: The case of Liechtenstein. *Corporate Reputation Review,* 7, 309–326

Pawelski, J.O. & Prilleltensky, I. 2005. 'That at which all things aim': happiness, wellness and the ethics of organizational life. In R.A. Giacalone, C.L. Jurkiewicz & C. Dunn (Eds.) *Positive psychology in business ethics and corporate responsibility.* Greenwich, CN: IAP.

Payne, N. 2004. Board effectiveness. *Directorship,* March: 6–7.

Peters, T.J. & Waterman, R.H. 1982. *In search of excellence: Lessons from America's best-run companies.* New York: Harper & Row.

Phasiwe, K. 2005. SAA, rival in hot water over R40 million fuel levy 'collusion'. *Business Day*. 23 March.

Phasiwe, K. 2006. SAA executives in illegal share deal, finds King. *Business Day*. 15 November.

Phillips, R. 2003. *Stakeholder theory and organizational ethics.* San Francisco: Berrett-Koehler.

Piaget, J. 1948. *The moral judgement of the child.* New York: Free Press.

Piliso, S. 2009. Minister probes SAA boss: Business partner of CEO Khaya Ngqula's wife lands lucrative airline deal. *Sunday Times*. 1 February.

Pless, N.M. 2007. Understanding responsible leadership: Role identity and motivational drivers. *Journal of Business Ethics*, 74:437–456.

Pless, N.M & Maak, T. 2005. Relational intelligence for leading responsibly in a connected world. In K.M. Weaver (Ed.) *Best paper proceedings of the sixty-fifth annual meeting of the Academy of Management*, Honolulu: Academy of Management.

Porras, J.I. & Silvers, R.C. 1991. Organization development and transformation. *Annual Review of Psychology*, 42:51–78.

PRI. 2006. Principles for responsible investment. [Online] Available: <http://www.unpri.org/principles/> [Accessed on 12 May 2009].

Prozesky, M. 2007. *Conscience: Ethical intelligence for global well-being.* Durban: University of KwaZulu-Natal Press.

Quinn, L. & D'Amato, A. 2008. *Globally responsible leadership: A leading edge conversation.* Colorado Springs, CO: Centre for Creative Leadership.

Quinn, R.E., Hildebrandt, H.W., Rogers, P.S. & Thompson, M.P. 1991. A competing values framework for analyzing presentational communication in management contexts. *Journal of Business Communication*, 28(3):213–232

Rawls, J. 1999. *A theory of justice.* Cambridge, MA: Belknapp.

Rasche, A. & Esser, D.E. 2007. Managing for compliance and integrity in practice. In C. Carter, S. Clegg, M. Kornberger, S. Laske & M. Messner (Eds.) *Business ethics as practice.* Cheltanham, Gloucestershire: Edward Elgar.

Reina, D.S. & Reina M.L. 1999. *Trust and betrayal in the workplace.* San Francisco: Berrett-Koehler.

Robbins, S.P. 1997. *Essentials of organizational behavior.* (5th ed.). Upper Saddle River, NJ: Prentice-Hall.

Rogovsky, N. & Schuler, R.S. 2007. *Socially sensitive enterprise restructuring in Asia.* Tokyo: Asian Productivity Organization.

Rossouw, D. 1994. *Business ethics: A southern African perspective.* Midrand: Southern Books.

Rossouw, D. 2000. *Business ethics in Africa* (2nd ed.). Cape Town: Oxford University Press.

Rossouw, D., Van der Watt, A. & Malan, D. 2002. Corporate governance in South Africa. *Journal of Business Ethics*, 37:289–302.

Rossouw, G.J. 1994. Rational interaction for moral sensitivity: A post-modern approach to moral decision-making in business. *Journal of Business Ethics,* 13:11–20.

Rossouw, G.J. 1997a. Strategy and skills for moral decision-making in business. *Koers,* 62(1):19–28.

Rossouw, G.J. 1997b. Etiese kodes in ondernemings: Ontwikkeling en implementering. *Koers,* 62(3):319–331.

Rossouw, G.J. 2002. Three approaches to teaching business ethics. *Teaching Business Ethics,* 6(4): 411–433.

Rossouw, G.J. 2005. Corporate governance and trust in business: A matter of balance. *African Journal of Business Ethics,* 1(1):1–7.

Rossouw, G.J. 2005. Business ethics and corporate governance in Africa. *Business & Society,* 44(1):94–106.

Rossouw, G.J. 2008a. *Beyond corporate social irresponsibility.* Paper presented at Second Lille World Forum on Corporate Social and Environmental Responsibility (9–11 October). Lille: France.

Rossouw, G.J. 2008b. Balancing corporate and social interests: Corporate governance theory and practice. *African Journal of Business Ethics,* 3(1):28–37.

Rossouw, G.J. 2009. The ethics of corporate governance: Crucial distinctions for global comparisons. *International Journal of Law and Management,* 51(1):5–9.

Rossouw, G.J. & Van Vuuren, L.J. 2003. Modes of managing morality: A descriptive model of strategies for managing ethics. *Journal of Business Ethics,* 46(4):389–402.

Ruettgers, M.C. 2003. *The integrity of management and management of integrity.* Raytheon Lectureship in Business Ethics. Waltham, MA: Bentley College.

SAA. 2009. SAA vision and values. [Online]. Available: http://ww1.flysaa.com/ Utility_Navigation/About/index.html [Accessed on 17 April 2009].

SABMiller. 2003. *Corporate accountability report.* Johannesburg: SABMiller.

Schein, E.H. 1978. *Career dynamics: Matching individual and organisational needs.* Reading, MA: Addison-Wesley.

Schein, E.H. 1992. *Organizational culture and leadership* (2nd ed.). San Francisco: Jossey-Bass.

Schmidt, F.L. & Hunter, J.E. 1998. The validity and utility of selection methods in personnel psychology: Practical and theoretical implications of 85 years of research findings. *Psychological Bulletin,* 124(2):262–274.

Schumpeter, J.A. 1942. *Capitalism, socialism and democracy.* New York: HarperPerennial.

Schwarz, M. 2001. The nature of the relationship between corporate codes of ethics and behaviour. *Journal of Business Ethics,* 32(3):247–262.

Schwartz, P. & Gibb, B.1999. *When good companies do bad things: Responsibility and risk in an age of globalisation.* New York: Wiley.

Schwartzel, J. 2008. *Conceptualising organisational ethics talk.* Unpublished doctoral thesis. Johannesburg: University of Johannesburg.

Seidenberg, I. 1998. *Ethics as a competitive edge.* The Sears Lectureship in Business Ethics. Waltham, MA: Bentley College.

Seidman, D. 2006. *The power of how: Achieving enduring success through ethics.* Raytheon Lectureship in Business Ethics. Waltham, MA: Bentley College.

Sen, A.K. 2000. *Development as freedom.* London: Anchor.

Senge, P.M. 1990. *The fifth discipline: The art and practice of the learning organization.* New York: Doubleday.

Sennett, R. 1998. *The corrosion of character: The personal consequences of work in the new capitalism.* New York: W.W. Norton.

Sharp Paine, L. 2002. Venturing beyond compliance. In L.P. Hartman (Ed.) *Perspectives in business ethics.* Boston: McGraw-Hill Irwin.

Sharp Paine, L. 2003. *Value shift.* New York: McGraw-Hill.

Shleifer, A. & Vishny, R.W. 1997. A survey of corporate governance. *The Journal of Finance,* 52(2):737–783.

Sims, R.S. & Brinkmann, J. 2003. Enron ethics (or: culture matters more than codes). *Journal of Business Ethics,* 45(3):243–256.

Smerden, R. 1998. *A practical guide to corporate governance.* London: Sweet & Maxwell.

Smith, A. 1776. *An inquiry into the nature and causes of the wealth of nations,* reprinted by R. Cambell & A. Skinner. Oxford: Claredon.

Smith, A. 1776. *The wealth of nations.* In R.L. Heilbronner (Ed.) *The essential Adam Smith.* New York: W.W. Norton.

Snowden, D.J. & Boone, M.E. 2007. A leader's framework for decision making. *Harvard Business Review,* 85(11):68–76.

Solidarity. 2005. Clover-bestuur sorg net vir hul eie sakke (Clover bosses look after themselves only). [Online]. Available: http://www.solidarity.co.za/home/content.asp [Accessed on 21 April 2005].

Solomon, R.C. & Martin, C. 2004. *Above the bottom line: An introduction to business ethics (3rd ed.).* Belmont, CA: Wadsworth/Thomson.

Sorlie, S. 2007. A complex task: Creating models for responsible leadership. *The Leadership in Action Journal,* 27(1): 21–23.

Steiner, G.A. & Miner, J.B. 1982. *Management policy and strategy* (2nd ed.). New York: Macmillan.

Steiner, G.A. & Steiner, J.F. (2003). *Business, government and society: A managerial perspective* (10th ed.). New York: McGraw-Hill.

Stevens, B. 1996. Using the competing values framework to assess corporate ethical codes. *Journal of Business Communication,* 33(1):71–83

Stone, C.D. 1975. *Where the law ends: the social control of corporate behaviour.* New York: Harper Collins.

Stone, C.D. 1992. The corporate social responsibility debate. In J. Olen & V. Barry (Eds.) *Applying ethics.* Belmont, CA: Wadsworth.

Sullivan, J.D. 2009. *The moral compass of companies: Business ethics and corporate governance as anti-corruption tools.* Washington, DC: International Finance Corporation.

SustainAbility. 1999. *The Social Reporting Report.* London: The Beacon Press.

SustainAbility, UNEP, Standard & Poor's. 2006. *Tomorrow's value: The Global reporters 2006 survey of corporate sustainability reporting.* London: The Beacon Press.

Szekely, F & Knirsch, M. 2005. Responsible leadership and corporate social responsibility: Metrics for sustainable performance. *European Management Journal,* 23(6):628–647.

The World Wealth Report. [Online]. Available: http://www.us.capgemini.com/worldwealthreport08 [Accessed in February 2009].

Thorne, L. & Jones, J. 2005. Organisational deviance and culture: Oversights and intentions. In R.E. Kidwell & C.L. Martin (Eds.) *Managing organisational deviance.* London: Sage.

Transparency International. 2009. [Online]. Available: http://www.transparency.org/policy_research/surveys_indices/cpi/2008 [Accessed on 28 May 2009].

Treviño, L.K., Butterfield, K.D. & McCabe, D.L. 2001. The ethical context in organisations: Influences on employee attitudes and behaviour. In J. Dienhart, D. Moberg & R. Duska (Eds.) *The next phase of business ethics: Integrating psychology and ethics.* Amsterdam: JAI/Elsevier.

Treviño, L.K., Weaver, G.R., Gibson, D.G. & Toffler, B.L. 1999. Managing ethics and legal compliance: What works and what hurts. *California Management Review,* 41(2):131.

Tromp, B. 2007. PSL top brass will find it hard to convince colleagues of payout. *Star* (Johannesburg). 2 October .

TSF (The Sustainability Forum). 2005. *The market value of reputation.* [Online]. Available: http://www.sustainability-zurich.org/en/p67000153.html> [Accessed on 7 June 2009].

UNEP Finance Initiative 2007. *Demystifying responsible investment performance: A review of key academic and broker research on ESG factors.* A joint report by the Asset Management Working Group of the United Nations Environment Programme Finance Initiative and Mercer. Geneva: UNEP R/Mercer.

United Nations Development Programme. UNHDI rankings. [Online]. Available: www.undp.org [Accessed in February 2009].

van der Watt, A. 2003. Identifying and managing risk (Part 3 of Governance, Risk and Ethics). Supplement to *Financial Mail,* 171(8):1–8.

van Rooyen, D. 2005. Laer melkprys stuur 'n sterk boodskap aan boere (Lower milk price sends a strong message to farmers). *Sake-Rapport.* 10 April.

van Vuuren, A. 2005. Kommissie kyk of suiwel saamspan (Commission investigates dairy collusion). *Beeld.* 8 April.

van Vuuren, L.J. & Crous, F. 2005. A shared meaning of ethics in organizations: An appreciative alternative. *Journal of Business Ethics,* 57:399–412.

Vergin, R.C. & Qouronfleh, M.W. 1998. Corporate reputation and the stock market. *Business Horizons*, 41(1):19–26.

Verschoor, C.C. 1998. A study of the link between and corporation's financial performance and its commitment to ethics. *Journal of Business Ethics*, 17:1509–1516.

Villere, M. & Hartman, S. 1989. What's affirmative about affirmative action? *Business Horizons*, September/October:22–27.

Visser, A. 2005. Melk is dik in die tribunaal se keel (Milk thick in tribunal's throat). *Beeld*. 8 April.

Visser, W. & Sunter, C. 2002. *Beyond reasonable greed: Why sustainable business is a much better idea!* Cape Town: Human & Rousseau Tafelberg.

Waddock, S. & Graves, S. 1997. The corporate social performance-financial performance link. *Strategic Management Journal*, 18(4):303–319.

Waters, J.A. & Bird, F. 1987. The moral dimension of organizational culture. *Journal of Business Ethics*, 6:15–22.

Weaver, G.R. 1993. Corporate codes of ethics: Purpose, process and content issues. *Business and Society*, 32(1):44–58.

Weaver, G.R. 2006. Virtue in organizations: Moral identity as a foundation for moral agency. *Organization Studies*, 27(3):341–368.

Webley, S. & More, E. 2003. *Does business ethics pay?* London: Institute of Business Ethics (IBE).

WEF. 2005. *Trust in governments, corporations and global institutions continues to decline.* [Online]. Available: http://www2.weforum.org/site/homepublic.nsf/ Content/Trust+in+Governments,+Corporations+and+Global+Institutions+C ontinues+to+Decline.html [Accessed on 7 December 2008].

Weiss, J.W. 2003. *Business ethics: A stakeholder and issues management approach* (3rd ed.). Mason, OH: Thomson-Southwestern.

Wieland J. 2005. Corporate governance, value management, and standards: A European perspective. *Business & Society*, 44(1):74–93.

Williams, F. 2007. Viljoen wil verslag se vlerke knip (Viljoen aims to contest report). *Sake-Rapport*. 17 November 2006.

Youssef, C.M. & Luthans, F. 2005. A positive organizational behavior approach to ethical performance. In R.A. Giacalone, C.L. Jurkiewicz & C. Dunn (Eds.) *Positive psychology in business ethics and corporate responsibility*. Greenwich, CN: IAP.

Zadek, S. 1998. Balancing performance, ethics, and accountability. *Journal of Business Ethics*, 7:1421–1441.

INDEX

Please note: Page numbers in *italics* refer to Tables and Figures.

A

B

C